The Babylonian Astr
Compendium MUL.A

MW00837679

MUL.APIN is the earliest surviving general work on astronomy in which a wide range of theoretical and practical information relating to the Sun, Moon, stars, and planets is presented. Hermann Hunger and John Steele have done us all an immense service in providing this up-to-date edition and accessible, yet accurate translation of a document of central importance for our understanding of the history of Mesopotamian astronomy, and more broadly of all pre-telescopic astronomy.

Alexander Jones, Institute for the Study of the Ancient World, New York University, USA

MUL.APIN, written sometime before the eighth century BC, was the most widely copied astronomical text in ancient Mesopotamia: a compendium including information such as star lists, descriptions of planetary phases, mathematical schemes for the length of day and night, a discussion of the luni-solar calendar and rules for intercalation, and a short collection of celestial omens. This book contains an introductory essay, followed by a new edition of the text and a facing-page transliteration and English translation. Finally, the book contains a new and detailed commentary on the text. This is a fascinating study, and an important resource for anyone interested in the history of astronomy.

Hermann Hunger is Emeritus Professor of Assyriology at the University of Vienna, Austria.

John Steele is Professor of the History of the Exact Sciences in Antiquity in the Department of Egyptology and Assyriology at Brown University, USA.

Scientific Writings from the Ancient and Medieval World

Series editor: John Steele, Brown University, USA

Scientific texts provide our main source for understanding the history of science in the ancient and medieval world. The aim of this series is to provide clear and accurate English translations of key scientific texts accompanied by up-to-date commentaries dealing with both textual and scientific aspects of the works and accessible contextual introductions setting the works within the broader history of ancient science. In doing so, the series makes these works accessible to scholars and students in a variety of disciplines including history of science, the sciences, and history (including Classics, Assyriology, East Asian Studies, Near Eastern Studies and Indology).

Texts will be included from all branches of early science including astronomy, mathematics, medicine, biology, and physics, and which are written in a range of languages including Akkadian, Arabic, Chinese, Greek, Latin, and Sanskrit.

Available titles:

The Foundations of Celestial Reckoning: Three Ancient Chinese Astronomical Systems
Christopher Cullen

The Babylonian Astronomical Compendium MUL.APIN
Hermann Hunger and John Steele

The Babylonian Astronomical Compendium MUL.APIN

Hermann Hunger and John Steele

Routledge
Taylor & Francis Group
LONDON AND NEW YORK

First published 2019
by Routledge
2 Park Square, Milton Park, Abingdon, Oxon OX14 4RN

and by Routledge
52 Vanderbilt Avenue, New York, NY 10017, USA

First issued in paperback 2020

Routledge is an imprint of the Taylor & Francis Group, an informa business

British Library Cataloguing-in-Publication Data
A catalogue record for this book is available from the British Library

Library of Congress Cataloging-in-Publication Data
Names: Hunger, Hermann, 1942- author. | Steele, John M., author.
Title: The Babylonian astronomical compendium MUL.APIN / Hermann Hunger and John Steele. Other titles: MUL APIN
Description: Abingdon, Oxon ; New York, NY : Routledge, 2018. | Series: Scientific writings from the ancient and Medieval world | Includes bibliographical references and index.
Identifiers: LCCN 2018004804 (print) | LCCN 2018007133 (ebook) | ISBN 9781315168722 (ebook) | ISBN 9781351686822 (web pdf) | ISBN 9781351686815 (epub) | ISBN 9781351686808 (mobi/kindle) | ISBN 9781138050471 (hardback : alk. paper)
Subjects: LCSH: Astronomy, Assyro-Babylonian. | Astronomy, Ancient. | Stars—Catalogs.
Classification: LCC QB19 (ebook) | LCC QB19 .H8625 2018 (print) | DDC 523.802/16—dc23
LC record available at https://lccn.loc.gov/2018004804

ISBN 13: 978-0-367-66618-7 (pbk)
ISBN 13: 978-1-138-05047-1 (hbk)

Typeset in Times New Roman
by Swales & Willis Ltd, Exeter, Devon, UK

MIX
Paper from responsible sources
FSC www.fsc.org FSC™ C013985

Printed in the United Kingdom
by Henry Ling Limited

Contents

Preface

Fragments of the Babylonian astronomical compendium known as MUL.APIN were first identified over one hundred years ago, but it was not until 1989 that a complete edition, with translation and study of the text, was published by H. Hunger and D. Pingree under the title *MUL.APIN: An Astronomical Compendium in Cuneiform*, Archiv für Orientforschung Beiheft 24 (Horn: Berger & Söhne, 1989). In the years since the publication of that volume, several new fragments of MUL.APIN have been identified. In addition, the publication of editions and studies of other works of early Babylonian astronomy that relate to MUL.APIN, as well as detailed studies of certain sections of MUL.APIN itself, has led to advances in our understanding of the text and its contents. With the earlier edition now being out of print, the time seems right to present an updated edition and translation of MUL.APIN, accompanied by a new study of its contents. The new edition incorporates several tablets of MUL. APIN that have been published since the 1989 edition, as well as a few previously unpublished tablets identified by ourselves.

Our work in both establishing the text of MUL.APIN and understanding its contents owes a large debt to the efforts of several scholars over the past century, in particular F. X. Kugler, E. Weidner, J. Schaumberger, B. L. van der Waerden, and D. Pingree. We also wish to record our sincere thanks to J. C. Fincke, who shared with us her article containing editions of several newly identified fragments and very generously provided us with photographs of all of the relevant tablets in the British Museum. She also drew H. Hunger's attention to a procedure for drawing copies of tablets from photos, which was developed by C. Wunsch and which is used for the copies in this book. We are grateful to St. Maul and A. Hätinen, who gave us access to tablets from Assur ahead of their publication. Previously unpublished tablets in the British Museum are published here by permission of the Trustees of the British Museum.

Abbreviations

CAD	The Assyrian Dictionary of the Oriental Institute of the University of Chicago (Chicago: Oriental Institute)
CT	Cuneiform texts from Babylonian tablets etc. in the British Museum (London: British Museum)
LBAT	Late Babylonian astronomical and related texts copied by T. G. Pinches and J. N. Strassmaier, prepared for publication by A. J. Sachs with the co-operation of J. Schaumberger (Providence: Brown University Press)

Introduction

The text known as MUL.APIN was the most widely copied work in the astral sciences written in ancient Mesopotamia.[1] It was composed sometime before the end of the eighth century BC, and copies of it have been found at many sites throughout Assyria and Babylonia, dating from the late Neo-Assyrian (eighth to seventh century BC) down to the Seleucid (third to first century BC) periods. In addition to being widely copied, MUL.APIN was clearly read and used by scholars throughout these periods: it is one of only a very few works of astral science identified by name in other cuneiform texts and provided the foundation for many later texts of what we term 'schematic astronomy'.[2] It is no exaggeration to say, therefore, that MUL.APIN was the most important work of early Babylonian astronomy.

Our knowledge of Mesopotamian astral science is based upon more than 5,000 cuneiform tablets containing texts ranging from collections of celestial omens, to reports of dated astronomical observations, to procedures for calculating astronomical phenomena. These tablets fall into two main groups: (1) tablets from the Neo-Assyrian period – dating to the late eighth and early seventh century BC and written either in Assyrian or Babylonian script – which mainly come from the last Assyrian capital, Nineveh, with small numbers having been found at the earlier capitals of Assur and Kalhu, all of which are in the Assyrian heartland, and at the site of the city of Huzirina in Anatolia, on the periphery of the Assyrian empire; and (2) tablets from Babylonia, ranging in date from the eighth century BC to the first century AD, mostly from the city of Babylon, but with a substantial number from Uruk in southern Babylonia, and a handful of tablets from other Babylonian cities. These sources show a thriving and multifaceted astronomical tradition that included the careful and regular observation of astronomical phenomena, the development of methods to predict those same phenomena, and the interpretation

1 The term 'astral sciences' is a catch-all to refer to scholarly activity that falls under the modern categories of astronomy, astrology and celestial divination, cosmology, and certain aspects of meteorology. For simplicity, we often use the term 'astronomy' in place of the longer 'astral sciences', with the understanding that astrology and celestial divination are part of astronomy.

2 Steele (in press a).

of astronomical phenomena through celestial omens and other systems of astrology, as well as texts such as MUL.APIN that provide schemes describing recurring astronomical events.

MUL.APIN contains a concise and generally well-organized collection of astronomical material covering all of the main topics we know to have been the subject of Babylonian astronomical concern in the second and early first millennium BC: lists of stars, the calendar, the synodic phases of the planets, the variation in the duration of visibility of the Moon and the length of day and night, the length of a shadow cast by a gnomon at different times of day throughout the year, and celestial omens. Copies of the work were often written in a two-tablet series, although the break between the two tablets was not fixed. Tablets containing the whole of the work on one tablet are also known, and it is possible that copies that extended over three tablets existed. The work is remarkably stable, with relatively few differences between the preserved copies.[3] This stands in contrast to another widely copied work of the astral sciences, the compendium of celestial omens *Enūma Anu Enlil*, which exhibits considerable variation, even to the extent of different traditions of the numbering of tablets between different cities.[4]

Modern scholarship on MUL.APIN began with the publication of a copy of BM 86378, a well-preserved manuscript for Tablet I, by King (1912: pls. 1–8). The publication of this copy led quickly to the publication of editions and studies of the tablet by Kugler (1913: 1ff.), Weidner (1915: 35ff. and 141ff.) and Bezold et al. (1913). Weidner (1923) identified and published further manuscripts of MUL.APIN, including sources that preserved parts of Tablet II. A full edition of the whole of MUL.APIN, accompanied by a short astronomical commentary, was finally published by Hunger and Pingree (1989). Since then, several new sources have been identified by Horowitz (1989–1990), Fincke (2014, 2017), Hätinen (forthcoming), and ourselves. The edition presented here is based upon all sources known to us as of September 2017.

In referring to lines within MUL.APIN, we follow the division of the work into two tablets adopted by Hunger and Pingree in their edition of 1989, with the exception of three additional lines in II Gap A. This line numbering is based upon two of the best-preserved sources, our source A (BM 86378) and source HH (VAT 9412+11279). It should be pointed out again, however, that this line numbering is essentially arbitrary. In particular, the division between 'Tablet I' and 'Tablet II' adopted here is a modern convention, only partly reflected in the ancient sources, and so it is unwise to form conclusions about the composition or structure of the work based upon this division.

3 For a study of the differences between the manuscripts that were published in Hunger and Pingree (1989), see Hobson (2012: 47–61). Most differences can be ascribed to simple scribal errors (especially in numbers) or minor orthographic variations.

4 Fincke (2001).

Structure and content of MUL.APIN

The preserved copies of MUL.APIN divide the text into sections that are separated from one another by horizontal rulings. In many cases, two or more sections can be grouped together to form large units of text that are subdivided into smaller parts. These larger units often contain one or more sections that contain factual statements, such as the names of stars or constellations, followed by a section containing a summary of the preceding sections: for example, giving the number of stars in the list, or a short mathematical procedure that draws upon the data given in the earlier section. We can therefore distinguish between larger units of text, which we will call 'sections', and the 'subsections' that make up this larger unit. No distinction is made between the appearance of the horizontal rulings that are used to separate sections and subsections. However, some general trends can be seen within sections. For example, sections often begin by giving lists of what can be thought of as astronomical data, such as the names of stars, the dates on which stellar phenomena occur, the intervals between the synodic phenomena of the planets, and the duration of visibility of the Moon and the length of night. Entries in these lists are usually indicated using the DIŠ sign (a single vertical wedge), which we translate using the symbol ¶.[5] Generally, entries in a list are given on separate lines, unless they are too long, in which case they extend on to a second line, or all the entries in the list are very short, in which case two entries are given per line, sometimes both marked with the DIŠ sign and arranged into two mini-columns, at other times simply following one another, without a separating DIŠ sign. Following a list of data, we often find one or more subsections that either summarize the preceding data or give a short procedure related to that data. These subsections can often be differentiated from the data subsections by the absence of the DIŠ sign at the beginning. Most of these procedures are not intended to tell the reader how to use the preceding data but instead to provide a justification for the data itself.

The basic contents of MUL.APIN can be summarized as follows:

I i 1 – I ii 35: Three lists of stars in the paths of Enlil, Anu, and Ea. These three paths divide the sky into northern, middle and southerly ranges of declination.

I ii 36 – I iii 12: A list of dates in the 360-day schematic calendar on which selected stars become visible for the first time (known as first visibility or heliacal rising).

I iii 13 – I iii 33: A list of stars which rise as other stars set.

I iii 34 – I iii 48: A list of the number of days between the rising (first visibility) of two stars.

5 The role of the DIŠ sign is discussed in detail by Watson and Horowitz (2011).

I iii 49 – I iv 9: A brief discussion of the culmination (*ziqpu*) of stars and a list of *ziqpu* stars.

I iv 10 – I iv 30: A list of dates in the 360-day schematic calendar on which one star culminates when another star rises at its first visibility.

I iv 31 – II i 8: A list of stars through which the Moon passes each month (i.e. the zodiacal constellations), followed by statements that the Sun and the planets move through the same path that the Moon travels.

II i 9 – II i 43: Statements concerning the motion of the Sun to the north and south and the change in the length of daylight. The dates of the solstices and equinoxes are placed on the 15th of Months I, IV, VII, and X in the 360-day schematic calendar.

II i 44 – II i 67: Statements of the duration of the visibility and invisibility periods of the five planets.

II i 68 – II Gap A 7: A brief discussion of the four seasons, which path the Sun is in during those seasons, and their characteristic weather. The seasons are set such that the solstices and equinoxes fall in their middle.

II Gap A 8 – II ii 20: An intercalation scheme governed by the date of conjunction of the Moon with the Pleiades and by the date of the first visibility of certain stars, followed by a mathematical explanation of the consequences of there being one intercalary month every three years.

II ii 21 – II ii 42: A mathematical scheme for the length of a shadow cast by a gnomon on the dates of the solstices and equinoxes.

II ii 43 – II iii 15: A mathematical scheme for the length of night and the daily change in the duration of visibility of the Moon.

II iii 16 – II iv 12: A short collection of celestial omens.

The macro structure of MUL.APIN largely follows a logical structure. The text begins by introducing the main stars of the night sky, before dividing these stars into three overlapping groups: stars for which the date of first visibility is given; stars whose culminations are to be used; and the zodiacal constellations through which the Moon, Sun, and the five planets pass. The latter two of these groups of stars are named according to their characteristics: the *ziqpu* ('culminating') stars (MUL^{meš} šá ziq-pi), and the stars that stand in the path of the Moon (DINGIR/MUL^{meš} ša i-na KASKAL ^{d}Sin GUB^{meš}). With the exception of the list of stars in the path of the Moon, the lists of stars are followed by further lists in which additional statements about some of these stars are given that tie phenomena of the stars either to one another or into a calendrical framework. The second half of MUL.APIN moves away from a concern with stars to present material relating to the calendar, the synodic phases of the planets, mathematical schemes for the length of shadow cast by a gnomon, the length of night, and the daily variation in the duration of visibility of the Moon. Finally, a small group of celestial omens is given at the end of the text. Although still following a broadly logical order, this second half of the work is not as well ordered as the first part. In particular, it is unclear why the section concerning the synodic phases of the planets appears between two sections that concern the calendar. It is tempting to see the planetary material as having become displaced from its original position, which may have been immediately following the statements that the planets travel the same path as the Moon; however, this may simply reflect a modern bias in what we think would make a logical order, rather than what made sense for the author of the text. On the whole, however, later sections of the composition build upon or rely upon data introduced earlier in the text.

Previous studies of MUL.APIN have tended to assume that the work is a compilation of texts, at least some of which may have been considerably earlier in date than MUL.APIN itself.[6] Although this is possible, several arguments count against this conclusion. First, the astronomical data throughout MUL.APIN are remarkably consistent between sections.[7] We would not necessarily expect that, if the work was put together from already existing texts, all of those texts would reflect a unified body of astronomical knowledge. Second, we know of no examples of earlier texts that contain exact parallels to sections of MUL.APIN. It seems more likely, therefore, that the whole of MUL.APIN was composed at a single moment in time, by a single author. This author certainly drew on earlier knowledge to produce his text, but did not simply edit together existing textual material. In composing MUL.APIN, the author attempted to produce a single, concise text that covered all of the topics of concern in the astronomy of the period.

As discussed by Watson and Horowitz (2011), the macro structure of MUL. APIN reflects not only an increasing complexity of topic as we move through the work, from simple star lists at the beginning to mathematical schemes and procedures for the length of the shadow cast by a gnomon and the daily change in the duration of lunar visibility towards the end, but also a parallel increasing complexity in the conceptual framework and language of the material. For example, we move from simple spatial relationships between two objects (e.g. one star in front of another) to more complex, abstract spatial relationships (e.g. the cardinal directions), and from third person statements to second person procedures in which the reader is instructed to do something, not just read the text. Watson and Horowitz further argue that this ordering of topics in MUL.APIN reflects the history of Babylonian astronomical activity, beginning with listing stars and moving

6 For example, Hunger and Pingree (1989: 9).

7 Indeed, there is only one clear contradiction within the text: in the list of dates of the first visibilities of stars in I ii 36 – I iii 12, the stars Eridu and the Raven are stated to have their first visibility on the 10th of Month VI, and the star ŠU.PA to have its first visibility on the 15th of Month VI. However, in the list of stars that culminate at the moment of the first visibility of another star, Eridu and ŠU.PA are said to have their first visibilities together on the 15th of Month VI (the first visibility of the Raven is not mentioned).

on to procedures for calculating intercalations and astronomical phenomena. We find this conclusion problematical, however, first because it assumes that science progresses in a direct, positive direction, from less accurate to more accurate, and from listing to procedures; second, because it does not fit in very well with what we know of the history of early Babylonian astronomy where, for example, numerical schemes that model the variation in the length of day and night are known from roughly the same time period as the earliest star lists; and third, because it projects on to the ancient scribe who composed MUL.APIN a modern concern with placing things in historical sequence. In our opinion, the ordering of topics within MUL.APIN can be better explained by the needs of the text itself. For example, the intercalation rules in II Gap A 8 – II ii 20 rely upon the list of dates of the rising of stars in I ii 36 – I iii 12.

Basic concepts and methods

Stars and constellations

The Babylonian night sky was populated by a large number of celestial objects that were designated by the Akkadian word *kakkabu*, normally translated into English as 'star'; *kakkabu*, however, is used to refer to a large range of celestial objects, rather than just single fixed stars. In addition to individual fixed stars, *kakkabu* could be used to refer to a constellation, a group of stars that constitute part of a constellation, or a planet, as well as transitory objects such as comets and meteors. Within MUL.APIN, *kakkabu* usually refers to individual stars, groups of stars, or constellations. Unless otherwise noted, we follow the convention of the text in referring to all of these as 'stars'.

By the time of the composition of MUL.APIN, a large number of constellations had been constructed by the fixed stars being grouped into patterns that were then identified with and named after a variety of human (or divine) figures, animals, and objects. These constellations appear in various lists, omen texts, and literary works. Some of the constellations are described in the preserved examples of what have been termed 'uranology texts', which give prose descriptions of the constellations.[8] Although the uranology texts clearly post-date the composition of MUL.APIN, there is no reason to suppose that the images of the constellations changed significantly over time.

Individual stars and small groups of stars were often identified as parts of constellations. For example, in addition to naming the Scorpion, MUL.APIN refers to two other stars that are part of the Scorpion: the Chest of the Scorpion and the Horn of the Scorpion. In this example, the stars are named by reference to the larger constellation. Sometimes, stars or small star groups could have individual names and also be part of a larger constellation. For example, within the Stag are two stars or star groups: the Vole, a group of scintillating stars that stand in the Stag's chest, and the Deleter, a bright red star that stands in its kidney. Cases

8 Beaulieu, Frahm, Horowitz, and Steele (2018).

such as these may suggest that, at some point in Mesopotamian history, there was a process of combining or overlaying on one another two or more traditions of constellations. Such a process may also explain what seem to be alternative traditions of how some star names, which were written using logograms, were read by the Babylonian scholars. For example, the name of the star written ^{mul}UD.KA.DUḪ.A was sometimes read as the Akkadian word *nimru*, 'panther', but in a uranology text this constellation is described as being a clothed human figure with two faces, almost certainly reflecting a literal Sumerian reading of the star name as the 'Demon with the gaping mouth'. Similarly, the star name written ^{mul}EN.TE.NA.BAR.ḪUM was sometimes read as the Akkadian word *ḫabaṣirānu*, 'mouse-like', but in the uranology text it is again said to be a human figure.

Several attempts have been made over the past 120 years to identify Babylonian stars and constellations with their modern equivalents. Only those stars that are used in Late Babylonian observational texts can be identified with certainty; the identity of many other stars and constellations can be guessed at with greater or lesser confidence, based upon their position relative to other stars and constellations, similarities in the names of the stars with those known from Greek and later sources, and visual analogues helped by the descriptive statements found in texts. Recent summaries of possible identifications, including some that are quite speculative, can be found in Hunger and Pingree (1999: 271–277) and Kurtik (2007). We deliberately avoid the question of star identifications in the present work.

The calendar

The Babylonian calendar used throughout the second and first millennia BC was a luni-solar calendar in which the 12 months of the year were defined by the first visibility of the new moon crescent, and the year was kept in line with the seasons by the addition of a thirteenth month slightly more often than once every three years.[9] The Babylonian day began at sunset. In the evening that would begin the thirtieth day, a watch was kept for the new moon. If the new crescent moon was seen, then the day that was just beginning would be renamed as the first day of the new month. However, if it was not seen, that day would remain as the thirtieth day of the current month, and a new month would begin the following evening, irrespective of whether the Moon was seen or not on that day. Thus, months had either 29 or 30 days, and the beginning of the month would not be delayed because bad weather prevented the Moon being seen on the thirty-first evening.

The Babylonian year began in the spring. Because 12 lunar months are about 11 days shorter than the solar year, the first day of the first month of a year will move earlier relative to the equinox (or, put another way, the date of the equinox will move later in the Babylonian calendar) by about 11 days per year, until an intercalation is performed by the addition of an extra month, which will then move the beginning of the next year forward by about 19 days (11 days back

9 It is likely that, for about one hundred years in the late second millennium BC, the Assyrian calendar was purely lunar without intercalation. See recently Bloch (2012) and Jeffers (2017).

plus 30 days forward) relative to the equinox. Thus, in a properly intercalated calendar, the beginning of the year falls within a range of about 30 days relative to the equinox (and relative to a purely solar calendar such as ours). Early in the first millennium, the new year took place before or around the time of the vernal equinox, but, presumably by intention, the beginning of the year was allowed to gradually slip to after the equinox by the beginning of the fifth century BC, after which it was kept stable.[10] The 12 months of the Babylonian calendar are:

Month I	Nisannu
Month II	Ajjaru
Month III	Simanu
Month IV	Du'uzu
Month V	Abu
Month VI	Ululu
Month VII	Tešritu
Month VIII	Araḫsamnu
Month IX	Kislimu
Month X	Ṭebetu
Month XI	Šabaṭu
Month XII	Addaru

Owing to the difficulty of making calendar-based calculations when months can be either 29 or 30 days in length and there may be either 12 or 13 months in a year, from as early as the late third millennium BC, a simplified 'schematic' calendar was often used in both astronomical and non-astronomical (e.g. economic) calculations.[11] In the schematic calendar, months are assumed to always contain 30 days, and the year to contain 12 months, making a total of 360 days in a year. It is important to stress that the schematic 360-day year never replaced the luni-solar calendar as a true calendar used in everyday life. Instead, the schematic calendar existed purely as a simplification of the true calendar, both to make calculation easier and to provide a fixed framework to place events (in our case, astronomical phenomena) in a schematic fashion. The schematic calendar already appeared in an astronomical context in texts that date to the Old Babylonian period, well before the composition of MUL.APIN. In those texts, the solstices and equinoxes are placed on the 15th days of Months III, VI, IX, and XII. In MUL.APIN and texts that follow it, however, the solstices and equinoxes are placed one month later, on the 15th of Months I, IV, VII, and X. The reason for this one-month shift in the dates of the solstices and equinoxes between the Old Babylonian and later texts is unknown. The schematic calendar is used extensively throughout MUL.APIN, in contrast to the true luni-solar calendar, which only appears in the context of intercalation rules.

10 Britton (2007).
11 For a summary of the use of the schematic calendar, see Brack-Bernsen (2007).

Numbers and quantities

The commonest types of number found in MUL.APIN are what are called 'quantities', that is, concrete numbers accompanied by a metrological unit that unambiguously represent the magnitude of a measurable item. Three types of quantity with their associated metrologies appear in MUL.APIN: intervals of time, weights, and lengths. Time intervals of less than a day are measured in bēru (DANNA), UŠ and NINDA, where there are 12 bēru in a day, 30 UŠ in a bēru, and 60 NINDA in an UŠ:

	12		30		60	
Day	↔	bēru	↔	UŠ	↔	NINDA

Weights are expressed in minas (MA.NA) and shekels (GÍN), where there are 60 shekels in a mina:

	60	
mina	↔	shekel

Lengths are expressed in cubits (KÙŠ).

The second type of number found in MUL.APIN is written using the floating-point sexagesimal place value system. In this system, each place is a factor of 60 larger than the place that follows it, but there is no indication of absolute magnitude. In our translation, we separate sexagesimal places using a comma. A number such as 23,5,56 can therefore be understood as $(23 \times 60^2) + (5 \times 60) + 56$ or $(23 \times 60) + 5 + (56 \times 60^{-1})$, or any multiple of 60 greater or smaller. In our commentary, we sometimes indicate the implied magnitude of a sexagesimal number by using a semicolon between integers and fractions.

In MUL.APIN, the floating-point sexagesimal place value system only appears within procedures as part of a calculation, never in the presentation of a piece of data. This is in accord with the use of the sexagesimal place value system within Babylonian mathematics, where it is used as an intermediary stage in performing calculations, but the initial problem and the final result are given as quantities with units.

Zigzag functions

A common mathematical tool employed in MUL.APIN, and within Babylonian astronomy more generally, is the zigzag function. Zigzag functions are used to model periodic variations by means of linear increases and decreases between maximum and minimum values in uniform steps. For example, the scheme for the variation in the time interval from sunrise to the rising moon on the fifteenth day of the month over the course of the year presented in II ii 43 – iii 12 follows a zigzag function, with a minimum value of 8 UŠ and a maximum value of 16 UŠ:

Month I	12 UŠ
Month II	10 UŠ 40 NINDA
Month III	9 UŠ 20 NINDA
Month IV	8 UŠ
Month V	9 UŠ 20 NINDA
Month VI	10 UŠ 40 NINDA
Month VII	12 UŠ
Month VIII	13 UŠ 20 NINDA
Month IX	14 UŠ 40 NINDA
Month X	16 UŠ
Month XI	14 UŠ 40 NINDA
Month XII	13 UŠ 20 NINDA

Each month, the time interval decreases by 1 UŠ 20 NINDA, until it reaches the minimum (*m*) of 8 UŠ, after which it increases by the same increment until it reaches the maximum (*M*) of 16 UŠ, after which it decreases again, so that the whole sequence begins again after 12 months. We refer to the increase per step as the difference (*d*) of the zigzag function. In this example, it takes 12 steps, or 12 months, to complete a full cycle of the sequence and return both to the same value and the same direction of increasing or decreasing values. Twelve months therefore constitute the *period* of the function (the interval in time after which the function repeats), and 12 steps constitute the function's *number period* (the number of steps after which the function repeats). In many zigzag functions used in later mathematical astronomy, the two periods are not equal: in such cases, the period of the function is not an integer; the function will not hit the minimum and maximum values in each cycle, because the difference between the minimum and maximum values is not an integer multiple of the function's difference *d*; and the number period will be significantly larger than the period, because it takes many cycles of increasing and decreasing values before the return to the same value. However, in MUL.APIN and other texts of early astronomy, the period and the number period are always equal, and the function reaches the maximum and minimum each cycle.

The place of MUL.APIN within Babylonian astral science

MUL.APIN is part of an astronomical tradition in Babylonia that stretches back to the early second millennium BC. Our knowledge of the earlier periods of Babylonian astral science, however, is largely dependent upon cuneiform tablets that were written in the eighth century BC or later. Although the content of these sources broadly accords with those of the few astronomical tablets preserved from earlier times, it is far from certain whether they provide us with an accurate picture of astronomical activity in the second and early first millennia BC. Put simply, the texts that are available to us are those that someone in the Neo-Assyrian and later periods considered worth copying, and therefore reflect the interests and biases of these late scribes. It is possible, for example, that whole other aspects of astronomical practice – for example, making and recording astronomical observations – existed but were not transmitted down into the late period. Thus, any characterizations of early Babylonian astronomy must remain tentative and preliminary.

Despite these words of caution, it is possible to identify several themes within early Babylonian astral science: the use of simple numerical schemes to model the variation of the length of day and night; the grouping of stars into three 'paths' associated with the gods Enlil, Anu, and Ea; the development of collections of celestial omens; and the use of the 360-day schematic calendar. Numerical schemes for the length of day and night are known from an Old Babylonian (early second millennium BC) tablet, BM 17175+17284,[12] the so-called 'Three Stars Each' texts,[13] the oldest known example of which dates to the twelfth century BC, and the fourteenth tablet of the celestial omen series *Enūma Anu Enlil*.[14] These schemes all assume a linear variation in the length of day and night between extremes in the ratio of 2:1, with the solstices and equinoxes placed in the middle of Months III, VI, IX, and XII of the schematic calendar. *Enūma Anu Enlil* tablet 14 also includes a scheme for the variation in the duration of visibility of the Moon over the course of a schematic equinoctial month: it assumes that the daily change in the Moon's visibility is equal to one-fifteenth of the length of night. The Three Stars Each texts contain lists of twelve stars in each of the three paths. Three stars, one from each path, are assigned to a month in the schematic calendar. These months are probably to be understood as the month in which the star makes its first appearance before sunrise (first visibility). Some of these texts add sections listing stars that rise and set simultaneously. Tablet 51 of *Enūma Anu Enlil* contains omens that utilize the lists of stars in the Three Stars Each texts.[15] Omens from a wide range of other types of celestial phenomenon, including the appearance of the Moon, lunar and solar eclipses, the appearance of the Sun, planetary phenomena, and metrological phenomena, are listed in other tablets of *Enūma Anu Enlil* – a large composition written on about seventy tablets – and its predecessors.[16]

All of the types of material contained in the texts just described are found in MUL.APIN as well: numerical schemes for the length of daylight and the duration of visibility of the Moon, star lists, and celestial omens. Furthermore, MUL.APIN and this other material share several basic principles such as the centrality of the schematic calendar and basic parameters, such as the 2:1 ratio for the length of the longest to the shortest day and the factor of one-fifteenth connecting the length of night and the daily change in the duration of visibility of the Moon. MUL.APIN goes further than this other material, however, by adding additional topics such as intercalation and the length of shadow cast by a gnomon, and by providing more precise information such as exact dates for the first appearance of stars, rather

12 Hunger and Pingree (1989: 163–164).
13 Horowitz (2014).
14 Al-Rawi and George (1991–1992).
15 Reiner and Pingree (1981).
16 For a survey of *Enūma Anu Enlil* and related material, see Koch-Westenholz (1995).

than simply the month in which this was expected to occur. Furthermore, there is one crucial difference between MUL.APIN and the Three Stars Each, *Enūma Anu Enlil* Tablet 14 and BM 17175+17284: MUL.APIN places the solstices and equinoxes in the middle of Months I, IV, VII, and X, whereas these other texts place them one month earlier. These two factors, the greater scope and precision of MUL.APIN and the change in the placement of the solstices and equinoxes in the schematic calendar, suggest, although do not prove, that MUL.APIN was composed later than these other texts.

MUL.APIN, the Three Stars Each, *Enūma Anu Enlil*, and similar texts present a fairly coherent picture of early Babylonian astronomy. These texts are all primarily descriptive rather than offering procedures for making astronomical calculations or recording accounts of specific observations. They present an overarching, largely self-consistent description of the universe that is mathematically ordered around the 360-day schematic calendar. Although based in part upon knowledge of observed astronomical phenomena, this description is not primarily empirical, and it is highly unlikely that observations were made specifically in order to produce this description. Rather, accumulated knowledge of simple astronomical phenomena that are easily seen without particular observations were combined with basic mathematical models such as the schematic calendar and the zigzag function, resulting in a description of the universe that, although based in astronomical reality, is simplified and schematized in order to produce a coherent model. One consequence of this simplification is that some parts of the resulting model are not very accurate. The clearest example of this inaccuracy is the 2:1 ratio for the length of longest to shortest day, which is a gross exaggeration for the latitude of either Babylonia or Assyria. Mathematical simplicity and the coherence between different parts of the overall description of the universe seem to have been given priority over accuracy here.[17] Furthermore, some of the gross inaccuracies in MUL.APIN may have been less important to the text's composer and reader than we tend to project on to them. Although the 2:1 ratio may be particularly bad, the function for the duration of visibility of the Moon that is derived from it, which may have been more important to the Babylonians, is not as bad.

The descriptive nature of MUL.APIN and other astronomical texts from the early period and the seeming inaccuracy of some of the contents lead to the question of what these texts were for. This question has no single answer: the texts almost certainly had a different function when they were written to the role they played in the late first millennium, for example. Two diametrically opposing views of how to understand the purpose of early Babylonian astronomy have been put forward in recent years. Brown (2000) has argued that MUL.APIN, the Three Stars Each, and other early texts present a model for an 'ideal' universe against which reality can be judged, with agreement being a positive omen and disagreement a negative omen. Brown's argument draws support from the story of the formation of the heavens in the Babylonian creation epic *Enūma Eliš*. The fifth tablet of this epic describes a universe that is created with a repeating order founded around a

17 Brown (2000).

30-day month and a 12-month year, exactly the schematic calendar used in early astronomical texts. Furthermore, *Enūma Eliš* makes a direct allusion to the Three Stars Each texts. Brown's argument is further supported by evidence from reports of divinatory practice that, for example, show that 29-day months were often considered unfavourable, whereas 30-day months were favourable. In Brown's interpretation, MUL.APIN was not intended to be used (and was not used) to calculate astronomical phenomena in the context of making astronomical predictions, but rather to provide an ideal that could be compared with observed reality purely for divinatory purposes. Brack-Bernsen (2005), however, argues that MUL.APIN was intended from its creation to be used to make astronomical (in the modern sense) predictions. In her view, the schemes that use the 360-day calendar provide a simple way to calculate phenomena that can then be adjusted to fit the actual luni-solar calendar by the two calendars being tied together through the dates of phenomena such as the solstices and equinoxes. Contrary to Brown's view, these two interpretations need not be mutually exclusive: the schemes found in MUL.APIN may have been used both to provide an ideal against which to judge reality for divinatory purposes and to simplify the calculation of astronomical phenomena by using schemes based upon the simple schematic calendar and nice numerical values for key parameters. Furthermore, it is quite possible that different readers of the text read it in different ways and used it for different purposes.

Our earliest sources for MUL.APIN date to the Neo-Assyrian period. A large number of tablets containing astronomical and astrological material are known from the last Assyrian capital of Nineveh, the earlier capitals of Assur and Kalhu, and other Assyrian cities, including Huzirina in Anatolia. In addition to MUL.APIN, these texts include works that can be thought of as standard reference works, such as copies of the celestial omen series *Enūma Anu Enlil* and other related omen material and commentaries, the Three Stars Each texts, and a variety of different star lists. There are also texts that are the result of astronomical and astrological practice, in particular, a large number of letters and reports sent by scholars to the kings Esarhaddon and Assurbanipal that concern the ominous interpretation of observed celestial phenomena. MUL.APIN was clearly already a well-known standard text by this period: it is referred to by name in a list of compositions (perhaps a library catalogue; K 12000d) and is mentioned as among the texts being copied for the king's library in a letter sent by the scholar Akkullanu to the king (Parpola 1993: No. 62). Passages from MUL.APIN are quoted in a handful of letters and reports (Hunger 1992: No. 507; Parpola 1993: No. 362), including one that identifies MUL.APIN as the source of the quotation (Parpola 1993: No. 62). A long quotation from MUL.APIN I iv 1–3 also appears at the head of a list of the distances between *ziqpu* stars (K 9794 and its late duplicate AO 6478).[18] Also from this period, we find excerpt texts that quote

18 The passage is lost on K 9794 but preserved on the duplicate AO 6478 from Seleucid Uruk. So far as they are preserved, the two tablets are exact duplicates, even in layout, and so there is no reason to believe that this passage was not found on K 9794.

whole sections from MUL.APIN: our sources NN and UU (see Table of sources), both from Assur, excerpt, respectively, the sections containing the scheme for the length of night and the duration of visibility of the Moon (II ii 43 – iii 12) and the intercalation scheme (II Gap A 8 – ii 6, although UU is broken at the beginning and so begins at II Gap A 13, and it ends unexpectedly at II ii 4 rather than at II ii 6). A later Babylonian excerpt, source M from Nippur, contains the list of the dates of first appearances of stars (I ii 36 – I iii 12; M is broken at the beginning and preserves only line I ii 42 onwards). These excerpt texts seem to extract from MUL.APIN the parts that are of most practical use, namely those that have to do with intercalation and the visibility of the Moon. Evidence from letters sent by scholars to the king show that one consideration in deciding if an intercalation was necessary was whether the first appearance of stars occurred at their expected time. Some of these letters quote visibility dates from I ii 36 – iii 12, and these dates were themselves used in the intercalation scheme described at II Gap A 8 – ii 6. The excerpt texts, therefore, provided ready access to those parts of MUL.APIN that were most commonly needed by the scholars. They also provide a strong indication that at least parts of MUL.APIN did indeed have a practical use and were not used only for divination.

Despite the existence of many other texts containing lists of stars that circulated during the Neo-Assyrian period, the repertoire of stars presented in MUL. APIN seems to have taken on a special status. For example, the uranology texts draw exclusively upon the constellations contained in MUL.APIN, and often quote from MUL.APIN their descriptions.[19] This again points to the central place held by MUL.APIN in early Mesopotamian astronomy.

Sources from Babylon and, to a lesser extent, Uruk and other cities show that extensive astronomical activity was undertaken in Babylonia from the latter part of the eighth century BC onwards. Babylonian astronomy quickly developed into a multifaceted endeavour that included the precise and systematic observation of individual celestial phenomena; the development and application of methods for the prediction of future phenomena by applying lunar and planetary periods to past observations; the construction of systems of mathematical astronomy that allowed certain lunar and planetary phenomena to be calculated using purely numerical methods, without direct empirical input; and new forms of astrology, including numerical schemes associating calendar dates with medical ingredients and cultic sites and systems of personal astrology. These new types of astronomy and astrology led to the production of new genres of astronomical texts, such as the Astronomical Diaries, which contain reports of night-by-night observations of certain celestial phenomena; Goal-Year Texts, which assemble observational data for predicting future astronomical phenomena; Almanacs and Normal Star Almanacs, which contain the results of these predictions; tables containing astronomical data calculated using the various systems of mathematical astronomy and

19 Beaulieu, Frahm, Horowitz, and Steele (2018).

procedure texts that explain how to make these predictions; and horoscopes that contain astronomical data for around the date of birth of an individual.

Given these extensive developments in Babylonian astronomy, it might be expected that MUL.APIN would have become redundant. The simple schemes modelling celestial phenomena, which relied upon the 360-day schematic calendar, would have quickly been seen to be crude and inaccurate once precise observations were systematically made and recorded, and the newly developed systems of mathematical astronomy were both more ambitious and more accurate than anything that could be achieved using the type of astronomy found in MUL.APIN. However, MUL.APIN continued to be copied and quoted until at least the last couple of centuries BC. Roughly half of the known sources for MUL.APIN are Late Babylonian, and quotations of the list of the dates of first visibilities of stars (I ii 36 – I iii 12), the statement concerning the daily change in which stars are visible (I iii 49 – I iii 50), and the statement that intercalation once every three years means that there are the equivalent of 10 extra days per year (II ii 13 – II ii 17) are known from other Late Babylonian astronomical texts.

MUL.APIN was not just copied, however, which could have implied that it survived only out of an antiquarian interest: new texts that drew directly from the astronomy of MUL.APIN were composed as well. These new texts continued the tradition of schematic astronomy, founded on the 360-day schematic year and the basic principles and parameters used in MUL.APIN, and include further expansions of the scheme for the length of shadow cast by a gnomon,[20] the lunar visibility scheme,[21] and the list of the dates of the first appearances of stars. Perhaps most surprisingly, a detailed mathematical scheme that gives the culmination of positions at or at specified distanced behind *ziqpu* stars at sunrise and sunset was developed, based upon the schematic calendar and the MUL.APIN scheme for the length of daylight. Remarkably, this scheme was then combined with the newly developed concept of the zodiac as a way of dividing the path of the Sun, Moon and planets into twelve equal parts to produce a so-called 'rising time scheme' that correlates the time it takes for a zodiacal sign to rise across the horizon with the range of distances behind *ziqpu* stars that culminate over the same time period.[22] This example shows that the astronomy of MUL.APIN remained part of a living tradition that existed alongside, and on occasions interacted with, the (what to us may seem incompatible) new developments in Babylonian astronomy during the last eight centuries BC.[23]

The continued importance of MUL.APIN in the late period is further demonstrated by a recently identified composition, partially preserved in at least two copies, that seems to rework sections of MUL.APIN, expanding on the

20 Steele (2013).
21 Brack-Bernsen and Hunger (2002: 72–75).
22 Steele (2017).
23 Steele (in press a).

information presented in the text and rewriting it in a deliberately different form.[24] Only a small fraction of the work can be reconstructed at present, but the preserved parts expand upon the list of dates in the schematic calendar of the first visibilities of stars in MUL.APIN I ii 36 – iii 12, the discussion of intercalation in II ii 13–17, and the scheme for the duration of lunar visibility in II ii 43 – II iii 15. Interestingly, the composition seems to parallel the overall structure of MUL.APIN, highlighting its direct relationship with the earlier text.

MUL.APIN holds an important place in the history of Babylonian astronomy. For the scholars of the Neo-Assyrian period onwards, the text represented the culmination of 'early' Babylonian astronomy, presenting a complete and self-consistent model of the celestial world. But, far from representing the end of this 'early' tradition of astronomy, MUL.APIN then became the foundation for later developments in schematic astronomy that existed alongside other types of astronomy in Babylonia.

Date and place of composition

The history of the composition of MUL.APIN – who composed it, when, and where – unfortunately remains uncertain. The earliest preserved copies date to the early seventh century BC: the colophon of source HH says that this tablet, which comes from Assur, was written in the eponym year of Sennacherib, corresponding to 687 BC, and the other Assur sources come from archives that date to around the same time. Similarly, archival context implies that the tablets from Nineveh were copied within a couple of decades of the middle of the seventh century BC, and that the tablets from Huzirina were written towards the end of the eighth century or during the first three-quarters of the seventh century BC.[25] The wide distribution of copies of the text and the fact that it was a composition that was referred to by name in other tablets from this period, however, suggest that MUL.APIN was not a new text at this time. It seems reasonable to suppose, therefore, the MUL.APIN could not have been composed any later than about 750 BC. How much earlier, however, is difficult to establish. The only firm piece of evidence placing a constraint on the age of MUL.APIN is the mention of the Kassites in line II ii 20, which places a *terminus post quem* for its composition in the middle of the second millennium BC when the Kassites gained control of Babylonia. Thus, the text could, in principle, have been composed any time between the middle of the second millennium and the end of the first quarter of the first millennium BC.

Two approaches have been used by earlier scholars to attempt to place narrower constraints upon the date of composition of MUL.APIN. Pingree,[26] Watson and

24 The work is partially preserved on BM 36315+37517, BM 36382, BM 37175, and BM 37200 and will be published in due course by J. M. Steele. For a description of these texts and a preliminary analysis, see Steele (in press a).

25 Pedersén (1995).

26 Reiner and Pingree (1981: 72–75) and Hunger and Pingree (1989: 11).

Horowitz,[27] and others have argued that it is possible to reconstruct a sequence of texts containing star lists, beginning with the Old Babylonian 'Prayer to the Gods of the Night', through the Three Stars Each texts (one of which is preserved on a tablet from the twelfth century BC), to MUL.APIN, with increasing accuracy in the sequence of first appearances of the stars. These authors therefore conclude that MUL.APIN was almost certainly written after the twelfth century. Although this conclusion is attractive, and very likely correct, there are methodological problems with this approach to dating. First, it assumes that a text that is astronomically more accurate is necessarily later than one that is less accurate. But this need not have been the case: accuracy in the modern sense may not have been the primary motivation underlying any of these lists. Second, the existence of a copy of the Three Stars Each text dating to the twelfth century BC does not imply that the Three Stars Each text was composed at that time: it is possible that the tablet contains a copy of a much earlier text.

The second approach to dating the composition of MUL.APIN has been to try to find the date that best fits some of the astronomical data contained in the composition. Most attempts have used either the list of dates of the first appearances of stars in I ii 36 – I iii 12 or the list of intervals of days between the first appearances of stars in I iii 34 – I iii 48, or both. Because the date of the first appearance of a star is dependent upon its celestial longitude and latitude and upon the geographical latitude of the observer, it should, in principle, be possible to find a date and latitude that provide the best agreement with modern computation. There are three obstacles to finding a correct result, however. First, the dates and the intervals in days given in MUL.APIN are reported using the schematic 360-day calendar, rather than a calendar that uses the true length of the solar year. Second, many of the 'stars' given in these lists are constellations or star groups. Does the first appearance of a constellation refer to the first appearance of one star of the constellation, or the appearance of enough stars to make the constellation readily identifiable, or even the appearance of the complete constellation? And third, can the ancient star names be confidently identified with modern counterparts, ideally without relying upon the list that is being analysed?

The first detailed attempt to date MUL.APIN astronomically was undertaken by van der Waerden (1949). He considered the intervals in days between the first appearances of the first star of a constellation and the first appearance of Sirius, concluding that the best fit was for dates between 1300 and 1000 BC and for an observer at the latitude of Babylon. Using a somewhat different set of identifications of stars, Papke (1978) proposed a much earlier date of around 2300 BC as best fitting the intervals between the first appearances of stars. Such an extremely early date does not seem plausible, however, and many of Papke's assumptions concerning the identification of stars do not hold up to close scrutiny. Reiner and Pingree (1981: 6) attempted to identify the Babylonian constellations visually using the Zeiss planetarium at the Adler Planetarium in Chicago, arriving at the

27 Watson and Horowitz (2011: 3–6).

conclusion that the best fitting date for the various star lists in MUL.APIN is about 1000 BC, and that the observations were made in Nineveh. Reiner and Pingree's approach relies heavily upon their own visual impressions and upon the (untestable) accuracy of the planetarium. More recently, de Jong (2007) has repeated the type of analysis done by van der Waerden, but using more detailed astronomical models of stellar visibility. De Jong concludes that the observations underlying the two lists of MUL.APIN can be dated to about 1300 BC with an uncertainty of about 150 years. He also concludes that the observations were probably made in Babylon, and that Nineveh can be excluded as a possible place of observation.

Although de Jong's analysis is the most convincing yet published, it still suffers from methodological problems that, in our view, cannot be overcome. First, when mapping dates in the text, which are given in the schematic 360-day calendar, on to the solar year, it is necessary either to alter those dates by stretching the 360-day year so that it reaches the length of the solar year (about 365¼ days) or to assume a period of 5¼ 'empty' days somewhere in the year (e.g. at the end). Although the effect of this assumption will be fairly small, it may nevertheless be sufficient to push the derived date too early or late. Second, and more serious, all attempts to use the dates of first appearances and the intervals between them acknowledge that the dates are given only to a precision of 5 days. However, they also tacitly assume that the dates have been obtained by simply rounding the date obtained from observation to the closest 5-day interval, and that the errors caused by such rounding balance out. In our opinion, this assumption is not justifiable on the basis of the available evidence. We do not know what strategies or techniques would have been used by the ancient scholars. Systematic rounding in one direction (e.g. always rounding up rather than rounding down or up to the nearest 5-day interval) would cause a significant bias in the data. Furthermore, it is possible that the dates given in the text were adjusted to make them fit into a scheme, rather than simply rounded, which would certainly bias the data. And finally, too many assumptions need to be made in the identification of stars and the interpretation of what first appearance means when constellations are mentioned.

Our conclusion must therefore be rather unsatisfactory: we simply do not know when MUL.APIN was composed. MUL.APIN's placement of the solstices and equinoxes one month later than in a text we can firmly date to the Old Babylonian period and in *Enūma Anu Enlil* and the Three Stars Each texts suggests that MUL.APIN is a later composition, and the fact that MUL.APIN was well known by the end of the eighth century BC provides a broad constraint on the date of the text, placing it in the late second or early first millennium BC, but no more than that. We lean towards an early first millennium BC date, but purely on impressionistic grounds.

We similarly have no definitive evidence for the place of composition of the text, although there are enough hints in the text to point towards a Babylonian rather than an Assyrian origin. An Assyrian origin would have important consequences for our understanding of scholarly activity in Assyria at this period,[28]

28 George (1991).

which is often downplayed in modern scholarship owing to lack of evidence and a default assumption that assigns scholarly developments to Babylonia when there is no compelling evidence to the contrary. As with establishing its date, the methodological problems with trying to answer the question of where MUL.APIN was composed by means of astronomical analysis are, in our opinion, too great to allow a firm conclusion to be drawn.

Three small pieces of non-astronomical evidence, however, provide modest support for concluding that MUL.APIN was a Babylonian composition. First, the three reigns associated with intercalary months (Šulgi, the Amorites, and the Kassites) in lines II ii 18 – II ii 20 make more sense from a Babylonian perspective than an Assyrian one: Šulgi was an important Sumerian king during the third dynasty of Ur, the Amorites ruled southern Babylonia during the early second millennium BC, and the Kassites ruled Babylonia during the second half of the first millennium BC. None of these kingdoms extended into Assyria. Second, if MUL.APIN was composed in the late second millennium BC in Assyria, as suggested by Pingree, this would almost coincide with the period in Assyrian history when intercalation was not performed in the Assyrian calendar (in contrast to the Babylonian calendar). It would therefore be difficult to understand why several intercalation rules are presented in the work. Finally, there are a few words in the text that are decidedly Babylonian: that is, they would be written differently in the Assyrian dialect:

I ii 29: be-let (Ass. bēlat)
I iii 8 and iii 50: li-la-a-ti (Ass. li-li-a-ti)
I iv 3: immaru (Ass. immuru)
I iv 38: annûtu (Ass. anniūtu)
II iii 36: lidekki (Ass. ludakki)

We therefore lean towards a Babylonian rather than an Assyrian origin for the work.

In conclusion, therefore, it seems likely that MUL.APIN was composed sometime in the late second or (more likely) early first millennium BC in Babylonia.

Edition

Table of sources

Single-letter sigla refer to tablets in Babylonian script, double-letter sigla to those in Assyrian script. In order to continue using the sigla from the earlier edition, it was necessary to introduce lower-case letters for most of the tablets identified since 1989. The choice of letters is therefore almost arbitrary.

Siglum	*Museum number*	*Lines preserved*
a	K 12376	I i 33–39, iv 21–26
A	BM 86378	I i 1–44, ii 1–47, iii 3–50, iv 1–39
AA	VAT 9429	I i 1–27, ii 16–36, iv 19–26
b	K 11816	I iii 14–23
B	K 13254	I i 1–6
BB	VAT 9435 (+) 19306	I i 1–16, 20–35, iii 12–24, iv 3–11
c	K 10719	I iii 17–20
C	BM 34814+35708	I i 8–20, ii 18–30
CC	K 11251	I i 1–10
d	BM 43849	I ii 25–34, iii 41–48
D	BM 42277	II i 1–16, i 58 – Gap A 11, iii 2–19, iv 3–12
DD	ND 4405/30	I i 1–23, iii 27–34
e	BM 43871	I ii 33–39
E	AO 7540+	I i 10–17, ii 47 – iii 26, iv 28 – II i 18, ii 19–30, iii 22–39
EE	ND 5497/22	I i 25–42, II ii 1–9
f	BM 59313	I ii 1–12, iv 15–20
F	K 3852	I i 19–28, iv 29–38
FF	Rm 2, 174+313	I i 37 – ii 9, iii 37–48, II iii 1–10, Gap B 6 – iv 12
g	BM 46871	I ii 13–22, iii 49 – iv 6
G	K 15929	I ii 2–12
GG	K 6558 + Sm 1907	I ii 39–42, iii 2–13, II Gap A 1–11
h	BM 73815	I iv 23–26
H	BM 76505	I ii 6–9, ii 31 – iii 36, iv 10–15

HH	VAT 9412+11279	II i 1–71, ii 1–54, iii 1–53, iv 1–12
j	Ashmolean 1924-1815	II ii 7–17
J	Rm 319	I ii 10–27, iii 29 – iv 15, II i 7–19
JJ	VAT 9527	I iii 48 – iv 5, II i 22–36, Gap A 12 – ii 8
k	BM 32427	I i 1–8, ii 14–18, iv 15–20
K	BM 32311	I ii 7–27, iii 44 – iv 6
KK	SU 52/72+	II i 9–43, ii 2–35, iii 15–27, iii 37 – iv 12
L	BM 45922	I iii 4–9, iv 5–6
LL	SU 51/16	II ii 51 – iii 6
m	W 18003f	I iii 20–33
M	N 1463	I ii 42 – iii 12
N	BM 33724+33779	I i 35–39, ii 41 – iii 5, iii 23–39
NN	VAT 8619	II ii 43–52, iii 4–12
O	K 3020	I iii 8–25, iv 17–27
OO	SU 52/50	II iii 16–22
P	BM 37325	II ii 12–23, ii 29–37
PP	SU 51/26A	II Gap B 4 – iv 2
Q	Rm 322	I ii 22–23, iv 2–12
QQ	SU 52/40	II iv 9–12
R	BM 35207	I iv 12–21
RR	SU 51/421	II iv 5–10
S	BM 36851	II i 6–15, i 69 – Gap A 4
SS	VAT 9415 (+) 10836 +11532 +11665 +11784	I iii 4–24, iv 7–19, II i 16–22, ii 8–10, iii 3–12
T	BM 41218	I i 27 – ii 1, iv 13–27
tt	K 20085	I i 14?–21?
TT	Rm 2, 380	I iii 3–12, II iii 27–33
U	BM 36627 + 37112 + 37144 + 37473	II iii 46 – Gap B, iv 1–9
UU	VAT 9893	II Gap A 12 – ii 4
V	BM 33791	I iii 1–14
VV	VAT 11270	I iii 39–43
W	BM 33728	I iii 34–47
WW	VAT 14424	I iii 2–9
X	BM 32626	I ii 19–27, iv 5–13
Y	K 8598	I ii 19 – iii 5
Z	BM 54817	I i 12–24

Description of sources

Copies and photos in the earlier edition are not listed here again.

A BM 86378
CDLI P479385
Copy: King, CT 33, 1–8

Selected bibliography: Bezold, Kopff and Boll 1913; Kugler 1913: 1ff. ; Weidner 1915: 35ff., 141ff.; van der Waerden 1968: 64–82.
Almost complete 4-column tablet. Labelled 'Tablet I' in its colophon.

a K 12376
Copy: Fincke (2017: 248).
Previous edition: Fincke (2017: 248–250).
Fragment from left edge.

AA VAT 9429
CDLI P496542
Copy: Hätinen (forthcoming).
Previous edition: Hätinen (forthcoming).
4-column tablet. From Assur, archive N2.

B K 13254
Upper left corner with beginning of Tablet I.

b K 11816
Copy: Fincke (2017: 256).
Previous edition: Fincke (2017: 255f.).
Flake from reverse.

BB VAT 9435 (+) 19306
CDLI P496543
Copy (of VAT 9435): Hätinen (forthcoming).
Previous edition: Hätinen (forthcoming).
From Assur.

C BM 34814+35708
CDLI P364246
Copy: LBAT No. 1496+1497.
Flake from obverse of 4-column tablet.

c K 10719
Copy: Fincke (2017: 256).
Previous edition: Fincke (2017: 255f.).
Flake from reverse.

CC K 11251
CDLI P399179
Copy: King, CT 26, 47.
Upper left corner.

D BM 42277
CDLI P496537
Upper half of a 4-column tablet. Called '2nd tablet' of MUL.APIN in its colophon.

E AO 7540 + W 3376q+3377p+3378i
CDLI P492525 (AO 7540 only)
Copies: Weidner (1923: 190f. (AO 7540); Falkenstein (1931) No. 113 (partial copy).

Obverse only of a 6-column tablet. From Uruk. Contrary to my remarks in the earlier edition, Falkenstein indicated by an * that the other side of the tablet was not preserved. In 1989, I had an excavation photo of the tablet (courtesy of the German Archaeological Institute). I could now read most of column ii but did not consider the very salt-encrusted remnants of col. i.

Oelsner (1986: 495) confirms the join of the two fragments. He also states that, according to the excavation records, this tablet is from the sixth or fifth century BC. The fragment W 18003f edited in Gehlken (1996) No. 240a has the upper edge preserved and cannot be joined to AO 7540 (against Ossendrijver 2012).

e BM 43871
Copy: Fincke (2014).
Previous edition: Fincke (2014).

EE ND 5497/22
CDLI P363443
Copy: Black and Wiseman (1996) No. 28
Probably fragment of a 4-column tablet. From Kalḫu.

F K 3852
CDLI P238299
Probably part of a 4-column tablet.

f BM 59313
Copy: Pls. III and IV.

FF Rm 2, 174+313
CDLI P426394
Copy: Virolleaud (1908–1911) Supp. 2 No. 67
6-column tablet.

G K 15929
CDLI P239410
Flake from right edge, probably 4-column tablet.

g BM 46871
Copy: Pls. V and VI.

GG K 6558 + Sm 1907
CDLI P396633
Copy: Weidner (1913/1923) Pl. I (of Sm 1907).
Probably 6-column tablet.

H BM 76505
CDLI P496539
Lower right part of a 4-column tablet containing Tablet I.

h BM 73815
Copy: Horowitz (1989–1990: 117).
Previous edition: Horowitz (1998–1990).

HH VAT 9412 + 11279
CDLI P496541
Copy: Hunger (1982).
4-column tablet; dated to 687 BC. From Assur.

J Rm 319
CDLI P240155
4-column tablet.

j Ashm 1924-1815
Copy: Gurney (1989) No. 86.

JJ VAT 9527
CDLI P496544
Copy: Hunger (1982).
Fragment of a 6-column tablet. From Assur.

K BM 32311
CDLI P496528
Upper right corner of a 4-column tablet.

k BM 32427
Copy: Pls. VII and VIII.

KK SU 52/72+
CDLI P338646
Copy: Gurney and Hulin (1963) No. 331–334.
4-column tablet, called 2nd (and last) tablet of MUL.APIN in its colophon.

L BM 45922
CDLI P496538
Lower edge of a 4-column tablet.

LL SU 51/16
CDLI P338653
Copy: Gurney and Hulin (1963) No. 338.

M N 1463
CDLI P276605
Small 1-column tablet. Reverse apparently not MUL.APIN.

m W 18003f
Copy and edition: Gehlken (1996) No. 240a.
Fragment from edge, probably 4-column tablet. From Uruk.

N BM 33724+33779
CDLI P496531
Copy: Fincke (2017: 252).
Previous edition: Kugler (1907) pl. 23 (BM 33779 only); Fincke (2017: 250–255).
Fragment of a 4-column tablet.

NN VAT 8619
CDLI P496540
Copy: Weidner (1939: 147) pl. XII.
Excerpt tablet.

O K 3020
CDLI P238245
Right middle part of a 4-column tablet.

OO SU 52/50
CDLI P338651
Copy: Gurney and Hulin (1963) No. 336.
Upper right corner.

P BM 37325
CDLI P496535
Probably 4-column tablet.

PP SU51/26A
CDLI P338652
Copy: Gurney and Hulin (1963) No. 337.
Flake from left edge.

Q Rm 322
CDLI P240157
Columns ii and iii of a 4-column tablet.

QQ SU52/40
CDLI P338628
Copy: Gurney and Hulin (1963) No. 313.

R BM 35207
CDLI P364247
Copy: LBAT No. 1498.
Flake from reverse of 4-column tablet.

RR SU 51/421
CDLI P338672
Copy: Gurney and Hulin (1963) No. 357
Flake, probably of reverse.

S BM 36851
CDLI P496533
Middle part of a 4-column tablet.

SS VAT 9415 (+) 10836+11532+11665+11784
Copy: Hätinen (forthcoming).
Previous edition: Hätinen (forthcoming).
6-column tablet. From Assur.

T BM 41218
CDLI P496536
Fragment of 4-column tablet.

TT Rm 2, 380
Mentioned Reiner (1998: 285).
Copy: Pls. IX and X.
8-column tablet?

U BM 36627+37112+37144+37473
CDLI P496534
Copy: Fincke (2017: 258).
Previous edition: Fincke (2017: 257–260).
Flake from reverse, left edge partly preserved.

UU VAT 9893
Copy: Hätinen (forthcoming).
Excerpt tablet. From Assur.

V BM 33791
CDLI P496532
Copy (by A. Sachs): Pl. XII.
Probably fragment of 4-column tablet.

VV VAT 11270
Copy: Hätinen (forthcoming).
Previous edition: Hätinen (forthcoming).
Fragment of 2-column tablet. From Assur.

W BM 33728
CDLI P496530
Copy (by A. Sachs): Pl. XI.
Fragment from edge of probably 4-column tablet.

WW VAT 14424
Copy: Hätinen (forthcoming).
Fragment of 4-column tablet. From Assur.

X BM 32626
CDLI P496529
Fragment of 4-column tablet.

Y K 8598
CDLI P238743
Lower left corner of 2-column tablet.

Z BM 54817
Copy and previous edition: Horowitz (1989–1990).

Concordance of museum numbers

Museum number	*Siglum*
AO 7540+	E
Ashm 1924-1815	j
BM 32311	K
BM 32427	k
BM 32626	X
BM 33724+33779	N
BM 33728	W
BM 33791	V
BM 34814+35708	C
BM 35207	R
BM 36627 + 37112 + 37144 + 37473	U
BM 36851	S
BM 37325	P
BM 41218	T
BM 42277	D
BM 43849	d
BM 43871	e
BM 45922	L
BM 46871	g
BM 54817	Z
BM 59313	f
BM 73815	h
BM 76505	H
BM 86378	A
K 10719	c
K 11251	CC

(continued)

(continued)

Museum number	*Siglum*
K 11816	b
K 12376	a
K 13254	B
K 15929	G
K 20085	tt
K 3020	O
K 3852	F
K 6558 + Sm 1907	GG
K 8598	Y
N 1463	M
ND 4405/30	DD
ND 5497/22	EE
Rm 2, 174+313	FF
Rm 2, 380	TT
Rm 319	J
Rm 322	Q
SU 51/16	LL
SU 51/26A	PP
SU 51/421	RR
SU 52/40	QQ
SU 52/50	OO
SU 52/72+	KK
VAT 8619	NN
VAT 9412+11279	HH
VAT 9415 (+) 10836 +11532 +11665 +11784	SS
VAT 9429	AA
VAT 9435 (+) 19306	BB
VAT 9527	JJ
VAT 9893	UU
VAT 11270	VV
VAT 14424	WW
W 18003f	m

Concordance of previously published tablets

The earlier edition of 1989 is not listed here.

Publication	*Siglum*
Black and Wiseman (1996) No. 27	DD
Black and Wiseman (1996) No. 28	EE

Falkenstein (1931) No. 113	E
Fincke (2017: 248)	a
Fincke (2017: 252)	N
Fincke (2017: 255f.)	c
Fincke (2017: 256)	b
Fincke (2017: 257–260)	U
Fincke (2014)	e
Gehlken (1996) No. 240a	m
Gurney and Hulin (1963) No. 313	QQ
Gurney and Hulin (1963) Nos 331–334	KK
Gurney and Hulin (1963) No. 336	OO
Gurney and Hulin (1963) No. 337	PP
Gurney and Hulin (1963) No. 338	LL
Gurney and Hulin (1963) No. 357	RR
Gurney (1989) No. 86	j
Horowitz (1989–1990: 116)	Z
Horowitz (1989–1990: 117)	h
Hunger (1982: 128–134)	HH
Hunger (1982: 135)	JJ
King, CT 33: 1–8	A
King, CT 26: 47	CC
Kugler (1907) pl. 23	N
LBAT No. 1496	C
LBAT No. 1497	C
LBAT No. 1498	R
Reiner (1998: 285)	TT
Virolleaud (1908–1911) 2nd Supp. 67	FF
Weidner (1913) pl. I	GG
Weidner (1923: 190f.)	E
Weidner (1927) pl. XII	NN

Tablet I

i 1		DIŠ $^{mul\ giš}$APIN ^{d}En-líl a-lik pa-ni MUL^{meš} šu-ut ^{d}En-líl
A i 1		[a-li]k pa-ni MUL^{meš} šu-ut ^{d}En-líl
B	1	[^{mu}]$^{l\ giš}$APIN ^{d}En-líl a-lik IGI [ ]
k i 1		[ ]-⸢ni$^{?}$ MUL$^{me?}$ ^{d}En-líl⸣
AA i 1		DIŠ ⸢^{mul}APIN⸣ [^{d}En-l]íl a-li[k IGI] ^{d}En-líl
BB	1	[ ] APIN ^{d}E[n]-l[íl a-li]k IGI [ ]
CC	1	^{mul}[ ]
DD	1	[DIŠ ^{m}]^{ul}APIN ^{d}En-líl a-lik IGI [ ]

Epinnu Enlil ālik pāni kakkabī šūt Enlil

¶ The Plough, Enlil, who goes in front of the stars of Enlil.

i 2		DIŠ ^{mul}UR.BAR.RA ^{giš}NÍNDA šá ^{mul}APIN
A i 2		[ ] ^{giš}NÍNDA šá ^{mul}APIN
B	2	[DIŠ ^{mul}]UR.BAR.RA ^{giš}NÍNDA [ ]
k i 2		[ ] ⸢šá⸣ ^{mul}APIN
AA i 2		DIŠ ⸢^{mul}UR⸣.BAR.RA ⸢^{giš}NÍNDA šá⸣ ^{mul}[API]N
BB	2	^{mul}UR.BAR.RA NÍNDA ^{m}[^{ul}APIN
CC	2	^{mul}UR.BAR.[RA]
DD	2	[DIŠ] ^{mul}UR.BAR.RA [^{giš}NÍ]NDA [ ]
		Barbaru ittû ša Epinni
		¶ The Wolf, the seed-funnel of the Plough.
i 3		DIŠ ^{mul}ŠU.GI ^{d}En-me-šár-ra
A i 3		[DIŠ ^{mul}ŠU].GI ^{d}En-me-šár-ra
B	3	[Š]U.GI [ ]
k i 3		[^{d}E]n-me-šár-ra
AA i 3		DIŠ ⸢^{mul}ŠU⸣.GI ^{d}En-me-šár-ra
BB	3	^{mul}ŠU.GI ^{d}[En]-me-š[ár-ra]
CC	3	^{mul}ŠU.[GI]
DD	3	DIŠ ^{mul}ŠU.GI ^{d}En-me-⸢šár⸣-ra
		Šību Enmešarra
		¶ The Old Man, Enmešarra.
i 4		[DIŠ] ^{mul}GÀM ^{d}Gam-lum
A i 4		[DIŠ ^{mul}]GÀM ^{d}Gam-lum
B	4	[GÀ]M [ ]
k i 4		[GÀ]M Gam-lum
AA i 3		^{mul}⸢GÀM⸣ ^{d}Gam-⸢lum⸣
BB	4	^{mul}GÀM [^{d}]Ga-[ ]
CC	4	^{mul}G[ÀM]
DD	3	^{mul}GÀM [ ]
		Gamlu Gamlu
		¶ The Crook, Gamlu.
i 5		DIŠ ^{mul}MAŠ.TAB.BA.GAL.GAL.LA ^{d}Lugal-ir$_{9}$-ra ù ^{d}Mes-lam-ta-è-a
A i 5		[ ] ⸢MAŠ.TAB.BA⸣.GAL.GAL ^{d}Lugal-ir$_{9}$-ra u ^{d}Mes-lam-ta-è-a
B	5	[.B]A.GAL.GAL.LA ^{d}Lugal-ir$_{9}$-ra ù ^{d}[ ]
k i 5		[^{d}Lugal-ir$_{9}$-r]a u ^{d}Mes-lam-ta-è-a
AA i 4		DIŠ ^{mul}⸢MAŠ.TAB.BA⸣.GAL.GAL ^{d}Lugal-ir$_{9}$-ra ^{d}Mes-lam-ta-⸢è-a⸣
BB	5	^{mul}MAŠ.TAB.BA.GAL.GAL ^{d}Lugal-[ir$_{9}$-ra] 6) ù ^{d}Mes-lam-ta-⸢è⸣-[a]
CC	5	^{mul}M[AŠ
DD	4	DIŠ ^{mul}MAŠ.TAB.BA.GAL.GAL.LA ^{d}Lugal-⸢ir$_{9}$⸣-ra ù ^{d}[ ]
		Tū'amū rabûtu Lugalirra u Meslamtaea
		¶ The Great Twins, Lugalirra and Meslamtaea.
i 6		DIŠ ^{mul}MAŠ.TAB.BA.TUR.TUR ^{d}Alammuš ù ^{d}Nin-EZEN×GUD
A i 6		[DIŠ ^{mul}MAŠ.TAB.B]A.TUR.TUR ^{d}Alammuš u ^{d}Nin-EZEN×GUD
B	6	[.TU]R.T[UR ^{d}Alam]muš ù [ ]

k i 6		[ ]^{d}Nin-EZEN×GUD
AA i 5		DIŠ ^{mul}MAŠ.[TA]B.BA.⸢TUR⸣.TUR ^{d}MÙŠ.LÀL ^{d}Nin- E[ZEN×GUD]
BB	7	^{mul}MAŠ.TAB.BA.TUR.TUR ^{d}Alammuš 8) ù ^{d}Nin-[EZEN×GUD]
CC	6	^{mul}[ ]
DD	5	[DIŠ] ^{mul}MAŠ.TAB.BA.TUR.TUR ^{d}Al[ammuš] ù ^{d}[Nin-]

Tūʾamū ṣeḫrūtu Alammuš u Nin-EZEN×GUD
¶ The Small Twins, Alammuš and Nin-gublaga.

<u>i 7</u> DIŠ ^{mul}AL.LUL šu-bat ^{d}A-nim

A i 7		[DIŠ ^{mul}AL.LU]L šu-bat ^{d}A-nim
k i 7		[ ] ⸢^{d}A⸣-nim
AA i 6		DIŠ ⸢^{mul}AL⸣.LUL šu-bat ^{d}⸢A-nim⸣
BB	9	^{mul}AL.LUL šu-⸢bat ^{d}A⸣-ni[m]
CC	7	^{mul}[ ]
DD	6	[DIŠ ^{mu}]^{l}AL.LUL šu-bat ^{d}A-nim

Alluttu šubat Anim
¶ The Crab, the seat of Anu.

<u>i 8</u> DIŠ ^{mul}UR.GU.LA ^{d}La-ta-ra-ak

A i 8		[DIŠ ^{mul}UR.G]U.LA ^{d}La-ta-ra-ak
C i 1′		[ ] ⸢x⸣ [ ]
k i 8		[-r]a-ak-a
AA i 7		DIŠ ^{mul}UR.GU.LA ^{d}La-ta-[ra]k
BB	10	^{mul}UR.GU.LA ^{d}La-⸢ta-rak⸣
CC	8	^{mu}[^{l}]
DD	6	^{mul}UR.GU.LA ^{d}[ ]

Urgulû Latarak
¶ The Lion, Latarak.

<u>i 9</u> DIŠ MUL šá ina GABA ^{mul}UR.GU.LA GUB-zu ^{mul}LUGAL

A i 9		[^{m}]^{ul}UR.GU.LA GUB-zu ^{mul}LUGAL
C i 2′		[ ] GUB-zu ^{múl}LUGAL
AA i 8		DIŠ MUL šá ina GABA ^{mul}UR.GU.LA GUB-zu ⸢^{mul}LUGAL⸣
BB	11	MUL ša ina GABA ^{mul}UR.GU.LA GUB-[zu] 12) ^{mul}⸢LUGAL⸣
CC	9	M[UL]
DD	7	[ ] GABA ^{mul}UR.GU.LA GUB-zu ^{m}[^{ul}LUGAL]

kakkabu ša ina irat Urgulî izzazzu Šarru
¶ The star which stands in the chest of the Lion: the King.

<u>i 10</u> DIŠ MUL^{meš} um-mu-lu-tu$_{4}$ šá ina KUN ^{mul}UR.GU.LA

A i 10		[um-mu-l]u-tu$_{4}$ šá ina KUN ^{mul}UR.GU.LA
C i 3′		[ ] ^{mul}UR.GU.LA
E i 1′		[ ].LA
AA i 9		DIŠ MUL um-mu-⸢lu⸣-tu$_{4}$ šá ina K[UN] ^{mul}UR.GU.LA
BB	13	MUL^{meš} um-mu-lu-tu šá ina KUN ^{mul}U[R.GU.LA]
CC	10	M[UL]
DD	8	[um-m]u-lu-tú šá ina KUN ^{mul}UR.GU.LA

kakkabū ummulūtu ša ina zibbat Urgulî
¶ The scintillating stars which stand in the tail of the Lion:

i 11 GUB-zu sis-sin-nu ^{d}E$_{4}$-ru$_{6}$ ^{d}Zar-pa-ni-tu$_{4}$

A i 11		[sis]-sin-nu ^{d}E$_{4}$-ru$_{6}$ ^{d}Zar-pa-ni-tu$_{4}$
C i 3′		G[UB] sis-sin-nu ^{d}E$_{4}$-ru$_{6}$ 4) ^{d}Zar-pa-ni-tu$_{4}$
E i 1′		GUB-zu 2) [^{d}Za]r-pa-ni-tu$_{4}$
AA i 9		⸢GUB⸣-zu 10) sis-sin-nu ^{d}E$_{4}$-ru$_{6}$ ^{d}⸢Zar⸣-pa-ni-tu$_{4}$
BB	14	GUB$^{meš\ si\text{-}si\text{-}nu}$sis-sin-⸢nu⸣ 15) ^{d}⸢E$_{4}$-ru$_{6}$⸣$^{e\text{-}ru}$ ^{d}Zar-pa-ni-⸢tu$_{4}$⸣
DD	8	GUB-zu [ ]

izzazzū sissinnu Eru Zarpanītu
The Frond (of the date palm) of Eru, Zarpanitu.

i 12 DIŠ ^{mul}ŠU.PA ^{d}En-líl šá ši-mat KUR i-šim-mu

A i 12		[^{d}En]-líl šá ši-mat KUR i-šim-mu
C i 5′		[ši]-mat KUR i-š[im]-me
E i 3′		[i]-šim-me
Z	1′	[DIŠ ^{mul}Š]U.[P]A ^{d}[En-líl]
AA i 11		DIŠ ⸢^{mul}ŠU⸣.PA ^{d}En-líl šá ši-mat KUR i-⸢šim-ma⸣
BB	16	^{mul}ŠU.PA ^{d}BE šá ši-mat ⸢KUR⸣ i-šim-m[u]
DD	9	[ ] ^{d}En-líl šá ši-mat KUR [ ]

ŠU.PA Enlil ša šīmat māti išimmu
¶ ŠU.PA, Enlil who decrees the fate of the land.

i 13 DIŠ MUL šá ina IGI-šú GUB-zu ^{mul}Ḫé-gál-a-a-ú SUKAL ^{d}Nin-líl

A 1 13		[-z]u ^{mul}Ḫé-gál-a-a SUKAL ^{d}Nin-líl
C i 6′		[ ] ^{múl}Ḫé-gál-la-a-a [SUKAL] ^{d}Nin-líl
E i 4′		[^{mul}Ḫé-gál-a]-a SUKAL ^{d}Nin-líl
Z	2′	[DIŠ M]UL šá ina IGI-šú GUB-⸢zu⸣ [ ]
AA i 12		DIŠ MUL [šá ina I]G[I-š]ú GUB-zu ^{mul}Ḫé-gál-a-a-ú SUKAL ^{d}Nin-líl
BB	17	MUL šá ina IGI.šú G [UB-zu ^{mul}Ḫé]-gál-a-a-[ú] 18) SUKAL [^{d}Nin-líl]
DD	10	[ ] IGI-šú GUB-zu ^{mul}Ḫé-gál-a-a [ ]

kakkabu ša ina pānišu izzazzu Ḫegalaju sukal Ninlil
¶ The star which stands in front of it: the Abundant One, the minister of Ninlil.

i 14 DIŠ MUL šá EGIR-šú GUB-zu MUL BAL.TÉŠ.A SUKAL ^{d}MÚŠ

A i 14		[M]UL BAL.TÉŠ.A SUKAL ^{d}MÚŠ
C i 7′		[ ] MUL BAL.TÉŠ.A SU[KAL] ^{d}MÚŠ
E i 5′		[BAL.TÉŠ].A SUKAL ^{d}MÚŠ
Z	3′	[DIŠ] MUL šá EGIR-šú GUB-zu MUL [ ]
AA i 13		DIŠ ⸢MUL šá⸣ EGIR-šú GUB-zu MUL BAL.TÉŠ.A SUKAL ^{d}MÚŠ
BB	19	MUL šá ina [ ] 20) SUKAL [^{d}MÚŠ]
DD	11	[ ] EGIR-šú GUB-zu MUL BAL.TÉŠ.A [ ]

kakkabu ša arkišu izzazzu Kakkab bāšti sukal Tišpak
¶ The star which stands behind it: the Star of Dignity, the minister of Tišpak.

i 15 DIŠ ^{mul}MAR.GÍD.DA ^{d}Nin-líl

A i 15		[ ].⸢DA⸣ ^{d}Nin-líl
C i 8′		[^{d}]Nin-líl

E i 6′ [ ] ^{d}Nin-líl
Z 4′ DIŠ ^{mul}MAR.GÍD.[DA]
AA i 14 DIŠ $^{mu[l}$M]AR.GÍD.DA ^{d}Nin-líl
BB 21 ^{mul}[ ]
DD 12 [MA]R.GÍD.DA [ ]

Ereqqu Ninlil
¶ The Wagon, Ninlil.

i 16 DIŠ MUL šá KI za-ri-i šá ^{mul}MAR.GÍD.DA GUB-zu

A i 16 [šá KI z]a-ri-i šá MAR.GÍD.DA GUB-zu
C i 9′ [šá ^{mul}M]AR.GÍD.DA GUB-zu
E i 7′ [ ] GUB-zu
Z 5′ DIŠ MUL šá KI za-re-e šá ^{mul}M[AR.GÍD.DA]
AA i 15 DIŠ M[UL] ⸢šá KI⸣ za-ri-⸢i šá⸣ ^{mul}MAR.GÍD.⸢DA GUB⸣-zu
BB 22 MU[L]
DD 13 [ ] šá KI za-re-e šá ⸢^{mul}MAR⸣.GÍD.DA GUB-zu

kakkabu ša ašar zarî ša Ereqqi izzazzu
¶ The star which stands in the shaft of the Wagon:

i 17 ^{mul}KA$_5$.A ^{d}Èr-ra gaš-ri DINGIR^{meš}

A i 17 [$^{m]ul}$KA$_5$.A ^{d}Èr-ra gaš-ri DINGIR^{meš}
C i 9′ ^{mul}KA$_5$.A ^{d}Èr-ra 10) gaš-ri DINGIR^{meš}
E i 8′ [gaš-r]i DINGIR^{meš}
AA i 16 DIŠ ^{mul}KA$_5$.A ^{d}Èr-ra gaš-ri DINGIR^{meš}
BB 23 $^{m[ul}$]

Šēlebu Erra gašri ilāni
the Fox, Erra, the strong one of the gods.

i 18 DIŠ MUL šá ina SAG.KI ^{mul}MAR.GÍD.DA GUB-zu ^{mul}U$_8$ ^{d}A-a

A i 18 DIŠ ⸢MUL šá⸣ ina ⸢SAG⸣.KI ^{mul}MAR.GÍD.DA GUB-zu ^{mul}U$_8$ ^{d}A-a
C i 11′ [GUB]-zu ^{mul}U$_8$ ^{d}A-a
Z 6′ DIŠ MUL šá ina SAG.KI ^{mul}MAR.GÍD.[DA]
AA i 17 ⸢DIŠ MUL⸣ šá ina ⸢SAG⸣.KI ^{mul}⸢MAR.GÍD.DA⸣ GUB-zu ^{mul}U$_8$ ^{d}A-a
BB 24 [ ]
DD 14 [ ] šá ina SAG.KI ^{mul}MAR.GÍD.DA GUB-zu [ ]

kakkabu ša ina pūt Ereqqi izzazzu Laḫru Aja
¶ The star which stands in the front part of the Wagon: the Ewe, Aja.

i 19 DIŠ ^{mul}MU.BU.KÉŠ.DA ^{d}A-num GAL-ú šá AN-e

A i 19 DIŠ ^{mul}MU.BU.KÉŠ.DA ^{d}A-num GAL-ú šá AN-e
C i 12′ [ ] GA[L-ú] šá AN-e
F 1′ DIŠ ^{mul}[ ]
Z 7′ DIŠ ^{mul}MU.BU.KÉŠ.DA $^{⸢d⸣}$[A-num]
AA i 18 ⸢DIŠ ^{mul}MU⸣.[B]U.KÉŠ.DA ^{d}A-nu-um GAL-u šá AN-e
BB 25 [ ]
DD 15 [M]U.BU.KÉŠ.DA ^{d}A-num GA[L-ú]

MU.BU.KÉŠ.DA Anu rabû ša šamê
¶ The Hitched Yoke, great Anu of heaven.

i 20		DIŠ ^{mul}MAR.GÍD.DA.AN.NA ^{d}Dam-ki-an-na

A i 20		DIŠ ^{mul}MAR.GÍD.DA.AN.NA ^{d}Dam-ki-an-na
C i 13′		[^{d}D]am-ki-an-na
F	2′	DIŠ ^{mul}MAR.GÍD.D[A].AN.[NA]
Z	8′	DIŠ ^{mul}MAR.GÍD.DA.AN.NA ⸢^{d}⸣[ ]
AA i 19		DIŠ ^{mul}M[AR.GÍ]D.DA.AN.NA ^{d}Dam-ki-an-na
BB	26	⸢^{mul}⸣ [ ]
DD	16	[DIŠ ^{m}]^{ul}MAR.GÍD.DA.AN.[N]A [ ]

Ereqqi šamê Damkianna
¶ The Wagon of Heaven, Damkianna.

i 21		DIŠ MUL šá ina ṭur-ri-šú GUB-zu ^{mul}IBILA.É.MAḪ

A i 21		DIŠ MUL šá ina ṭur-ri-šú GUB-zu ^{mul}IBILA.É.MAḪ
F	3′	DIŠ MUL šá ina ṭur-ri-šú GU[B-zu]
Z	9′	DIŠ MUL šá ina DUR-šú GUB-⸢za ^{mul}⸣[ ]
AA i 20		DIŠ MUL [šá ina ṭu]r-ri-šú GUB-zu ^{mul}IBILA ⸢MAḪ ÀM$^{?}$⸣
BB	27	MUL ša [ ] 28) [^{m}]^{ul}IBILA [ ]
DD	17	[DIŠ M]UL šá ina ṭur-ri-šú GUB-zu IBILA M[AḪ$^{?}$]

kakkabu ša ina ṭurrišu izzazzu Ibila-Emaḫ
¶ The star which stands in its knot: the Heir of the Sublime Temple,

i 22		DUMU res-tu-ú šá ^{d}A-nu-um

A i 22		DUMU res-tu-ú šá ^{d}A-nu-um
F	4′	DUMU res-tu-ú [ ]
AA i 21		⸢MUL⸣ [DUMU] ⸢reš-tu-ú⸣ šá ^{d}A-nim
BB	28	[DUMU reš-tu-ú] 29) ša [ ]

māru rēštû ša Anim
the first-ranking son of Anu.

i 23		DIŠ ^{mul}DINGIR.GUB.BA^{meš} šu-ut É-kur <DIŠ> ^{mul}DINGIR.TUŠ.A^{meš} šu-ut É-kur

A i 23		DIŠ ^{mul}DINGIR.GUB.BA^{meš} šu-ut É-kur ^{mul}DINGIR.TUŠ.A^{meš} šu-ut É-kur
F	5′	DIŠ ^{mul}DINGIR.GUB.BA^{meš} [ ] 6) DIŠ ^{mul}DINGIR.TUŠ.A^{meš} [ ]
Z	10′	DIŠ ^{mul}DINGIR.GUB.BA^{m}[^{eš}]
AA i 22		[DIŠ ^{m}]^{ul}DINGIR.⸢GUB.BA⸣^{meš} šu-ut É-kur DINGIR.TUŠ.A šu-ut É-kur
BB	30	^{mul}DINGIR.GU[B.BA] 31) ^{mul}DINGIR.TU[Š.A^{meš}]
DD	18	[DIŠ ^{m}]^{ul}DINGIR.GUB.BA^{meš} [ ] 19) [DIŠ ^{mul}DINGIR.TU]Š.A^{meš} š[u-ut]

dingirgubbû šūt Ekur dingirtušû šūt Ekur
¶ The Standing Gods of Ekur. ¶ The Sitting Gods of Ekur.

i 24		DIŠ ^{mul}ÙZ ^{d}Gu-la

A i 24		DIŠ ^{mul}ÙZ ^{d}Gu-la
F	7′	DIŠ ^{mul}ÙZ [ ]
Z	11′	DIŠ ^{mul}⸢ÙZ⸣ [ ]
AA i 23		[DIŠ ^{mu}]^{l}ÙZ ^{d}⸢Nin-kar⸣-ra-ak

BB 32 ^{mul}ÙZ [ ]
EE i 1′ [ ] ⌜x x⌝ [x x]

Enzu Gula
¶ The Goat, Gula.

i 25 DIŠ MUL šá ina IGI ^{mul}ÙZ GUB-zu ^{mul}UR.KU

A i 25 DIŠ MUL šá ina IGI ^{mul}ÙZ GUB-zu ^{mul}UR.KU
F 8′ DIŠ MUL ša [ ]
AA i 24 [DIŠ MU]L šá ina IGI ^{mul}ÙZ GUB-zu ^{mul}⌜UR.KU⌝
BB 33 MUL šá ina IGI ^{mul}Ù[Z]
EE i 2′ [^{m}]^{ul}⌜UR⌝.K[U]

kakkabu ša ina pān Enzi izzazzu Kalbu
¶ The star which stands in front of the Goat: the Dog.

i 26 DIŠ MUL né-bu-ú šá ^{mul}ÙZ ^{d}LAMMA SUKAL ^{d}Ba-Ú

A i 26 DIŠ MUL né-bu-ú šá ^{mul}ÙZ ^{d}LAMMA SUKAL ^{d}Ba-Ú
F 9′ DIŠ MUL [ ]
AA i 25 [DIŠ MU]L né-bu-u šá ^{mul}ÙZ ^{d}LAMMA SUKAL [ ]
BB 34 [MUL né-bu-ú š[a ^{mul}ÙZ] 35) ^{d}LAMMA SUKAL [ ]
EE i 3′ [ ] ^{mul}ÙZ 4) [^{d}]Ba-Ú

kakkabu nebû ša Enzi Lamassu sukal Baba
¶ The bright star of the Goat: Lamma, the minister of Baba.

i 27 DIŠ 2 MUL^{meš} šá EGIR-šú GUB^{meš}-zu ^{d}Nin-SAR u ^{d}Èr-ra-gal

A i 27 DIŠ 2 MUL^{meš} šá EGIR-šú GUB^{meš}-zu ^{d}Nin-SAR u ^{d}Èr-ra-gal
F 10′ DIŠ 2 [ ]
T i 1′ [^{d}Ni]n-[S]AR u ^{d}Èr-ra-gal
AA i 26 [ ] šá EGIR-šú ⌜GUB-zu⌝ [ ]
BB 36 2 MUL^{meš} ša EGIR-š[u GUB^{meš}] 37) ^{d}Nin-SAR ù ^{d}[Èr-ra-gal]
EE i 5′ [GU]B-zu 6) [ ] ^{d}Èr-ra-gal

2 kakkabū ša arkišu izzazzū Nin-SAR u Erragal
¶ The two stars which stand behind it: Nin-nisig and Erragal.

i 28 DIŠ ^{mul}UD.KA.DUḪ.A ^{d}U.GUR

A i 28 DIŠ ^{mul}UD.KA.DUḪ.A ^{d}U.GUR
F 11′ DIŠ [ ]
T i 2′ [ ] ^{d}U.GUR
BB 38 ^{mul}KA.DUḪ.A ⌜^{d}⌝[U.GUR]
EE i 7′ [ ] ^{d}U.GUR

Nimru Nergal
¶ The Panther, Nergal.

i 29 DIŠ MUL šá ina ZAG-šú GUB-zu ^{mul}ŠAḪ ^{d}Da-mu

A i 29 DIŠ MUL šá ina ZAG-šú GUB-zu ^{mul}ŠAḪ ^{d}Da-mu
T i 3′ [ ] ^{mul}ŠAḪ ^{d}Da-mu

BB 41 MUL šá ina ZAG-šú GUB ^{mul}ŠÁḪ [ ]
EE i 9′ [ ] ⸢GUB$^{?}$⸣ ^{mul}ŠAḪ ^{d}Da-mu

kakkabu ša ina imittišu izzazzu Šaḫû Damu
¶ The star which stands on its right: the Pig, Damu.

<u>i 30</u> DIŠ MUL šá ina GÙB-šú GUB-zu ^{mul}ANŠE.KUR.RA

A i 30 DIŠ MUL šá ina GÙB-šú GUB-zu ^{mul}ANŠE.KUR.RA
T i 4′ [ ] GU[B-zu] ^{mul}ANŠE.KUR.RA
BB 39 MUL šá ina GÙB-šu [GUB] 40) ^{mul}⸢ANŠE⸣.[KUR.RA]
EE i 8′ [GUB]-zu ^{mul}ANŠE.KUR.RA

kakkabu ša ina šumēlišu izzazzu Sīsû
¶ The star which stands on its left: the Horse.

<u>i 31</u> DIŠ MUL šá EGIR-šú GUB-zu ^{mul}lu-lim SUKAL MUL.MUL

A i 31 DIŠ MUL šá EGIR-šú GUB-zu ^{mul}lu-lim SUKAL MUL.MUL
T i 5′ [ ] GUB-z[u ^{m}]^{ul}lu-lim SUKAL MUL.MUL
BB 42 MUL šá EGI[R]-⸢šú⸣ GUB ^{mul}[lu-lim] 43) SUKAL MUL.[MUL]
EE i 10′ [EGIR]-šú GUB ^{mul}lu-lim 11) [SUKA]L MUL.MUL

kakkabu ša arkišu izzazzu Lulīmu sukal Zappi
¶ The star which stands behind it: the Stag, the minister of the Stars.

<u>i 32</u> DIŠ MUL^{meš} um-mu-lu-tu$_{4}$ šá ina GABA ^{mul}lu-lim

A i 32 DIŠ MUL^{meš} um-mu-lu-tu$_{4}$ šá ina GABA ^{mul}lu-lim
a 1′ ⸢DIŠ⸣ [MU]L^{m}[^{eš}]
T i 6′ [um-m]u-lu-tu$_{4}$ šá ina GA[BA] ^{mul}lu-lim
BB 44 MUL^{meš} um-mu-lu-t[u] šá ina [ ]
EE i 12′ [um]-mu-lu-tu šá ina GABA ^{mul}lu-lim

kakkabū ummulūtu ša ina irat Lulīmi
¶ The scintillating stars which stand in the chest of the Stag:

<u>i 33</u> GUB^{meš}-zu ^{d}Ḫar-ri-ru ^{d}TIR.AN.NA

A i 33 GUB^{meš}-zu ^{d}Ḫar-ri-ru ^{d}TIR.AN.NA
a 2′ [ ] ^{d}⸢Ḫar⸣-[ ]
T i 6′ GUB-zu ^{d}Ḫar-ri-ri 7) ^{d}TIR.AN.NA
BB 45 GUB^{meš} ^{d}Ḫar-[ri-ru ^{d}TIR.AN.NA]
EE i 13′ [^{d}]Ḫar-ri-ru ^{d}TIR.AN.NA

izzazzū Ḫarriru Manzât
The Vole, the Rainbow god.

<u>i 34</u> DIŠ MUL SA$_{5}$ né-bu-ú šá ina BIR ^{mul}lu-lim

A i 34 DIŠ MUL SA$_{5}$ né-bu-ú šá ina BIR ^{mul}lu-lim
a 3′ DIŠ MUL SA$_{5}$ n[é-bu-ú]
T i 8′ [né-bu]-⸢ú⸣ šá ina BIR ^{mul}lu-lim

BB 46 MUL SA$_5$ né-bu-[ú]
EE i 14′ [DIŠ MUL S]A$_5$ né-bu-ú šá ina BIR ^{mul}lu-lim

kakkabu sāmu nebû ša ina kalīt Lulīmi
¶ The bright red star which stands in the kidney of the Stag:

i 35 GUB-zu ^{mul}ZÚ.MUŠ.Ì.KÚ.E

A i 35 GUB-zu ^{mul}ZÚ.MUŠ.Ì.KÚ.E
N i 1′ [ ].E
T i 8′ [GU]B-zu ^{mul}ZÚ.MUŠ.Ì.KÚ.E
BB 47 GUB $^{mu[l}$]
EE i 15′ [GUB-z]u ^{mul}ZÚ.MUŠ.Ì.KÚ.E

izzazzu Pāšittu
The Deleter.

i 36 ki-ma MUL^{meš} šu-ut ^{d}En-líl ug-dam-mi-ru-ni

A i 36 ki-ma MUL^{meš} šu-ut ^{d}En-líl ug-dam-mi-ru-ni
a 4′ GIM MUL$^{me[š}$]
N i 2′ [n]i
T i 9′ [ki-ma MUL$^{me]š}$ šu-ut ^{d}En-líl ug-dam-mi-ru-[ni]
EE i 16′ [ki-ma] MUL^{meš} šu-ut 50 ug-da-me-ru-ni

kīma kakkabū šūt Enlil ugdammirūni
When the stars of Enlil have been finished,

i 37 1 MUL GAL UD.DA-su da-aʾ-mat AN-e BAR-ma GUB-zu MUL ^{d}AMAR.UD né-bi-ri

A i 37 1 MUL GAL UD.DA-su da-aʾ-mat AN-e BAR-ma GUB-zu MUL ^{d}AMAR.UD né-bi-ri
a 5′ 1 MUL GAL U[D.DA] 7′) MUL ^{d}[ ]
N i 3′ [-r]i
T i 10′ [1 MUL GAL UD.DA-s]u da-aʾ-mat AN-e BAR-ma GUB-ma M[UL]
EE i 17′ [1 MU]L GAL-ú UD.DA-su da-aʾ-mat 18) AN-e BAR-ma GUB-iz 19) [MU]L ^{d}AMAR.UD ^{d}Né-be-ru
FF i 1′ [-m]a ⸢GUB-ma⸣ M[UL]

ištēn kakkabu rabû ṣēssu daʾmat šamê uštamšalma izzaz kakkab Marduk Nēberu
one big star – (although) its light is dim – divides the sky in half and stands there: (that is) the star of Marduk, the Ford.

i 38 DIŠ ^{mul}SAG.ME.GAR KI.GUB-su KÚR.KÚR-ir AN-e ib-bir

A i 38 DIŠ ^{mul}SAG.ME.GAR KI.GUB-su KÚR.KÚR-ir AN-e ib-bir
a 7′ DIŠ ^{mul}SA[G.ME.GAR]
N i 4′ [ib-bi]r
T i 11′ [ ] KI.GUB-su KÚR.KÚR-ma A[N]
EE i 20′ [DIŠ $^{m]ul}$SAG.ME.GAR KI.GUB-su KÚR.KÚR-ir 21) AN-e ib-bir
FF i 2′ [DIŠ] ^{mul}SAG.ME.GAR K[I.GUB]

SAG.ME.GAR manzāssu ittanakkir šamê ibbir
¶ Jupiter keeps changing its position and crosses the sky.

<u>i 39</u> 33 MUL^{meš} šu-ut ^{d}En-líl

A i 39		33 MUL^{meš} šu-ut ^{d}En-líl
a	8′	33 MU[L^{meš}]
N i 5′		[^{d}En-lí]l
T i 12′		[MUL^{me}]^{š} šu-ut [^{d}En-líl]
EE i 22′		[x]+1 MUL^{meš} šu-ut ^{d}En-líl
FF i 3′		33 MUL^{meš} [ ]

33 kakkabū šūt Enlil
33 stars of Enlil.

<u>i 40</u> DIŠ ^{mul}AŠ.IKU šu-bat ^{d}É-a a-lik IGI MUL^{meš} šu-ut ^{d}A-nim

A i 40		DIŠ ^{mul}AŠ.IKU šu-bat ^{d}É-a a-lik IGI MUL^{meš} šu-ut ^{d}A-nim
a	9′	⸢DIŠ⸣ ^{m}[^{ul}]
T i 13′		[šu]-bat ^{d}É-a a-lik IGI MUL šu-ut [^{d}A-nim]
EE i 23′		[DIŠ ^{mu}]^{l}AŠ.IKU šu-bat ^{d}É-a 24) a-lik pa-an MUL^{meš} šu-ut [^{d}A-nim]
FF i 4′		DIŠ ^{mul}AŠ.IKU šu-bat ^{d}É-⸢a⸣ [ ]

Ikû šubat Ea ālik pān kakkabī šūt Anim
¶ The Field, the seat of Ea, who goes in front of the stars of Anu.

<u>i 41</u> DIŠ MUL šá ina IGI-et ^{mul}AŠ.IKU GUB-zu ^{mul}Ši-nu-nu-tu$_4$

A i 41	DIŠ MUL šá ina IGI-et ^{mul}AŠ.IKU GUB-zu ^{mul}Ši-nu-nu-tu$_4$
T i 14′	[IGI-e]t ^{mul}AŠ.IKU GUB-zu ^{mul}Ši-nu-[nu-tu$_4$]
EE i 25′	[DIŠ MU]L šá ina IGI-et ^{mul}AŠ.IK[U GUB-zu] 25) ^{mul}Ši-nu-nu-tu$_4$
FF i 5′	DIŠ MUL šá ina IGI-et ^{mul}AŠ.IK[U]

kakkabu ša ina meḫret Ikî izzazzu Šinūnūtu
¶ The star which stands opposite the Field: the Swallow.

<u>i 42</u> DIŠ MUL šá EGIR ^{mul}AŠ.IKU GUB-zu ^{mul}A-nu-ni-tu$_4$

A i 42	DIŠ MUL šá EGIR ^{mul}AŠ.IKU GUB-zu ^{mul}A-nu-ni-tu$_4$
T i 15′	[DIŠ MUL šá EGI]R ^{mul}AŠ.IKU GUB-zu ^{mul}A-nu-[ni-tu$_4$]
EE i 25′	[DIŠ MU]L šá EGIR ^{mul}AŠ.IKU [GUB-zu] 26) [^{mul}A-n]u-n[i-tu$_4$]
FF i 6′	DIŠ MUL šá EGIR ^{mul}AŠ.IKU [ ]

kakkabu ša arki Ikî izzazzu Anunītu
¶ The star which stands behind the Field: Anunitu.

<u>i 43</u> DIŠ MUL šá EGIR-šú GUB-zu $^{\text{mul lú}}$Ḫ̮UN.GÁ ^{d}Dumu-zi

A i 43	DIŠ MUL šá EGIR-šú GUB-zu $^{\text{mul lú}}$Ḫ̮UN.GÁ ^{d}Dumu-zi
T i 16′	[EGIR-š]ú GUB-zu ^{mul}Ḫ̮UN.GÁ ^{d}Dumu-[zi]
EE i 27′	[ ]-⸢šú$^{?}$ GUB$^{?}$⸣ [ ]
FF i 7′	DIŠ MUL šá EGIR-šú GUB-zu $^{\text{mul lú}}$Ḫ̮UN.GÁ ^{d}D[umu-zi]

kakkabu ša arkišu izzazzu Agru Dumuzi
¶ The star which stands behind it: the Hired Man, Dumuzi.

i 44		DIŠ MUL.MUL ^{d}7.BI DINGIR^{meš} GAL^{meš}
A i 44		DIŠ MUL.MUL ^{d}7.BI DINGIR^{meš} GAL^{meš}
T i 17′		[ ] DINGIR^{meš} [ ]
FF i 8′		DIŠ MUL.MUL ^{d}7.BI DINGIR^{meš} GAL$^{\text{⸢meš⸣}}$

Zappu Sebettu ilū rabûtu
¶ The Stars, the Seven, the great gods.

ii 1		DIŠ ^{mul}GU$_4$.AN.NA ^{d}is le-e AGA ^{d}A-nim
A ii 1		DIŠ ^{mul}GU$_4$.AN.NA ^{d}is l[e-e]
f	1′	DIŠ M[UL]
T i 18′		[^{d}i]s [le-e]
FF i 9′		DIŠ ^{mul}GU$_4$.AN.NA is le-e AGA ^{d}A-nim

alû is lê agê Ani
¶ The Bull of Heaven, the Jaw of the Bull, the crown of Anu.

ii 2		DIŠ ^{mul}SIPA.ZI.AN.NA ^{d}Pap-sukal SUKAL ^{d}A-nim u INNIN
A ii 2		DIŠ ^{mul}SIPA.ZI.AN.NA ^{d}Pap-sukal SUK[AL ^{d}A-nim u INNIN]
f	2′	DIŠ ^{mul}[ ]
G	1′	[ ] u ^{d}I[NNIN]
FF i 10′		DIŠ ^{mul}SIPA.ZI.AN.NA ^{d}Pap-sukal SUKAL ^{d}A-nim u INNIN

Šidallu Papsukal sukal Ani u Ištar
¶ The True Shepherd of Anu, Papsukal, the minister of Anu and Ištar.

ii 3		DIŠ ^{mul}MAŠ.TAB.BA šá ina IGI-it ^{mul}SIPA.ZI.AN.NA
A ii 3		DIŠ ^{mul}MAŠ.TAB.BA šá ina IGI-it $^{\text{mu[l}}$SIPA.ZI.AN.NA]
f	3′	DIŠ ^{mul}MAŠ.[TAB.BA]
FF i 11′		DIŠ ^{mul}MAŠ.TAB.BA šá ina IGI-it ^{mul}SIPA.ZI.AN.NA

Tū'amū ša ina meḫret Šidalli
¶ The twin stars which stand opposite the True Shepherd of Anu:

ii 4		GUB^{meš}-zu ^{d}LÚ.LÀL u ^{d}La-ta-ra-ak
A ii 4		GUB^{meš}-zu ^{d}LÚ.LÀL u ^{d}La-[ta-ra-ak]
G	2′	[ ] ^{d}La-ta-ra-ak
FF i 11′		GUB-zu 12) ^{d}LÚ.LÀL u ^{d}La-ta-ra-ak

izzazzū Lulal u Latarak
Lulal and Latarak.

ii 5		DIŠ MUL šá EGIR-šú GUB-zu ^{mul}DAR.LUGAL
A ii 5		DIŠ MUL šá EGIR-šú GUB-zu ^{mul}[DAR.LUGAL]
f	4′	DIŠ MUL ša EGI[R]
G	3′	[ ] ^{d}DAR.LUGAL
FF i 13′		DIŠ MUL šá EGIR-šú GUB-zu ^{mul}DAR.LUGAL

kakkabu ša arkišu izzazzu Tarlugallu
¶ The star which stands behind it: the Rooster.

<u>ii 6</u> DIŠ ^{mul}KAK.SI.SÁ šil-ta-ḫu UR.SAG GAL-ú ^{d}Nin-urta

A ii 6		DIŠ ^{mul}KAK.SI.SÁ šil-ta-ḫu UR.SAG GAL-ú [^{d}Nin-urta]
f	5′	DIŠ ^{mul}KAK.SI.S[Á]
G	4′	[ ] ^{d}MAŠ
H i 1′		[^{d}Nin-u]rta
FF i 14′		DIŠ ^{mul}KAK.SI.SÁ šil-ta-ḫu UR.SAG GAL-ú ^{d}Nin-urta

Šukūdu šiltaḫu qarrādu rabû Ninurta
¶ The Arrow, the arrow of the great warrior Ninurta.

<u>ii 7</u> DIŠ ^{mul}BAN ^{d}Iš-tar NIM.MA-tu$_{4}$ DUMU.SAL ^{d}En-líl

A ii 7		DIŠ ^{mul}BAN ^{d}Iš-tar NIM.MA-tu$_{4}$ DUMU.SAL [^{d}En-líl]
f	6′	DIŠ ^{mul}BAN ^{d}Iš-[tar]
G	5′	[ ] DUMU.SAL ^{d}En-líl
H i 2′		[^{d}E]n-líl
K ii 1′		[ ] e-la-ma-tú ⸢DUMU.SAL⸣ ^{d}En-[líl]
FF i 15′		DIŠ ^{mul}BAN ^{d}Iš-tar NIM.MA-tu$_{4}$ DUMU.SAL ^{d}En-líl

Qaštu Ištar elammatu mārat Enlil
¶ The Bow, the Elamite Ištar, the daughter of Enlil.

<u>ii 8</u> DIŠ $^{mul\ d}$MUŠ ^{d}Nin-giš-zi-da EN er-ṣe-tu$_{4}$

A ii 8		DIŠ $^{mul\ d}$MUŠ ^{d}Nin-giš-zi-da EN er-ṣe-tu$_{4}$
f	7′	DIŠ ^{mul}MUŠ ^{d}Ni[n-giš-zi-da]
G	6′	[ ] EN KI-tì
H i 3′		[er-ṣe]-tu$_{4}$
K ii 2′		[^{d}Ni]n-giš-zi-da EN KI-[ ]
FF i 16′		DIŠ $^{mul\ d}$MUŠ ^{d}Nin-giš-zi-da EN KI-tì

Niraḫ Ningišzida bēl erṣeti
¶ The Snake, Ningišzida, lord of the Netherworld.

<u>ii 9</u> DIŠ ^{mul}UGA^{mušen} a-ri-bu MUL ^{d}IM

A ii 9		DIŠ ^{mul}UGA^{mušen} a-ri-bu MUL ^{d}IM
f	8′	DIŠ ^{mul}UGA^{mušen} [ ]
G	7′	[ ] MUL ^{d}IM
H i 4′		[ ] ^{d}IM
K ii 3′		[DIŠ ^{múl}UG]A^{mušen} a-ri-bi MUL ^{d}⸢IM⸣
FF i 17′		DIŠ ^{mul}[UGA^{mušen} MU]L ^{d}IM

Āribu kakkab Adad
¶ The Raven, the star of Adad.

<u>ii 10</u> DIŠ ^{mul}AB.SÍN ^{d}Ša-la šu-bu-ul-tu$_{4}$

A ii 10		DIŠ ^{mul}AB.SÍN ^{d}Ša-la šu-bu-ul-tu$_{4}$
f	9′	DIŠ ^{mul}AB.SÍN ^{d}Ša-l[a]
G	8′	[ ] šu-bul-tu$_{4}$

J i 1′ [ ]-tu$_4$
K ii 4′ [DIŠ ^{múl}AB.S]ÍN ^{d}Ša-la ^{d}Šu-bu-lá

Šer'u Šala šubultu
¶ The Furrow, Šala, the ear of grain.

ii 11 DIŠ ^{mul}ZI.BA.AN.NA SI ^{mul}GÍR.TAB

A ii 11 DIŠ ^{mul}ZI.BA.AN.NA SI ^{mul}GÍR.TAB
f 10′ DIŠ ^{mul}ZI.BA.AN.NA S[I]
G 9′ [ ] ^{mul}GÍR.TAB
g 1′ [S]I$^{?}$ ⸢x⸣ [ ]
J i 2′ [^{mul}]GÍR.TAB
K ii 4′ DIŠ ^{múl}ZI.BA.[AN.NA]

Zibānītu qaran Zuqāqīpi
¶ The Scales, the horn of the Scorpion.

ii 12 DIŠ MUL ^{d}Za-ba$_4$-ba$_4$ ^{mul}TI$_8^{mušen}$ u ^{mul}AD$_6$

A ii 12 DIŠ MUL ^{d}Za-ba$_4$-ba$_4$ ^{mul}TI$_8^{mušen}$ u ^{mul}AD$_6$
f 11′ DIŠ MUL ^{d}Za-ba$_4$-ba$_4$ [ ] ⸢x x⸣ [ ]
G 10′ [$^{m]ul}$AD$_6$
g 2′ [$^{mu]l}$⸢TI$_8^{mušen}$⸣ [ ]
J i 3′ [$^{m]ul}$AD$_6$
K ii 5′ [DIŠ MÚL ^{d}Za]-ba$_4$-ba$_4$ ^{múl}TI$_8^{mušen}$ u ^{múl}[AD$_6$]

Kakkab Zababa Erû u Pagru
¶ The star of Zababa, the Eagle, and the Corpse.

ii 13 DIŠ ^{mul}Dili-bat KI.GUB-su KÚR.KÚR-ir-ma AN-e ib-bir

A ii 13 DIŠ ^{mul}Dili-bat KI.GUB-su KÚR.KÚR-ir AN-e ib-bir
g 3′ [DIŠ ^{mul}]Dili-bat KI.GUB-su KÚR.K[ÚR-ir-]
J i 4′ [ ]-⸢e⸣ ib-bir
K ii 6′ [KI.GUB-s]u KÚR.KÚR-ir-ma AN-e ib-bir

Dilibat manzāssu ittanakkirma šamê ibbir
¶ Venus keeps changing its position and crosses the sky.

ii 14 DIŠ ^{mul}Ṣal-bat-a-nu KI.GUB-su KÚR.KÚR-ir-ma AN-e ib-bir

A ii 14 DIŠ ^{mul}Ṣal-bat-a-nu KI.GUB-su KÚR.KÚR-ir AN-e ib-bir
g 4′ DIŠ $^{m]ul}$Ṣal-bat-⸢a-nu⸣ KI.GUB-su KÚR.[ ]
J i 5′ [ ]-ir-ma AN-e ib-bir
K ii 7′ [ ] KI.GUB-su KÚR.KÚR-ir-ma AN-e ib-bir
k ii 1 DIŠ ^{mul}Ṣal-bat-a-[nu]

Ṣalbatānu manzāssu ittanakkirma šamê ibbir
¶ Mars keeps changing its position and crosses the sky.

ii 15 DIŠ ^{mul}UDU.IDIM.SAG.UŠ KI.GUB-su KÚR.KÚR-ir-ma AN-e ib-bir

A ii 15 DIŠ ^{mul}UDU.IDIM.SAG.UŠ KI.GUB-su KÚR.KÚR-ir AN-e ib-bir
g 5′ [DIŠ $^{m]ul}$⸢UDU.IDIM.SAG⸣.UŠ KI.GUB-su KÚR.⸢KÚR⸣ [ ]

J i 6′ [ ]-ir-ma AN-e ib-bir
K ii 8′ [DIŠ ^{mul}UDU.IDIM.SA]G.[U]Š KI.GUB-su KÚR.KÚR-ir-ma AN-e ib-bir
k ii 2 DIŠ ^{mul}UDU.IDIM.[SAG.UŠ]

Kajamānu manzāssu ittanakkirma šamê ibbir
¶ Saturn keeps changing its position and crosses the sky.

ii 16 DIŠ ^{mul}UDU.IDIM.GU$_4$.UD šá ^{d}MAŠ MU.NI lu-ú ina ^{d}UTU.È.A

A ii 16 DIŠ ^{mul}UDU.IDIM.GU$_4$.UD šá ^{d}MAŠ MU.NI lu ina ^{d}UTU.È
g 6′ [DIŠ $^{mu]l}$UDU.IDIM.GU$_4$.UD šá ⸢^{d}MAŠ MU⸣-šú lu [ ]
J i 7′ [ ] lu ina ^{d}UTU.È
K ii 9′ [ ] ⸢^{d}MAŠ⸣ MU-šú lu-ú ina ^{d}UTU.È.A
k ii 3 DIŠ ^{mul}UDU.IDIM.G[U$_4$.UD]
AA ii 1 ⸢DIŠ⸣ $^{m[ul}$]

Šiḫṭu ša Ninurta šumšu lu ina ṣīt Šamši
¶ Mercury, whose name is Ninurta, rises or sets in the east

ii 17 lu-ú ina ^{d}UTU.ŠÚ.A e-ma ITI IGI.LÁ-ma e-ma ITI TÙM

A ii 17 lu ina ^{d}UTU.ŠÚ.A e-ma ITI IGI.LÁ-ma e-ma ITI TÙM
g 7′ [ ] e-ma ITI IGI.LÁ-ma e-[ma]
J i 8′ [m]a e-ma ⸢ITI⸣ TÙM
K ii 9′ lu-ú ina ^{d}UTU.ŠÚ.A e-ma ITI IGI.LÁ e-ma ITI TÙM
k ii 4 e-[ ]
AA ii 1 [^{d}UT]U.ŠÚ 2) ⸢e⸣-ma [ITI] ⸢IGI.LÁ-ma⸣ [e-ma ITI] TÙM

lu ina ereb Šamši ēma arḫi innammarma ēma arḫi itabbal
or in the west within a month.

---

ii 18 23 MUL^{meš} šu-ut ^{d}A-nim

A ii 18 23 MUL^{meš} šu-ut ^{d}A-nim
C ii 1′ 23 MUL^{meš} [ ]
g 8′ [ ] MUL^{meš} [ ]
J i 9′ [šu-u]t ^{d}A-nim
K ii 10′ [š]u-ut ^{d}A-nim
k ii 5 23 [ ]
AA ii 3 ⸢23 MUL⸣[^{meš}] šu-⸢ut⸣ ^{d}A-nim

23 kakkabū šūt Anim
23 stars of Anu.

---

ii 19 DIŠ ^{mul}KU$_6$ ^{d}É-a a-lik IGI MUL^{meš} šu-ut ^{d}É-a

A ii 19 DIŠ ^{mul}KU$_6$ ^{d}É-a a-lik IGI MUL^{meš} šu-ut ^{d}É-a
C ii 2′ DIŠ ^{mul}KU$_6$ ^{d}É-[a]
g 9′ [ ] ^{d}É-a a-lik IGI MU[L^{meš}]
J i 10′ [MUL]^{meš} šu-ut ^{d}BE
K ii 11′ [M]UL šu-ut ^{d}É-a
k ii 6 DIŠ [ ]

X ii 1′		[^{d}]É-a a-lik ⸢IGI⸣ M[UL^{meš}]
Y	1′	DIŠ ^{m}[^{ul}KU$_{6}$]
AA ii 4		⸢DIŠ⸣ [^{mul}KU$_{6}$] ⸢^{d}É⸣-[a] šu-ut ^{d}É-a

Nūnu Ea ālik pān kakkabī šūt Ea
¶ The Fish, Ea, who goes in front of the stars of Ea.

ii 20 DIŠ ^{mul}GU.LA ^{d}É-a ^{mul}NUN^{ki} ^{d}É-a

A ii 20		DIŠ ^{mul}GU.LA ^{d}É-a ^{mul}NUN^{ki} ^{d}É-a
C ii 3′		DIŠ ^{mul}GU.LA ^{d}[É-a]
g	10′	[ ] ^{d}É-a ^{mul}N[UN^{ki}]
J i 11′		[^{mul}NUN^{k}]^{i} ^{d}É-a
K ii 12′		[^{mul}NUN^{k}]^{i} ^{d}É-a
X ii 2′		DIŠ ^{mul}G[U.L]A [ ] 3) DIŠ ^{mul}NUN^{ki} [ ]
Y	2′	DIŠ ^{m}[^{ul}GU.LA]
AA ii 5		DIŠ ⸢^{mul}⸣GU.LA ^{d}É-a ⸢^{mul}⸣NUN^{ki} ^{d}É-⸢a⸣

GU.LA Ea Eridu Ea
¶ The Great One, Ea; Eridu, Ea.

ii 21 DIŠ MUL šá ina 15-šú GUB-zu ^{mul}Nin-maḫ

A ii 21		DIŠ MUL šá ina 15-šú GUB-zu ^{mul}Nin-maḫ
C ii 4′		DIŠ MUL šá ina 15-šú GUB-[zu]
g	11′	[G]UB-zu [ ]
J i 12′		[ ]Nin-maḫ
K ii 13′		[ ]
X ii 4′		DIŠ MUL šá ina 15-šú GUB-zu [ ]
Y	3′	DIŠ M[UL]
AA ii 6		DIŠ ⸢MUL šá⸣ ina [15-šú G]UB-zu ^{mul}Nin-maḫ

kakkabu ša ina imittišu izzazzu Ninmaḫ
¶ The star which stands at its right: Ninmaḫ.

ii 22 DIŠ ^{mul}EN.TE.NA.BAR.ḪUM ^{d}Nin-gír-su

A ii 22		DIŠ ^{mul}EN.TE.NA.BAR.ḪUM ^{d}Nin-gír-su
C ii 5′		[ ]
g	12′	[ ] ⸢x⸣ [ ]
J i 13′		[^{d}]Nin-gír-su
K ii 13′		[DIŠ ^{mul}E]N.TE.NA.BAR.ḪUM ^{d}Nin-gír-su
Q ii 1′		[DIŠ ^{mul}]EN.TE.N[A].B[AR.ḪUM]
X ii 5′		DIŠ ^{mul}EN.TE.NA.BAR.ḪUM [ ]
Y	4′	DIŠ ^{m}[^{ul}]
AA ii 7		[DIŠ ^{mul}E]N.T[E].NA.BAR.Ḫ[UM] ^{d}Nin-gír-su

Ḫabaṣīrānu Ningirsu
¶ The Mouse, Ningirsu.

ii 23 DIŠ MUL šá ina Á-šú GUB-zu $^{mul\ giš}$GÁN.ÙR ^{giš}TUKUL šá ^{d}A É

A ii 23		DIŠ MUL šá ina Á-šú GUB-zu $^{mul\ giš}$GÁN.ÙR ^{giš}TUKUL šá ^{d}A É
C ii 5′		DIŠ MUL šá ina Á-šú G[UB-zu]

J i 14′		[$^{\text{mul giš}}$GÁN.Ù]R ^{giš}TUKUL 15) [ ]
K ii 14′		[D]UMU É
Q ii 2′		[DIŠ MU]L šá ina Á-šú GU[B]-z[u]
X ii 6′		DIŠ MUL šá ina Á-šú ⌜GUB⌝-zu $^{\text{mùl giš}}$GÁN.Ù[R]
Y	5′	DIŠ MUL [ ]
AA ii 8		⌜DIŠ MUL šá⌝ ina Á-šú ⌜GUB-zu⌝ $^{\text{mul giš}}$GÁN.Ù[R]$^{?}$ ^{giš}TUKUL šá DUMU ⌜x⌝

kakkabu ša ina idišu izzazzu Maškakātu kakku ša Mār-bīti
¶ The star which stands at its side: the Harrow, the weapon of Mār-bīti,

<u>ii 24</u> šá ina lìb-bi-šú ZU.AB i-bar-ru-ú

A ii 24		šá ina lìb-bi-šú ZU.AB i-bar-ru-ú
d	1′	[ ] ⌜x⌝ [ ]
J i 15′		[ZU.A]B i-bar-ru-ú
K ii 14′		šá ina ŠÀ-šú ZU.AB i-bar-ru-ú
AA ii 9		šá ina ŠÀ-šú ZU.AB i-bar-ru-[ú]

ša ina libbišu apsâ ibarrû
by means of which he sees the subterranean waters.

<u>ii 25</u> DIŠ 2 MUL^{meš} šá EGIR-šú GUB^{me}-zu ^{d}Šúllat u ^{d}Ḫániš ^{d}UTU u ^{d}IM

A ii 25		DIŠ 2 MUL^{meš} šá EGIR-šú GUB^{me}-zu ^{d}Šúllat u ^{d}Ḫániš ^{d}UTU u ^{d}IM
C ii 6′		DIŠ 2 MUL^{meš} šá E[GIR-šú]
d	2′	[GUB^{me}]^{š}-zu ^{d}Šúllat u ^{d}Ḫ[ániš]
J i 16′		[ ] u ^{d}Ḫániš ^{d}[UTU u] ^{d}IM
K ii 15′		[ ] u ^{d}IM
X ii 7′		DIŠ 2 MUL^{meš} šá EGIR-šú GUB-zu [ ] 8) ^{d}U[TU u ^{d}IM]
Y	6′	2 MUL^{meš} [ ]
AA ii 10		DIŠ 2 MUL^{meš} šá EGIR-šú ⌜GUB⌝-zu ^{d}Šúllat ^{d}[Ḫániš] ^{d}UTU u [^{d}IM]

2 kakkabū ša arkišu izzazzū Šullat u Ḫaniš Šamaš u Adad
¶ The two stars which stand behind it: Šullat and Ḫaniš, Šamaš and Adad.

<u>ii 26</u> DIŠ MUL šá EGIR-šú-nu GUB-zu GIM ^{d}É-a KUR-ḫa

A ii 26		DIŠ MUL šá EGIR-šú-nu GUB-zu GIM ^{d}É-a KUR-ḫa
C ii 7′		DIŠ MUL šá EGIR-šú-nu [ ]
d	3′	[GUB-z]u GIM ^{d}É-a KUR-ḫa
J i 17′		[ ]-ḫa
X ii 9′		DIŠ MUL šá EGIR-šú-nu GUB-z[u]
Y	7′	DIŠ MUL šá E[GIR-šú-nu]
AA ii 11		DIŠ MUL šá EGIR-šu-nu GUB-zu ⌜GIM⌝ ^{d}É-[a KUR-ḫa]

kakkabu ša arkišunu izzazzu kīma Ea inappaḫa
¶ The star which stands behind them rises like Ea

<u>ii 27</u> GIM ^{d}É-a ŠÚ-bi ^{mul}Nu-muš-da ^{d}IM

A ii 27		GIM ^{d}É-a ŠÚ^{meš} ^{mul}Nu-muš-da ^{d}IM
d	3′	[GIM] ⌜^{d}⌝[É-a] 4) [^{mul}N]u-muš-da [ ]
J i 17′		GIM ^{d}É-[a] ŠÚ-ú 18) [ ] ⌜x ^{d}IM⌝
K ii 16′		[^{m}]^{ul}Nu-muš-[da] ^{d}IM
AA ii 12		GIM ^{d}É-a ŠÚ-bi ^{mul}Nu-muš-d[a ^{d}IM]

kīma Ea irabbi Numušda Adad
and sets like Ea: Numušda, Adad.

<u>ii 28</u> DIŠ MUL šá ina GÙB ^{mul}GÍR.TAB GUB-zu ^{mul}UR.IDIM ^{d}Kù-sù

A ii 28		DIŠ MUL šá ina GÙB ^{mul}GÍR.TAB GUB-zu ^{mul}UR.IDIM ^{d}Kù-sù
C ii 8′		DIŠ MUL [šá ina] GÙB [ ]
d	5′	[^{mul}GÍ]R.TAB GUB-zu ^{mul}UR.IDIM ^{d}[Kù-sù]
K ii 10′		[DIŠ M]U[L šá ina G]Ù[B]
Y	8′	DIŠ MUL šá ina GÙ[B]
AA ii 13		DIŠ MUL šá ina GÙB ^{mul}GÍR.TAB GUB-zu ^{mul}UR.I[DIM]

kakkabu ša ina šumēl Zuqāqīpi izzazzu Uridimmu Kusu
¶ The star which stands at the left of the Scorpion: the Wild Dog, Kusu.

<u>ii 29</u> DIŠ ^{mul}GÍR.TAB ^{d}Iš-ḫa-ra be-let da-ád-me

A ii 29		DIŠ ^{mul}GÍR.TAB ^{d}Iš-ḫa-ra be-let da-ád-me
C ii 9′		DIŠ ^{mul}[GÍR.TAB]
d	6′	[ ] ^{d}Iš-ḫa-⸢ra⸣ [be]-le$^{?}$-[et$^{?}$]
Y	9′	DIŠ ^{mul}GÍR.[TAB]
AA ii 14		DIŠ ^{mul}GÍR.TAB ^{d}Iš-ḫa-ra be-let d[a-ád-me]

Zuqāqīpu Išḫara bēlet dadmē
¶ The Scorpion, Išḫara, lady of all inhabited regions.

<u>ii 30</u> DIŠ ^{mul}GABA GÍR.TAB ^{d}Li$_{9}$-si$_{4}$ ^{d}AG

A ii 30		DIŠ ^{mul}GABA GÍR.TAB ^{d}Li$_{9}$-si$_{4}$ ^{d}AG
C ii 10′		DIŠ [ ]
d	7′	[ ] ^{d}Li$_{9}$-si$_{4}$ [ ]
Y	10′	DIŠ ^{mul}GAB[A]
AA ii 15		DIŠ ^{mul}GABA GÍR.TAB ^{d}⸢Li$_{9}$-si$_{4}$⸣ [^{d}AG]

Irat Zuqāqīpi Lisi Nabû
¶ The Chest of the Scorpion: Lisi, Nabû.

<u>ii 31</u> DIŠ 2 MUL^{meš} šá ina zi-qit ^{mul}GÍR.TAB GUB^{meš}-zu

A ii 31		DIŠ 2 MUL^{meš} šá ina zi-qit ^{mul}GÍR.TAB GUB^{meš}-zu
d	7′	[ ]GÍR.TAB GUB^{me}-zu
H ii 1′		[GU]B^{me}[^{š}]
Y	11′	DIŠ 2 MUL^{meš} šá [ ]
AA ii 16		DIŠ 2 MUL^{meš} šá ina zi-qit ^{mul}GÍR.TAB GUB-zu

2 kakkabū ša ina ziqit Zuqāqīpi izzazzū
¶ The two stars which stand in the sting of the Scorpion:

<u>ii 32</u> ^{d}Šár-ur$_{4}$ u ^{d}Šár-gaz

A ii 32		^{d}Šár-ur$_{4}$ u ^{d}Šár-gaz
d	8′	^{d}Šár-ur$_{4}$ u [ ]
H ii 1′		^{d}Šár-ur$_{4}$ u ^{d}[ ]
AA ii 16		⸢^{d}⸣[ ]

Šarur u Šargaz
Šarur and Šargaz.

ii 33 DIŠ MUL šá EGIR-šú-nu GUB-zu ^{mul}Pa-bil-sag

A ii 33 DIŠ MUL šá EGIR-šú-nu GUB-zu ^{mul}Pa-bil-sag
d 9′ [GUB-z]u ^{mul}Pa-bil-sag
e 1′ ⸢DIŠ MUL^{meš} šá EGIR-šú⸣-n[u GUB-zu]
H ii 2′ [ ] ^{mul}Pa-b[il-sag]
Y 12′ DIŠ MUL šá EG[IR-šú-nu]
AA ii 17 DIŠ MUL^{meš} šá EGIR^{meš}-šú-nu ⸢GUB-zu⸣ ^{mul}[Pa-bil-sag]

kakkabu ša arkišunu izzazzu Pabilsag
¶ The star(s) which stand(s) behind them: Pabilsag,

ii 34 DIŠ ^{mul}MÁ.GUR$_8$ u ^{mul}SUḪUR.MÁŠ$^{ku}_6$

A ii 34 DIŠ ^{mul}MÁ.GUR$_8$ u ^{mul}SUḪUR.MÁŠ$^{ku}_6$
d 9′ ^{mul}[ ] 10) ^{mul}SUḪ[UR]
e 2′ [ ]
H ii 3′ [ ] ^{mul}SUḪUR.[MÁŠ]
Y 13′ DIŠ ^{mul}MÁ.[GUR$_8$]
AA ii 18 ^{mul}MÁ.GUR$_8$ ^{mul}[SUḪUR.MÁŠ]

Makurru u Suḫurmāšu
¶ the Barge, and the Goat-Fish.

---

ii 35 15 MUL^{meš} šu-ut ^{d}É-a

A ii 35 15 MUL^{meš} šu-ut ^{d}É-a
e 3′ [1]5 MUL^{meš} [ ]
H ii 4′ [ ] šu-ut ^{d}⸢É⸣-[a]
Y 14′ 15 MUL[^{meš}]
AA ii 19 15 MUL^{meš} šu-[ut ^{d}É-a]

15 kakkabū šūt Ea
15 stars of Ea.

---

ii 36 DIŠ ina ^{iti}BÁR UD 1 KAM $^{mul\ lú}$ḪUN.GÁ IGI.LÁ

A ii 36 DIŠ ina ^{iti}BÁR UD 1 KAM $^{mul\ lú}$ḪUN.GÁ IGI.LÁ
e 4′ ⸢DIŠ⸣ ina ^{iti}BÁR UD 1 KAM [ ]
H ii 5′ [ ] $^{mul\ lú}$ḪUN.GÁ [IGI.LÁ]
Y 15′ DIŠ ina ^{iti}B[ÁR]
AA ii 20 [DIŠ ina ^{it}]^{i}BÁR U[D 1 KAM]

ina Nisanni UD 1 Agru innammar
¶ On the 1st day of Month I the Hired Man becomes visible.

ii 37 DIŠ ina ^{iti}BÁR UD 20 KAM ^{mul}GÀM IGI.LÁ

A ii 37 DIŠ ina ^{iti}BÁR UD 20 KAM ^{mul}GÀM IGI.LÁ
e 5′ ⸢DIŠ⸣ ina ^{iti}BÁR UD 20 KAM [ ]

H ii 6′ [ ] ^{mul}GÀM [ ]
Y 16′ DIŠ ina ^{iti}BÁR [ ]

ina Nisanni UD 20 Gamlu innammar
¶ On the 20th day of Month I the Crook becomes visible.

ii 38 DIŠ ina ^{iti}GU$_4$ UD 1 KAM MUL.MUL IGI.LÁ

A ii 38 DIŠ ina ^{iti}GU$_4$ UD 1 KAM MUL.MUL IGI.LÁ
e 6′ ⸢DIŠ⸣ ina ^{iti}GU$_4$ UD 1 KAM [ ]
H ii 7′ [ ] MUL.MUL [ ]
Y r. 1 DIŠ ina [ ]

ina Ajjari UD 1 Zappu innammar
¶ On the 1st day of Month II the Stars become visible.

ii 39 DIŠ ina ^{iti}GU$_4$ UD 20 KAM ^{mul}is le-e IGI.LÁ

A ii 39 DIŠ ina ^{iti}GU$_4$ UD 20 KAM ^{mul}is le-e IGI.LÁ
e 7′ ⸢DIŠ ina ^{iti}GU$_4$ UD 20⸣ K[AM]
H ii 8′ [ ] ^{mul}is le-e [IGI.LÁ]
Y r. 2 DIŠ ina [ ]
GG ii 1 DIŠ ina ^{iti}GU$_4$ UD 20 KAM ^{mul}is le-e IGI.[LÁ]

ina Ajjari UD 20 is lê innammar
¶ On the 20th day of Month II the Jaw of the Bull becomes visible.

ii 40 DIŠ ina ^{iti}SIG$_4$ UD 10 KAM ^{mul}SIPA.ZI.AN.NA u ^{mul}MAŠ.TAB.BA.GAL.GAL IGI^{me}

A ii 40 DIŠ ina ^{iti}SIG$_4$ UD 10 KAM ^{mul}SIPA.ZI.AN.NA u ^{mul}MAŠ.TAB.BA.GAL.GAL IGI^{me}
H ii 9′ [^{mul}SI]PA.ZI.AN.NA u ^{mul}MAŠ.TAB.BA.GAL.GAL [ ]
Y r. 3 DIŠ ina ⸢[^{iti}SIG$_4$]
GG ii 2 DIŠ ina ^{iti}SIG$_4$ UD 10 KAM ^{mul}SIPA.ZI.AN.NA ^{mul}MAŠ.TAB.BA.GAL.[GAL]

ina Simāni UD 10 Šidallu u Tū᾽amū rabûtu innammarū
¶ On the 10th day of Month III the True Shepherd of Anu and the Great Twins become visible.

ii 41 DIŠ ina ^{iti}ŠU UD 5 KAM ^{mul}MAŠ.TAB.BA.TUR.TUR u ^{mul}AL.LUL IGI^{me}

A ii 41 DIŠ ina ^{iti}ŠU UD 5 KAM ^{mul}MAŠ.TAB.BA.TUR.TUR u ^{mul}AL.LUL IGI^{me}
H ii 10′ [^{m}]^{ul}MAŠ.TAB.BA.TUR.TUR u ^{mul}AL.LUL I[GI^{me}]
N ii 1′ ⸢DIŠ⸣ ina [ ]
Y r. 4 DIŠ ina ^{iti}[ŠU]
GG ii 3 [ ] ^{mul}MAŠ.TAB.BA.TUR.TUR ^{mul}AL.[LUL]

ina Du᾽ūzi UD 5 Tū᾽amū ṣeḫrūtu u Alluttu innammarū
¶ On the 5th day of Month IV the Small Twins and the Crab become visible.

ii 42 DIŠ ina ^{iti}ŠU UD 15 KAM ^{mul}KAK.SI.SÁ ^{mul}MUŠ u ^{mul}UR.GU.LA

A ii 42 DIŠ ina ^{iti}ŠU UD 15 KAM ^{mul}KAK.SI.SÁ ^{mul}MUŠ u ^{mul}UR.GU.LA
H ii 11′ [ ] ^{mul}KAK.SI.SÁ ^{mul}MUŠ u ^{mul}UR.GU.L[A]
M 1 [DIŠ ina ^{iti}]ŠU U[D 15 KAM [2) u ^{mul}U[R.G]U.L[A]
N ii 2′ DIŠ ina ^{iti}⸢ŠU UD 15⸣ [ ]

Y	r. 5	DIŠ ina ^{iti}[ŠU]
GG ii 4		[KAK].SI.SÁ ^{mu}[^{l}M]UŠ ^{m}[^{ul}]

ina Du'ūzi UD 15 Šukūdu Niraḫ u Urgulû
¶ On the 15th day of Month IV the Arrow, the Snake, and the Lion

<u>ii 43</u> IGI^{me}-ma 4 MA.NA EN.NUN u$_4$-me 2 MA.NA EN.NUN GI$_6$

A ii 43		IGI^{me}-ma 4 MA.NA EN.NUN u$_4$-me 2 MA.NA EN.NUN GI$_6$
H ii 12′		[ ] 4 MA.NA EN.NUN u$_4$-mi 2 MA.NA EN.NUN G[I$_6$]
M	3	[ ]
N ii 2′		[ ] 3) 4 MA.NA EN.NUN ⸢u$_4$⸣-m[e]
Y	r. 6	[ ]

innammarūma 4 mana maṣṣarti ūmi 2 mana maṣṣarti mūši
become visible; 4 minas is the watch of the day, 2 minas is the watch of the night.

<u>ii 44</u> DIŠ ina ^{iti}IZI UD 5 KAM ^{mul}BAN u ^{mul}LUGAL IGI^{me}

A ii 44		DIŠ ina ^{iti}IZI UD 5 KAM ^{mul}BAN u ^{mul}LUGAL IGI^{me}
H ii 13′		[ ] ⸢5⸣ KAM ^{mul}BAN u ^{mul}LUGAL IGI^{me}[^{š}]
M	4	DIŠ ina ^{iti}IZI UD 15 KAM [ ]
N ii 4′		DIŠ ina ^{iti}IZI UD 15 KAM ^{múl}⸢BAN$^{?}$⸣ [ ]
Y	r. 7	DIŠ ina ^{iti}[ ]

ina Abi UD 5 (var. 15) Qaštu u Šarru innammarū
¶ On the 5th (var. 15th) of Month V, the Bow and the King become visible.

<u>ii 44a</u> DIŠ ina ^{iti}KIN UD 1 KAM ^{mul}[ ]

M	5	DIŠ ina ^{iti}[KIN] UD 1 K[AM [ ]
N ii 5′		DIŠ ina ^{iti}KIN UD 1 KAM ^{mul}⸢x⸣ [ ]

ina Ulūli UD 1 [ ]
¶ On the 1st day of Month VI, [ ]

<u>ii 45</u> DIŠ ina ^{iti}KIN UD 10 KAM ^{mul}NUN^{ki} u ^{mul}UGA^{mušen} IGI^{me}

A ii 45		DIŠ ina ^{iti}KIN UD 10 KAM ^{mul}NUN^{ki} u ^{mul}⸢UGA⸣^{mušen} IGI^{me}
H ii 14′		[ ] 10 KAM ^{mul}NUN^{ki} u ^{mul}UGA^{mušen} IGI^{meš}
M	6	DIŠ ina ^{iti}KIN UD 10 KAM [ ]
N ii 6′		DIŠ ina ^{iti}KIN UD 10 KAM ^{mul}N[UN^{ki}]
Y	r. 8	DIŠ [ina] ^{iti}KIN U[D]

ina Ulūli UD 10 Eridu u Āribu innammarū
¶ On the 10th day of Month VI Eridu and the Raven become visible.

<u>ii 46</u> DIŠ ina ^{iti}KIN UD 15 KAM ^{mul}ŠU.PA ^{d}En-líl IGI

A ii 46		DIŠ ina ^{iti}KIN UD 15 KAM ^{mul}ŠU.PA ^{d}En-líl [IGI]
H ii 15′		[U]D 15 KAM ^{mul}ŠU.PA ^{d}En-líl IGI
M	7	DIŠ ina ^{iti}KIN UD 15 KA[M]
N ii 7′		DIŠ ina ^{iti}KIN UD 15 KAM ^{mul}ŠU.PA [ ]
Y	r. 9	[DIŠ ina] ^{iti}KIN U[D]

ina Ulūli UD 15 ŠU.PA Enlil innammar

¶ On the 15th day of Month VI ŠU.PA, Enlil, becomes visible.

ii 47		DIŠ ina ^{iti}KIN UD 25 KAM ^{mul}AB.SÍN IGI
A ii 47		DIŠ ina [^{iti}KIN] UD 25 ^{mul}AB.SÍN [IGI]
E ii 1		DIŠ ina ^{iti}KIN UD 25 KAM ^{mul}AB.SÍN IGI
H ii 16′		[ ] UD 25 KAM ^{mul}AB.SÍN IGI
M	8	DIŠ ina ^{iti}KIN [U]D 10+[x]
N ii 8′		DIŠ ina ^{iti}KIN UD 25 KAM ^{mul}AB.SÍ[N IGI]
Y	r. 10	DIŠ ina ^{iti}[KIN] U[D]

ina Ulūli UD 25 Šer'u innammar

¶ On the 25th day of Month VI the Furrow becomes visible.

iii 1		DIŠ ina ^{iti}DU$_6$ UD 15 KAM ^{mul}zi-ba-ni-tu$_4$ ^{mul}UR.IDIM ^{mul}EN.TE.NA.BAR.ḪUM
E ii 2		DIŠ ina ^{iti}DU$_6$ UD 15 KAM ^{mul}zi-ba-ni-tu$_4$ ^{mul}UR.IDIM ^{mul}EN.TE.NA.BAR.ḪUM
H ii 17′		[DIŠ ina ^{iti}D]U$_6$ UD 15 KAM ^{mul}zi-ba-ni-tu$_4$ ^{mul}UR.I[DIM] 18) ^{mul}EN.TE.NA.BAR. ḪUM
M	9	DIŠ ina ^{iti}DU$_6$ UD 15 [KAM ^{mul}zi-ba]-ni-[tu$_4$]
N ii 9′		DIŠ ina ^{iti}DU$_6$ UD 15 KAM ^{mul}zi-ba-n[i-t]u$_4$ ^{m}[^{ul}]
V	1′	[EN].TE.N[A.BAR.ḪUM]
Y	r. 11	DIŠ ina ^{iti}DU$_6$ [U]D [ ]
WW	1′	[ ] ⌜x⌝ [ ]

ina Tašrīti UD 15 Zibānītu Uridimmu Ḫabaṣīrānu

¶ On the 15th day of Month VII the Scales, the Wild Dog, the Mouse,

iii 2		u ^{mul}UR.KU IGI^{me}-ma 3 MA.NA EN.NUN u$_4$-mi 3 MA.NA EN.NUN GI$_6$
E ii 3		u ^{mul}UR.KU IGI^{me}-ma 3 MA.NA EN.NUN u$_4$-mi 3 MA.NA EN.NUN GI$_6$
H ii 18′		ù ^{mul}UR.KU IGI^{meš}-m[a] 19) 3 MA.NA EN.NUN u$_4$-mi 3 MA.NA EN.NUN G[I$_6$]
M	10	u ^{mul}UR.KU IGI^{me}-ma 3 MA.NA EN.[NUN]
N ii 10′		u ^{mul}UR.KU IGI.LÁ-ma 3 E.NA EN.NUN u$_4$-m[u]
V	2′	[u$_4$-m]u 3 MA.N[A]
Y	r. 12	[ ]
GG ii 1′		[ ]-ma 3 [ ]
WW	2′	[ ] ⌜MA.NA⌝ [ ]

u Kalbu innammarūma 3 mana maṣṣarti ūmi 3 mana maṣṣarti mūši

and the Dog become visible; 3 minas is the watch of the day, 3 minas is the watch of the night.

iii 3		DIŠ ina ^{iti}APIN UD 5 KAM ^{mul}GÍR.TAB IGI
A iii 3		DIŠ ina [^{mu}]^{l}GÍR.[TAB]
E ii 4		DIŠ ina ^{iti}APIN UD 5 KAM ^{mul}GÍR.TAB IGI
H ii 20′		[DIŠ ina ^{it}]^{i}APIN UD 5 KAM ^{mul}GÍR.TAB IGI
M	11	DIŠ ina ^{iti}APIN UD 15 KAM ^{mul}GÍR.TAB [IGI]
N ii 11′		[DIŠ] ina ^{iti}APIN UD 15 KAM ^{mul}G[ÍR.T[AB]
V	3′	[ ] $^{mul?}$ [ ]
Y	r. 13	DIŠ [ina] ^{iti}A[PIN]
GG ii 2′		[DIŠ ina ^{iti}API]N UD 5 KAM ^{mul}GÍ[R.TAB]

TT	1′	[^{m}]^{ul}GÍR-TAB [ ]
WW	3′	[^{mu}]^{l}GÍR.TAB [ ]

ina Araḫsamni UD 5 (var. 15) Zuqāqīpu innammar

¶ On the 5th (var. 15th) day of Month VIII the Scorpion becomes visible.

<u>iii 4</u> DIŠ ina ^{iti}APIN UD 15 KAM ^{mul}ÙZ u ^{mul}GABA GÍR.TAB IGI^{me}

A iii 4		DIŠ ina ⸢^{iti}APIN UD 15 KAM⸣ ^{mul}ÙZ u ^{mul}[ ]
E ii 5		DIŠ ina ^{iti}APIN UD 15 KAM ^{mul}ÙZ u ^{mul}GABA GÍR.TAB IGI^{me}
H ii 21′		[DIŠ] ina ^{iti}APIN UD 15 KAM ^{mul}ÙZ u ^{mul}GABA GÍR.TAB IGI[^{meš}]
L iii 1		DIŠ ina ^{iti}[API]N UD 25 KAM ^{mul}[ÙZ]
M	12	DIŠ ina ^{iti}APIN UD 15 KAM ^{mul}ÙZ u ^{mul}[GABA]
N ii 12′		[DIŠ ina ^{i}]^{ti}A[PIN ^{mu}]^{l}Ù[Z]
V	4′	[^{mul}Ù]Z u ^{mul}GABA GÍR.T[AB]
Y	r. 14	DIŠ ina ^{iti}AP[IN]
GG ii 3′		[DIŠ ina] ^{iti}APIN UD 15 KAM ^{mul}ÙZ ^{mul}⸢GABA GÍR.TAB⸣ [ ]
SS i 1′		[^{mu}]^{l}ÙZ u] 2′) [^{mul}GABA GÍR-TA]B IGI.L[Á^{meš}]
TT	2′	[ ] ^{mul}ÙZ ^{mul}G[ABA]
WW	4′	[^{m}]^{ul}ÙZ ^{mul}GAB[A]

ina Araḫsamni UD 15 (Var. 25) Enzu u Irat Zuqāqīpi innammarū

¶ On the 15th (var. 25th) day of Month VIII the Goat and the Chest of the Scorpion become visible.

<u>iii 5</u> DIŠ ina ^{iti}GAN UD 15 KAM ^{mul}UD.KA.DUḪ.A ^{mul}TI$_8^{mušen}$

A iii 5		DIŠ ina ^{iti}GAN UD 15 KAM ^{mul}UD.KA.DUḪ.A ^{mul}TI$_8^{mušen}$
E ii 6		DIŠ ina ^{iti}GAN UD 15 KAM ^{mul}UD.KA.DUḪ.A ^{mul}TI$_8^{mušen}$
H ii 22′		[DIŠ] ina ^{iti}GAN UD 15 KAM ^{mul}UD.KA.DUḪ.A ^{mul}TI$_8^{mušen}$
L iii 2		DIŠ ina ^{iti}GAN UD 15 KAM ^{d}UD.K[A.DUḪ.A]
M	13	DIŠ ina ^{iti}GAN UD 15 KAM ^{mul}UD.KA.DUḪ.A [ ]
V	5′	[^{mu}]^{l}UD.KA.DUḪ.A ^{mul}T[I$_8^{mušen}$]
Y	r. 15	[DIŠ] ina ^{iti}G[AN]
GG ii 4′		[DIŠ ina ^{it}]^{i}GAN UD 15 KAM ^{mul}UD.KA.DUḪ.A ^{mul}TI$_8^{mušen}$
SS i 3′		[KA]M [^{mu}]^{l}K[A].DUḪ.[A] 4′) [ ]
TT	3′	[K]AM ^{mul}UD.KA.DUḪ.A [ ]
WW	5′	[^{m}]^{ul}UD.KA.DUḪ.A ^{mul}T[I$_8^{mušen}$]

ina Kislīmi UD 15 Nimru Erû

¶ On the 15th day of Month IX the Panther, the Eagle

<u>iii 6</u> u ^{mul}Pa-bil-sag IGI^{meš}

A iii 6		u ^{mul}Pa-bil-sag IGI^{meš}
E ii 7		u ^{mul}Pa-bil-sag IGI^{me}
H ii 22′		u ^{mul}Pa-bil-sag I[GI^{meš}]
L iii 2		[ ]
M	14	u ^{mul}Pa-bil-sag [IGI^{meš}]
GG ii 4′		^{mul}Pa-bil-sag [ ]
SS i 4′		^{mul}Pa-bíl-sag ⸢IGI^{meš}⸣
TT	4′	[^{mul}Pa]-bil-sag [ ]
WW	6′	[^{mul}Pa-b]il-sag IGI[^{meš}]

u Pabilsag innammarū

and Pabilsag become visible.

iii 7		DIŠ ina ^{iti}AB UD 15 KAM ^{mul}SIM.MAḪ ^{mul}ši-nu-nu-tu$_4$ ^{mul}IM.ŠEŠ

A iii 7		DIŠ ina ^{iti}AB UD 15 KAM ^{mul}SIM.MAḪ ^{mul}ši-nu-nu-tu$_4$ ^{mul}IM.ŠEŠ
E ii 8		DIŠ ina ^{iti}AB UD 15 KAM ^{mul}SIM.MAḪ ^{mul}ši-nu-nu-tu$_4$ ^{mul}IM.ŠEŠ
H ii 23′		DIŠ ina ^{iti}AB UD 15 KAM ^{mul}SIM.MAḪ ^{mul}ši-nu-nu-tu$_4$ u ^{mul}IM.[ŠEŠ]
L iii 3		DIŠ ina [^{it}]^{i}AB UD 15 KAM ^{mul}S[IM.MAḪ]
M	15	DIŠ ina ^{iti}AB UD 15 <KAM> ^{mul}SIM.MAḪ ^{mu}[^{l}ši-nu-nu-tu$_4$] 16) ^{mul}IM.Š[EŠ]
V	6′	[ ]SIM.MAḪ u ^{mùl}ši-[nu-nu-tu$_4$]
GG ii 5′		[DIŠ ina ^{iti}A]B UD 15 KAM ^{mul}SIM.MAḪ ^{mul}ši-nu-nu-⸢tu$_4$⸣ ^{mul}IM.ŠEŠ
SS i 5′		[^{m}]^{ul}⸢SIM.MAḪ⸣ ^{d}ši-nu-nu-tu$_4$ 6′) [^{mul}IM.ŠE]Š
TT	5′	[1]5 KAM ^{mul}SIM.MAḪ u [ ] 6′) [^{mul}IM.Š]EŠ
WW	7′	[^{m}]^{ul}SIM.MAḪ ^{mul}ši-nu-nu-tú ^{mu}[^{l}IM.ŠEŠ]

ina Ṭebēti UD 15 SIM.MAḪ Šinūnūtu Marratu
¶ On the 15th day of Month X SIM.MAḪ, (i.e.) the Swallow (or) IM.ŠEŠ,

iii 8		ina GIŠ.NIM IGI.LÁ u ^{mul}KAK.SI.SÁ ina li-la-a-ti

A iii 8		ina GIŠ.NIM IGI.LÁ u ^{mul}KAK.SI.SÁ ina li-la-a-ti
E ii 9		ina GIŠ.NIM IGI^{me} u ^{mul}KAK.SI.[SÁ ina l]i-lá-a-ta
H ii 24′		ina GIŠ.NIM IGI.LÁ ù ^{mul}KAK.SI.SÁ ina li-la-a-ti
L iii 3		[ ] 4) u ^{mùl}KAK.SI.SÁ ina li-la-a-[ti]
M	16	ina GIŠ.N[IM$^{?}$] 17) u ^{mul}KAK.SI.SÁ ina l[i-la]-⸢a⸣-tú
O ii 1′		[ina GIŠ.NI]M IGI.L[Á]
V	7′	[KA]K.SI.SÁ ina li-[ ]
GG ii 5′		ina G[IŠ.NIM] 6) [K]AK.SI.SÁ ina li-[l]a-[t]i$^{?}$
SS i 6′		ina GI[Š].⸢NIM⸣ {x} IGI 7′) [u ^{mul}KAK].SI.⸢SÁ⸣ ina li-la-ti
TT	6′	ina GIŠ.NIM IGI.LÁ u ^{mu}[^{l}KAK.SI.SÁ]
WW	8′	[^{mu}]^{l}KAK.SI.SÁ ⸢ina li⸣-[la-ti]

ina ṣītān innammar u Šukūdu ina līlâti
becomes visible in the east, and the Arrow

iii 9		IGI.LÁ-ma 2 MA.NA EN.NUN u$_4$-me 4 MA.NA EN.NUN GI$_6$

A iii 9		IGI.LÁ-ma 2 MA.NA EN.NUN u$_4$-me 4 MA.NA EN.NUN GI$_6$
E ii 9		IGI^{me}-ma 10) 2 MA.NA EN.NUN u$_4$-mi 4 MA.NA EN.NUN GI$_6$
H ii 24′		I[GI.LÁ-ma] 25) 2 MA.NA EN.NUN u$_4$-mi 4 MA.NA EN.NUN G[I$_6$]
L iii 5		[x] ⸢x x⸣ [ ]
M	17	[18) 2 MA.[NA E]N.NUN [ ] 19) 4 MA.[N]A E[N].NUN [GI$_6$]
O ii 2′		[-m]a 2 MA.NA EN.NUN ⸢u$_4$⸣-[ ]
V	8′	[E]N. NUN [ ]
GG ii 6′		⸢x x x x x x x 4⸣ MA.NA ⸢EN⸣.N[UN GI$_6$]
SS i 7′		IGI.LÁ-ma 8′) [2 MA EN].NUN UD 4 ⸢MA⸣ EN.NUN GI$_6$
TT	7′	[IGI.L]Á$^{?}$-ma 2 MA.NA EN.NUN u$_4$-mi 4 M[A.NA]
WW	9′	[u$_4$]-⸢mi⸣ [ ]

innammarma 2 mana maṣṣarti ūmi 4 mana maṣṣarti mūši
becomes visible in the evening; 2 minas is the watch of the day, 4 minas is the watch of the night.

iii 10		DIŠ ina ^{iti}ZÍZ UD 5 KAM ^{mul}GU.LA ^{mul}AŠ.IKU u ^{mul}lu-lim IGI^{meš}

A iii 10		DIŠ ina ^{iti}ZÍZ UD 5 KAM ^{mul}GU.LA ^{mul}AŠ.IKU u ^{mul}lu-lim IGI^{meš}
E ii 11		DIŠ ina ^{iti}ZÍZ UD 5 KAM ^{mul}GU.LA ^{mul}AŠ.IKU u ^{mul}lu-lim IGI^{me}
H ii 26′		DIŠ ina ^{iti}ZÍZ UD 5 KAM ^{mul}GU.LA ^{mul}[AŠ.IKU u] ^{mul}lu-lim IGI^{m}[^{eš}]

M	20	[DIŠ ina $^{it]i}$ZÍZ UD 15 KAM ^{mul}AŠ.IKU $^{mu[l}$]u-lim [IGI^{meš}]
O ii 3′		[DIŠ ina ^{iti}ZÍZ UD] 5 KAM ^{mul}GU.LA ^{mul}AŠ.IKU u ^{mul}l[u-lim IGI^{meš}]
V	9′	[DIŠ ina ^{iti}ZÍZ UD 5 KA]M $^{⸢mul⸣}$GU.LA ^{mul}AŠ.IKU u $^{m[ul}$lu-lim IGI^{meš}]
GG ii 7′		[DIŠ ina ^{iti}ZÍZ] UD 5 KAM ^{mul}GU.LA ^{mul}AŠ.IKU u ^{mul}lu-lim IGI^{me}
SS i 9′		[UD] ⸢5 KAM⸣ ^{mul}GU.LA 10′) [^{mul}AŠ.IK]U ^{mul}⸢lu⸣-lim IGI^{meš}
TT	8′	[ ]GU.LA ^{mul}AŠ.IKU u $^{mu[l}$]

ina Šabāṭi UD 5 (var. 15) GU.LA Ikû u Lulīmu innammarū
¶ On the 5th (var. 15th) day of Month XI the Great One, the Field, and the Stag become visible.

<u>iii 11</u> DIŠ ina ^{iti}ZÍZ UD 25 KAM ^{mul}A-nu-ni-tu$_4$ IGI.LÁ

A iii 11		DIŠ ina ^{iti}ZÍZ UD 25 KAM ^{mul}A-nu-ni-tu$_4$ IGI.LÁ
E ii 12		DIŠ ina ^{iti}ZÍZ UD 25 KAM ^{mul}A-nu-ni-tu$_4$ IGI.LÁ
H ii 27		DIŠ ina ^{iti}ZÍZ UD 25 KAM ^{mul}A-nu-ni-tu$_4$ IGI.[LÁ]
M	21	[DIŠ ina ^{iti}ZÍ]Z$^{?}$ UD 25 KAM $^{m[ul}$]A-nu-[ni-tu$_4$]
O ii 4		[ ] UD 25 KAM $^{mul\ d}$A-nu-ni-tu$_4$ IGI.L[Á]
V	10′	[x]+5 KAM $^{mul\ d}$A-<nu>-ni-tu$_4$ I[GI.LÁ]
GG ii 8′		[U]D 25 KAM ^{mul}A-nu-n[i]-tu$_4$ IGI.LÁ
TT	9′	[$^{m]ul}$A-nu-ni-tu$_4$ [ ]

ina Šabāṭi UD 25 Anunītu innammar
¶ On the 25th day of Month XI Anunitu becomes visible.

<u>iii 12</u> DIŠ ina ^{iti}ŠE UD 15 KAM ^{mul}KU$_6$ u ^{mul}ŠU.GI IGI.LÁ^{me}

A iii 12		DIŠ ina ^{iti}ŠE UD 15 KAM ^{mul}KU$_6$ u ^{mul}ŠU.GI IGI.LÁ^{me}
E ii 13		DIŠ ina ^{iti}ŠE UD 15 KAM ^{mul}KU$_6$ u ^{mul}ŠU.GI IGI^{me}
H ii 28′		DIŠ ina ^{iti}ŠE UD 15 KAM ^{mul}KU$_6$ u ^{mul}ŠU.GI IGI^{meš}
M	22	[ ] 15 KAM [x] ⸢x⸣ [ ]
O ii 5′		[ ] UD 15 KAM ^{mul}KU$_6$ ù ^{mul}ŠU.GI IGI.LÁ
V	11′	[x]+5 KAM ^{mul}KU$_6$ u ^{múl}ŠU.GI I[GI]
BB	B 1′	[ ] ^{mul}KU$_6$ [u $^{mu]l}$Š[U.GI]
GG ii 9′		[x]+5 [ŠU.G]I IGI.LÁ$^{m[e]}$
SS i 11′		[KA]M ^{mul}KU$_6$ 12′) [u ^{mul}]ŠU.⸢GI⸣ IGI.LÁ$^{m[e]š}$
TT	10′	[ ]⸢KU$_6$ u ^{mul}⸣[ ]

ina Addari UD 15 Nūnu u Šību innammarū
¶ On the 15th day of Month XII the Fish and the Old Man become visible.

<u>iii 13</u> DIŠ MUL.MUL KUR-ma ^{mul}GÍR.TAB ŠÚ-bi

A iii 13		DIŠ MUL.MUL KUR-ma ^{mul}GÍR.TAB ŠÚ-bi
E ii 14		DIŠ MUL.MUL KUR-ma ^{mul}GÍR.TAB ŠÚ-bi
H iii 1		DIŠ MUL.MUL KUR-ma ^{mul}GÍR.TAB ŠÚ-b[i]
O ii 6′		[DIŠ MUL.MU]L KUR-ma ^{mul}GÍR.TAB ŠÚ-bi
V	12′	[KU]R-ḫa-ma ^{múl}[GÍ]R.TAB [ ]
BB	B 2′	[KU]R-ma [$^{m]ul}$GÍ[R.T]AB [ ]
GG ii 10′		[ ] Š[Ú]
SS i 13′		[ ] KUR-ma [$^{m]ul}$G[Í]R.TAB ŠÚ

Zappu inappaḫma Zuqāqīpu irabbi
¶ The Stars rise and the Scorpion sets.

<u>iii 14</u> DIŠ ^{mul}GÍR.TAB KUR-ma MUL.MUL ŠÚ-bi

A iii 14		DIŠ ^{mul}GÍR.TAB KUR-ma MUL.MUL ŠÚ-bi
b	1	[M]UL.⌜MUL ŠÚ-bi⌝
E ii 15		DIŠ ^{mul}GÍR.TAB KUR-ma MUL.MUL ŠÚ-bi
H iii 2		DIŠ ^{mul}GÍR.TAB KUR-ma MUL.MUL ŠÚ-[bi]
O ii 7		[DIŠ ^{mul}GÍR].TAB KUR-ma MUL.MUL ŠÚ-bi
V	13	[KUR-ḫ]a-ma MÚL.MÚ[L]
BB	B 3′	[KUR-m]a MUL.M[U]L Š[Ú-bi]
SS i 14′		[ ] KUR-ma MUL.MUL ŠÚ

Zuqāqīpu inappaḫma Zappu irabbi
¶ The Scorpion rises and the Stars set.

<u>iii 15</u> DIŠ ^{mul}GU$_4$.AN.NA KUR-ma ^{mul}ŠU.PA ŠÚ-bi

A iii 15		DIŠ ^{mul}GU$_4$.AN.NA KUR-ma ^{mul}ŠU.PA ŠÚ-bi
b	2′	A]N.NA KU[R]
E ii 16		[DIŠ] ^{mul}GU$_4$.AN.NA KUR-ma ^{mul}ŠU.PA ŠÚ-bi
H iii 3		DIŠ ^{mul}GU$_4$.AN.NA KUR-ma ^{mul}ŠU.PA ŠÚ-b[i]
O ii 8′		[^{mu}]^{l}GU$_4$.AN.NA KUR-ma ^{mul}⌜x⌝ ŠÚ-bi
BB	B 4′	[ ] KUR-ma [^{m}]^{ul}ŠU.⌜PA⌝ [ ]
SS i 15′		[AN.N]A ⌜KUR⌝-ma ^{mul}ŠU.PA ŠÚ

Alû inappaḫma ŠU.PA irabbi
¶ The Bull of Heaven rises and ŠU.PA sets.

<u>iii 16</u> DIŠ ^{mul}SIPA.ZI.AN.NA KUR-ma ^{mul}Pa-bil-sag ŠÚ-bi

A iii 16		DIŠ ^{mul}SIPA.ZI.AN.NA KUR-ma ^{mul}Pa-bil-sag ŠÚ-bi
b	3′	[SI]PA.ZI.AN.NA KUR-[ma]
E ii 17		[DIŠ ^{mu}]^{l}SIPA.ZI.AN.NA KUR-ma ^{mul}Pa-bil-sag ŠÚ-bi
H iii 4		DIŠ ^{mul}SIPA.ZI.AN.NA KUR-ma ^{mul}Pa-bil-sag ŠÚ-[bi]
O ii 9		[DIŠ ^{m}]^{ul}SIPA.ZI.AN.NA KUR-ma ^{mul}Pa-bil-sag ŠÚ-bi
BB	B 5′	[^{mul}SIPA.ZI.A]N.NA KUR-ma ^{mul}Pa-b]íl-sag ŠÚ-bi]
SS i 16′		[SIPA.Z]I.AN.NA KUR-⌜ma⌝ 17′) [^{mul}Pa-bí]l-sag [ŠÚ]

Šidallu inappaḫma Pabilsag irabbi
¶ The True Shepherd of Anu rises and Pabilsag sets.

<u>iii 17</u> DIŠ ^{mul}KAK.SI.SÁ $^{mul\ d}$MUŠ u ^{mul}UR.GU.LA KUR^{me}-nim-ma

A iii 17		DIŠ ^{mul}KAK.SI.SÁ $^{mul\ d}$MUŠ u ^{mul}UR.GU.LA KUR^{me}-ma
b	4′	[KA]K.SI.SÁ ^{mul}MUŠ ^{mul}U[R.GU.LA]
c	1′	[KA]K.SI.SÁ ^{mul}MUŠ u ^{mul}UR.GU.L[A]
E ii 18		[DIŠ ^{mul}KA]K.S[I.S]Á ^{mul}MUŠ u ^{mul}UR.GU.LA KUR^{meš}-ma
H iii 5		DIŠ ^{mul}KAK.SI.SÁ ^{mul}MUŠ u ^{mul}UR.GU.LA K[UR^{me}-nim$^{?}$-ma]
O ii 10′		[DIŠ] ^{mul}KAK.SI.SÁ $^{mul\ d}$MUŠ u ^{mul}UR.GU.LA KUR^{me}-nim-ma
BB	B 6′	[^{m}]^{ul}MUŠ ^{mul}U[R.GU.LA]
SS i 18′		[SI.S]Á ⌜^{mul}⌝[^{d}MUŠ u] 19′) [^{mul}UR].⌜GU.LA⌝ [ ]

Šukūdu Niraḫ u Urgulû inappaḫūnimma
¶ The Arrow, the Snake, and the Lion rise, and

<u>iii 18</u> ^{mul}GU.LA u ^{mul}TI$_8^{\text{mušen}}$ ŠÚ^{meš}

A iii 18		^{mul}GU.LA u ^{mul}TI$_8^{\text{mušen}}$ ŠÚ^{meš}
c	2′	[^{mul}G]U.LA u ⸢^{mul}⸣[ ]
E ii 19		[^{mul}G]U.LA u ^{mul}TI$_8^{\text{mušen}}$ ⸢ŠÚ⸣^{meš}
H iii 6		^{mul}GU.LA u [ ]
O ii 11′		^{mul}GU.LA ù ^{mul}TI$_8$⸢^{mušen}⸣ ŠÚ^{meš}
BB	B 7′	[^{mu}]^{l}TI$_8^{\text{mušen}}$ ŠÚ^{meš}
SS i 20′		[^{mul}GU.L]A ^{mu}[^{l}TI$_8^{\text{mušen}}$]

GU.LA u Erû irabbû
the Great One and the Eagle set.

<u>iii 19</u> DIŠ ^{mul}BAN u ^{mul}LUGAL KUR^{me}-ma ^{mul}ÙZ ŠÚ-bi

A iii 19		DIŠ ^{mul}BAN u ^{mul}LUGAL KUR^{me}-ma ^{mul}ÙZ ŠÚ-bi
b	5′	[DIŠ ^{mul}B]AN u ^{mul}LUGAL KUR-ḫa-nim-[ma ^{mul}ÙZ]
c	3′	[DIŠ ^{mul}B]AN u [^{mul}LUGAL KUR^{me}-ma ^{m}]^{ul}Ù[Z]
E ii 20		[ ] u ^{mul}⸢LUGAL⸣ KUR^{meš}-ma ^{mul}ÙZ ŠÚ-bi
H iii 7		DIŠ ^{mul}BAN u ^{mul}LUGAL KUR^{meš}-ma ^{mul}Ù[Z]
O ii 12′		[DIŠ ^{m}]^{ul}BAN u ^{mul}LUGAL KUR^{me}-nim-ma ^{mul}ÙZ ŠÚ-bi
BB	B 8′	[^{mul}LUGA]L KUR^{meš}-ma ^{mul}Ù[Z]
SS i 21′		[ ] ^{mul}L[UGAL] 22′) [^{mul}ÙZ] ŠÚ

Qaštu u Šarru inappaḫūnimma Enzu irabbi
¶ The Bow and the King rise, and the Goat sets.

<u>iii 20</u> DIŠ ^{mul}NUN^{ki} u ^{mul}UGA^{mušen} KUR^{meš}-ma ^{mul}UD.KA.DUḪ.A ŠÚ-bi

A iii 20		DIŠ ^{mul}NUN^{ki} u ^{mul}UGA^{mušen} KUR^{meš}-ma ^{mul}UD.KA.DUḪ.A ŠÚ-bi
b	6′	[DIŠ ^{mul}N]UN^{ki} u ^{mul}UGA^{muš}[^{en}]
c	4′	[DIŠ ^{mul}NU]N[^{ki} KUR^{meš}-n]im-m[a]
E ii 21		[NUN]^{ki} u ^{mul}UGA[^{mu}]^{šen} [KU]R^{meš}-m[a ^{m}]^{ul}UD.KA.DUḪ.⸢A⸣ ŠÚ-bi
H iii 8		[DIŠ ^{m}]^{ul}NUN^{ki} u ^{mul}UGA^{mušen} KUR^{meš}-ma ^{mul}UD.K[A.DUḪ.A] ŠÚ-bi
m	1	[^{m}]^{ul}UD.KA.DUḪ.A [ŠÚ-bi]
O ii 13′		[DIŠ ^{mu}]^{l}NUN^{ki} u ^{mul}UGA^{mušen} KUR^{me}-nim-ma ^{mul}UD.KA.DUḪ.A ŠÚ-bi
BB	B 9′	[^{mu}]^{l}UGA⸢^{mušen}⸣ [ ] 10′) [^{mul}K]A.DUḪ.A ŠÚ^{meš}
SS i 23′		[NUN^{k}]^{i} ⸢^{mul}⸣UGA^{mušen} 24′) [^{mu}]^{l}KA.DUḪ.A ŠÚ

Eridu u Āribu inappaḫūnimma Nimru irabbi
¶ Eridu and the Raven rise, and the Panther sets.

<u>iii 21</u> DIŠ ^{mul}ŠU.PA ^{d}En-líl KUR-ma ^{mul}AŠ.IKU ŠÚ-bi

A iii 21		DIŠ ^{mul}ŠU.PA ^{d}En-líl KUR-ma ^{mul}AŠ.IKU ŠÚ-bi
b	7′	[DIŠ ^{mul}Š]U.PA ^{d}En-líl KUR-ma ^{mu}[^{l}]
E ii 22		[ ]ŠU.PA ^{d}En-líl KUR-ma ^{mul}AŠ.IKU ŠÚ-bi
H iii 9		[DIŠ ^{mu}]^{l}ŠU.PA ^{d}En-líl KUR-ḫa-ma ^{mul}AŠ.IKU [ŠÚ-bi]
m	2	[^{m}]^{ul}AŠ.IKU [ŠÚ-bi]
O ii 14′		[DIŠ ^{mul}Š]U.PA ^{d}En-líl KUR-ma ^{mul}AŠ.IKU ŠÚ-bi
BB	B 11′	[ ] KUR-ma ^{mul}AŠ.IKU ŠÚ-[bi]
SS i 25′		[^{d}En-lí]l KUR-ma ^{mul}AŠ.IKU ŠÚ

ŠU.PA Enlil inappaḫma Ikû irabbi
¶ ŠU.PA, Enlil, rises and the Field sets.

<u>iii 22</u> DIŠ ^{mul}Nin-maḫ KUR-ma ^{mul}A-nu-ni-tu$_4$ ŠÚ-bi

A iii 22		DIŠ ^{mul}Nin-maḫ KUR-ma ^{mul}A-nu-ni-tu$_4$ ŠÚ-bi
b	8′	[DIŠ ^{mul}Ni]n-maḫ KUR-ma ^{mu}[^{l}]
E ii 23		[DIŠ ^{mul}]Nin-maḫ KUR-ma ^{mul}A-nu-ni-tu$_4$ ŠÚ-bi
H iii 10		[DIŠ ^{mul}]Nin-maḫ KUR-ma ^{mul}A-nu-ni-tu$_4$ ŠÚ-b[i]
m	3	[KUR-ma ^{m}]^{ul}A-nu-ni-tu$_4$ [ŠÚ-bi]
O ii 15′		[DIŠ ^{mul}Nin-m]aḫ KUR-ma $^{mul\ d}$A-nu-ni-tu$_4$ ŠÚ-bi
BB	B 12′	[^{m}]^{ul}A-⸢nu⸣-ni-t[u$_4$]
SS i 26′		[^{m}]^{ul}A-nu-ni-tu$_4$ ŠÚ

Ninmaḫ inappaḫma Anunītu irabbi
¶ Ninmaḫ rises and Anunitu sets.

<u>iii 23</u> DIŠ ^{mul}zi-ba-ni-tu$_4$ ^{mul}UR.IDIM u ^{mul}EN.TE.NA.BAR.ḪUM

A iii 23		DIŠ ^{mul}zi-ba-ni-tu$_4$ ^{mul}UR.IDIM u ^{mul}EN.TE.NA.BAR.ḪUM
b	9′	[DIŠ ^{mul}z]i-ba-ni-⸢tu$_4$ ^{mul}UR.IDIM u⸣ ^{m}[^{ul}]
E ii 24		[DIŠ] ^{mul}zi-ba-ni-tu$_4$ ^{mul}UR.IDIM u ^{mul}EN.TE.NA.BAR.ḪUM
H iii 11		[DIŠ ^{mul}z]i-ba-ni-tu$_4$ ^{mul}UR.IDIM u ^{mul}EN.TE.NA.BAR.ḪUM
m	4	[^{mul}E]N.⸢TE.NA⸣.BAR.ḪUM
N iii 1′		[DIŠ ^{múl}z]i-ba-ni-tu$_4$ ^{múl}UR.IDIM ^{múl}[
O ii 16′		[DIŠ ^{mul}zi-ba-ni-t]u$_4$ ^{mul}UR.IDIM u ^{mul}E[N.T]E.[NA].BAR.ḪUM
BB	B 13′	[. . . ^{mul}Zi-ba-ni-t]u$_4$ ⸢^{mul}⸣UR.⸢IDIM⸣ ^{m}[^{ul}EN.TE.NA.BAR.ḪUM]
SS i 27′		[^{m}]^{ul}⸢UR⸣.IDIM 28′) [^{mul}EN.TE.NA.BA]R.ḪUM

Zibānītu Uridimmu u Ḫabaṣīrānu
¶ The Scales, the Wild Dog, and the Mouse

<u>iii 24</u> KUR^{me}-ma $^{mul\ lú}$ḪUN.GÁ ŠÚ-bi

A iii 24		KUR^{me}-ma $^{mul\ lú}$ḪUN.GÁ ŠÚ-bi
E ii 24		KUR^{meš}-ma $^{mul\ lú}$ḪUN.GÁ ŠÚ-bi
H iii 11		KUR^{meš}-ma $^{mul\ lú}$ḪUN.GÁ ŠÚ-[bi]
m	4	KUR^{me}-ma $^{mul\ l}$[^{ú}ḪUN.GÁ ŠÚ-bi]
O ii 16′		⸢KUR^{meš}-ma⸣ 17) [^{mul}] ^{lú}ḪUN.GÁ ŠÚ-bi
BB	B 14′	[$^{mul\ l}$]^{ú}⸢ḪUN.GÁ⸣ [ŠÚ-bi]
SS i 28′		KUR⸢^{meš}⸣-[ma] 29′) [ ]

inappaḫūma Agru irabbi
rise, and the Hired Man sets.

<u>iii 25</u> DIŠ ^{mul}GÍR.TAB u ^{mul}UR.KU KUR^{me}-ma ^{mul}NUN^{ki} u MUL.MUL ŠÚ^{meš}

A iii 25		DIŠ ^{mul}GÍR.TAB u ^{mul}UR.KU KUR^{me}-ma ^{mul}NUN^{ki} u MUL.MUL ŠÚ^{meš}
E ii 25		[DIŠ] ^{mul}GÍR.TAB u ^{mul}UR.KU KUR^{meš}-ma ^{mul}NUN^{ki} u MUL.MUL KUR^{meš}
H iii 12		[DIŠ ^{mul}GÍR].TAB u ^{mul}UR.KU KUR^{meš}-ma ^{mul}NUN^{ki} u MUL.MUL ŠÚ[^{meš}]
m	5	[^{mu}]^{l}NUN^{ki} <u> MUL.MUL Š[Ú^{meš}]
N iii 2′		[DIŠ ^{múl}GÍ]R.TAB u ^{múl}UR.KU ḫa-KUR-nim-ma ^{m}[^{úl}]
O ii 18′		[-m]a ^{mul}NU[N^{ki}]$^{meš?}$

Zuqāqīpu u Kalbu inappaḫūma Eridu u Zappu irabbû
¶ The Scorpion and the Dog rise, and Eridu and the Stars set.

iii 26 DIŠ ^{mul}GABA GÍR.TAB u ^{mul}ÙZ KUR^{meš}-ma ^{mul}ŠU.GI u ^{mul}SIPA.ZI.AN.NA ŠÚ^{meš}

A iii 26 DIŠ ^{mul}GABA GÍR.TAB u ^{mul}ÙZ KUR^{meš}-ma ^{mul}ŠU.GI u ^{mul}SIPA.ZI.AN.NA ŠÚ^{meš}
E ii 26 [DIŠ] ^{mul}GABA GÍR.TAB u ^{mul}ÙZ KUR^{meš}-ma ^{mul}ŠU.GI u ^{mul}SIPA.ZI.A[N.NA ŠÚ]^{meš}
H iii 13 [GÍ]R.TAB u ^{mul}ÙZ KUR^{meš}-ma ^{mul}ŠU.GI u ^{mul}SIPA.Z[I.AN.NA ŠÚ^{meš}]
m 6 [$^{mu]l}$ŠU.PA^{sic} u ^{mul}SIPA.ZI.A[N.NA ŠÚ^{meš}]
N iii 3′ [DIŠ ^{mul}G]ABA GÍR.TAB ^{mul}ÙZ KUR-ḫa-nim-m[a]
O ii 19′ [ ] ⸢ŠÚ^{meš}⸣

Irat Zuqāqīpi u Enzu inappaḫūma Šību u Šidallu irabbû
¶ The Chest of the Scorpion and the Goat rise, and the Old Man and the True Shepherd of Anu set.

iii 27 DIŠ ^{mul}Pa-bil-sag ^{mul}Za-ba$_4$-ba$_4$ u DINGIR.GUB.BA^{meš} KUR^{meš}-ma

A iii 27 DIŠ ^{mul}Pa-bil-sag ^{mul}Za-ba$_4$-ba$_4$ u DINGIR.GUB.BA^{meš} KUR^{meš}-ma
E ii 27 [DIŠ] ^{mul}Pa-bil-sag ^{mul}Za-ba$_4$-ba$_4$ u ^{mul}DINGIR.GUB.BA^{meš} ⸢KUR^{meš}-ma⸣
H iii 14 [DIŠ ^{mul}Pa-bil-s]ag ^{mul}Za-ba$_4$-ba$_4$ u ^{mul}DINGIR.GUB.BA^{meš} KUR[^{meš}-ma]
m 7 [ ]DINGIR.GUB.BA^{meš} KUR^{me}-[ma]
N iii 4′ [DIŠ $^{mu]l}$Pa-bil-sag ^{mul}Za-ba$_4$-ba$_4$ u $^{\text{mú}[l}$]
DD r. 1′ [DIŠ $^{mu]l}$[Pa-bil-sag ^{mul}]Za-ba$_4$-ba$_4$ DINGIR.[GUB.BA]

Pabilsag Zababa u Dingirgubbû inappaḫūma
¶ Pabilsag, Zababa, and the Standing Gods rise, and

iii 28 ^{mul}KAK.SI.SÁ ^{mul}BAN u ^{mul}GÀM ŠÚ^{meš}

A iii 28 ^{mul}KAK.SI.SÁ ^{mul}BAN u ^{mul}GÀM ŠÚ^{meš}
E ii 28 ^{mul}KAK.SI.SÁ ^{mul}BAN u ^{mul}GÀM ŠÚ^{meš}
H iii 15 [^{mul}]KAK.SI.SÁ ^{mul}BAN u ^{mul}G[ÀM]
m 8 [^{mul}G]ÀM ŠÚ[^{meš}]
N iii 5′ [^{múl}KAK.SI.⸢SÁ⸣ ^{múl}BAN u ^{múl}GÀM [ ]
DD r. 2′ [ ] ⸢x⸣ [ ]

Šukūdu Qaštu u Gamlu irabbû
the Arrow, the Bow, and the Crook set.

iii 29 DIŠ ^{mul}UD.KA.DUḪ.A u ^{mul}TI$_8^{\text{mušen}}$ KUR^{meš}-ma

A iii 29 DIŠ ^{mul}UD.KA.DUḪ.A u ^{mul}TI$_8^{\text{mušen}}$ [KUR]^{meš}-ma
E ii 29 [DIŠ] ^{mul}UD.KA.DUḪ.A u ^{mul}TI$_8^{\text{mušen}}$ KUR^{meš}-ma
H iii 16 [ ] u ^{mul}TI$_8^{\text{mušen}}$ KUR^{meš}-[ma]
J ii 1′ DIŠ ^{mul}UD.KA.DUḪ.A [ ]
m 9 [ ]-nim-m[a]
N iii 6′ [DIŠ $^{\text{m]úl}}$UD.KA.DUḪ.A u ^{múl}T[I$_8^{\text{mušen}}$]
DD r. 3′ [DIŠ $^{m]ul}$[ ] ù $^{mu[l]}$⸢TI$_8$⸣^{mušen} KUR$^{m[\text{eš}}$-ma]

Nimru u Erû inappaḫūma
¶ The Panther and the Eagle rise, and

iii 30 ^{mul}MAŠ.TAB.BA.GAL.GAL u ^{mul}MAŠ.TAB.BA.TUR.TUR ŠÚ^{meš}

A iii 30 ^{mul}MAŠ.TAB.BA.GAL.GAL u ^{mul}MAŠ.TAB.BA.TUR.TUR ŠÚ^{meš}
E ii 30 ^{mul}MAŠ.TAB.BA.GAL.GAL u ^{mul}MAŠ.TAB.BA.TUR.TUR ŠÚ^{meš}

H iii 17		[^{mul}MAŠ.TAB.B]A.GAL.GAL.LA u ^{mul}MAŠ.TAB.BA.[TUR.TUR ŠÚ^{meš}]
J ii 2′		^{mul}MAŠ.TAB.BA.GAL.GAL [ ]
m	10	[^{mul}MAŠ.TAB.BA.T]UR.TUR ŠÚ[^{meš}]

Tū᾿āmū rabûtu u Tū᾿āmū ṣeḫrūtu irabbû
the Great Twins and the Small Twins set.

iii 31 DIŠ ^{mul}AŠ.IKU ^{mul}GU.LA u ^{mul}lu-lim KUR^{meš}-ma

A iii 31		DIŠ ^{mul}AŠ.IKU ^{mul}GU.LA u ^{mul}lu-lim KUR^{meš}-ma
E ii 31		DIŠ ^{mul}AŠ.IKU ^{mul}GU.LA u ^{mul}lu-lim KUR^{meš}-ma
H iii 18		[^{mul}GU.L]A u ^{mul}lu-lim KUR^{meš}-[ma]
J ii 3′		DIŠ ^{mul}AŠ.IKU ^{mul}GU.LA u [ ]
m	11	[ ] KUR^{me}-[ma]
N iii 7′		DIŠ ^{mul}AŠ.IKU ^{mul}GU.LA u ^{mul}lu-l[im]
DD	r. 4′	[DIŠ ^{m}]^{ul}[AŠ.IKU ^{mul}]GU.LA ^{mul}lu-lim [ ]

Ikû GU.LA u Lulīmu inappaḫūma
¶ The Field, the Great One, and the Stag rise, and

iii 32 ^{mul}UR.GU.LA $^{\text{mul d}}$MUŠ u ^{mul}EN.TE.NA.BAR.ḪUM ŠÚ^{meš}

A iii 32		^{mul}UR.GU.LA $^{\text{mul d}}$MUŠ u ^{mul}EN.TE.NA.BAR.ḪUM ŠÚ^{meš}
E ii 32		^{mul}UR.GU.LA ⸢$^{\text{mul d}}$MUŠ u ^{mul}EN.TE.NA.BAR.ḪUM⸣ ŠÚ^{meš}
H iii 19		[^{mul}UR.GU.LA ^{m}]^{ul}MUŠ u ^{mul}EN.[TE.NA.BAR.ḪUM ŠÚ^{meš}]
J ii 4′		^{mul}UR.GU.LA ^{m}[^{ul}]
m	12	[^{mul}EN.TE.NA.BAR.Ḫ]UM Š[Ú^{meš}]
N iii 7′		[ ] 8) $^{\text{múl d}}$MUŠ ^{múl}EN.TE.EN.NA.BAR.Ḫ[UM]
DD	r. 5′	[^{mul}UR.GU.LA $^{\text{mul d}}$MUŠ u] ^{mul}EN.TE.[NA]

Urgulû Niraḫ u Ḫabaṣīrānu irabbû
the Lion, the Snake, and the Mouse set.

iii 33 DIŠ ^{mul}KU$_{6}$ u ^{mul}ŠU.GI KUR^{meš}-ma ^{mul}AB.SÍN u ^{mul}UR.IDIM ŠÚ^{meš}

A iii 33		DIŠ ^{mul}KU$_{6}$ u ^{mul}ŠU.GI KUR^{meš}-ma ^{mul}AB.SÍN u ^{mul}UR.IDIM ŠÚ^{meš}
E ii 33		[DIŠ] ^{mul}KU$_{6}$ u ⸢x x x x x x x x x x x x x x⸣ ⸢ŠÚ$^{\text{meš?}}$⸣
H iii 20		[KUR^{me}]^{š}-ma ^{mu}[^{l}AB.SÍN]
J ii 5′		DIŠ ^{mul}KU$_{6}$ u ^{mul}ŠU.GI KUR^{meš}-nim-ma [ ]
m	13	[ ] ⸢x⸣ [ ]
N iii 9′		DIŠ ^{múl}KU$_{6}$ ^{múl}ŠU.GI KUR-ḫa-nim-ma ^{mú}[^{l}AB.SÍN]
DD	r. 6′	[DIŠ] ^{mul}[KU$_{6}$ u ^{mul}]ŠU.GI KUR^{meš}-nim-[ma]

Nūnu u Šību inappaḫūnimma Šer᾿u u Uridimmu irabbû
¶ The Fish and the Old Man rise, and the Furrow and the Wild Dog set.

---

iii 34 DIŠ TA KUR šá ^{mul}KAK.SI.SÁ 55 UD^{meš} ana KUR šá ^{mul}NUN^{ki}

A iii 34		DIŠ TA KUR šá ^{mul}KAK.SI.SÁ 55 UD^{meš} ana KUR šá ^{mul}NUN^{ki}
E ii 34		(illegible)
H iii 21		[ ] 55 UD^{meš} [ ]
J ii 6′		DIŠ TA KUR-ḫa šá ^{mul}KAK.SI.SÁ 55 [ ]
N iii 10′		DIŠ TA KUR-ḫa šá ^{múl}KAK.SI.SÁ 55 u$_{4}$-m[u]

W 1′ [NU]N^{ki}
DD r. 7′ [ ] ⸢x⸣ [ ] ^{mul}KAK.SI.SÁ 55 U[D^{meš}]

ultu napāḫi ša Šukūdi 55 ūmū ana napāḫi ša Eridu
¶ From the rising of the Arrow 55 days to the rising of Eridu.

iii 35 DIŠ TA KUR šá ^{mul}KAK.SI.SÁ 1 ŠU UD^{meš} ana KUR šá ^{mul}ŠU.PA

A iii 35 DIŠ TA KUR šá ^{mul}KAK.SI.SÁ 1 ŠU UD^{meš} ana KUR šá ^{mul}ŠU.PA
E ii 35 ⸢x x x x x x x x x x⸣ ⸢UD^{meš} ana KUR [ ]
H iii 22 [Š]U UD^{meš} [ ]
J ii 7′ DIŠ TA KUR-ḫa šá ^{mul}KAK.SI.SÁ 1 ŠU [ ]
N iii 11′ DIŠ TA KUR-ḫa šá ^{mul}KAK.SI.SÁ 1 ŠU u$_4$-m[u]
W 2′ [^{mul}]ŠU.PA

ultu napāḫi ša Šukūdi šūš ūmū ana napāḫi ša ŠU.PA
¶ From the rising of the Arrow 60 days to the rising of ŠU.PA.

iii 36 DIŠ TA KUR šá ^{mul}ŠU.PA 10 UD^{meš} ana KUR šá ^{mul}AB.SÍN

A iii 36 DIŠ TA KUR šá ^{mul}ŠU.PA 10 UD^{meš} ana KUR šá ^{mul}AB.SÍN
E ii 36 (illegible)
H iii 23 [ ] ⸢10⸣ UD[^{meš}]
J ii 8′ DIŠ TA KUR-ḫa šá ^{mul}ŠU.PA 10 [ ]
N iii 12′ DIŠ TA KUR-ḫa šá ^{mul}ŠU.PA 10 u$_4$-mu [ ]
W 3′ [$^{m]ul}$AB.SÍN

ultu napāḫi ša ŠU.PA 10 ūmū ana napāḫi ša Šerʾi
¶ From the rising of ŠU.PA 10 days to the rising of the Furrow.

iii 37 DIŠ TA KUR šá ^{mul}AB.SÍN 20 UD^{meš} ana KUR šá ^{mul}zi-ba-ni-tu$_4$

A iii 37 DIŠ TA KUR šá ^{mul}AB.SÍN 20 UD^{meš} ana KUR šá ^{mul}zi-ba-ni-tu$_4$
E ii 37 ⸢DIŠ TA KUR x x x x x⸣ ⸢UD^{meš} ana KUR šá⸣ ^{mul}zi-ba-ni-tu$_4$
J ii 9′ DIŠ TA KUR-ḫa šá ^{mul}AB.SÍN 20 [ ]
N iii 13′ [DIŠ T]A KUR-ḫa šá ^{mul}AB.SÍN 20 u$_4$-m[u]
W 4′ [z]i-ba-ni-tú
FF ii 1′ [DIŠ] TA KU[R]

ultu napāḫi ša Šerʾi 20 ūmū ana napāḫi ša Zibānīti
¶ From the rising of the Furrow 20 days to the rising of the Scales.

iii 38 DIŠ TA KUR šá ^{mul}zi-ba-ni-tu$_4$ 30 UD^{meš} ana KUR šá ^{mul}ÙZ

A iii 38 DIŠ TA KUR šá ^{mul}zi-ba-ni-tu$_4$ 30 UD^{meš} ana KUR šá ^{mul}ÙZ
E ii 38 ⸢DIŠ TA KUR x x x x x x x⸣ ⸢UD^{meš} ana KUR šá ^{mul}ÙZ⸣
J ii 10′ DIŠ TA KUR-ḫa šá ⸢^{mul}zi-ba-ni⸣-tu$_4$ 30 [ ]
N iii 14′ [š]á ^{mul}zi-ba-ni-t[u$_4$]
W 5′ [ ] šá ^{múl}ÙZ
FF ii 2′ [DIŠ] TA KUR šá [ ]

ultu napāḫi ša Zibānīti 30 ūmū ana napāḫi ša Enzi
¶ From the rising of the Scales 30 days to the rising of the Goat.

<u>iii 39</u> DIŠ TA KUR šá ^{mul}ÙZ 30 UD^{meš} ana KUR šá ^{mul}UD.KA.DUḪ.A

A iii 39 DIŠ TA KUR šá ^{mul}ÙZ 30 UD^{meš} ana KUR šá ^{mul}UD.KA.DUḪ.A
E ii 39 ⸢DIŠ TA KUR x x x x x x x x x x x x x x x x⸣
J ii 11′ DIŠ TA KUR-ḫa šá ^{mul}ÙZ 30 [ ]
N iii 15′ [š]á ^{múl}ÙZ 30 u_4-[mu]
W 6′ [ ]UD.KA.DUḪ
FF ii 3′ DIŠ TA KUR šá ^{mul}[ÙZ]
VV 1′ [ ] ⸢ša⸣ ^{mul}ÙZ ⸢30⸣ U[D^{meš}] 2) [ ] ^{mul}KA.DUḪ.A

ultu napāḫi ša Enzi 30 ūmū ana napāḫi ša Nimri
¶ From the rising of the Goat 30 days to the rising of the Panther.

<u>iii 40</u> DIŠ TA KUR šá ^{mul}UD.KA.DUḪ.A 30 UD^{meš} ana KUR šá ^{mul}SIM.MAḪ

A iii 40 DIŠ TA KUR šá ^{mul}UD.KA.DUḪ.A 30 UD^{meš} ana KUR šá ^{mul}SIM.MAḪ
E ii 40 ⸢DIŠ TA KUR x x x x x⸣ [ ]
J ii 12′ DIŠ TA KUR-ḫa šá ⸢^{mul}⸣UD.K[A.DUḪ].A 30 [ ]
W 7′ [ ]SIM.MAḪ
FF ii 4′ DIŠ TA KUR šá ^{mul}UD.K[A.DUḪ.A]
VV 3′ [ ] ^{mul}⸢KA.DUḪ⸣.A 30 [ ] 4) [^{mul}]⸢SIM.MAḪ⸣

ultu napāḫi ša Nimri 30 ūmū ana napāḫi ša Šinūnūti
¶ From the rising of the Panther 30 days to the rising of the Swallow.

<u>iii 41</u> DIŠ TA KUR šá ^{mul}SIM.MAḪ 20 UD^{meš} ana KUR šá ^{mul}AŠ.IKU

A iii 41 DIŠ TA KUR šá ^{mul}SIM.MAḪ 20 UD^{meš} ana KUR šá ^{mul}AŠ.IKU
d r. 1′ [ ] ⸢šá ^{mu}[^{l}⸣]
E ii 41 ⸢DIŠ TA KUR x x x x⸣ [ ]
J ii 13′ DIŠ TA KUR-ḫa šá ^{mul}SIM.MAḪ 10 U[D^{meš}]
W 8′ [ ] ^{múl}AŠ.IKU
FF ii 5′ DIŠ TA KUR šá ^{mul}SIM.M[AḪ]
VV 5′ [^{mul}]SIM.MAḪ ⸢20?⸣ UD^{m}[^{eš}] 6) [ ]AŠ.IKU

ultu napāḫi ša Šinūnūti 20 ūmū ana napāḫi ša Ikî
¶ From the rising of the Swallow 20 (var. 10) days to the rising of the Field.

<u>iii 42</u> DIŠ TA KUR šá ^{mul}AŠ.IKU 40 UD^{meš} ana KUR šá ^{mul}KU$_6$

A iii 42 DIŠ TA KUR šá ^{mul}AŠ.IKU 40 UD^{meš} ana KUR šá ^{mul}KU$_6$
d r. 2′ [UD^{m}]^{eš} ana KUR šá ^{mul}[ ]
E ii 42 ⸢x x⸣ [ ]
J ii 14′ DIŠ TA KUR-ḫa šá ^{mul}AŠ.IKU 40 [ ]
W 9′ [ ] ^{múl}KU$_6$
FF ii 6′ DIŠ TA KUR šá ^{mul}AŠ.IKU ⸢40⸣ [ ]
VV 7′ [A]Š.IKU [ ] 8) [^{mul}]KU$_6$

ultu napāḫi ša Ikî 40 ūmū ana napāḫi ša Nūni
¶ From the rising of the Field 40 days to the rising of the Fish.

iii 43		DIŠ TA KUR šá ^{mul}KU$_{6}$ 35 UD^{meš} ana KUR šá ^{mul}GÀM

A iii 43		DIŠ TA KUR šá ^{mul}KU$_{6}$ 35 UD^{meš} ana KUR šá ^{mul}GÀM
d	r. 3′	[U]D^{meš} ana KUR šá ^{mul}G[ÀM]
J ii 15′		DIŠ TA KUR-ḫa šá ^{mul}KU$_{6}$ 20+[x]
W	10′	[ ] šá ^{múl}GÀM
FF ii 7′		DIŠ TA KUR šá ^{mul}KU$_{6}$ 35 [ ]
VV	9′	[DIŠ TA KUR šá ^{m}]^{ul}KU$_{6}$ 10+[x]

ultu napāḫi ša Nūni 35 ūmū ana napāḫi ša Gamli
¶ From the rising of the Fish 35 days to the rising of the Crook.

iii 44		DIŠ TA KUR šá ^{mul}GÀM 10 UD^{meš} ana KUR šá MUL.MUL

A iii 44		DIŠ TA KUR šá ^{mul}GÀM 10 UD^{meš} ana KUR šá MUL.⸢MUL⸣
d	r. 4′	[U]D^{meš} ana KUR šá MUL.[MUL]
J ii 16′		DIŠ TA KUR-ḫa šá ^{mul}GÀM [ ]
K iii 1′		[ ] ana KUR šá M[ÚL.MÚL]
W	11′	[ ] šá MÚL.MÚL
FF ii 8′		DIŠ TA KUR šá ^{mul}GÀM 10 [ ]

ultu napāḫi ša Gamli 10 ūmū ana napāḫi ša Zappi
¶ From the rising of the Crook 10 days to the rising of the Stars.

iii 45		DIŠ TA KUR šá MUL.MUL 20 UD^{meš} ana KUR šá ^{mul}GU$_{4}$.AN.NA

A iii 45		DIŠ TA KUR šá MUL.MUL 20 UD^{meš} ana KUR šá ^{mul}[GU$_{4}$.AN.NA]
d	r. 5′	[ ] ⸢KUR⸣ šá ^{mul}GU$_{4}$.[AN.NA]
J ii 17′		DIŠ TA KUR-ḫa šá MUL.MUL 10+[x]
K iii 2′		[ ] ana KUR šá ^{múl}GU$_{4}$.A[N.N]A
W	12′	[ ] šá ^{múl}GU$_{4}$.AN.NA
FF ii 9′		DIŠ TA KUR šá MUL.MUL 20 UD^{m}⸢^{eš}]

ultu napāḫi ša Zappi 20 ūmū ana napāḫi ša Alî
¶ From the rising of the Stars 20 days to the rising of the Bull of Heaven.

iii 46		DIŠ TA KUR šá ^{mul}GU$_{4}$.AN.NA 20 UD^{meš} ana KUR šá ^{mul}SIPA.ZI.AN.NA

A iii 46		DIŠ TA KUR šá ^{mul}GU$_{4}$.AN.NA 20 UD^{meš} ana KUR šá ^{mu}[^{l}SIPA.ZI.AN.NA]
d	r. 6′	[ ] ⸢šá⸣ ^{mul}SIPA.Z[I.AN.NA]
J ii 18′		DIŠ TA KUR-ḫa šá ^{mul}GU$_{4}$.AN.NA 20 [ ]
K iii 3′		[u$_{4}$-m]u ana KUR šá ^{múl}SIPA.ZI.AN.NA
W	13′	[ ] šá ^{múl}SIPA
FF ii 10′		[DIŠ TA] KUR šá ^{mul}GU$_{4}$.AN.NA 20 UD^{meš} ana [ ]

ultu napāḫi ša Alî 20 ūmū ana napāḫi ša Šidalli
¶ From the rising of the Bull of Heaven 20 days to the rising of the True Shepherd of Anu.

iii 47		DIŠ TA KUR šá ^{mul}SIPA.ZI.AN.NA 35 UD^{meš} ana KUR šá ^{mul}KAK.SI.SÁ

A iii 47		DIŠ TA KUR šá ^{mul}SIPA.ZI.AN.NA 35 UD^{meš} ana KUR šá [ ]
d	r. 7′	[^{m}]^{ul}KAK.S[I.SÁ]
J ii 19′		DIŠ TA KUR-ḫa šá ^{mul}[SIPA].ZI.AN.NA [ ]

K iii 4′ [DIŠ TA KUR šá ^{mul}SIPA.ZI.AN.N]A 35 u$_4$-mu ana KUR šá ^{múl}KAK.SI.SÁ
W 14′ [š]á ^{múl}KAK.SI.SÁ
FF ii 11′ [^{mul}S]IPA.ZI.AN.NA 35 UD^{meš} ana KUR [ ]

ultu napāḫi ša Šidalli 35 ūmū ana napāḫi ša Šukūdi
¶ From the rising of the True Shepherd of Anu 35 days to the rising of the Arrow.

iii 48 DIŠ TA KUR šá ^{mul}KAK.SI.SÁ 20 UD^{meš} ana KUR šá ^{mul}BAN

A iii 48 DIŠ TA KUR šá ^{mul}KAK.SI.SÁ 20 UD^{meš} ana KUR šá [ ]
d r. 8′ [^{mu}]^{l}[BAN]
J ii 20′ DIŠ T[A] KUR-ḫa šá ^{mul}KAK.SI.S[Á]
K iii 5′ [ ] u$_4$-mu ana KUR šá ^{múl}BAN
FF ii 12′ [^{mul}KAK.S]I.SÁ 20 UD^{meš} ana KUR [ ]
JJ ii 1′ [^{mu}]^{l}BAN

ultu napāḫi ša Šukūdi 20 ūmū ana napāḫi ša Qašti
¶ From the rising of the Arrow 20 days to the rising of the Bow.

---

iii 49 u$_4$-mu 1 UŠ.TA.ÀM MUL^{meš} ina šèr-ti ana GI$_6$ KU$_4$^{meš}-ni

A iii 49 ⸢u$_4$⸣-mu 1 UŠ.TA.ÀM MUL^{meš} ina šèr-t[i]
g r. 1′ [ ].⸢ÀM⸣ MUL^{meš} [ ]
J iii 1 u$_4$-[mu 1 U]Š.TA.ÀM MUL[^{meš}]
K iii 6′ [š]èr-tú ana GI$_6$ KU$_4$^{meš}-ni
FF ii 13′ [ ] ⸢x x x⸣ [ ]
JJ ii 2′ [ ] KU$_4$^{meš}-ni

ūmu 1 UŠ kakkabū ina šērti ana mūši irrubūni
The stars enter into the night in the morning 1 UŠ each day.

iii 50 u$_4$-mu 1 UŠ.TA.ÀM MUL^{meš} ina li-la-a-ti ana u$_4$-me È^{meš}-ni

A iii 50 ⸢u$_4$⸣-mu 1 UŠ.TA.ÀM MUL^{meš} ina li-la-a-t[i]
g r. 2′ [ ] ⸢1 UŠ⸣.TA.ÀM MUL^{meš} ina [ ]
J iii 2 u$_4$-[mu 1 UŠ.T]A.ÀM MUL^{m}[^{eš}]
K iii 7′ [ ] li-la-a-tú ana u$_4$-me È^{meš}-ni
JJ ii 3′ [u$_4$-m]i È^{meš}-ni

ūmu 1 UŠ kakkabū ina līlâti ana ūmi uṣṣûni
The stars come out into the day in the evening 1 UŠ each day.

---

iv 1 DIŠ MUL^{meš} šá ziq-pi šá ina KASKAL šu-ut ^{d}En-líl ina MURUB$_4$ AN-e

A iv 1 MUL^{meš} šá ziq-pi šá ina KASKAL šu-ut ^{d}En-líl ina [ ]
g r. 3′ [DIŠ M]UL^{meš} šá ziq-pi šá ina KASKAL šu-u[t]
J iii 3 DIŠ MUL^{meš} ziq-pi šá ina [ ]
K iii 8′ [^{d}En]-líl ina MURUB$_4$ AN-e
JJ ii 4′ [^{d}E]n-líl [ ]

kakkabū ša ziqpi ša ina ḫarrān šūt Enlil ina qabal šamê
¶ The *ziqpu* stars that stand in the path of Enlil in the middle of the sky

iv 2 ina IGI-et GABA šá ŠEŠ AN-e GUB^{meš}-ma GI$_6$ KUR u ŠÚ-bi

A iv 2 ina IGI-et GABA šá ŠEŠ AN-e GUB^{meš}-ma GI$_6$ KU[R]
g r. 4′ ina IGI-et GABA šá ŠEŠ AN-e GU[B^{meš}-ma] 5) GI$_6$ KUR u ŠÚ^{meš}
J iii 4 ina IGI-[et] GABA šá ŠEŠ A[N-e] 5) u ŠÚ-bi
K iii 8′ ina IGI-et GABA 9) [GUB]-az-ma GI$_6$ KUR u ŠÚ
Q iii 1′ [ina IGI-e]t GABA š[á$^{?}$]
JJ ii 5′ [GUB-a]z-ma [ ]

ina meḫret irti ša nāṣir šamê izzazzūma mūša nipḫa u rība
opposite the chest of the observer of the sky, and

iv 3 šá MUL^{meš} ina lìb-bi-šú-nu im-ma-ru

A iv 3 šá MUL^{meš} ina lìb-bi-šú-nu im-ma-r[u]
g r. 5′ šá MUL^{meš} [ ]
J iii 5 šá MUL^{meš} ina lìb-[bi-šú-nu]
K iii 9′ šá MUL ina lìb-bi-šú-nu IGI-mar
Q iii 2′ [šá] MUL^{mes} ina lì[b-bi-šú-nu]
BB B r.1′ [ ] ⸢i-na⸣ l[ìb-bi-šú-nu]
JJ ii 6′ [im-m]a-ru

ša kakkabī ina libbišunu immaru
by means of which he observes the rising and setting of the stars at night:

---

iv 4 DIŠ ^{mul}ŠU.PA MUL BAL.TÉŠ.A ^{mul}DINGIR.GUB.BA^{meš} ^{mul}UR.KU

A iv 4 ^{mul}ŠU.PA MUL BAL.TÉŠ.A ^{mul}DINGIR.GUB.BA^{meš} ^{mul}UR.KU
g r. 6′ ⸢DIŠ ^{mul}ŠU⸣.[PA] ⸢MUL⸣ BAL.TÉŠ.A ^{m}[^{ul}DINGIR.GUB.BA^{meš}] 7) ⸢^{mul}UR⸣.KU]
J iii 6 DIŠ ^{mul}ŠU.PA MUL BAL.TÉ[Š.A]
K iii 10′ [DIŠ ^{mul}ŠU.PA MUL BAL.T]ÉŠ.A ^{múl}DINGIR.GUB.BA^{meš} ^{múl}UR.KU u
Q iii 3′ [DIŠ ^{mul}ŠU].PA MUL BAL.TÉŠ.[A] 4) [^{mul}U]R.KU
BB B r. 2′ [BAL.TÉ]Š.A ^{mul}DINGIR.GU[B.BA^{meš}] 3′) [ ]
JJ ii 7′ [ ]

ŠU.PA Kakkab bāšti Dingirgubbû Kalbu
¶ ŠU.PA, the Star of Dignity, the Standing Gods, the Dog,

iv 5 ^{mul}ÙZ ^{mul}UD.KA.DUḪ.A ^{mul}lu-lim ^{mul}ŠU.GI ^{mul}GÀM

A iv 5 ^{mul}ÙZ ^{mul}UD.KA.DUḪ.A ^{mul}lu-lim ^{mul}ŠU.GI ^{mul}GÀM
g r. 7′ ^{mul}Ù[Z]
J iii 7 ^{mul}ÙZ ^{mul}UD.KA.[ ]
K iii 10′ ^{múl}ÙZ 11) [^{múl}UD.KA.DUḪ].A ^{múl}lu-lim ^{múl}ŠU.GI ^{múl}GÀM
L iv 1′ ^{mul}ÙZ 2) [ ]
Q iii 4′ ^{mul}ÙZ [ ] 5) [^{mul}l]u-lim ^{mul}ŠU.GI ^{m}[^{ul}GÀM]
X iii 1′ [^{múl}]UD.KA.DUḪ.A ^{mú}[^{l}lu-lim]
BB B r. 3′ [^{mul}Ù]Z ^{mul}KA.DU[Ḫ.A] 4′) [^{mul}Lu-lim ^{mu}]^{l}ŠU.GI ^{mul}GÀM
JJ ii 7′ [^{mul}Ù]Z 8) [ ] ⸢x⸣

Enzu Nimru Lulīmu Šību Gamlu
the Goat, the Panther, the Stag, the Old Man, the Crook,

iv 6 ^{mul}MAŠ.TAB.BA.GAL.GAL ^{mul}AL.LUL ^{mul}UR.GU.LA ^{mul}E$_{4}$-ru$_{6}$ u ^{mul}Ḫé-gál-la-a-a

A iv 6 ^{mul}MAŠ.TAB.BA.GAL.GAL ^{mul}AL.LUL ^{mul}UR.GU.LA ^{mul}E$_{4}$-ru$_{6}$ u ^{mul}Ḫé-gál-la-a-a
g r. 8′ [x] ⸢x x x⸣ [ ]
J iii 8 ^{mul}MAŠ.TAB.BA.GAL.GAL ^{mu}[^{l}AL.LUL]
K iii 11′ ^{múl}MAŠ.TAB.BA.GAL.GAL 12) [^{múl}U]R.GU.LA ^{múl}E$_{4}$-ru$_{6}$ u ^{múl}Ḫé-gál-la-a-a
L iv 2′ [^{mul}MAŠ].TAB.BA.GAL.GAL 3) [^{mul}AL.LUL ^{mul}UR.GU.LA ^{mul}E$_{4}$-ru$_{6}$ u ^{mul}Ḫé-gá]l-la-a-a
Q iii 6′ [^{mul}MAŠ.TAB].BA.GAL.GAL ^{mul}AL.[LUL] 7) [^{mul}UR.G]U.LA ^{mul}E$_{4}$-ru$_{6}$ [ ]
X iii 2′ [^{múl}]UR.GU.LA ^{múl}[E$_{4}$-ru$_{6}$]
BB B r. 5′ [ ]$^{meš\ mul}$⸢AL⸣.L[UL] 6′) [ ] ⸢^{mul}⸣E$_{4}$-ru$_{6}$ ^{mul}Ḫé-gál-⸢a⸣-[a]

Tū'āmū rabûtu Alluttu Urgulû Eru u Ḫegalaju
the Great Twins, the Crab, the Lion, Eru, and the Abundant One.

---

iv 7 PAP an-nu-tu MUL^{meš} šá ziq-pi šá KASKAL šu-ut ^{d}En-líl šá ina MURUB$_{4}$ AN-e

A iv 7 PAP an-nu-tu MUL^{meš} šá ziq-pi šá KASKAL šu-ut ^{d}En-líl šá ina MURUB$_{4}$ AN-e
J iii 9 PAP DIŠ an-nu-tu$_{4}$ MUL^{meš} ziq-pi šá KASKAL š[u-ut]
Q iii 8′ [ ] MUL^{meš} šá ziq-pi šá [KASKAL šu-ut ^{d}En-líl] 9) [šá ina MURUB$_{4}$ AN]-e
X iii 3′ [ ] MUL ziq-pi šá KA[SKAL]
BB B r. 7′ [M]UL^{meš} ša zi-iq-pi 8′) [AN]-e
SS ii 1′ PAP a[n-nu-tu] 2′) ⸢šá⸣ [ ]

napḫar annûtu kakkabū ša ziqpi ša ḫarrān šūt Enlil ša ina qabal šamê
All these are the *ziqpu* stars of the path of the stars of Enlil that stand in the middle of the sky

iv 8 ina IGI-et GABA-ka GUB^{me}-zu-ma GI$_{6}$ SAR^{meš} u ŠÚ^{meš}

A iv 8 ina IGI-et GABA-ka GUB^{me}-zu-ma GI$_{6}$ MÚ^{meš} u ŠÚ^{meš}
J iii 10 ina IGI-et GABA-ka GUB^{meš}-m[a]
Q iii 9′ IGI-et GABA-ka iz-⸢za-az⸣-[zu-ma]
X iii 4′ [t]i šá EN.NUN AN-e GU[B]
BB B r. 8′ IGI-et GABA-ka ⸢GUB-zu⸣ 9′) [ŠÚ^{m}]^{eš}
SS ii 2′ [GUB-z]u-[m]a 3′) M[Ú^{meš}]

ina meḫret irtika izzazzūma mūša nipḫāti u rībī
opposite your chest, and by means of which you observe at night

iv 9 šá MUL^{meš} ina lìb-bi-šú-nu tam-ma-ru

A iv 9 šá MUL^{meš} ina lìb-bi-šú-nu tam-ma-ru
J iii 11 šá MUL^{me} ina lib-bi-šú-nu ta[m-ma-ru]
Q iii 10′ [x] u GI$_{6}$ ina lìb-bi-šú-nu tam-ma-[ru]
X iii 5′ [-š]ú-nu [ ]
BB B r. 9′ ša MUL^{meš} ù$^{?}$ [ ] 10′) [ina lìb-bi-šú-n]u tam-⸢ma⸣-[ru]
SS ii 3′ [ša MU]L^{meš} 4′) ⸢ù⸣ [GI$_{6}$] tam-ma-ru

ša kakkabī ina libbišunu tammaru
the risings and settings of the stars.

---

iv 10		BE-ma zi-iq-pa a-na a-ma-ri-ka ina ^{iti}BÁR UD 20 KAM

A iv 10		BE-ma zi-iq-pa a-na a-ma-ri-ka ina ^{iti}BÁR UD 20 KAM
H iv 1		[^{iti}BÁ]R UD 20 KAM
J iii 12		BE-ma ziq-pi ana IGI-k[a]
Q iii 11′		[ ] ana a-ma-ri-ka ina ^{iti}BÁR UD 10+[x KAM]
X iii 6′		[ ] ziq-pi ana IGI-ka ina [ ]
BB	B r. 11′	[^{iti}BÁ]R UD-20$^{?}$-[KAM]
SS ii 5′		BE-ma z[i-i]q-pa a-n[a a-m]a-ri-ka 6′) ina ^{iti}[BÁ]R UD 20 KAM

šumma ziqpa ana amārika ina Nisanni UD 20
If you are to observe the *ziqpu*, on the 20th of Month I you stand

iv 11		ina šèr-ti la-am ^{d}UTU KUR-ḫa GUB-ma ZAG-ka ^{im}MAR.TU

A iv 11		ina šèr-ti la-am ^{d}UTU KUR-ḫa GUB-ma ZAG-ka ^{im}MAR.TU
H iv 2		[GU]B$^{?}$-ma [ ]
J iii 13		[ ] la-am ^{d}UTU KUR-ḫa [ ]
Q iii 12′		[l]a-am ^{d}UTU KUR-ḫa GUB-az-ma ZAG-k[a] 13) [^{im}MAR.TU]
X iii 7′		[la-a]m ^{d}UTU KUR-ḫa GUB-[ma]
BB	B r. 12′	[ ] ⸢la⸣-a[m ^{d}UTU] ⸢x⸣ [x]
SS ii 6′		⸢i-na šèr-ti 7′) ⸢la-am⸣ ^{d}UTU KUR-ḫ[a] GUB-ma 8′) [ZAG-k]a ^{im}MAR.TU

ina šērti lam Šamaš ippuḫa tazzazma imittaka Amurru
in the morning before sunrise, your right to the West,

iv 12		GÙB-ka ^{im}KUR.RA ni-iš IGI-ka ^{im}U$_{18}$.LU

A iv 12		GÙB-ka ^{im}KUR.RA ni-iš IGI-ka ^{im}U$_{18}$.LU
H iv 3		[.R]A 4) [ ]
J iii 14		GÙB-ka ^{im}KUR.R[A]
Q iii 13′		[G]ÙB-ka ^{im}KUR.RA ni-iš pa-ni-k[a]
R	1′	[ ] ⸢x⸣ [ ]
X iii 8′		[GÙB-ka ^{im}]KUR.RA ÍL IGI-k[a]
SS ii 8′		GÙB-ka ^{im}KUR.RA 9′) [Í]L IGI-ka ⸢^{im}⸣U$_{18}$.LU

šumēlka Šadû nīš pānīka Šūtu
your left to the East, your face directed towards South;

iv 13		qú-ma-ru šá ^{mul}UD.KA.DUḪ.A ina MURUB$_{4}$ AN-e

A iv 13		qú-ma-ru šá ^{mul}UD.KA.DUḪ.A ina MURUB$_{4}$ AN-e
H iv 4		[qú-ma-ru šá ^{mul}UD.K]A.DUḪ.A 5) [ina MURUB$_{4}$ AN-e]
J iii 15		qú-ma-ru šá ^{mul}[ ]
R	2′	[ ]⸢UD.⸣[K]A.DUḪ.A [ ]
T iv 1′		[ ] ina MURUB$_{4}$ [ ]
X iii 9′		[ ] ⸢AN-e⸣
SS ii 10′		[qú-ma-r]u ša ^{mul}KA.DUḪ.A ina ⸢MURUB$_{4}$⸣ AN-e

qumāru ša Nimri ina qabal šamê
the shoulder of the panther stands in the middle of the sky

iv 14		ina IGI-et GABA-ka GUB-ma ^{mul}GÀM KUR-ḫa

A iv 14		ina IGI-et GABA-ka GUB-ma ^{mul}GÀM KUR-ḫa
H iv 5		[ ]-ḫa

J iii 16		ina IGI-et GA[BA-ka]
k iii 1′		⸢x x x⸣ [ ]
R	3′	[m]a ^{múl}G[À]M KUR-ḫa
T iv 2′		[m]a ^{mul}GÀM [ ]
X iii 9′		⸢ina IGI-et⸣ [ ]
SS ii 11′		[GABA-k]a ⸢GUB⸣-ma ^{mul}GÀM KUR-ḫa

ina meḫret irtika izzazma Gamlu inappaḫa
opposite your chest, and the Crook rises.

<u>iv 15</u> DIŠ ina ^{iti}GU$_4$ UD 1 KAM GABA šá ^{mul}UD.KA.DUḪ.A ina MURUB$_4$ AN-e

A iv 15		DIŠ ina ^{iti}GU$_4$ UD 1 KAM GABA šá ^{mul}UD.KA.DUḪ.A ina MURUB$_4$ AN-e
f	r. 1	DIŠ ina ^{iti}GU$_4$ UD 1 KAM GABA ⸢šá⸣ [ ] 2) ina MURUB AN-e
H iv 6		[ ]-⸢e$^?$⸣
J iii 17		[ ] ^{iti}[ ]
k iii 2′		DIŠ ina GU$_4$ UD ⸢5$^?$ KAM GABA šá⸣ [ ]
R	4′	[^{mul}U]D.KA.DUḪ.A ina MURUB$_4$ AN-e
T iv 3′		[ ] šá ^{mul}UD.KA.D[UḪ.A]
SS ii 12′		[UD] 1 KAM GABA ša [^{mul}]KA.DUḪ.A 13′) ina MURUB$_4$ AN-e

ina Ajjari UD 1 irtu ša Nimri ina qabal šamê
¶ On the 1st day of Month II, the chest of the Panther stands in the middle of the sky

<u>iv 16</u> IGI-et GABA-ka GUB-ma MUL.MUL KUR-ḫa

A iv 16		IGI-et GABA-ka GUB-ma MUL.MUL KUR-ḫa
f	r. 2	ina IGI-et GABA-[ka]
R	4′	ina IGI-et 5) [ ] MÚL.MÚL KUR-ḫa
T iv 4′		IGI-et GABA-ka GUB-ma [ ]
SS ii 13′		[GU]B-ma 14′) [KUR]-ḫa

meḫret irtika izzazma Zappu inappaḫa
opposite your chest, and the Stars rise.

<u>iv 17</u> DIŠ ina ^{iti}GU$_4$ UD 20 KAM ki-in-ṣu šá ^{mul}UD.KA.DUḪ.A

A iv 17		DIŠ ina ^{iti}GU$_4$ UD 20 KAM ki-in-ṣu šá ^{mul}UD.KA.DUḪ.A
f	r. 3	DIŠ ina ^{iti}GU$_4$ UD 20 KAM ki-in-ṣ[i]
k iii 3′		DIŠ ina SIG$_4$ UD 20$^?$ KAM kin-ṣi šá ^{m}[^{úl}]
O iii 1′		[^{mul}]⸢UD.KA.DUḪ.A⸣
R	6′	[ ] ⸢x⸣ kin-ṣa šá ^{múl}UD.KA.DUḪ.A
T iv 5′		[ ] ⸢kin⸣-ṣi šá ^{mul}UD.KA.[DUḪ.A]
SS ii 15′-17′		[ ]

ina Ajjari UD 20 kinṣu ša Nimri
¶ On the 20th day of Month II, the Knee of the Panther

<u>iv 18</u> ina MURUB$_4$ AN-e IGI-et GABA-ka GUB-ma ^{mul}is le-e KUR-ḫa

A iv 18		ina MURUB$_4$ AN-e IGI-et GABA-ka GUB-ma ^{mul}is le-e KUR-ḫa
f	r. 4	ina MURUB$_4$ AN-e ina IGI-et GAB[A-ka]
O iii 1′		⸢ina MURUB$_4$⸣ [A]N-e 2) [^{mul}is l]e-e KUR-ḫa

R 7′ [IGI-e]t GABA-ka GUB-zu-ma ^{múl}is l[e-e]
T iv 6′ [ ] IGI-et GABA-ka GUB-ma ^{mul}i[s le-e]

ina qabal šamê meḫret irtika izzazma Is lê inappaḫa
stands in the middle of the sky opposite your chest, and the Jaw of the Bull rises.

---

iv 19 DIŠ ina ^{iti}SIG$_4$ UD 10 KAM a-si-du šá ^{mul}UD.KA.DUḪ.A ina MURUB$_4$ AN-e

A iv 19 DIŠ ina ^{iti}SIG$_4$ UD 10 KAM a-si-du šá ^{mul}UD.KA.DUḪ.A ina MURUB$_4$ AN-e
f r. 5 DIŠ ina ^{iti}SIG$_4$ UD 10 KAM [ ] 6) ina ⸢MURUB$_4$$^{?}$ x x⸣
k iii 4′ ⸢DIŠ ina SIG$_4$⸣ UD 10$^{?}$ KAM a-si-du šá ^{múl}U[D.KA.DUḪ.A]
O iii 3′ [ ].KA.DUḪ(tablet: GABA) ina MURUB$_4$ AN-e
R 8′ [ ] a-si-du šá ^{múl}UD.KA.DUḪ.A ina MU[RUB$_4$ AN-e]
T iv 7′ [ ] a-si-du šá ^{mul}UD.KA.D[UḪ.A]
AA iii 1′ [DIŠ] ina ^{iti}S[IG$_4$]
SS iv 18′ DIŠ ina [ ]

ina Simāni UD 10 asīdu ša Nimri ina qabal šamê
¶ On the 10th day of Month III, the Heel of the Panther stands in the middle of the sky

iv 20 IGI-et GABA-ka GUB-ma ^{mul}SIPA.ZI.AN.NA KUR-ḫa

A iv 20 IGI-et GABA-ka GUB-ma ^{mul}SIPA.ZI.AN.NA KUR-ḫa
O iii 4′ [GA]BA-k[a . Z]I.AN.NA KUR-ḫa
R 9′ [ ] GUB-ma ^{múl}SIPA.Z[I.AN.NA]
T iv 8′ [IGI-e]t GABA-ka GUB-ma ^{mul}SI[PA.ZI.AN.NA]
AA iii 2′ IGI-et G[ABA]

meḫret irtika izzazma Šidallu inappaḫa
opposite your chest, and the True Shepherd of Anu rises.

---

iv 21 DIŠ ina ^{iti}ŠU UD 15 KAM MUL^{m}]^{eš} um-mu-lu-tú šá ^{mul}ŠU.GI ina MURUB$_4$ AN-e

A iv 21 DIŠ ina ^{iti}ŠU UD 15 KAM MUL né-bu-ú šá ^{mul}ŠU.GI ina MURUB$_4$ AN-e
a r. 1′ ⸢DIŠ⸣ [ ] 2) ⸢MIN⸣ [ ]
O iii 5′ [DIŠ ina ^{iti}ŠU] UD 15 [šá ^{m}]^{ul}ŠU.GI ina MURUB$_4$ AN-e
T iv 9′ [MUL^{m}]^{eš} um-mu-lu-tú šá ^{mul}[ŠU.GI]
R 10′ [u]m-mu-lu-tú šá ^{múl}⸢x⸣ [ ]
AA iii 3′ DIŠ ina ^{iti}ŠU UD ⸢15⸣ KAM ⸢MUL né⸣-b[u-ú šá ^{mul}ŠU.GI] 4) [ina MURUB$_4$ A]N-e

ina Du'ūzi UD 15 kakkabū ummulūtu (var. kakkabu nebû) ša Šībi ina qabal šamê
¶ On the 15th day of Month IV the scintillating stars (var. bright star) of the Old Man stand in the middle of the sky

IGI-et GABA-ka GUB-ma ^{mul}KAK.SI.SÁ KUR-ḫa

A iv 21 MIN MIN ^{mul}KAK.⸢SI.SÁ KUR-ḫa⸣
O iii 6′ [IGI-et GA]BA-k[a ^{mul}KAK].SI.SÁ KUR-ḫa
T iv 10′ [IGI-et GA]BA-ka GUB-ma ^{mul}KAK.S[I.SÁ]
AA iii 4′ IGI-et GABA-k[a]

meḫret irtika izzazma Šukūdu inappaḫa
opposite your chest, and the Arrow rises.

---

iv 22 DIŠ ina ^{iti}IZI UD 15 KAM MUL né-bu-ú šá ^{mul}ŠU.GI

A iv 22 DIŠ ina ^{iti}IZI UD 15 KAM MUL^{meš} um-mu-lu-tu$_4$ šá ^{mul}ŠU.GI
a r. 3′ DIŠ ina ^{it}⌜^{i}IZI
O iii 7′ [^{iti}IZ]I UD 15 [KAM um-mu-lu]-ti šá ^{mul}ŠU.GI
T iv 11′ [MUL n]é-bu-ú šá ^{mul}ŠU.GI
AA iii 5′ [DIŠ ina ^{iti}IZ]I UD 5 KAM MUL um-m[u-lu-tu$_4$]

ina Abi UD 15 (var. 5) kakkabu nebû (var. kakkabū ummulūtu) ša Šībi
¶ On the 15th (var. 5th) day of Month V the bright star (var. scintillating stars) of the Old Man

iv 23 ina MURUB$_4$ AN-e IGI-et GABA-ka GUB-ma ^{mul}BAN KUR-ḫa

A iv 23 MIN MIN ^{mul}BAN ⌜KUR-ḫa⌝
a r. 4′ MIN MIN ^{m}⌜^{ul}BAN]
h 1′ [ ] ⌜^{mul}BAN⌝ KUR-ḫa
O iii 7′ ina MURUB$_4$ AN-e 8) [IGI-e]t GABA-ka G[UB-ma ^{mul}]BAN KUR-ḫa
T iv 12′ [G]UB-ma ^{mul}BAN [ ]
AA iii 6′ [A]N-e KIMIN ^{mul}B[AN]

ina qabal šamê meḫret irtika izzazzūma Qaštu inappaḫa
stand in the middle of the sky opposite your chest, and the Bow rises.

---

iv 24 DIŠ ina ^{iti}KIN UD 15 KAM ^{mul}MAŠ.TAB.BA.GAL.GAL ina MURUB$_4$ AN-e

A iv 24 DIŠ ina ^{iti}KIN UD 15 KAM ^{mul}MAŠ.TAB.BA.GAL.GAL MIN
a r. 5′ DIŠ ina ^{iti}KIN [ ]
h 2′ [^{mul}]⌜MAŠ⌝.TAB.BA.GAL.GAL ina MURUB$_4$ AN-e
O iii 9′ [DIŠ ina ^{iti}KI]N UD 15 KAM ^{mul}MAŠ.⌜TAB⌝.BA.GAL.GAL ina MURUB$_4$ AN-e
T iv 13′ [MAŠ].TAB.BA.GAL.GAL.LA [ ]
AA iii 7′ [UD] 15 KAM ^{mul}MAŠ.TAB.BA.GAL.G[AL]

ina Ulūli UD 15 Tūʾāmū rabûtu ina qabal šamê
¶ On the 15th day of Month VI the Great Twins stand in the middle of the sky

IGI-et GABA-ka GUB-ma ^{mul}ŠU.PA u ^{mul}NUN^{ki} KUR^{meš}-ni

A iv 24 MIN ^{mul}ŠU.PA u ^{mul}⌜NUN^{ki} KUR^{meš}-ni⌝
a r. 6′ IGI-et GABA-ka GUB-m[a]
h 3′ [GU]B$^{?}$-ma ^{mul}ŠU.PA u ^{mul}NUN^{ki} KUR^{meš}-ni
O iii 10′ [IGI-e]t GABA-ka GUB-ma ^{mul}ŠU.PA u ^{mul}NUN^{ki} KUR^{me}-ni
T iv 14′ [^{mu}]^{l}NUN^{ki} KUR^{me}-[ni]
AA iii 7′ [KIMIN] 8) [^{mul}Š]U.PA ^{mul}NUN^{ki} K[UR^{meš}-ni]

meḫret irtika izzazūma ŠU.PA u Eridu inappaḫūni
opposite your chest, and ŠU.PA and Eridu rise.

---

iv 25		DIŠ ina ^{iti}DU$_6$ UD 15 KAM ^{mul}UR.GU.LA ina MURUB$_4$ AN-e

A iv 25		DIŠ ina ^{iti}DU$_6$ UD 15 KAM ^{mul}UR.GU.LA MIN
a	r. 7′	DIŠ ina ^{iti}DU$_6$ U[D] 8) MIN
h	4′	[ ] ^{mul}UR.GU.LA ina MURUB$_4$ AN-e
O iii 11′		[DIŠ ina ^{iti}D]U$_6$ UD 15 KAM ^{mul}UR.GU.LA ina MURUB$_4$ AN-e
T iv 15′		[DIŠ ina ^{iti}DU$_6$ UD 15] ⸢x⸣ ^{mul}UR.GU.LA [ ]
AA iii 9′		[K]AM ^{mul}UR.G[U].L[A]

ina Tešrīti UD 15 Urgulû ina qabal šamê
¶ On the 15th day of Month VII the Lion stands in the middle of the sky

IGI-et GABA-ka GUB-ma ^{mul}zi-ba-ni-tu$_4$ KUR-ḫa

A iv 25		MIN ^{mul}zi-ba-ni-⸢tu$_4$ KUR-ḫa⸣
a	r. 8′	MIN ^{mu}⸢[
h	5′	[ ] ⸢^{mul}zi⸣-ba-ni-tu$_4$ KUR-ḫ[a]
O iii 12′		[IGI-et GAB]A-ka GUB-ma ^{mul}zi-ba-ni-tu$_4$ KUR-ḫa
T iv 16′		[ ]
AA iii 9′		[KIMIN] 10) ^{mul}⸢zi-ba⸣-[n]i-tu$_4$ KUR-ḫa

meḫret irtika izzazma Zibānītu inappaḫa
opposite your chest, and the Scales rise.

---

iv 26		DIŠ ina ^{iti}APIN UD 15 KAM ^{mul}E$_4$-ru$_6$ ina MURUB$_4$ AN-e IGI-et GABA-ka GUB-ma ^{mul}ÙZ KUR-ḫa

A iv 26		⸢DIŠ ina ^{iti}APIN⸣ UD 15 KAM ^{mul}E$_4$-ru$_6$ MIN MIN ^{mul}ÙZ KUR-ḫa
a	r. 9′	DIŠ ina [ ]
h	6′	[^{mul}E$_4$-r]u$_6$ ina MURUB$_4$ [AN-e]
O iii 13′		[DIŠ ina ^{iti}APIN UD] 15 KAM ^{mul}E$_4$-ru$_6$ ina MUR[UB$_4$ AN-e] 14) [ ] GUB-ma ^{mul}Ù[Z KUR-ḫa]
T iv 17′		[^{mul}E$_4$]-ru$_6$ MIN MIN ^{mul}Ù[Z KUR-ḫa]
AA iii 11′		[DIŠ] ina ^{iti}AP[IN U]D 15 K[AM] 12) ^{mul}Ù[Z KUR-ḫa]

ina Araḫsamni UD 15 Eru ina qabal šamê meḫret irtika izzazma Enzu inappaḫa
¶ On the 15th day of Month VIII, Eru stands in the middle of the sky opposite your chest, and the Goat rises.

---

iv 27		[DIŠ ina ^{iti}G]AN UD 15 KAM ^{mul}ŠU.PA MIN MIN ^{mul}UD.KA.DUḪ.A KUR-ḫa

A iv 27		[DIŠ ina ^{iti}G]AN UD 15 KAM ^{mul}ŠU.PA MIN MIN ^{mul}UD.KA.DUḪ.A KUR-ḫa
O iii 15′		[^{mu}]^{l}ŠU.PA [ ]
T iv 18′		[ ] MIN MIN ^{mul}[UD.KA.DUḪ.A

ina Kislīmi UD 15 ŠU.PA ina qabal šamê meḫret irtika izzazma Nimru inappaḫa
¶ On the 15th day of Month IX ŠU.PA stands in the middle of the sky opposite your chest, and the Panther rises.

---

iv 28 DIŠ ina ^{iti}AB UD 15 KAM ^{mul}DINGIR.GUB.BA^{meš} MIN

A iv 28 [DIŠ ina ^{iti}A]B UD 15 KAM ^{mul}DINGIR.GUB.BA^{meš} MIN
E iii 1 DIŠ ina ^{iti}AB [ ]

ina Ṭebēti UD 15 Dingirgubbû ina qabal šamê
¶ On the 15th day of Month X the Standing Gods stand in the middle of the sky

IGI-et GABA-ka GUB^{meš} ^{mul}SIM.MAḪ KUR-ḫa

A iv 28 MIN ^{mul}SIM.MAḪ KUR-ḫa
E iii 2 IGI-et GABA-ka [ ]

meḫret irtika izzazzūma Šinūnūtu inappaḫa
opposite your chest, and the Swallow rises.

---

iv 29 DIŠ ina ^{iti}ZÍZ UD 15 KAM ^{mul}UR.KU MIN IGI-et GABA-ka GUB-ma ^{mul}AŠ.IKU KUR-ḫa

A iv 29 [DIŠ ina ^{iti}]ZÍZ UD 15 KAM ^{mul}UR.KU MIN MIN ^{mul}AŠ.IKU KUR-ḫa
E iii 3 DIŠ ina ^{iti}ZÍZ UD [ ] 4) IGI-et GABA-[ka]
F r. 1′ DIŠ ina [ ]

ina Šabāṭi UD 15 Kalbu ina qabal šamê meḫret irtika izzazma Ikû inappaḫa
¶ On the 15th (error for 5th) day of Month XI the Dog stands in the middle of the sky opposite your chest, and the Field rises.

---

iv 30 DIŠ ina ^{iti}ŠE UD 15 KAM ^{mul}ÙZ MIN IGI-et GABA-ka GUB-ma ^{mul}KU$_6$ KUR-ḫa

A iv 30 [DIŠ ina ^{iti}]ŠE UD 15 KAM ^{mul}ÙZ MIN IGI-et GABA-ka GUB-ma ^{mul}KU$_6$ KUR-ḫa
E iii 5 DIŠ ina ^{iti}ŠE UD [ ] 6) IGI-et [ ]
F r. 2′ DIŠ ina ^{iti}[ŠE]

ina Addari UD 15 Enzu ina qabal šamê meḫret irtika izzazma Nūnu inappaḫa
¶ On the 15th day of Month XII the Goat stands in the middle of the sky opposite your chest, and the Fish rises.

---

iv 31 DINGIR^{meš} ša i-na KASKAL ^{d}Sin GUB^{meš}-ma ^{d}Sin e-ma ITI

A iv 31 [DINGIR]^{meš} ša i-na KASKAL ^{d}Sin GUB^{meš}-ma ^{d}Sin e-ma ITI
E iii 7 DINGIR^{meš} šá ina KASKAL ^{d}Sin [ ]
F r. 3′ MUL^{m}[^{eš}] 4) e-ma I[TI]

ilāni ša ina ḫarrān Sin izzazzūma Sin ēma arḫi
The gods (var. stars) who stand in the path of the Moon, through whose region the Moon during a month

iv 32 {ina} pi-rik-šú-nu DIB^{meš}-ma TAG^{meš}-šú-nu-ti

A iv 32 [ina pi]-rik-šú-nu DIB^{meš}-ma TAG^{meš}-šú-nu-ti
E iii 8 ina pi-ri[k-šú-nu]
F r. 4′ [ ]

{ina} pirikšunu ītenettiquma iltanappatušunūti
passes repeatedly and keeps touching them:

---

iv 33 MUL.MUL ^{mul}GU$_4$.AN.NA ^{mul}SIPA.ZI.AN.NA ^{mul}ŠU.GI

A iv 33 [MUL.M]UL ^{mul}GU$_4$.AN.NA ^{mul}SIPA.ZI.AN.NA ^{mul}ŠU.GI
E iii 9 MUL.MUL [ ]
F r. 5′ MUL.M[UL] 6) ^{mul}ŠU.[GI]

Zappu Alû Šidallu Šību
The Stars, the Bull of Heaven, the True Shepherd of Anu, the Old Man,

iv 34 ^{mul}GÀM ^{mul}MAŠ.TAB.BA.GAL.GAL ^{mul}AL.LUL ^{mul}UR.GU.LA

A iv 34 [^{mul}]GÀM ^{mul}MAŠ.TAB.BA.GAL.GAL ^{mul}AL.LUL ^{mul}UR.GU.LA
E iii 10 ^{mul}GÀM [ ] 11) ^{mul}UR.GU.LA
F r. 6′ [ ] 7) ^{mul}A[L.LUL]

Gamlu Tū'āmū rabûtu Alluttu Urgulû
the Crook, the Great Twins, the Crab, the Lion,

iv 35 ^{mul}AB.SÍN ^{mul}zi-ba-ni-tu$_4$ ^{mul}GÍR.TAB ^{mul}Pa-bil-sag

A iv 35 [^{mul}]zi-ba-ni-tu$_4$ ^{mul}GÍR.TAB ^{mul}Pa-bil-sag
E iii 11 [ ] 12) ^{mul}Pa-bil-sag
F r. 7′ [ ] 8) ^{mul}zi-b[a-ni-tu$_4$]

Šir'u Zibānītu Zuqāqīpu Pabilsag
the Furrow, the Scales, the Scorpion, Pabilsag,

iv 36 ^{mul}SUḪUR MÁŠ ^{mul}GU.LA KUN^{meš} ^{mul}SIM.MAḪ

A iv 36 [^{mul}SUḪUR MÁŠ ^{mu}]^{l}GU.LA KUN^{meš} ^{mul}SIM.MAḪ
E iii 12 [ ]
F r. 9′ ^{mul}SUḪUR [MÁŠ]

Suḫurmāšu GU.LA Zibbāt Šinūnūti
the Goat-Fish, the Great One, the Tails of the Swallow,

iv 37 ^{mul}A-nu-ni-tu$_4$ u $^{\text{mul lú}}$ḪUN.GÁ

A iv 37 [^{mul}A-nu-ni-t]u$_4$ u $^{\text{mul lú}}$ḪUN.GÁ
E iii 13 ^{mul}A-nu-ni-tu$_4$ [ ]
F r. 10′ ^{mul}A-nu-[ni-tu$_4$]

Anunītu u Agru
Anunitu, and the Hired Man.

---

iv 38 PAP an-nu-tu$_4$ DINGIR^{meš} šá ina KASKAL ^{d}Sin GUB^{meš}-ma ^{d}Sin e-ma ITI

A iv 38 [ ] šá ina KASKAL ^{d}Sin GUB^{meš}-ma ^{d}Sin e-ma ITI
E iii 14 PAP an-nu-tu$_4$ DINGIR^{meš} [ ]
F r. 11′ PAP an-nu-t[u] 12) ⸢e⸣-[ma ITI]

naphar annûtu ilāni ša ina ḫarrān Sin izzazzūma Sin ēma arḫi
All these are the gods who stand in the path of the Moon, through whose region the Moon during a month

iv 39

A iv 39 [pi-rik-šú-nu DIB]^{meš}-ma TAG^{meš}-šú-nu-ti

pirikšunu ītenettiquma iltanappatušunūti
passes repeatedly and keeps touching them.

Tablet II

i 1 DIŠ KASKAL ^{d}Sin DU-ku ^{d}UTU DU-ak

A iv 40 [D]U-ak
D i 1 DIŠ KASKAL ^{d}Sin DU-ku ^{d}[UTU]
E iii 15 DIŠ KASKAL ^{d}Sin DU-[ku]
HH i 1 [ ] ^{d}UTU [ ]

ḫarrān Sin illaku Šamaš illak
¶ The Sun travels the (same) path the Moon travels.

i 2 DIŠ KASKAL ^{d}Sin DU-ku ^{d}Šul-pa-è-a DU-ak

D i 2 DIŠ KASKAL ^{d}Sin DU-ku ^{d}Šu[l-pa-è]-a DU-ak
E iii 16 DIŠ KASKAL ^{d}Sin DU-[ku]
HH i 2 [^{d}Šul-p]a-è-a [DU-ak]

ḫarrān Sin illaku Šulpaea illak
¶ Jupiter travels the (same) path the Moon travels.

i 3 DIŠ KASKAL ^{d}Sin DU-ku ^{d}Dili-bat DU-ak

D i 3 DIŠ KASKAL ^{d}Sin DU-ku MUL [ ] DU-ak
E iii 17 DIŠ KASKAL ^{d}Sin DU-[ku]
HH i 3 [ ] ^{d}Dili-bat [ ]

ḫarrān Sin illaku Dilibat illak
¶ Venus travels the (same) path the Moon travels.

i 4 DIŠ KASKAL ^{d}Sin DU-ku ^{d}Ṣal-bat-a-nu DU-ak

D i 4 DIŠ KASKAL ^{d}Sin DU-ku ^{mul}Ṣal-[bat]-a-nu DU-ak
E iii 18 DIŠ KASKAL ^{d}Sin DU-[ku]
HH i 4 [ ] ^{d}Ṣal-bat-a-nu [DU-ak]

ḫarrān Sin illaku Ṣalbatānu illak
¶ Mars travels the (same) path the Moon travels.

i 5 DIŠ KASKAL ^{d}Sin DU-ku ^{mul}UDU.IDIM.GU$_4$.UD šá ^{d}Nin-urta MU-šú DU-ak

D i 5 DIŠ KASKAL ^{d}Sin DU-ku ^{mul}UDU.IDIM.GU$_4$.UD šá ^{d}Nin-urta MU-šú D[U-ak]
E iii 19 DIŠ KASKAL ^{d}Sin DU-[ku]
HH i 5 [^{mul}UDU].IDIM.GU$_4$.UD [šá] ^{d}MAŠ MU-šú [DU-ak]

ḫarrān Sin illaku Šiḫṭu ša Ninurta šumšu illak
¶ Mercury whose name is Ninurta travels the (same) path the Moon travels.

i 6 DIŠ KASKAL ^{d}Sin DU-ku ^{mul}UDU.IDIM.SAG.UŠ DU-ak

D i 6 DIŠ KASKAL ^{d}Sin DU-ku ^{mul}UDU.IDIM.SAG.UŠ DU-a[k]
E iii 20 DIŠ KASKAL ^{d}Sin DU-k[u]
S i 1′ [^{mul}UDU.IDIM.SA]G.⌜UŠ⌝ DU-ak
HH i 6 [^{mul}UDU.IDIM.SA]G.U[Š]

ḫarrān Sin illaku Kajamānu illak
¶ Saturn travels the (same) path the Moon travels.

---

i 7 PAP 6 DINGIR^{meš} šá 1-en NA^{meš}-su-nu MUL^{me} AN-e

D i 7 PAP 6 DINGIR^{meš} šá 1-en NA^{meš}-su-nu MUL^{me} AN-e
E iii 21 PAP 6 DINGIR^{meš} šá [ ]
J iv 1 [ ] AN-e
HH i 7 PAP ⌜x⌝ [ ] MUL [ ]

napḫar 6 ilāni ša ištēn manzāssunu kakkabī šamê
Together six gods whose places are one, (and) who touch the stars of the sky

i 8 TAG^{meš} NA^{meš}-su-nu KÚR.KÚR-ru

D i 7 TAG^{meš} NA^{meš}-su-nu KÚR.KÚR-r[u]
E iii 22 TAG^{meš} u [ ]
J iv 1 TAG^{me} 2) [ ] KÚR^{meš}
S i 2′ [ ] KÚR.KÚR-ru
HH i 8 [-su-n]u KÚR[ ]

ilappatū manzāssunu ittanakkirū
(and) keep changing their positions.

---

i 9 DIŠ ina ^{iti}ŠU UD 15 KAM ^{mul}KAK.SI.SÁ IGI.LÁ-ma
D i 8 DIŠ ina ^{iti}ŠU UD 15 KAM ^{mul}KAK.SI.SÁ IGI.LÁ-ma
E iii 23 DIŠ ina ^{iti}ŠU UD 1[5]
J iv 3 [^{mul}KAK.S]I.SÁ IGI-ma
HH i 9 [ ] KAM ^{mul}KAK.SI.SÁ [ ]
KK i 1 DIŠ ina ^{iti}ŠU UD 15 KAM ^{mul}KAK.SI.SÁ IGI.[LÁ-ma]

ina Du'ūzi UD 15 Šukūdu innammarma
¶ On the 15th day of Month IV the Arrow becomes visible, and

i 10 4 MA.NA EN.NUN u$_{4}$-mi 2 MA.NA EN.NUN GI$_{6}$

D i 8 4 MA.NA EN.NUN u$_{4}$-mu 2 MA.N[A GI$_{6}$$^{?}$]
E iii 24 4 MA.NA E[N.NUN]
J iv 3 4 MA.NA E[N.N]UN [ ]
S i 3′ [EN].NUN GI$_{6}$
HH i 10 [EN.NU]N u$_{4}$-mi 2 MA.NA E[N.NUN]
KK i 2 4 MA.NA EN.NUN u$_{4}$-mi 2 MA.NA EN.NUN [GI$_{6}$]

4 mana maṣṣarti ūmi 2 mana maṣṣarti mūši
4 minas is the watch of the day, 2 minas is the watch of the night.

i 11 ^{d}UTU šá ina id ^{im}SI.SÁ KI SAG.DU ^{mul}UR.GU.LA KUR-ḫa

D i 9 ^{d}UTU šá ina id ^{im}SI.SÁ KI SAG.DU ^{mul}UR.GU.LA KUR-ḫa
E iii 25 ^{d}U[TU]
J iv 4 [^{d}]UTU šá ina id 5) [^{mul}UR].GU.LA KUR-ḫa
HH i 11 [^{im}]SI.SÁ KI SAG.DU ^{m}[^{ul}]
KK i 3 ^{d}UTU šá ina id ^{im}SI.⌜SÁ⌝ KI SAG.DU ^{mul}UR.GU.[LA]

Šamaš ša ina id iltāni itti qaqqad Urgulî inappaḫa
The Sun which rises in the North with the head of the Lion

i 12 GUR-ma ana id ^{im}U$_{18}$.LU u$_{4}$-mu 40 NINDA.TA.ÀM ul-ta-nap-pal

D i 10 GUR-ma ana id ^{im}U$_{18}$.LU u$_{4}$-me 40 NINDA.TA.ÀM ul-ta-nap-p[al]
E iii 26 GUR-ma ana [ ] 27) ul-ta-[nap-pal]
J iv 5 GUR-ma 6) [ ].ÀM ul-ta-nap-pal
S i 4′ [ ]U$_{18}$.LU 5) [ ]
HH i 12 [ ] ^{im}U$_{18}$.LU u$_{4}$-mu 40 [ ]
KK i 4 GUR-ma ana id ^{im}U$_{18}$.LU UD 40 NINDA.TA.ÀM ul-ta-[nap-pal]

itârma ana id šūti ūma 40 ninda ultanappal
turns and keeps moving down towards the South 40 NINDA per day.

i 13 UD^{meš} LUGÚD.DA^{meš} GI$_{6}$^{meš} GÍD.DA^{meš}

D i 11 UD^{meš} LUGÚD.DA^{meš} GI$_{6}$^{meš} GÍD.DA^{meš}
J iv 7 [UD^{meš} LUGÚD.DA^{meš}] GI$_{6}$ GÍD.DA^{meš}
S i 5′ [GÍD.D]A^{meš}
HH i 13 [UD^{meš}] LUGÚD.DA^{meš} [ ]
KK i 5 UD^{me} LUGÚD.DA^{me} GI$_{6}$^{meš} GÍD.DA[^{meš}]

ūmū ikarrÛ mūšātu irrikā
The days become shorter, the nights become longer.

---

i 14 DIŠ ina ^{iti}DU$_{6}$ UD 15 KAM ^{d}UTU ina lìb-bi ^{mul}zi-ba-ni-tu$_{4}$ ina ^{d}UTU.È KUR-ḫa

D i 12 [ ] 15 KAM ^{d}UTU ina lìb-bi ^{mul}zi-ba-ni-tu$_{4}$ ina ^{d}UTU.È KUR-ḫa
E iii 28 DIŠ ina ^{iti}D[U$_{6}$]
J iv 8 [i ^{mu}]^{l}zi-ba-ni-tú KUR-ḫa
HH i 14 DIŠ ina ^{i}[^{ti}DU$_{6}$ UD 1]5 KAM ^{d}UTU ina lìb-b[i ^{mul}z]i-b[a-n]i-tú [ ]
KK i 6 DIŠ ina ^{iti}DU$_{6}$ UD 15 KAM ^{d}UTU ina ŠÀ ^{mul}zi-ba-ni-t[u$_{4}$] 7) KUR-ḫa

ina Tešrīti UD 15 Šamaš ina libbi Zibānīti ina ṣīt Šamši inappaḫa
¶ On the 15th day of Month VII the Sun rises within the Scales in the East,

i 15	u ^{d}Sin ina IGI MUL.MUL EGIR $^{mul\ lú}$ḪUN.GÁ GUB-az-ma

D i 13	[M]UL.MUL EGIR $^{mul\ lú}$ḪUN.GÁ GUB-ma
E iii 29	u ^{d}S[in]
J iv 9	[Ḫ]UN.GÁ GUB-az-ma
S i 6′	u ^{d}Sin 7) [ ]
HH i 15	u ^{d}[Sin M]UL.MUL EGIR ^{mul}[Ḫ]UN.GÁ GUB-ma
KK i 7	u ^{d}Sin ina IGI MUL.MUL [EGI]R $^{mul\ lú}$ḪUN.GÁ 8) GUB-ma

u Sin ina pān Zappi arki Agri izzazma
and the Moon stands in front of the Stars behind the Hired Man,

	3 MA.NA EN.NUN u$_{4}$-mi 3 MA.NA EN.NUN GI$_{6}$
D i 14	[ ] u$_{4}$-mi 3 MA.NA EN.NUN [GI$_{6}$]
E iii 30	3 M[A.NA]
J iv 10	[EN.NU]N GI$_{6}$
S i 7′	[MA.N]A EN.NUN ⌜GI$_{6}$⌝
HH i 15	3 MA.NA EN.NUN u$_{4}$-mi 3 MA.NA EN.N[UN GI$_{6}$]
KK i 8	3 [M]A.NA EN.NUN u$_{4}$-mi 3 MA.NA EN.NUN GI$_{6}$

3 mana maṣṣarti ūmi 3 mana maṣṣarti mūši
3 minas is the watch of the day, 3 minas is the watch of the night.

---

i 16	DIŠ ina ^{iti}AB UD 15 KAM ^{mul}KAK.SI.SÁ ina li-la-a-ti IGI.LÁ-ma

D i 15	[li-l]a-ti IG[I.L]Á-ma
E iii 31	DIŠ ina ^{iti}A[B]
J iv 11	[l]i-la-a-ti IGI-ma
HH i 16	DIŠ ina $^{i[ti}$AB UD 15 KAM $^{mu]l}$KAK.SI.SÁ ina li-la-ti IGI.LÁ-ma
KK i 9	DIŠ ina $^{i[ti}$A]B UD 15 KAM ^{mul}KAK.SI.SÁ ina li-lá$^{?}$-x-ti 10) [IGI].LÁ-ma
SS iii 1′	⌜DIŠ⌝ ina [ ] 2) IG[I.LÁ-ma]

ina Ṭebēti UD 15 Šukūdu ina līlâti innammarma
¶ On the 15th day of Month X, the Arrow becomes visible in the evening.

	2 MA.NA EN.NUN u$_{4}$-mi 4 MA.NA EN.NUN GI$_{6}$
D i 15	2 M[A.NA]
E iii 32	[x] ⌜x⌝ [ ]
J iv 12	[ ] ⌜x⌝
HH i 16	2 MA.NA EN.NUN u$_{4}$-mi 4 MA.NA EN.NUN [GI$_{6}$]
KK i 10	2 MA.NA EN.NUN u$_{4}$-mi 4 MA.NA EN.[NUN] GI$_{6}$

2 mana maṣṣarti ūmi 4 mana maṣṣarti mūši
2 minas is the watch of the day, 4 minas is the watch of the night.

i 17	^{d}UTU šá ina id ^{im}U$_{18}$.LU KI SAG.DU ^{mul}UR.GU.LA KUR-ḫa GUR-ma ana id ^{im}SI.SÁ

E iii 33	^{d}[UTU] 34) ana id [ ]
J iv 12	^{d}UTU šá ina id 13) [ ] ana id 14) [^{im}SI.SÁ]
HH i 17	[^{im}U$_{18}$.]LU KI SAG.DU ^{mul}UR.GU.LA KUR-ḫa GUR-ma ana id ^{im}SI.SÁ

KK i 11 ^{d}UTU šá ina id ^{im}U$_{18}$.LU KI SAG.DU ^{mul}U[R.G]U.LA ⌜KUR-ḫa⌝ 12) GUR-ma ana id ^{im}SI.SÁ
SS iii 3′ ^{d}[UTU] 4) KUR G[UR-ma]

Šamaš ša ina id šūti itti qaqqad Urgulî (error for:GU.LA) inappaḫa itârma ana id iltāni
The Sun which rises in the South with the head of the Lion (error for: Great One?) turns and

i 18 UD 40 NINDA.TA.ÀM un-da-na-ḫar UD^{meš} GÍD.DA^{meš} GI$_6$^{meš} LUGÚD.DA^{meš}

E iii 34 [ ] 35) UD^{meš} [ ]
J iv 14 [un-da-na]-ḫar 15) [ ]^{meš}
HH i 18 [UD 40 NINDA.T]A.À[M] un-da-na-ḫar UD^{meš} GÍD.DA^{meš} GI$_6$^{meš} LUGÚD.DA^{meš}
KK i 12 UD 40 NINDA.TA.ÀM 13) un-da-na-ḫar UD^{meš} GÍD^{meš} GI$_6$^{meš} LUGÚD^{meš}
SS iii 5′ ⌜u$_4$⌝-u[m] 6) [U]D$^{me[š}$]

ūma 40 ninda undanaḫḫar ūmū irrikū mūšâtu ikarrâ
keeps coming up towards the North 40 NINDA per day. The days become longer, the nights become shorter.

---

i 19 DIŠ ina ^{iti}BÁR UD 15 KAM ^{d}Sin ina li-la-a-ti ina ŠÀ

J iv 16 [-t]u$_4$
HH i 19 DIŠ [ ] ^{d}Sin ina li-lá-a-ti ina ŠÀ
KK i 14 DIŠ ina ^{iti}BÁR UD 15 K[AM] ^{d}Sin ina li-la-a-ti ina ŠÀ
SS iii 7′ DIŠ ina ^{iti}BÁR [ ] 8) ina ⌜ŠÀ⌝

ina Nisanni UD 15 Sin ina līlâti ina libbi
¶ On the 15th day of Month I the Moon stands in the evening within

i 20 ^{mul}zi-ba-ni-tú ina ^{d}UTU.È u ^{d}UTU ina ^{d}UTU.ŠÚ.A

HH i 20 ^{m}[^{ul}zi-ba-ni]-tú ina ^{d}UTU.È u ^{d}UTU ina ^{d}UTU.ŠÚ.A
KK i 14 ^{mul}zi-b[a]-n[i-tú] 15) u ^{d}UTU È$^{?}$.ŠÚ$^{?}$.A
SS iii 8′ [ ] 9) ina ^{d}UTU.⌜È⌝ [ ] 10) ina ^{d}⌜UTU.ŠÚ⌝

zibānīti ina ṣīt Šamši u Šamaš ina ereb Šamši
the Scales in the East, and the Sun in the West in front of the Stars behind

i 21 ina IGI MUL.MUL EGIR ^{mul}ḪUN.GÁ GUB-ma 3 MA.NA EN.NUN u$_4$-mi 3 MA.NA EN.NUN GI$_6$

HH i 21 ina [ ] GUB-ma 3 MA.NA <EN.NUN> u$_4$-mi 3 MA.NA EN.NUN GI$_6$
KK i 15 ina IGI MUL.MUL EGIR ^{mul}ḪUN.GÁ GUB-ma 3 MA.NA [ ]
SS iii 10′ [ ] 11) 3 MA [ ]

ina pān Zappi arki Agri izzazma 3 mana maṣṣarti ūmi 3 mana maṣṣarti mūši
the Hired Man. 3 minas is the watch of the day, 3 minas is the watch of the night.

---

i 22 DIŠ ina ^{iti}BÁR UD 15 KAM ina ^{iti}ŠU UD 15 KAM ina ^{iti}DU$_6$ UD 15 KAM ina ^{iti}AB UD 15 KAM

HH i 22 [K]AM ina ^{iti}ŠU UD 15 KAM ina ^{iti}DU$_6$ UD 15 KAM ina ^{iti}AB UD 15 KAM
JJ iii 1′ [ ] ina ^{i}[^{ti}]D[U$_6$] U[D]

KK i 16 DIŠ ina ^{iti}BÁR UD 15 KAM ina ^{iti}ŠU UD 15 KAM ina ^{iti}DU$_{6}$ UD 15 [KAM] 17) ina ^{i}[^{ti}A]B UD 15 KAM
SS iii 12′ DIŠ ina [ ]

ina Nisanni UD 15 ina Du'ūzi UD 15 ina Tešrīti UD 15 ina Ṭebēti UD 15
¶ On the 15th day of Month I, on the 15th day of Month IV, on the 15th day of Month VII, on the 15th day of Month X,

i 23 KUR^{meš} šá ^{d}UTU NA^{meš} šá ^{d}Sin IGI.DUḪ.A^{meš} šá ^{mul}KAK.SI.SÁ

HH i 23 [KUR^{meš} šá] ^{d}UTU NA^{meš} šá ^{d}Sin IGI.DUḪ.A^{meš} šá ⸢^{mul}⸣KAK.SI.SÁ
JJ iii 2′ [^{d}S]in IGI.DUḪ.A^{meš} [ ]
KK i 17 KUR^{meš} šá ^{d}UTU NA^{meš} šá ^{d}Sin IGI.DUḪ.A[^{meš}] 18) ša ^{mul}KAK.SI.SÁ

nipḫāti ša Šamaš manzāzī ša Sin tāmarāti ša Šukūdi
you observe the risings of the Sun, the positions of the Moon, the appearances of the Arrow,

i 24 ŠEŠ-ár UD^{meš} DIRI^{meš} IGI.LÁ

HH i 24 [ŠEŠ-ár] UD^{meš} DIRI^{meš} IGI.LÁ
JJ iii 3′ [U]D^{meš} DIRI^{meš} [ ]
KK i 18 ŠEŠ-ár UD^{meš} DIRI^{meš} IGI.LÁ

tanaṣṣar ūmī atrūti tammar
and you will find the days in excess.

----

i 25 DIŠ ina ^{iti}KIN UD 10 KAM ^{mul}NUN^{ki} UD 15 KAM ^{mul}ŠU.PA IGI^{meš}

HH i 25 [DIŠ ina ^{iti}KI]N UD 10 KAM ^{mul}NUN^{ki} UD 15 KAM ^{mu}⸢^{l}ŠU.PA] IGI^{meš}
JJ iii 4′ [DIŠ ina] ^{it}⸢^{i}KIN U]D 10 KAM ^{mul}NUN^{ki} UD 15 KAM ^{mul}ŠU.PA I[GI^{meš}]
KK i 19 DIŠ ina ^{iti}K[IN UD] 10 KAM ^{mul}NUN^{ki} UD 15 KAM ^{mul}ŠU.PA 20) AN$^{?}$ [x x] ⸢x⸣

ina Ulūli UD 10 Eridu UD 15 ŠU.PA innammarū
¶ On the 10th day of Month VI Eridu (and) on the 15th ŠU.PA become visible;

i 26 MUL^{meš}-šú-nu ina u$_{4}$-mi IGI^{meš} MÚ^{meš}-šú-nu zi-me-šú-nu

HH i 26 [MUL^{meš}-š]ú-nu ina u$_{4}$-mi IGI^{meš} MÚ^{meš}-šú-nu [zi-me]-šú-nu
JJ iii 5′ MUL^{meš}-šú-nu ina u$_{4}$-mi IGI^{meš} zi-me-šú-nu
KK i 20 MUL-šú-nu ina u$_{4}$-mi IGI^{meš} zi-me-šú-nu

kakkabūšunu ina ūm innammarū nipḫātišunu zīmēšunu
on the day their stars become visible you observe their risings, their glow, and

i 27 ri-is-ni-šú-nu ù IM šá DU-ku ŠEŠ ANŠE.KUR.RA^{meš}

HH i 27 [ri-i]s-ni-šú-nu ù IM šá DU-ku ŠE[Š ANŠE.KUR.R]A^{meš}
JJ iii 5′ ri-is-ni-[šú-nu] 6) ù IM šá DU-ku ŠEŠ ANŠE.KUR.RA
KK i 21 r[i-is-ni-šú-nu ù IM] šá DU-ku ⸢ŠEŠ⸣ ANŠE.KUR.RA^{meš}

risnīšunu u šāra ša illaku tanaṣṣar sīsê
their 'soakings', and the wind that blows; you guard$^{?}$ the horses

i 28 ina ÍD A^{meš} NU NAG^{meš}

HH i 28 [tu$^{?}$-n]a-an-ṣar-ma ina ÍD A^{meš} ⸢x⸣ [x x] NAG^{meš}
JJ iii 6′ tu-na-a[ṣ-] 7) ina ÍD A^{meš} NU NAG-ú
KK i 22 [ina] ÍD ⸢A⸣^{meš} NU NAG^{meš}

tunaṣṣar$^{?}$-ma ina nāri mê la išattû
so that they do not drink water from the river.

i 29 ki-i MUL^{meš}-šú-nu ul-ta-ta-pu-ni

HH i 29 [k]i MUL^{meš}-šú-nu ul-t[a-ta-p]u$^{?}$-ni
JJ iii 7′ ki-i MUL^{meš}-šú-nu [ ]
KK i 23 [ ] ul-ta-ta-pu-ni

kî kakkabūšunu ultātapûni
When their stars have been made visible,

i 30 maḫ-ḫu-ri-šú-nu tu-maḫ-ḫar ANŠE.KUR.RA^{meš}

HH i 30 [maḫ-ḫu-r]i-šú-nu tu-maḫ-ḫar [ANŠE.KUR.R]A^{meš}
JJ iii 8′ maḫ-ri-šú-nu tu-maḫ ANŠE.KUR.RA^{meš}
KK i 23 maḫ-ḫu-ri-šú-nu 24) [ANŠE.KUR.R]A^{meš}

maḫḫurišunu tumaḫḫar sīsê
you present offerings to them; horses

i 31 ESIR TAG^{meš}-ma ina ÍD A^{meš} NAG^{meš}

HH i 31 ESIR TAG^{meš}-ma ina ÍD [A^{meš}] NAG^{meš}
JJ iii 8′ ESIR T[AG]
KK i 24 ESIR ⸢x⸣ ÍD A^{meš} NAG^{meš}

ittâ ilappatūma ina nāri mê išattû
may touch bitumen and drink water from the river.

---

i 32 DIŠ ina ^{iti}APIN UD 5 KAM ^{mul}GÍR.TAB UD 15 KAM ^{mul}GABA GÍR.TAB

HH i 32 DIŠ ina ^{iti}APIN UD 5 KAM ^{mul}GÍR.TAB UD 15 K[AM ^{mul}]GABA GÍR.TAB
JJ iii 9′ DIŠ ina ^{iti}APIN UD 5 KAM ^{mul}GÍR.TAB U[D]
KK i 25 [DIŠ ina ^{iti}APIN UD 5 KAM ^{mul}GÍR.TAB U]D [1]5 KAM ⸢^{mul}GABA⸣ GÍR.[TAB]

ina Araḫsamni UD 5 Zuqāqīpu UD 15 irat Zuqāqīpi
¶ On the 5th day of Month VIII the Scorpion (and) on the 15th day the Chest of the Scorpion become visible;

i 33 IGI^{meš} ina u$_4$-me IGI^{meš} IM šá [DU-ku ŠE]Š-ár

HH i 33 ⸢IGI^{meš}⸣ ina u$_4$-me IGI^{meš} IM šá [DU-ku ŠE]Š-ár
JJ iii 10′ [ ] ina u$_4$-mi IGI^{meš} IM [ ]

innammarū ina ūm innammarū šāra ša [illaku] tanaṣṣar
on the day they become visible you observe the wind that blows.

<u>i 34</u> DIŠ ina ^{iti}ŠE UD 15 KAM ^{mul}KU$_6$ ina še-ri [IGI] ina li-la-a-ti ^{mul}NUN[^{ki} IGI]

HH i 34 DIŠ ina ^{iti}ŠE UD 15 KAM ^{mul}KU$_6$ ina še-r[i ^{mu}]^{l}NU[N^{ki} IGI]
JJ iii 11′ DIŠ ina ^{iti}ŠE UD 15 KAM ^{mul}KU$_6$ [ ] 12) ina li-la-a-ti ^{mul}NUN[^{ki} IGI]

ina Addari UD 15 Nūnu ina šēri [innammar] ina līlâti Eridu [innammar]
¶ On the 15th day of Month XII the Fish [becomes visible] in the morning, in the evening Eridu [becomes visible;]

<u>i 35</u> MUL^{meš}-šú-nu MUL^{meš} ra ba [ ]

HH i 35 MUL^{meš}-šú-nu MUL^{meš} ra ba [ ]
JJ iii 13′ MUL^{meš}-šu-nu MUL^{m}[^{eš}]

kakkabūšunu kakkabī ra ba [ ]
their stars . . . [. . .];

<u>i 36</u> ina u$_4$-me IGI^{meš} MÚ^{meš}-šú-nu zi-[ ]

HH i 36 [ina] u$_4$-me IGI^{meš} MÚ^{meš}-šú-nu zi-[ ]
JJ iii 14′ ina u$_4$-mi ⸢IGI⸣^{m}[^{eš} [ ]

ina ūm innammarū niphātišunu zī[mīšunu]
on the day they become visible you observe their risings, their glow,

<u>i 37</u>

HH i 37 [r]i-is-ni-šú-nu IM š[á D]U-ku Š[EŠ-ár]

risnīšunu šāra ša illaku t[anaṣṣar]
their ‘soakings’, (and) the wind that blows.

<u>i 38</u>

HH i 38 ^{mul}Sag-me-gar ^{mul}Dili-bat ^{mul}[UDU.ID]IM.GU$_4$.UD šá ^{d}MAŠ MU-šú

Sagmegar Dilibat Šiḫṭu ša Ninurta šumšu
Jupiter, Venus, Mercury, whose name is Ninurta,

^{mul}Ṣal-bat-a-nu ^{mul}UDU.IDIM.SAG.UŠ

HH i 38 ^{mul}Ṣal-bat-a-nu ^{mul}UDU.IDIM.⸢SAG.UŠ⸣
KK i 31 [^{mul}]UDU.IDIM.S[AG].UŠ

Ṣalbatānu Kajamānu
Mars, Saturn,

<u>i 39</u> [KIMIN] ^{mul}zi-ba-ni-tu$_4$ MUL ^{d}UTU

HH i 39 [KIMIN] ^{mul}zi-ba-ni-t[u$_4$] MUL ^{d}UTU
KK i 32 [ ] MUL ^{d}UTU

[KIMIN] Zibānītu kakkab Šamaš
[also called] 'the Scales' (or) 'Star of the Sun'.

---

i 40 [N]A^{meš}-šú-nu u zi-me-šú-nu KÚR.KÚR-ru

HH i 40 [x x x x] ⸢x⸣ [x N]A^{meš}-šú-nu u zi-me-šú-nu KÚR.KÚR-ru
KK i 33 [z]i-me-šú-nu 34) [ ]

[. . . man]zāzīšunu u zīmēšunu ittanakkirū
[ ] keep changing their positions and their glow, (and)

i 41 [MUL^{meš} AN]-e TAG^{meš} MUL^{meš}-šú-nu ina u$_4$-me IGI^{meš} KUR^{me}-šú-nu SUḪ^{meš}-šú-nu

HH i 41 [ ] TAG^{meš} MUL^{meš}-šú-nu ina u$_4$-me IGI^{meš} KUR^{me}-šú-nu SUḪ^{meš}-šú-nu
KK i 34 [MUL^{meš} AN]-⸢e⸣ TAG^{me} 35) [z]i-me-šú-nu

[kakkabī šam]ê ilappatū kakkabūšunu ina ūm innammarū niphātišunu zīmēšunu
touch [the stars of the sky]; on the day their stars become visible, you observe their risings, their glow,

i 42 [ri-is-ni-šú-nu K]I IGI^{meš} IM šá DU-ku ŠEŠ-ár ina UD IGI^{meš} muḫ-ḫu-ri-šú-nu

HH i 42 [K]I IGI^{meš} IM šá DU-ku ŠEŠ-ár ina UD IGI^{meš} muḫ-ḫu-ri-šú-nu
KK i 36 [ ] ŠEŠ$^{?}$ 37) [ ]

[risnīšunu as]ar innammarū šāra ša illaku tanaṣṣar ina ūm innammarū muḫḫurišunu
[their 'soakings',] where they become visible, (and) the wind that blows; on the day they become visible,

i 43 [tu-maḫ]-ḫa-ru ANŠE.KUR.RA^{meš} ESIR TAG^{meš}

HH i 43 [tu-maḫ]-ḫa-ru ANŠE.KUR.RA^{meš} ESIR TAG^{meš}
KK i 37 [ ] ESIR$^{?}$ T[AG]^{meš}

tumaḫḫaru sīsê ittâ ilappatū
you present offerings to them; horses may touch bitumen.

---

i 44
HH i 44 [DIŠ ^{mul}Di]li-bat <ina> ^{d}UTU.È TÙM-ma ITI ina AN-e uḫ-ḫa-ra
Dilibat <ina> ṣīt Šamši itabbalma arḫa ina šamê uḫḫara
¶ Venus disappears in the East and remains (invisible) in the sky for a month,

i 45
HH i 45 [KIMIN] 1 ITI UD 15 KAM u$_4$-mi KIMIN 2 ITI uḫ-ḫa(over erasure)-ram-ma
KIMIN arḫa šapatti ūmī KIMIN 2 arḫī uḫḫaramma
or for 1 month and 15 days, or it remains for 2 months, and

i 46
HH i 46 [ina] ^{d}UTU.ŠÚ.A IGI.LÁ

ina ereb Šamši innammar
becomes visible in the West.

---

i 47
HH i 47 DIŠ mulDili-bat ina dUTU.ŠÚ.A TÙM-ma ina u4-me TÙM ina dUTU.È KUR-ḫa KIMIN 3 u4-mi

Dilibat ina ereb Šamši itabbalma ina ūm itabbalu ina ṣīt Šamši inappaḫa KIMIN 3 ūmī
¶ Venus disappears in the West and rises (again) in the East on the day it disappears; or, for 3 days,

i 48
HH i 48 KI.3 7 u4-mi KI.4 14 u4-mi uḫ-ḫa-ram.ma KUR-ḫa

KI.3 7 ūmī KI.4 14 ūmī uḫḫaramma inappaḫa
thirdly, for 7 days, fourthly, for 14 days, it remains (invisible) and then rises.

---

i 49
HH i 49 DIŠ mulSag-me-gar ina dUTU.ŠÚ.A TÙM-ma 20 u4-me ina AN-e uḫ-ḫa-ra

Sagmegar ina ereb Šamši itabbalma 20 ūmī ina šamê uḫḫara
¶ Jupiter disappears in the West and remains (invisible) in the sky for 20 days,

i 50
HH i 50 KIMIN ITI uḫ-ḫa-ram-ma ina dUTU.È ina KASKAL dUTU MÚ-ḫa IGI.LÁ

KI)MIN arḫa uḫḫaramma ina ṣīt Šamši ina ḫarrān Šamši inappaḫa innammar
or remains for a month, and rises and becomes visible in the East in the path of the Sun.

---

i 51
HH i 51 DIŠ mulṢal-bat-a-nu ina dUTU.ŠÚ.A TÙM-ma 2 ITI KIMIN 3 ITI 10 u4-mi KIMIN 6 ITI

Ṣalbatānu ina ereb Šamši itabbalma 2 arḫī KIMIN 3 arḫī 10 ūmī KIMIN 6 arḫī
¶ Mars disappears in the West and remains (invisible) in the sky for 2 months, or for 3 months and 10 days, or for 6 months

i 52
HH i 52 20 u4-mi ina AN-e uḫ-ḫa-ram-ma ina dUTU.È ina KASKAL dUTU MÚ-ḫa IGI.LÁ

20 ūmī ina šamê uḫḫaramma ina ṣīt Šamši ina ḫarrān Šamši inappaḫa innammar
and 20 days, and then rises and becomes visible in the East in the path of the Sun.

---

i 53
HH i 53 DIŠ dUDU.IDIM.SAG.UŠ ina dUTU.ŠÚ.A TÙM-ma 20 u4-mi ina AN-e uḫ-ḫa-ram-ma ina KASKAL dUTU IGI.LÁ
Kajamānu ina ereb Šamši itabbalma 20 ūmī ina šamê uḫḫaramma ina ḫarrān Šamši innammar
¶ Saturn disappears in the West, remains (invisible) in the sky for 20 days, and becomes visible in the path of the Sun.

---

i 54
HH i 54 DIŠ ^{mul}UDU.IDIM.GU$_4$.UD šá ^{d}MAŠ MU-šú lu ina ^{d}UTU.È lu ina ^{d}UTU.ŠÚ.A IGI.LÁ-ma

Šiḫṭu ša Ninurta šumšu lu ina ṣīt Šamši lu ina ereb Šamši innammarma
¶ Mercury, whose name is Ninurta, becomes visible either in the East or in the West, and

i 55
HH i 55 7 u$_4$-mi KIMIN 14 u$_4$-mi KIMIN UD 21 KAM KI.4 ITI KI.5 ITI 15 u$_4$-mi ina AN-e GUB-ma

7 ūmī KIMIN 14 ūmī KIMIN 21 ūmī KI.4 arḫa KI.5 arḫa 15 ūmī ina šamê izzazma
stands in the sky for 7 days, or for 14 days, or for 21 days, fourthly, for a month, fifthly, for a month and 15 days,

---

i 56
HH i 56 ki-ma TÙM ma-la u$_4$-mi šá ina AN-e GUB-zu uḫ-ḫa-ram-ma lu ina ^{d}UTU.È

kīma itabbalu mala ūmī ša ina šamê izzizu uḫḫaramma lu ina ṣīt Šamši
and when it disappears it remains (invisible) for as many days as it stood in the sky,

i 57
HH i 57 lu ina ^{d}UTU.ŠÚ.A ina KASKAL ^{d}UTU MÚ-ḫa IGI.LÁ MUL BI ina EN.TE.NA IGI.LÁ-ma
A.AN u A.KAL

lu ina ereb Šamši ina ḫarrān Šamši inappaḫa innammar kakkabu šū ina kuṣṣi innammarma zunnu u mīlu
and rises and becomes visible either in the East or in the West in the path of the Sun. (If) this star becomes visible in winter, (there will be) rain and flood;

i 58 ina BURU$_{14}$ IGI.LÁ-ma zi-me-šú ri-is-ni-šú KI IGI.LÁ ù IM šá DU-ku ŠEŠ-ár

D ii 1 [ ] ⌜x⌝ [ ]
HH i 58 ina BURU$_{14}$ IGI.LÁ-ma zi-me-šú ri-is-ni-šú KI IGI.LÁ ù IM šá DU-ku ŠEŠ-ár

ina ebūri innammarma zīmīšu risnīšu ašar innammaru u šāra ša illaku tanaṣṣar

(if) it becomes visible at harvest time, you observe its glow, its 'soakings', where it becomes visible, and the wind that blows.

i 59 MUL BI BE-ma SA$_5$ u ba-il BE-ma SIG$_7$ u GI$_6$

D ii 2 [MUL B]I šum-[ma]
HH i 59 MUL BI BE-ma SA$_5$ u ba-il BE-ma SIG$_7$ u GI$_6$

kakkabu šū šumma sām u ba᾿il šumma aruq u ṣalim
This star is either red and bright, or yellow and dark.

---

i 60 [DIŠ] ^{mul}Sag-me-gar ina ^{d}UTU.È IGI-ma MU 1 KAM ina AN-e GUB-ma ina ^{d}UTU.ŠÚ.A TÙM

D ii 3 [S]ag-me-gar ina ^{d}[UTU.È]
HH i 60 [DIŠ] ^{mul}Sag-me-gar ina ^{d}UTU.È IGI-ma MU 1 KAM ina AN-e GUB-ma {1} ina ^{d}UTU.ŠÚ.A TÙM

Sagmegar ina ṣīt Šamši innammarma šanat ina šamê izzazma ina ereb Šamši itabbal
¶ Jupiter becomes visible in the East, stands in the sky for one year, and disappears in the West.

---

i 61 DIŠ ^{mul}Dili-bat lu ina ^{d}UTU.È lu ina ^{d}UTU.ŠÚ.A IGI.LÁ-ma 9 ITI^{meš} ina AN-e GUB-ma i-tab-bal

D ii 4 [DIŠ ^{mu}]^{l}Dili-bat lu ina ^{d}UTU.[È]
HH i 61 DIŠ ^{mul}Dili-bat lu ina ^{d}UTU.È lu ina ^{d}UTU.ŠÚ.A IGI.LÁ-ma 9 ITI^{meš} ina AN-e GUB-ma i-tab-bal

Dilibat lu ina ṣīt Šamši lu ina ereb Šamši innammarma 9 arḫī ina šamê izzazma itabbal
¶ Venus becomes visible either in the East of in the West, stands in the sky for 9 months, and disappears.

---

i 62 DIŠ ^{mul}Ṣal-bat-a-nu ina ^{d}UTU.È IGI.LÁ-ma MU 1 KAM 6 ITI KIMIN MU 1 KAM 10 ITI KIMIN 2 MU.AN.NA^{meš}

D ii 5 [DIŠ ^{mu}]^{l}Ṣal-bat-a-nu ina ^{d}UTU.È [ ]
HH i 62 DIŠ ^{mul}Ṣal-bat-a-nu ina ^{d}UTU.È IGI.LÁ-ma MU 1 KAM 6 ITI KIMIN MU 1 KAM 10 ITI KIMIN 2 MU.AN.NA^{meš}

Ṣalbatānu ina ṣīt Šamši innammarma šanat 6 arḫī KIMIN šanat 10 arḫī KIMIN 2 šanāti
¶ Mars becomes visible in the East, stands in the sky for one year (and) 6 months, or for one year (and) 10 months, or for 2 years,

i 63 ina AN-e GUB-ma ina ^{d}UTU.ŠÚ.A TÙM MUL BI BE-ma SA$_5$ GAR u ba-ìl BE-ma un-nu-un u TUR

D ii 6 [ina A]N-e GUB-ma ina ^{d}UTU.ŠÚ.A [ ]
HH i 63 ina AN-e GUB-ma ina ^{d}UTU.ŠÚ.A TÙM MUL BI BE-ma SA$_5$ GAR u ba-ìl BE-ma un-nu-un u TUR

ina šamê izzazma ina ereb Šamši itabbal kakkabu šū šumma sūma šakin u ba'il šumma unnun u ṣeḫer
and disappears in the West. This star shows either redness and is bright, or is . . . and small.

---

i 64 DIŠ ^{mul}UDU.IDIM.SAG.UŠ KIMIN ^{mul}zi-ba-ni-tu$_4$ MUL ^{d}UTU ina ^{d}UTU.È IGI.LÁ-ma

D ii 7 [DIŠ ^{mu}]^{l}UDU.IDIM.SAG.UŠ KIMIN ^{mul}z[i-ba-ni-tu$_4$]
HH i 64 DIŠ ^{mul}UDU.IDIM.SAG.UŠ KIMIN ^{mul}zi-ba-ni-tu$_4$ MUL ^{d}UTU ina ^{d}UTU.È IGI.LÁ-ma

Kajamānu KIMIN Zibānītu kakkab Šamaš ina ṣīt Šamši innammarma
¶ Saturn, also (called) the Scales (or) star of the Sun, becomes visible in the East,

i 65 MU 1 KAM ina AN-e GUB-ma ina ^{d}UTU.ŠÚ.A TÙM MUL BI BE-ma SA$_{5}$ BE-ma BABBAR

D ii 8 [M]U 1 KAM ina AN-e GUB-ma ina ^{d}UTU.ŠÚ.A T[ÙM]
HH i 65 MU 1 KAM ina AN-e GUB-ma ina ^{d}UTU.ŠÚ.A TÙM MUL BI BE-ma SA$_{5}$ BE-ma BABBAR

šanat ina šamê izzazma ina ereb Šamši itabbal kakkabu šū šumma sām šumma peṣi
stands in the sky for one year, and disappears in the West. This star is either red or white.

---

i 66 DIŠ ^{mul}UDU.IDIM.GU$_{4}$.UD šá ^{d}Nin-urta MU-šú lu ina ^{d}UTU.È lu ina ^{d}UTU.ŠÚ.A

D ii 9 DIŠ ^{mul}UDU.IDIM.GU$_{4}$.UD šá ^{d}Nin-urta MU-šú lu ina [ ]
HH i 66 DIŠ ^{mul}UDU.IDIM bi-ib-bu šá ^{d}MAŠ MU-šú lu ina ^{d}UTU.È lu ina ^{d}UTU.ŠÚ.A

Šiḫṭu ša Ninurta šumšu lu ina ṣīt Šamši lu ina ereb Šamši
¶ Mercury, whose name is Ninurta, becomes visible within a month and disappears

i 67
HH i 67 e-ma ITI IGI.LÁ-ma e-ma ITI TÙM

ēma arḫi innammarma ēma arḫi itabbal
within a month, either in the East or in the West.

---

i 68 BE-ma mu-ṣe-e IM^{meš} ana IGI.LÁ-ka ^{mul}MAR.GÍD.DA ina ZI ^{im}SI.SÁ G[IL-á]t

D ii 10 šum-ma mu-ṣe-e IM^{meš} [ ] 11) ^{mul}MAR.GÍD.DA ina Z[I]
HH i 68 BE-ma mu-ṣe-e IM^{meš} ana IGI.LÁ-ka ^{mul}MAR.GÍD.DA ina ZI ^{im}SI.SÁ G[IL-á]t

šumma mūṣē šārī ana amārika Ereqqu ina tīb iltāni parkat
If you are to see the direction of the winds: the Wagon lies across where the North wind rises,

i 69 ^{mul}KU$_{6}$ ina ZI ^{im}U$_{18}$.LU GIL ^{mul}GÍR.TAB ina ZI ^{im}MAR.TU GIL-[á]t

D ii 12 ^{mul}KU$_{6}$ ina ZI ^{im}U$_{18}$.[LU GIL] 13) ^{mul}GÍR.TAB ina ZI ^{im}MAR.T[U]
S ii 2′ [ ] 2) ^{mul}GÍR.[TAB]
HH i 69 ^{mul}KU$_{6}$ ina Z[I ^{i}]^{m}U$_{18}$.LU GIL ^{mul}GÍR.TAB ina ZI ^{im}MAR.TU GIL-[á]t

Nūnu ina tīb šūti parik Zuqāqīpu ina tīb amurri parkat
the Fish lies across where the South wind rises, the Scorpion lies across where the West wind rises,

i 70 ^{mul}ŠU.GI u MUL.MUL ina ZI ^{im}KUR.RA GUB^{meš}-z[u]

D ii 14 ^{mul}ŠU.GI u MUL.MUL ina ZI ^{im}KUR.RA G[UB^{meš}-zu]
S ii 3′ ^{mul}ŠU.G[I]

HH i 70 ^{mul}[ŠU.GI u MU]L.MUL ina ZI ^{im}KUR.RA GUB^{meš}-z[u]

Šību u Zappu ina tīb šadî izzazzū
the Old Man and the Stars stand where the East wind rises.

i 71 ina u$_{4}$-me EN.NUN-ka IM šá DU-ku MUL^{meš} ú-kal-la-mu-k[a]

D ii 15 ina u$_{4}$-me EN.NUN-ka IM šá DU-ku MUL^{meš} ú-kal-la-[mu-ka]
S ii 4′ ina u$_{4}$-me {1} EN.NUN-k[a]
HH i 71 [ina u$_{4}$-me EN.NUN-k]a IM šá DU-ku MUL^{meš} ú-kal-la-mu-k[a]

ina ūm maṣṣartika šāra ša illaku kakkabū ukallamūka
On the day of your watch the stars will show you which wind blows.

Gap A 1 [DIŠ] TA UD 1 KAM šá ^{iti}ŠE EN UD 30 KAM šá ^{iti}GU$_{4}$ ^{d}UTU ina KASKAL šu-ut ^{d}A-nim

D ii 16 [DIŠ] TA UD 1 KAM šá ^{iti}ŠE EN UD 30 KAM šá ^{iti}GU$_{4}$ ^{d}UTU ina KASKAL šu-ut ^{d}A-nim
S ii 5′ TA UD 1 KAM šá ^{iti}Š[E] 6) ^{d}UTU ina KASKAL šu-u[t]
GG iv 1′ [ ] ina KASKAL šu-ut ^{d}[A-nim]

ultu UD 1 ša Addari adi UD 30 ša Ajjari Šamaš ina ḫarrān šūt Anim
¶ From the 1st day of Month XII until the 30th day of Month II the Sun stands in the path of those of Anu:

Gap A 2 GUB-ma zi-qu u UD.D[A]

D ii 16 G[UB]
GG iv 2′ [ ] zi-qu u UD.D[A]

izzazma zīqu u ṣētu
wind and warm weather.

Gap A 3 [DIŠ] TA UD 1 KAM šá ^{iti}SIG$_{4}$ EN UD 30 KAM šá ^{iti}IZI ^{d}UTU

D ii 17 [DIŠ T]A UD 1 KAM šá ^{iti}SIG$_{4}$ EN UD 30 KAM šá ^{iti}IZI ^{d}UTU
S ii 7′ TA UD 1 KAM šá ^{iti}S[IG$_{4}$] 8) ^{d}UTU
GG iv 3′ [^{iti}S]IG$_{4}$ EN UD 30 KAM šá ^{iti}IZI ^{d}UTU

ultu UD 1 ša Simāni adi UD 30 ša Abi Šamaš
¶ From the 1st day of Month III until the 30th day of Month V, the Sun

Gap A 4 ina KASKAL šu-ut ^{d}En-líl GUB-ma BURU$_{14}$ u uš-šú

D ii 17 ina KASKAL šu-ut ^{d}En-líl G[UB-ma]
S ii 8′ [ ] šu-u[t]
GG iv 4′ [ina KASKA]L šu-ut ^{d}En-líl GUB-ma BURU$_{14}$ u uš-šú

ina ḫarrān šūt Enlil izzazma ebūru u uššu
stands in the path of those of Enlil: harvest and heat.

Gap A 5 [DIŠ T]A UD 1 KAM šá ^{iti}KIN EN UD 30 KAM šá ^{iti}APIN ^{d}UTU

D ii 18 [DIŠ T]A UD 1 KAM šá ^{iti}KIN EN UD 30 KAM šá ^{iti}APIN ^{d}UTU
GG iv 5′ [DIŠ TA UD] 1 KAM šá ^{iti}KIN EN UD 30 KAM šá ^{iti}APIN ^{d}UTU

ultu UD 1 ša Ulūli adi UD 30 ša Araḫsamni Šamaš
¶ From the 1st day of Month VI until the 30th day of Month VIII, the Sun

Gap A 6 ina KASKAL šu-ut ^{d}A-nim GUB-ma zi-qu u UD.DA

D ii 18 ina KASKAL šu-ut ^{d}A-nim GUB-m[a]
GG iv 6′ [ ] šu-ut ^{d}A-nim GUB-ma zi-qu u UD.DA

ina ḫarrān šūt Anim izzazma zīqu u ṣētu
stands in the path of those of Anu: wind and warm weather.

Gap A 7 [DIŠ TA UD 1 K]AM šá ^{iti}GAN EN UD 30 KAM šá ^{iti}ZÍZ ^{d}UTU ina KASKAL šu-ut ^{d}É-a GUB-ma EN.TE.NA

D ii 19 [DIŠ TA UD 1 K]AM šá ^{iti}GAN EN UD 30 KAM šá ^{iti}ZÍZ ^{d}UTU ina KASKAL šu-ut ^{d}É-a GUB-[ma EN.TE.NA]
GG iv 7′ [DIŠ TA UD 1 KAM šá ^{it}]^{i}GAN EN UD 30 KAM šá ^{iti}ZÍZ ^{d}UTU ina KASKAL šu-ut ^{d}É-a GUB-ma EN.TE.NA

[ultu UD 1] ša Kislīmi adi UD 30 ša Šabāṭi Šamaš ina ḫarrān šūt Ea izzazma kuṣṣu
[¶ From the 1st day] of Month IX until the 30th day of Month XI, the Sun stands in the path of those of Ea: winter.

Gap A 8 [DIŠ ina ^{iti}BÁR$^{?}$ UD 1$^{?}$ K]AM MUL.MUL u ^{d}Sin šit-qu-lu MU BI GI.NA-ta

D ii 20 [K]AM MUL.MUL u ^{d}Sin šit-qu-lu MU BI GI.[NA-ta]
GG iv 8′ [ ] MUL.MUL u ^{d}Sin LÁL MU BI GI.NA-ta

[ina Nisanni UD 1] Zappu u Sin šitqulū šattu šī kīnat
[¶ On the 1st$^{?}$ day of Month I$^{?}$] the Stars and the Moon are balanced; this year is normal.

Gap A 9 [BE-ma$^{?}$ ina ^{iti}BÁR$^{?}$ U]D 3 KAM MUL.MUL u ^{d}Sin LÁL MU BI DIRI-át

D ii 21 [K]AM MUL.MUL u ^{d}Sin LÁL MU BI D[IRI-át]
GG iv 9′ [U]D 3 KAM MUL.MUL u ^{d}Sin LÁL MU BI DIRI-át

[šumma ina Nisanni U]D 3 Zappu u Sin šitqulū šattu šī atrat
[If] on the 3rd d[ay of Month I$^{?}$] the Stars and the Moon are balanced, this year is intercalary.

Gap A 10 [DIŠ ina ^{iti}GU$_{4}$ UD 1 KAM] MUL.MUL IGI.LÁ MU BI GI.NA-ta

D ii 22 [L]Á MU BI GI.N[A]
GG iv 10′ [ ] MUL.MUL IGI.LÁ MU BI GI.NA-ta

[ ] Zappu innammar šattu šī kīnat
[¶ In Month II on the 1st day] the Stars become visible; this year is normal.

Gap A 11	[BE-ma ina ^{iti}SIG$_4$ U]D 1 KAM MUL.MUL IGI.LÁ MU BI D[IRI-át]
D ii 23	[MUL.MU]L IGI.LÁ M[U B]I [DIRI-át]
GG iv 11′	[U]D 1 KAM MUL.MUL MIN M[U B]I D[IRI-át]
	[šumma ina Simani U]D 1 Zappu innammar šattu šī atrat
	[If in Month III] on the 1st day the Stars become visible, this year is intercalary.
Gap A 12	[DIŠ ina ^{iti}ŠU UD 15 KAM ^{mul}KAK.SI.SÁ IGI.LÁ]
	[¶ In Month IV on the 15th day the Arrow becomes visible;]
Gap A 13	[^{d}UTU šá ina id ^{im}SI.SÁ KUR-ḫa]
UU 1′	[ ] ⸢x⸣ [ ]
	[Šamaš ša ina id iltāni inappaḫa]
	[the Sun which rises in the North]
Gap A 14	
UU 2′	[GUR-ma ana] ⸢id⸣ IM.⸢U$_{18}$⸣.L[U ultanappal$^{?}$]
	[turns and keeps moving down towards] the South.
Gap A 15	
JJ iv 1′	[ ] ⸢x⸣ [MU BI GI.NA-át]
UU 3′	[0] ⸢MU BI⸣ [GI.NA-át]
	[ ] ⸢šattu šī⸣ [kīnat]
	[ ] this year [is normal.]

Gap A 16	[B]E-ma ina ^{iti}IZI UD ⸢15⸣ KAM ^{mul}KAK.SI.SÁ IGI.LÁ MU BI DIRI-[át]
JJ iv 2′	[ ] ^{mul}KAK.SI.SÁ <IGI.LÁ> MU BI [ ]
UU 4′	[B]E-ma ina ^{iti}IZI UD ⸢15⸣ KAM ^{m}[^{ul}KAK.SI.SÁ IGI.LÁ] 5′) MU BI DIRI-[át]
	šumma ina Abi UD 15 Šukūdu innammar šattu šī atrat
	If in Month V on the 15th day the Arrow becomes visible, this year is intercalary.

Gap A 17	DIŠ ina ^{iti}KIN UD 15 KA[M] ^{mul}ŠU.PA IGI.LÁ MU BI [GI.NA-át]
JJ iv 3′	[^{mul}]ŠU.PA IGI.LÁ MU BI [GI.NA-át]
UU 6′	DIŠ ina ^{iti}KIN UD 15 KA[M] ^{mul}ŠU.P[A]
	ina Ulūli UD 15 ŠU.PA innammar šattu šī [kīnat]
	¶ In Month VI on the 15th day ŠU.PA becomes visible; this year [is normal.]
Gap A 18	[B]E-ma ina ^{iti}DU$_6$ UD 15 KAM ^{mul}ŠU.PA IGI.LÁ MU BI [DIRI-át]
JJ iv 4′	[ ] KAM ^{mul}ŠU.PA IGI.LÁ MU BI [DIRI-át]
UU 7′	[B]E-ma ina ^{iti}DU$_6$ UD 15 KAM MU[L$^{?}$] 8′) [(x)] ⸢LÁL⸣ MU BI ⸢x⸣ [ ]

šumma ina Tešrīti UD 15 ŠU.PA innammar šattu šī [atrat]
If in Month VII on the 15th day ŠU.PA becomes visible, this year [is intercalary.]

---

ii 1 [DIŠ ina ^{i}]^{ti}DU$_6$ UD 15 KAM MUL.MUL u ^{d}Sin LÁL MU BI [GI.N]A-át

EE r. 1′ [ ] ^{d}[Sin]
HH ii 1′ [GI.N]A-á[t]
JJ iv 5′ [ ] MUL.MUL u ^{d}Sin LÁL MU BI G[I.NA-át]
UU 9′ [ina ^{i}]^{ti}DU$_6$ UD 15 KAM MU[L.MUL]

[ina] Tešrīti UD 15 Zappu u Sin šitqulū šattu šī kīnat
[¶ In] Month VII on the 15th day the Stars and the Moon are balanced; this year is normal.

---

ii 2 [BE-m]a ina ^{iti}APIN UD 15 KAM MUL.MUL u ^{d}Sin LÁL MU BI DIRI-át

EE r. 2′ [ ] ^{d}Sin L[ÁL]
HH ii 2′ [D]IRI-át
JJ iv 6′ [ ] 15 KAM MUL.MUL u ^{d}Sin LÁL MU BI D[IRI-át]
KK ii 1′ B[E MUL].MUL ⌜x⌝ [ ]
UU 10′ [BE-m]a ina ^{iti}APIN UD 1[5 KAM] 11′) LÁL [ ]

[šumm]a ina Araḫsamni UD 15 Zappu u Sin šitqulū šattu šī atrat
[If] in Month VIII on the 15th day the Stars and the Moon are balanced, this year is intercalary.

---

ii 3 [DIŠ ina ^{iti}A]B UD 1[5 KA]M ^{mul}KAK.SI.SÁ ina li-la-a-ti ina ^{d}UTU.È [IGI.LÁ ^{d}UTU]
EE r. 3′ [A]B UD 1[5 4) [ ].È [ ]
HH ii 3′ [ ]
JJ iv 7′ [KA]M ^{mul}KAK.SI.SÁ ina li-la-a-ti ina ^{d}UTU.È [ ]
KK ii 2′ DIŠ [^{m}]^{ul}KAK.SI.SÁ ina l[i-la-a-ti]
UU r.1′ [ ] ⌜x⌝ [ ] r.2′) [ina l]i-la-ti I[GI$^{?}$.LÁ ^{d}UTU]

[ina Ṭebēti UD 15 Šukūdu ina līlâti ina ṣīt Šamši [innammar Šamaš]
[¶ In Month X on the 15th] the Arrow [becomes visible] in the evening in the East; [the Sun]

[šá] ina id ^{im}U$_{18}$.LU KUR-ḫa GUR-ma ana id ^{im}SI.SÁ un-da-na-ḫar [MU B]I GI.NA-át

EE r. 5′ [i]d ^{i}[^{m}U$_{18}$.LU] 6) [^{i}]^{m}SI.S[Á] 7) [MU B]I GI.NA-át

HH ii 3′ [G]I.NA-át
JJ iv 8′ [^{i}]^{m}U$_{18}$.LU KUR-ḫa GUR-ma ana id ^{im}SI.SÁ un-da-[na-ḫar]
KK ii 3′ ⌜šá⌝ [^{im}U$_{18}$.L]U KUR-ḫa GUR-ma ana ⌜id ^{im}⌝S[I.S]Á [ ]
UU r. 3′ [šá] ina id ^{im}U$_{18}$.LU <KUR>$^{?}$ GUR-[ma ana id ^{im}SI.SÁ] r. 4′) un-da-na-ḫar [ ]

[ša] ina id šūti inappaḫa itârma ana id iltāni undanaḫḫar šattu šī kīnat
[which] rises in the South turns and keeps coming up towards the North: this [year] is normal.

ii 4		BE-ma ina ^{iti}ZÍZ UD 15 KAM ^{mul}KAK.SI.SÁ ina li-la-a-ti IGI MU BI DIRI-át

EE	r. 8′	[^{mu}]^{l}KAK.SI.SÁ ina l[i-] r. 9) [M]U BI D[IRI-át]
HH ii 4′		[M]U BI DIRI-át
JJ iv 9′		[ ] ^{iti}ZÍZ UD 15 KAM ^{mul}KAK.SI.SÁ ina li-la-a-ti IGI [ ]
KK ii 4′		[ ] ^{mul}KAK.SI.SÁ [ina l]i-la-a-ti [ ]
UU	r. 5′	BE-ma ina ^{iti}ZÍZ UD 15 KAM ^{mul}[KAK.SI.SÁ] r. 6) ina li-la-ti IGI-ma MU B[I]

šumma ina Šabāṭi UD 15 Šukūdu ina līlâti innammarma šattu šī atrat
If in Month XI on the 15th day the Arrow becomes visible in the evening, this year is intercalary.

---

ii 5		[DIŠ ina ^{iti}Š]E UD 15 KAM ^{mul}KU$_6$ ^{mul}ŠU.GI IGI.LÁ MU BI GI.NA-át

EE	r. 10′	[DIŠ ina ^{iti}Š]E$^?$ UD 15 KAM ^{mu}⸢^{l}] 11) [ina l]i-la-ti ina ^{d}[ ] 12) [MU B]I [GI.NA-át]
HH ii 5′		[M]U BI GI.NA-át
JJ iv 10′		[K]AM ^{mul}KU$_6$ ^{mul}ŠU.PA MU BI [GI.NA-át]
KK ii 5′		[DIŠ ina ^{iti}ŠE] UD 15 KAM ^{mul}KU$_6$ ^{mul}ŠU.GI IGI.LÁ [M]U B[I GI.NA-át]

[ina Add]ari UD 15 Nūnu Šību innammarū šattu šī kīnat
¶ The Fish (and) the Old Man become visible (var.: at night) on the 15th day of Month XII; this year is normal.

ii 6		[BE-ma] ina ^{iti}BÁR UD 15 KAM ^{mul}KU$_6$ ^{mul}ŠU.GI IGI^{meš} MU BI DIRI-át

EE	r. 13′	[BE-ma] ina ^{iti}BAR [14) [IGI^{me}]^{š} M[U]
HH ii 6′		[ ] MU BI DIRI-át
JJ iv 11′		[U]D 15 KAM ^{mul}KU$_6$ ^{mul}ŠU.GI IGI^{meš} M[U]
KK ii 6′		[BE-ma ina ^{it}]^{i}BÁR UD 15 KAM ^{mul}KU$_6$ ^{mul}ŠU.GI IGI.LÁ MU BI DI[RI-át]

[šumma] ina Nisanni UD 15 Nūnu u Šību innammarū šattu šī atrat
[If] in Month I on the 15th day the Fish (and) the Old Man become visible, this year is intercalary.

---

ii 7		MÚ^{meš} MUL^{meš} šá šu-ut ^{d}É-a šu-ut ^{d}A-nim šu-ut ^{d}En-líl

j	1′	[ ] ⸢x x x⸣ [ ]
EE	r. 15′	⸢x⸣ ^{meš} MUL⸢^{meš}⸣ [ ] 16) [šu-u]t ^{d}A-nim [ ]
HH ii 7′		⸢MÚ⸣ [ ] ^{d}A-nim šu-ut ^{d}50
JJ iv 12′		[š]u-u[t] ^{d}A-nim šu-ut ^{d}E[n-líl]
KK ii 7′		[x x MU]L^{meš} šá šu-ut ^{d}É-a šu-ut ^{d}⸢A-nim⸣ šu-ut ^{d}En-[líl]
SS iv 1′		MÚ[^{meš}] 2) š[u-ut ^{d}A-nim]

niphāt kakkabī ša šūt Ea šūt Anim šūt Enlil
The risings of the stars of Ea, Anu and Enlil.

ii 8		[. . .] u MÚ^{meš}-šú-nu [K]IN.KI[N-m]a MU BI ta-nam-bi

j	2′	[MU B]I ta-nam-[bi]
EE	r.17′	[x] ⸢MÚ$^{?}$⸣^{meš}-šú-nu [ ]
HH ii 8′		M[Ú$^?$]⸢^{meš}⸣-šú-[nu$^?$ -m]a MU BI ta-nam-bi
JJ iv 13′		[-m]a MU BI ta-[ ]
KK ii 8′		[x x MU]L$^?$ u MÚ^{meš}-šú-nu KI[N$^?$.KIN$^?$-m]a$^?$ ⸢MU⸣ [B]I ta-nab-b[i]
SS iv 3′		MU[L^{meš}] 4) [K]IN.KI[N-ma]

. . . u nipḫātišunu teš[tene’’i-m]a šatta šâti tanabbi
You se[arch] for [. . .] and their risings, and you name this year.

---

ii 9 ki-ma MUL^{meš} š[á . . . IT]I u MU.AN.NA tuš-tab-bal-ma

j 3′ [ ] MU tuš-tab-b[al-ma]
EE r. 18′ [ki]-ma [ ]
HH ii 9′ ki-ma MUL[^{meš}] šá ma$^{?}$ ⌜x x⌝ [x x M]U.AN.NA tuš-tab-bal-ma
KK ii 9′ [IT]I$^{?}$ u MU.AN.NA tus-ta-bal-ma
SS iv 5′ ki-ma MUL⌜^{meš}⌝ š[á] 6) tuš-tab-bal-ma

kīma . . . [. . .] . . . [. . .] arḫi$^{?}$ u šatti tuštabbalma
When the stars . . ., you compute [. . . of] Month$^{?}$ and year, and

ii 10 ina 3 MU^{meš} ME-a GAR-ma MU [BI DI]RI.GA ME-bi

j 4′ [ ] ⌜x x⌝ [ ]
HH ii 10′ ina 3 MU^{meš} ME-a GAR-ma MU [BI DI]RI.GA ME-bi
KK ii 9′ ina MU 3 KAM 10) [M]E-a GAR-ma M[U DIRI].GA ta-qab-bi
SS iv 6′ [ ] 7) MU BI [ ]

ina šalušti šatti qība tašakkanma šatta [šâti a]tarta taqabbi
in the third year (var. in three years) you make a pronouncement, and pronounce this year as intercalary.

---

ii 11 ana UD.NÁ.A 12 ITI^{meš} šu-ta-ku-lu ina 3 MU^{meš} ITI DIRI.GA ta-qab-bi

j 5′ [šu]-ta-ku-lu ina MU 3 KAM ITI DIRI.G[A]
HH ii 11′ UD.NÁ.A 12 ITI šu-ta-ku-[lu ina] 3 MU^{meš} ITI DIRI.GA ME-[bi]
KK ii 11′ ana UD.NÁ.ÀM 12 ITI^{meš} šu-ta-ku-lu 12) ina MU 3 KAM ITI DIRI.GA ta-qab-bi
SS iv 8′ ana UD.NÁ.A ana ⌜12⌝ [ ] 9) ina 3 MU^{m}[^{eš}]

ana ūm bubbuli 12 arḫī šutākulu ina 3 šanāti arḫa atra taqabbi
To . . . the day of disappearance of the Moon for 12 months, you pronounce an intercalary month in the third year (var. in three years);

ii 12 ina 12 ITI^{meš} 10 UD^{meš} DIRI^{meš} ŠID-at MU.AN.NA

j 6′ [UD]^{meš} DIRI^{meš} ŠID^{meš} MU IGI-[mar]
P ii 1′ ⌜x⌝ [ ]
HH ii 12′ ina 12 ITI^{meš} 10 UD^{meš} DIRI^{meš} ŠID-at MU.AN.N[A]
KK ii 13′ ina 12 ITI^{meš} 10 UD^{meš} DIRI^{meš} ŠID MU.AN.NA

ina 12 arḫī 10 ūmū atrūtu minât šatti
10 days in excess in 12 months is the amount for one year.

---

ii 13 šum-ma UD.DA.ZAL.LÁ-e u_4-mi ITI u MU.AN.NA ana IGI-ka

j 1′ [ ] ITI u MU ⌜x⌝ a ⌜x⌝ -ri-ka$^{?}$ 40$^{?}$ UD.DA.ZA[L.LÁ]
P ii 2′ BE-ma ⌜x⌝ [ ]
HH ii 13′ šum-ma UD.DA.ZAL.LÁ-e u_4-[m]u ITI u MU ana IGI-ka
KK ii 14′ BE-ma UD.DA.ZAL-e u_4-mi ⌜ITI⌝ u MU.AN.NA ana IGI-[ka]

šumma udazallê ūmi arḫi u šatti ana amārika
If you are to see the correction for day, month, and year:

ii 14 1,40 UD.DA.ZAL.LÁ-e u$_4$-me ana ITI ÍL-ma

P ii 3′ 1,40 UD.DA.[ZAL]
HH ii 14′ 1,40 UD.DA.ZAL.LÁ-e [u$_4$]-me ana ITI ÍL-ma
KK ii 15′ 1,40 UD.DA.ZAL-e u$_4$-mi ana ITI ÍL-ma

1,40 udazallê ūmi ana arḫi tanaššīma
you multiply 1,40, the correction for a day, by a month, and

ii 15 50 UD.DA.ZAL.LÁ-e ITI IGI 50 UD.DA.ZAL.LÁ-e ITI

j 8′ [UD].DA.ZAL.LÁ ITI IGI 50 UD.DA.ZAL.LÁ ITI
P ii 4′ 50 UD.DA.ZAL.[ ]
HH ii 15′ [50] UD.DA.ZAL.LÁ-e ITI IGI 50 UD.DA.ZAL.LÁ-e ITI
KK ii 16′ 50 UD.DA.ZAL.LÁ ITI IGI 50 UD.DA.ZAL.L[Á] ITI

50 udazallê arḫi tammar 50 udazallê arḫi
you find 50, the correction for a month; you multiply 50, the correction for a month,

ii 16 ana 12 ITI ÍL-ma 10 UD^{meš} DIRI^{meš} ŠID-at MU.AN.NA tam-mar
j 9′ [ ]-ma 10 UD$^{⸢\text{meš}⸣}$ D[IRI]^{me} ŠID^{meš} MU IGI-mar
P ii 4′ [ ] 5) ŠID-at MU.AN.NA [ ]
HH ii 16′ [ana 12] ITI ÍL-ma 10 UD^{meš} DIRI^{meš} ŠID-at MU tam-mar
KK ii 16′ ana 12 [ITI] ÍL-ma 17) 10 UD[^{meš} DI]RI[^{meš}] ⸢x⸣ MU.AN.NA

ana 12 arḫī tanaššīma 10 ūmī atrūti minât šatti tammar
by 12 months, and you find 10 days in excess, the amount for a year.

ii 17 ina 3 MU^{meš} MU BI DIRI.GA ME-bi

j 10′ [ ] ⸢MU$^{?}$⸣ [x x] ta-DIRI-bi
HH ii 17′ [ina] 3 MU^{meš} MU BI DIRI.GA ME-bi
KK ii 17′ ina MU 3 KAM MU DIRI.GA t[a]-qab-[bi]

ina 3 šanāti šatta šâti atarta taqabbi
In the third year (var.: in three years) you pronounce this year as intercalary.

---

ii 18 DIŠ ^{iti}BÁR.ZAG.GAR 2 KAM-ma BAL-e ^{d}Šul-gi

P ii 6′ DIŠ ^{iti}BÁR.ZAG.GAR [ ]
HH ii 18′ DIŠ ina ^{iti}BÁR.ZAG.GAR 2 KAM-ma BAL-e ^{d}Šul-gi
KK ii 18′ [ ] 2 KAM BAL ^{d}Šul-g[i]

Nisannu šanû palê Šulgi
¶ An intercalary Month I (belongs to) the reign of Šulgi;

ii 19 DIŠ ^{iti}DIRI.ŠE.GUR$_{10}$.KU$_5$ BAL-e MAR.TU-i

E iv 1′ DIŠ [x x] ⸢x⸣ [ ]
P ii 7′ DIŠ ^{iti}KIN.^{d}INNIN [ ]

HH ii 19′	DIŠ ina ^{iti}DIRI.ŠE.GUR$_{10}$.KU$_5$ BAL-e MAR.TU-i
KK ii 19′	[DIŠ ^{iti}DI]RI.[ŠE].GUR$_{10}$.KU$_5$ BAL MAR.K[I]$^?$
	Addaru arkû palê Amurrî
	¶ an intercalary Month XII (belongs to) the Amorite reign;
<u>ii 20</u>	DIŠ ^{iti}KIN.^{d}INNIN 2 KAM-ma BAL-e kaš-ši-i
E iv 2′	DIŠ [^{iti}KIN].^{d}INNIN [ ]
P ii 8′	DIŠ ^{iti}DIRI.ŠE.[ ]
HH ii 20′	DIŠ ina ^{iti}KIN.^{d}INNIN 2 KAM-ma BAL-e kaš-ši-i
KK ii 20′	[DIŠ ^{it}]^{i}KI[N.^{d}INN]IN 2 K[AM]$^?$ BAL kaš-š[i-i]
	Ulūlu šanû palê Kaššî
	¶ an intercalary Month VI (belongs to) the Kassite reign.

<u>ii 21</u>	DIŠ ina ^{iti}BÁR UD 15 KAM 3 MA.NA EN.NUN u$_4$-mi 3 MA.NA EN.NUN GI$_6$
E iv 3′	DIŠ ina ^{iti}BÁR UD ⸢15⸣ [ ]
P ii 9′	DIŠ ina ^{iti}BÁR [ ]
HH ii 21′	DIŠ ina ^{iti}BÁR UD 15 KAM 3 MA.NA <EN.NUN> u$_4$-mi 3 MA.NA EN.NUN GI$_6$
KK iii 1	[ ] KAM 3 MA.NA ⸢EN.NUN⸣ u$_4$-mi 3 M[A.N]A EN.[NUN] ⸢GI$_6$⸣
	ina Nisanni UD 15 3 mana maṣṣarti ūmi 3 mana maṣṣarti mūši
	¶ On the 15th day of Month I, 3 minas is the watch of the day, 3 minas is the watch of the night.
<u>ii 22</u>	1 ina 1 KÙŠ GIŠ.MI 2½ DANNA u$_4$-mu
E iv 4′	1 ina 1 KÙŠ GIŠ.[ ]
P ii 10′	1 ina 1 [ ]
HH ii 22′	1 ina 1 KÙŠ GIŠ.MI 2½ DANNA u$_4$-mu
KK iii 2	[1] ina 1 KÙŠ GIŠ.MI 2½ DANNA u$_4$-⸢mu⸣
	1 ina ammati ṣillu 2½ bēr ūmu
	1 cubit shadow 2½ bēru of daytime
<u>ii 23</u>	2 ina 1 KÙŠ GIŠ.MI 1 DANNA 7 UŠ 30 NINDA u$_4$-mu
E iv 5′	2 ina 1 KÙŠ GIŠ.[ ]
P ii 11′	2 ina [ ]
HH ii 23′	2 ina 1 KÙŠ GIŠ.MI 1 DANNA 7 UŠ 30 NINDA u$_4$-mu
KK iii 3	[2] ina 1 KÙŠ ⸢GIŠ.MI⸣ 1 DANNA 7 UŠ ⸢30 NINDA⸣ u$_4$-mu
	2 ina ammati šillu 1 bēr 7 UŠ 30 NINDA ūmu
	2 cubits shadow 1 bēru 7 UŠ 30 NINDA daytime
<u>ii 24</u>	3 ina 1 KÙŠ GIŠ.MI ⅔ DANNA 5 UŠ u$_4$-mu
E iv 6′	3 ina 1 KÙŠ GIŠ.[ ]
HH ii 24′	3 ina 1 KÙŠ GIŠ.MI ⅔ DANNA 5 UŠ u$_4$-mu
KK iii 4	[3 ina] 1 KÙŠ GIŠ.M[I] ⅔ [DANNA] 5 U[Š] u$_4$-mu

3 ina ammati ṣillu ⅔ bēr 5 UŠ ūmu
3 cubits shadow ⅔ bēru 5 UŠ daytime

----

ii 25 DIŠ ina ^{iti}ŠU UD 15 KAM 4 MA.NA EN.NUN u$_4$-mi 2 [MA.NA] EN.NUN GI$_6$

E iv 7′ DIŠ ina ^{iti}ŠU UD ⸢15⸣ [ ]
HH ii 25′ DIŠ ina ^{iti}ŠU UD 15 KAM 4 MA.NA EN.NUN u$_4$-mi 2 [MA.NA E]N.[N]UN GI$_6$
KK iii 5 [^{iti}Š[U] UD ⸢15 KAM⸣ [ ] EN.N[UN GI$_6$]
TT vi 1′ DIŠ ina ⸢^{iti}⸣[ŠU] 2′) 2 M[A.NA]

ina Du'ūzi UD 15 4 mana maṣṣarti ūmi 2 mana maṣṣarti mūši
¶ On the 15th day of Month IV, 4 minas is the watch of the day, 2 [minas] is the watch of the night.

ii 26 1 ina 1 KÙŠ GIŠ.MI 2 DANNA u$_4$-mu 2 ina 1 KÙŠ GI[Š.MI 1 DAN]NA u$_4$-mu

E iv 8′ 1 ina 1 K[ÙŠ] 9) 2 ina 1 K[ÙŠ]
HH ii 26′ 1 ina 1 KÙŠ GIŠ.MI 2 DANNA u$_4$-mu 2 ina 1 KÙŠ GI[Š.MI 1 DAN]NA u$_4$-mu
KK iii 6 [1] ina 1 KÙŠ GI[Š.MI] 2 [DANNA u$_4$]-mu 7) [2 ina] 1 K[ÙŠ] GI[Š.MI 1 DANNA u]$_4$-mu
TT vi 3′ 1 ina 1 [4′) 2 i[na]

1 ina ammati ṣillu 2 bēr ūmu 2 ina ammati ṣi[llu 1 b]ēr ūmu
1 cubit shadow 2 bēru daytime
2 cubits shadow [1] bēru daytime

ii 27 3 ina 1 KÙŠ GIŠ.MI ⅔ DANNA u$_4$-mu 4 ina 1 KÙŠ GIŠ.MI ½ DANNA u$_4$-mu

E iv 10′ 3 ina 1 KÙŠ GIŠ.M[I] 11) 4 ina 1 KÙŠ GIŠ.MI [ ]
HH ii 27′ 3 ina 1 KÙŠ GIŠ.MI ⅔ DANNA u$_4$-mu 4 ina 1 KÙŠ GIŠ.⸢MI ½⸣ [DA]NNA u$_4$-m[u]
KK iii 8 [ ] ⸢x⸣ [ ] 9) [ ] 1 K[ÙŠ]
TT vi 5′ 3 [ ]

3 ina ammati ṣillu ⅔ bēr ūmu 4 ina ammati ṣillu mišil bēr ūmu
3 cubits shadow ⅔ bēru daytime
4 cubits shadow ½ bēru daytime

ii 28 5 ina 1 KÙŠ GIŠ.MI 12 UŠ u$_4$-mu 6 ina 1 KÙŠ GIŠ.MI 10 UŠ u$_4$-mu

E iv 12′ 5 ina 1 KÙŠ GIŠ.MI 1[2] 13) 6 ina 1 KÙŠ GIŠ.MI 10 [ ]
HH ii 28′ 5 ina 1 KÙŠ GIŠ.MI 12 UŠ u$_4$-mu 6 ina 1 KÙŠ GIŠ.MI 10 UŠ u$_4$-m[u]
KK iii 10 [GI]Š.M[I] 11) [GIŠ.M]I [ ]

5 ina ammati ṣillu 12 UŠ ūmu 6 ina ammati ṣillu 10 UŠ ūmu
5 cubits shadow 12 UŠ daytime
6 cubits shadow 10 UŠ daytime

ii 29 8 ina 1 KÙŠ GIŠ.MI 7 UŠ 30 NINDA u$_4$-mu

E iv 14′ 8 ina 1 KÙŠ GIŠ.MI 7 U[Š]
P iii 1′ 8 ina 1 KÙ[Š]
HH ii 29′ 8 ina 1 KÙŠ GIŠ.MI 7 UŠ 30 NINDA u$_4$-mu
KK iii 12 [ ] NINDA [ ]

8 ina ammati ṣillu 7 UŠ 30 NINDA ūmu
8 cubits shadow 7 UŠ 30 NINDA daytime

<u>ii 30</u> 9 ina 1 KÙŠ GIŠ.MI 6 UŠ 40 NINDA u$_4$-mu 10 ina 1 KÙŠ GIŠ.MI 6 UŠ u$_4$-mu

E iv 15′ 9 ina 1 KÙŠ GIŠ.MI 6 UŠ [ ] 16) 10 ina 1 KÙŠ GIŠ.MI 6 U[Š]
P iii 2′ 9 ina 1 KÙŠ GIŠ.[MI] 3) 10 ina 1 KÙŠ GIŠ.[MI]
HH ii 30′ 9 ina 1 KÙŠ GIŠ.MI 6 UŠ 40 NINDA u$_4$-mu 10 ina 1 KÙŠ GIŠ.MI 6 UŠ u$_4$-mu
KK iii 13 [ ] 14) [ ]

9 ina ammati ṣillu 6 UŠ 40 NINDA ūmu 10 ina ammati ṣillu 6 UŠ ūmu
9 cubits shadow 6 UŠ 40 NINDA daytime
10 cubits shadow 6 UŠ daytime

<u>ii 31</u> DIŠ ina ^{iti}DU$_6$ UD 15 KAM 3 MA.NA EN.NUN u$_4$-mi 3 MA.NA EN.NUN GI$_6$

P iii 4′ DIŠ ina [^{iti}]DU$_6$ UD 1[5]
HH ii 31′ DIŠ ina ^{iti}DU$_6$ UD 15 KAM 3 MA.NA EN.NUN u$_4$-mi 3 MA.NA EN.NUN GI$_6$
KK iii 15 [ ] ⸢x⸣ MA.NA EN.⸢NUN x x x⸣ [ ]

ina Tešrīti UD 15 3 mana maṣṣarti ūmi 3 mana maṣṣarti mūši
¶ On the 15th day of Month VII, 3 minas is the watch of the day, 3 minas is the watch of the night.

<u>ii 32</u> 1 ina 1 KÙŠ GIŠ.MI 2½ DANNA u$_4$-mu

P iii 5′ 1 ina [1 KÙ]Š GIŠ.M[I]
HH ii 32′ 1 ina 1 KÙŠ GIŠ.MI 2½ DANNA u$_4$-mu
KK iii 16 [M]I 2½ DANNA [ ]

1 ina ammati ṣillu 2½ bēr ūmu
1 cubit shadow 2½ bēru daytime

<u>ii 33</u> 2 ina 1 KÙŠ GIŠ.MI 1 DANNA 7 UŠ 30 NINDA u$_4$-mu

P iii 6′ 2 ina [ ] GIŠ.MI [ ]
HH ii 33′ 2 ina 1 KÙŠ GIŠ.MI 1 DANNA 7 UŠ 30 NINDA u$_4$-mu
KK iii 17 [M]I ½ DANNA ⸢x x x⸣ [ ]

2 ina ammati šillu 1 bēr 7 UŠ 30 NINDA ūmu
2 cubits shadow 1 bēru 7 UŠ 30 NINDA daytime

<u>ii 34</u> 3 ina 1 KÙŠ GIŠ.MI ⅔ DANNA 5 UŠ u$_4$-mu

P iii 7′ 3 ina 1 KÙŠ GIŠ.M[I]
HH ii 34′ 3 ina 1 KÙŠ GIŠ.MI ⅔ DANNA 5 UŠ u$_4$-mu
KK iii 18 [ ] ⅔ DAN[NA] ⸢x x x⸣ [ ]

3 ina ammati ṣillu ⅔ bēr 5 UŠ ūmu
3 cubits shadow ⅔ bēru 5 UŠ daytime

<u>ii 35</u> DIŠ ina ^{iti}AB UD 15 KAM 2 MA.NA EN.NUN u_4-mi 4 MA.NA EN.NUN GI_6

P iii 8′ [DIŠ ina ^{it}]^{i}AB UD 15 KAM 2 [ ]
HH ii 35′ DIŠ ina ^{iti}AB UD 15 KAM 2 MA.NA EN.NUN u_4-mi 4 MA.NA EN.NUN GI_6
KK iii 19 [ ] ⸢x x x⸣ [ ]

ina Ṭebēti UD 15 2 mana maṣṣarti ūmi 4 mana maṣṣarti mūši
¶ On the 15th day of Month X, 2 minas is the watch of the day, 4 minas is the watch of the night.

<u>ii 36</u> 1 ina 1 KÙŠ GIŠ.MI 3 DANNA u_4-mu 2 ina 1 KÙŠ GIŠ.MI 1½ DANNA u_4-mu

P iii 9′ [ ] 1 KÙŠ GIŠ.MI [ ] 10) [GI]Š.M[I]
HH ii 36′ 1 ina 1 KÙŠ GIŠ.MI 3 DANNA u_4-mu 2 ina 1 KÙŠ GIŠ.MI 1½ DANNA u_4-mu

1 ina ammati ṣillu 3 bēr ūmu 2 ina ammati ṣillu 1½ bēr ūmu
1 cubit shadow 3 bēru daytime
2 cubits shadow 1½ bēru daytime

<u>ii 37</u> 3 ina 1 KÙŠ GIŠ.MI 1 DANNA u_4-mu 4 ina 1 KÙŠ GIŠ.MI ⅔ DANNA 2 UŠ 30 NINDA u_4-mu

P iii 11′ [GI]Š.M[I]
HH ii 37′ 3 ina 1 KÙŠ GIŠ.MI 1 DANNA u_4-mu 4 ina 1 KÙŠ GIŠ.MI ⅔ DANNA 2 UŠ 30 NINDA u_4-mu

3 ina ammati ṣillu 1 bēr ūmu 4 ina ammati ṣillu ⅔ bēr 2 UŠ 30 NINDA ūmu
3 cubits shadow 1 bēru daytime
4 cubits shadow ⅔ bēru 2 UŠ 30 NINDA daytime

<u>ii 38</u>
HH ii 38′ 5 ina 1 KÙŠ GIŠ.MI 18 UŠ u_4-mu 6 ina 1 KÙŠ GIŠ.MI ½ DANNA u_4-mu

5 ina ammati ṣillu 18 UŠ ūmu 6 ina ammati ṣillu ½ bēr ūmu
5 cubits shadow 18 UŠ daytime
6 cubits shadow ½ bēru daytime

<u>ii 39</u>
HH ii 39′ 8 ina 1 KÙŠ GIŠ.MI 11 UŠ 15 NINDA u_4-mu 9 ina 1 KÙŠ GIŠ.MI 10 UŠ u_4-mu

8 ina ammati ṣillu 11 UŠ 15 NINDA ūmu 9 ina ammati ṣillu 10 UŠ ūmu
8 cubits shadow 11 UŠ 15 NINDA daytime
9 cubits shadow 10 UŠ daytime

<u>ii 40</u>
HH ii 40′ 10 ina 1 KÙŠ GIŠ.MI 9 UŠ u_4-mu

10 ina ammati ṣillu 9 UŠ ūmu
10 cubits shadow 9 UŠ daytime
----

ii 41

HH ii 41′ BE-ma nap(!)-pal-ti 1 KÙŠ GIŠ.MI ana IGI-ka 40 nap-pal-ti u$_4$-m[i]

šumma nappalti ammat ṣilli ana amārika 40 nappalti ūmi
If you are to see the interval-number for 1 cubit of shadow, you multiply 40, the interval-number for daytime

ii 42

HH ii 42′ u GI$_6$ ana 7,30 ÍL-ma 5(!) nap-pal-ti GIŠ.MI 1 KÙŠ tam-[mar]

u mūši ana 7,30 tanaššīma 5 nappalti ṣilli ammat tam[mar]
and nighttime, by 7,30, and you see 5, the interval-number for a shadow of 1 cubit.

---

ii 43 DIŠ ina ^{iti}BÁR UD 1 KAM 3 MA.NA 10 GÍN EN.NUN GI$_6$ 12 UŠ 40 NINDA ŠÚ šá Sin

HH ii 43′ DIŠ ina ^{iti}BÁR UD 1 KAM 3 MA.NA 10 GÍN EN.NUN GI$_6$ 12 UŠ 40 NINDA ŠÚ šá [Sin]
NN 1 [DIŠ ina ^{iti}B]ÁR UD 1 KAM 3 MA.NA 10 GÍN EN.NUN GI$_6$ 12 UŠ 40 NINDA ŠÚ šá Sin

ina Nisanni UD 1 3 mana 10 šiqil maṣṣarti mūši 12 UŠ 40 NINDA rabû ša Sin
¶ On the 1st day of Month I, 3 minas 10 shekels is the watch of the night; 12 UŠ 40 NINDA setting of the Moon.

ii 44 DIŠ ina ^{iti}BÁR UD 15 KAM 3 MA.NA EN.NUN GI$_6$ 12 UŠ KUR šá Sin

HH ii 44′ DIŠ ina ^{iti}BÁR UD 15 KAM 3 MA.NA EN.NUN <GI$_6$> 12 UŠ KUR šá [Sin]
NN 2 [DIŠ ina ^{iti}BÁ]R UD 15 KAM 3 MA.NA EN.NUN GI$_6$ 12 UŠ KUR šá Sin

ina Nisanni UD 15 3 mana maṣṣarti mūši 12 UŠ napāḫu ša Sin
¶ On the 15th day of Month I, 3 minas is the watch of the night; 12 UŠ rising of the Moon.

---

ii 45 DIŠ ina ^{iti}GU$_4$ UD 1 KAM 2⅚ MA.NA EN.NUN GI$_6$ 11 UŠ 20 NINDA ŠÚ šá Sin

HH ii 45′ DIŠ ina ^{iti}GU$_4$ UD 1 KAM 2⅚ MA.NA EN.NUN GI$_6$ 11 UŠ 20 NINDA ŠÚ šá [Sin]
NN 3 [DIŠ ina ^{iti}G]U$_4$ UD 1 KAM 2⅚ MA.NA EN.NUN GI$_6$ 11 UŠ 20 NINDA ŠÚ šá Sin

ina Ajjari UD 1 2⅚ mana maṣṣarti mūši 11 UŠ 20 NINDA rabû ša Sin
¶ On the 1st day of Month II, 2⅚ minas is the watch of the night; 11 UŠ 20 NINDA setting of the Moon.

ii 46 DIŠ ina ^{iti}GU$_4$ UD 15 KAM 2⅔ MA.NA EN.NUN GI$_6$ 10 UŠ 40 NINDA KUR šá Sin

FF v 1′ [KA]M 2 [ ]
HH ii 46′ DIŠ ina ^{iti}GU$_4$ UD 15 KAM 2⅔ MA.NA EN.NUN GI$_6$ 10 UŠ 40 NINDA KUR [šá Sin]

NN 4 [DIŠ ina ^{iti}GU$_4$ U]D 15 KAM 2⅔ MA.NA EN.NUN GI$_6$ 10 UŠ 40 NINDA KUR šá Sin

ina Ajjari UD 15 2⅔ mana maṣṣarti mūši 10 UŠ 40 NINDA napāḫu ša Sin

¶ On the 15th day of Month II, 2⅔ minas is the watch of the night; 10 UŠ 40 NINDA rising of the Moon.

---

ii 47 DIŠ ina ^{iti}SIG$_4$ UD 1 KAM 2½ MA.NA EN.NUN GI$_6$ 10 UŠ ŠÚ šá Sin

FF v 2′ [DIŠ ina ^{iti}SI]G$_4$ UD 1 KAM 2½ MA ⌜EN.NUN⌝ [ ]

HH ii 47′ DIŠ ina ^{iti}SIG$_4$ UD 1 KAM 2½ MA.NA EN.NUN GI$_6$ 10 UŠ ŠÚ [šá Sin]

NN 5 [DIŠ ina ^{iti}SIG$_4$ U]D 1 KAM 2½ MA.NA EN.NUN GI$_6$ 10 UŠ ŠÚ šá Sin

ina Simāni UD 1 2½ mana maṣṣarti mūši 10 UŠ rabû ša Sin

¶ On the 1st day of Month III, 2½ minas is the watch of the night; 10 UŠ setting of the Moon.

ii 48 DIŠ ina ^{iti}SIG$_4$ UD 15 KAM 2⅓ MA.NA EN.NUN GI$_6$ 9 UŠ 20 NINDA KUR šá Sin

FF v 3′ [DIŠ ina ^{iti}]SIG$_4$ UD 15 KAM 2 ⅓ GÍN EN.NUN GI$_6$ 9 UŠ 20 NINDA KU[R šá Sin]

HH ii 48′ DIŠ ina ^{iti}SIG$_4$ UD 15 KAM 2⅔ GÍN EN.NUN GI$_6$ 9 UŠ 20 NINDA [KUR šá Sin]

NN 6 [DIŠ ina ^{iti}SIG$_4$ U]D 15 KAM 2⅓ MA.NA EN.NUN GI$_6$ 9 UŠ 20 NINDA KUR šá Sin

ina Simāni UD 15 2⅓ mana maṣṣarti mūši 9 UŠ 20 NINDA napāḫu ša Sin

¶ On the 15th day of Month III, 2⅓ minas is the watch of the night; 9 UŠ 20 NINDA rising of the Moon.

---

ii 49 DIŠ ina ^{iti}ŠU UD 1 KAM 2 MA.NA 10 GÍN EN.NUN GI$_6$ 8 UŠ 40 NINDA ŠÚ šá Sin

FF v 4′ [DIŠ ina ^{iti}Š]U UD 1 KAM 2 MA 10 GÍN EN.NUN GI$_6$ 8 UŠ 40 NINDA Š[Ú šá Sin]

HH ii 49′ DIŠ ina ^{iti}ŠU UD 1 KAM 2 MA.NA 10 GÍN EN.NUN GI$_6$ 8 [UŠ 40 NINDA ŠÚ šá Sin]

NN 7 [DIŠ ina ^{iti}ŠU U]D 1 KAM 2 MA.NA 10 GÍN EN.NUN GI$_6$ 8 UŠ 40 NINDA ŠÚ š[á Sin]

ina Du'ūzi UD 1 2 mana 10 šiqil maṣṣarti mūši 8 UŠ 40 NINDA rabû ša Sin

¶ On the 1st day of Month IV, 2 minas 10 shekels is the watch of the night; 8 UŠ 40 NINDA setting of the Moon.

ii 50 DIŠ ina ^{iti}ŠU UD 15 KAM 2 MA.NA EN.NUN GI$_6$ 8 UŠ [KUR šá Sin]

FF v 5′ [DIŠ ina ^{iti}Š]U UD 15 KAM 2 MA EN.NUN GI$_6$ 8 U[Š KUR šá Sin]

HH ii 50′ DIŠ ina ^{iti}ŠU UD 15 KAM 2 MA.NA EN.NUN GI$_6$ 8 [UŠ KUR šá Sin]

NN 8 [DIŠ ina ^{iti}ŠU U]D 15 KAM 2 MA.NA EN.NUN GI$_6$ 8 UŠ [KUR šá Sin]

ina Du'ūzi UD 15 2 mana maṣṣarti mūši 8 UŠ napāḫu ša Sin

¶ On the 15th day of Month IV, 2 minas is the watch of the night; 8 UŠ [rising of the Moon.]

---

ii 51 DIŠ ina ^{iti}IZI UD 1 KAM 2 MA.NA 10 GÍN EN.NUN GI$_6$ [8 UŠ 40 NINDA ŠÚ šá Sin]

FF v 6′ [DIŠ ina ^{iti}IZ]I UD 1 KAM 2 MA 10 GÍN EN.NUN GI$_6$ [ ]]

HH ii 51′ DIŠ ina ^{iti}IZI UD 1 KAM 2 MA.NA 10 GÍN EN.N[UN GI$_6$ 8 UŠ 40 NINDA ŠÚ šá Sin]

LL 1′ [E]N.N[UN]
NN 9 [ ] UD 1 KAM 2 MA.NA 10 GÍN EN.NUN GI$_6$ [8 UŠ 40 NINDA ŠÚ šá Sin]

ina Abi UD 1 2 mana 10 šiqil maṣṣarti mūši 8 UŠ 40 NINDA rabû ša Sin
¶ On the 1st day of Month V, 2 minas 10 shekels is the watch of the night; 8 UŠ 40 NINDA setting of the Moon.

ii 52 DIŠ ina ^{iti}IZI UD 15 KAM 2⅓ MA.NA EN.NUN GI$_6$ 9 U[Š 20 NINDA KUR šá Sin]

FF v 7′ [DIŠ ina ^{iti}IZ]I UD 15 KAM 2 MA ⅓ GÍN EN.NUN GI$_6$ [ ]
HH ii 52′ DIŠ ina ^{iti}IZI UD 15 KAM 2 MA.NA ⅔ E[N.NUN GI$_6$ 9 UŠ 20 NINDA KUR šá Sin]
LL 2′ [MA].NA EN.NUN GI$_6$ 9 U[Š]
NN 10 [U]D 15 KAM 2⅓ MA.NA EN.NUN [ ]

ina Abi UD 15 2⅓ mana maṣṣarti mūši 9 U[Š 20 NINDA napāḫu ša Sin]
¶ On the 15th day of Month V, 2⅓ minas is the watch of the night; 9 U[Š 20 NINDA rising of the Moon.]

---

ii 53 DIŠ ina ^{iti}KIN UD 1 KAM 2½ MA.NA EN.NUN GI$_6$ 10 UŠ ŠÚ [šá Sin]

FF v 8′ [DIŠ ina ^{iti}KI]N UD 1 KAM 2½ MA.NA EN.NUN GI$_6$ [ ]
HH ii 53′ DIŠ ina ^{iti}KIN UD 1 KAM 2½ MA.NA [ ]
LL 3′ [2]½ MA.NA [E]N.NUN GI$_6$ 10 UŠ ŠÚ [šá Sin]

ina Ulūli UD 1 2½ mana maṣṣarti mūši 10 UŠ rabû ša Sin
¶ On the 1st day of Month VI, 2½ minas is the watch of the night; 10 UŠ setting of the Moon.

ii 54 DIŠ ina ^{iti}KIN UD 15 KAM 2⅔ MA.NA EN.NUN GI$_6$ 10 UŠ 40 NINDA KUR [šá Sin]

FF v 9′ [DIŠ ina ^{iti}KI]N UD 15 KAM 2⅔ MA EN.NUN [ ]
HH ii 54′ DIŠ ina ^{iti}KIN UD 15 KAM 2⅔ M[A.NA]
LL 4′ [ ] 2⅔ MA.NA EN.NUN GI$_6$ 10 UŠ 40 NINDA KUR [šá Sin]

ina Ulūli UD 15 2⅔ mana maṣṣarti mūši 10 UŠ 40 NINDA napāḫu [ša Sin]
¶ On the 15th day of Month VI, 2⅔ minas is the watch of the night; 10 UŠ 40 NINDA rising [of the Moon.]

---

iii 1 DIŠ ina ^{iti}DU$_6$ UD 1 KAM 2⅚ MA.NA EN.NUN GI$_6$ 11 UŠ 20 NINDA ŠÚ [šá Sin]

FF v 10′ DIŠ [ina ^{iti}D]U$_6$ UD 1 KAM 2⅚ MA E[N.NUN]
HH iii 1 DIŠ ina ^{iti}DU$_6$ UD 1 KAM 2 ⸢⅚⸣ MA.⸢NA⸣ E[N.NUN]
LL 5′ [ ] 2⅚ MA.NA EN.NUN GI$_6$ 11 UŠ 20 NINDA ŠÚ [šá Sin]

ina Tešrīti UD 1 2⅚ mana maṣṣarti mūši 11 UŠ 20 NINDA rabû [ša Sin]
¶ On the 1st day of Month VII, 2⅚ minas is the watch of the night; 11 UŠ 20 NINDA setting [of the Moon.]

<u>iii 2</u> DIŠ ina $^{iti}DU_6$ UD 15 KAM 3 MA.NA EN.NUN GI_6 12 UŠ KUR [šá Sin]

D iii 1′ [KA]M 3 MA.NA EN.NUN GI_6 12 U[Š]
FF v 11′ DIŠ ina $^{iti}DU_6$ [ ]
HH iii 2 DIŠ ina $^{iti}DU_6$ UD 15 KAM 3 MA.NA E[N.NUN]
LL 6′ [ ] 3 MA.NA EN.NUN GI_6 12 UŠ KUR [šá Sin]

ina Tešrīti UD 15 3 mana maṣṣarti mūši 12 UŠ napāḫu ša Sin
¶ On the 15th day of Month VII, 3 minas is the watch of the night; 12 UŠ rising of the Moon.

<u>iii 3</u> DIŠ ina ^{iti}APIN UD 1 KAM 3 MA.NA 10 GÍN EN.NUN GI_6 12 UŠ 40 NINDA ŠÚ šá Sin

D iii 2′ [DIŠ ina ^{iti}]APIN UD 1 KAM 3 MA.NA 10 GÍN EN.NUN GI_6 12 UŠ 40 NINDA ŠÚ š[á Sin]
FF v 12′ DIŠ ina ^{iti}APIN [ ]
HH iii 3 DIŠ ina ^{iti}APIN UD 1 KAM 3 MA.NA 10 G[ÍN] E[N.NUN]
LL 7′ [ ] 3 MA.NA 10 GÍN EN.NUN GI_6 12 UŠ 40 NINDA ŠÚ [šá Sin]
SS v 1′ [ ] ša ⸢^{d}Sin⸣

ina Araḫsamni UD 1 3 mana 10 šiqil maṣṣarti mūši 12 UŠ 40 NINDA rabû ša Sin
¶ On the 1st day of Month VIII, 3 minas 10 shekels is the watch of the night; 12 UŠ 40 NINDA setting of the Moon.

<u>iii 4</u> DIŠ ina ^{iti}APIN UD 15 KAM 3⅓ MA.NA EN.NUN GI_6 13 UŠ 20 NINDA KUR šá Sin

D iii 3′ [DIŠ ina ^{it}]^{i}APIN UD 15 KAM 3⅓ MA.NA EN.NUN GI_6 13 UŠ 20 NINDA KUR šá Sin
FF v 13′ DIŠ ina ^{iti}APIN [ ]
HH iii 4 DIŠ ina ^{iti}APIN UD 15 KAM 3 MA.NA ⅓ GÍN E[N].N[UN]
LL 8′ [3]⅓ MA.NA EN.NUN GI_6 13 UŠ 20 NINDA [KUR šá Sin]
NN r. 1′ [ ] šá Sin
SS v 2′ [ ] ⸢3⅓⸣ MA EN.NUN GI_6 3) [13 UŠ 20] NINDA KUR ša ^{d}Sin

ina Araḫsamni UD 15 3⅓ mana maṣṣarti mūši 13 UŠ 20 NINDA napāḫu ša Sin
¶ On the 15th day of Month VIII, 3⅓ minas is the watch of the night; 13 UŠ 20 NINDA rising of the Moon.

<u>iii 5</u> DIŠ ina ^{iti}GAN UD 1 KAM 3½ MA.NA EN.NUN GI_6 14 UŠ ŠÚ šá Sin

D iii 4′ [DIŠ] ina ^{iti}GAN UD 1 KAM 3½ MA.NA EN.NUN GI_6 14 UŠ ŠÚ šá Sin
FF v 14′ DIŠ ina ^{iti}GAN [ ]
HH iii 5 DIŠ ina ^{iti}GAN UD 1 KAM 3½ MA.NA EN.NUN GI_6 1[4 UŠ]
LL 9′ [3]½ MA.NA EN.NUN GI_6 14 UŠ ŠÚ [šá Sin]
NN r. 2′ [U]D 1 KAM 3½ M[A.N]A [ ] ŠÚ šá Sin
SS v 4′ [ ] 3½ MA [E]N.NUN GI_6 5) [14 UŠ] ŠÚ ⸢ša ^{d}Sin⸣

ina Kislīmi UD 1 3½ mana maṣṣarti mūši 14 UŠ rabû ša Sin
¶ On the 1st day of Month IX, 3½ minas is the watch of the night; 14 UŠ setting of the Moon.

<u>iii 6</u> DIŠ ina ^{iti}GAN UD 15 KAM 3⅔ MA.NA EN.NUN GI$_6$ 14 UŠ 40 NINDA KUR šá Sin

D iii 5′ DIŠ ina ^{iti}GAN UD 15 KAM 3⅔ MA.NA EN.NUN GI$_6$ 14 UŠ 40 NINDA KUR šá Sin
FF v 15′ DIŠ ina ^{iti}GAN [ ]
HH iii 6 DIŠ ina ^{iti}GAN UD 15 KAM 3⅔ MA.NA EN.NUN GI$_6$ 14 [ ]
LL 10′ [M]A.NA EN.NUN G[I$_6$]
NN r. 3′ [U]D 15 KAM 3⅔ MA.NA EN.NUN GI$_6$ 14 UŠ 40 NINDA KUR šá Sin
SS v 6′ [DIŠ ina ^{iti}G]AN UD 15 K[AM] 3[⅔ MA] ⸢EN⸣.NUN GI$_6$ 7) [14] UŠ 40 NINDA KUR ša ^{d}Sin

ina Kislīmi UD 15 3⅔ mana maṣṣarti mūši 14 UŠ 40 NINDA napāḫu ša Sin
¶ On the 15th day of Month IX, 3⅔ minas is the watch of the night; 14 UŠ 40 NINDA rising of the Moon.

<u>iii 7</u> DIŠ ina ^{iti}AB UD 1 KAM 3⅚ MA.NA EN.NUN GI$_6$ 15 UŠ 20 NINDA ŠÚ šá Sin

D iii 6′ DIŠ ina ^{iti}AB UD 1 KAM 3⅚ MA.NA EN.NUN GI$_6$ ½ DANNA 20 NINDA ŠÚ šá Sin
FF v 16′ DIŠ ina ^{iti}AB [ ]
HH iii 7 DIŠ ina ^{iti}AB UD 1 KAM 3⅓ MA.NA EN.NUN GI$_6$ ½ DANNA [ ]
NN r. 4′ [U]D 1 KAM 3⅚ MA.NA EN.NUN GI$_6$ 15 UŠ 20 NINDA ŠÚ šá Sin
SS v 8′ [DIŠ ina ^{it}]^{i}AB UD 1 KAM 3⅚ MA EN.NUN GI$_6$ 9) [½] DANNA 20 NINDA ŠÚ ša ^{d}Sin

ina Ṭebēti UD 1 3⅚ mana maṣṣarti mūši 15 UŠ (Variant: mišil bēr) 20 NINDA rabû ša Sin
¶ On the 1st day of Month X, 3⅚ minas is the watch of the night; 15 UŠ (variant: half a bēru) 20 NINDA setting of the Moon.

<u>iii 8</u> DIŠ ina ^{iti}AB UD 15 KAM 4 MA.NA EN.NUN GI$_6$ 16 UŠ KUR šá Sin

D iii 7′ DIŠ ina ^{iti}AB UD 15 KAM 4 MA.NA EN.NUN GI$_6$ 16 UŠ {20 NINDA} KUR šá Sin
FF v 17′ DIŠ ina ^{iti}[AB]
HH iii 8 DIŠ ina ^{iti}AB UD 15 KAM 4 MA.NA EN.NUN GI$_6$ 16 UŠ [ ]
NN r. 5′ [UD] 15 KAM 4 MA.NA EN.NUN GI$_6$ 16 UŠ KUR šá Sin
SS v 10′ ⸢DIŠ⸣ ina $^{⸢iti⸣}$AB UD 15 K[AM] 4 M[A E]N.NUN GI$_6$ 11) 16 ⸢UŠ⸣ KUR ša ^{d}Sin

ina Ṭebēti UD 15 4 mana maṣṣarti mūši 16 UŠ napāḫu ša Sin
¶ On the 15th day of Month X, 4 minas is the watch of the night; 16 UŠ rising of the Moon.

<u>iii 9</u> DIŠ ina ^{iti}ZÍZ UD 1 KAM 3⅚ MA.NA EN.NUN GI$_6$ 15 UŠ 20 NINDA ŠÚ šá Sin

D iii 8′ DIŠ ina ^{iti}ZÍZ UD 1 KAM 3⅚ MA.NA EN.NUN GI$_6$ ½ DANNA 20 NINDA ŠÚ šá Sin
FF v 18′ DIŠ ina ^{it}[^{i}ZÍZ]
HH iii 9 DIŠ ina ^{iti}ZÍZ UD 1 KAM 3 MA.NA ⅚ GÍN EN.NUN GI$_6$ ½ DANNA [ ]
NN r. 6′ [U]D 1 KAM 3⅚ MA.NA EN.NUN GI$_6$ 15 UŠ 20 NINDA ŠÚ šá Sin
SS v 12′ DIŠ ina ^{iti}ZÍZ UD 1 K[AM] 3⅚ MA ⸢EN.NUN⸣ GI$_6$ 13) ½ DANNA [20 NINDA] ŠÚ ⸢ša ^{d}Sin⸣

ina Šabāṭi UD 1 3⅚ mana maṣṣarti mūši 15 UŠ (variant: mišil bēr) 20 NINDA rabû ša Sin
¶ On the 1st day of Month XI, 3⅚ minas is the watch of the night; 15 UŠ (variant: half a bēru) 20 NINDA setting of the Moon.

iii 10 DIŠ ina ^{iti}ZÍZ UD 15 KAM 3⅔ MA.NA EN.NUN GI$_6$ 14 UŠ 40 NINDA KUR šá Sin

D iii 9′ DIŠ ina ^{iti}ZÍZ UD 15 KAM 3⅔ MA.NA EN.NUN GI$_6$ 14 UŠ 40 NINDA KUR šá Si[n]
FF v 19′ DIŠ ina ^{i}[^{ti}ZÍZ]
HH iii 10 DIŠ ina ^{iti}ZÍZ UD 15 KAM 3⅔ MA.NA EN.NUN GI$_6$ 14 UŠ 40 NI[NDA]
NN r. 7′ [ ] UD 15 KAM 3⅔ MA.NA EN.NUN GI$_6$ 14 UŠ 40 NINDA KUR šá Sin
SS v 14′ DIŠ ina ^{iti}ZÍZ [U]D 15 KAM ⸢3⅔ MA EN⸣.N[UN GI$_6$] 15) 14 UŠ 40 NINDA KUR [ša ^{d}Sin]

ina Šabāṭi UD 15 3⅔ mana maṣṣarti mūši 14 UŠ 40 NINDA napāḫu ša Sin
¶ On the 15th day of Month XI, 3⅔ minas is the watch of the night; 14 UŠ 40 NINDA rising of the Moon.

---

iii 11 DIŠ ina ^{iti}ŠE UD 1 KAM 3½ MA.NA EN.NUN GI$_6$ 14 UŠ ŠÚ šá Sin

D iii 10′ DIŠ ina ^{iti}ŠE UD 1 KAM 3½ MA.NA EN.NUN GI$_6$ 14 UŠ ŠÚ šá Si[n]
HH iii 11 DIŠ ina ^{iti}ŠE UD 1 KAM 3½ MA.NA EN.NUN GI$_6$ 14 UŠ ŠÚ šá Sin
NN r. 8′ [U]D 1 KAM 3½ MA.NA EN.NUN GI$_6$ 14 UŠ ŠÚ šá Sin
SS v 16′ ⸢DIŠ⸣ [ina] ^{iti}Š[E] UD 1 KAM 3½ ⸢MA⸣ E[N.NUN GI$_6$] 17) [1]4 UŠ ŠÚ š[a ^{d}Sin]

ina Addari UD 1 3½ mana maṣṣarti mūši 14 UŠ rabû ša Sin
¶ On the 1st day of month XII, 3½ minas is the watch of the night; 14 UŠ setting of the Moon.

iii 12 DIŠ ina ^{iti}ŠE UD 15 KAM 3⅓ MA.NA EN.NUN GI$_6$ 13 UŠ 20 NINDA KUR šá Sin

D iii 11′ DIŠ ina ^{iti}ŠE UD 15 KAM 3⅓ MA.NA EN.NUN GI$_6$ 13 UŠ 20 NINDA KU[R]
HH iii 12 DIŠ ina ^{iti}ŠE UD 15 KAM 3⅔ GÍN EN.NUN GI$_6$ 13 UŠ 20 NINDA KUR šá Sin
NN r. 9′ [U]D 15 KAM 3⅓ MA.NA EN.NUN GI$_6$ 13 UŠ 20 NINDA KUR šá Sin
SS v 18′ [DIŠ ina ^{it}]^{i}ŠE UD 15 KAM [3]⅓ MA EN.[NUN GI$_6$] 19) ⸢13⸣ [U]Š 20 NI[NDA] KUR [ša ^{d}Sin]

ina Addari UD 15 3⅓ mana maṣṣarti mūši 13 UŠ 20 NINDA napāḫu ša Sin
¶ On the 15th day of Month XII, 3⅓ minas is the watch of the night; 13 UŠ 20 NINDA rising of the Moon.

---

iii 13 4 igi-gub-bé-e IGI.DUḪ.A šá ^{d}Sin 3 MA.NA EN.NUN GI$_6$

D iii 12′ 4 igi-gub-BA IGI.DUḪ.A šá ^{d}Sin 3 MA.NA EN.NUN [GI$_6$]
HH iii 13 4 igi-gub-bé-e IGI.DUḪ.A šá ^{d}Sin 3 MA.NA EN.NUN GI$_6$

4 igigubbê tāmarti ša Sin 3 mana maṣṣarti mūši
4 is the coefficient for the visibility of the Moon; you multiply 3 minas, the night-time watch,

iii 14 ana 4 ÍL-ma 12 IGI.DUḪ.A šá ^{d}Sin IGI

D iii 13′ [ana] 4 ÍL-ma 12 IGI.D[UḪ].A š[á] ^{d}Sin IGI
HH iii 14 ana 4 ÍL-ma 12 IGI.DUḪ.A šá Sin IGI

ana 4 tanaššīma 12 tāmarta ša Sin tammar
by 4, and you find 12, the visibility of the Moon.

<u>iii 15</u> 40 NINDA nap-pal-ti u$_4$-mi u GI$_6$ ana 4 ÍL-ma 2,40 nap-pal-ti IGI.DUḪ.A IGI

D iii 14′ [4]0 NINDA nap-pal-ti u$_4$-mi u GI$_6$ ana 4 Í[L-ma] 15) [2],40 nap-pal-ti IGI.DUḪ.A [IGI]
HH iii 15 40 nap-pal-ti UD u GI$_6$ ana 4 ÍL-ma 2,40 nap-pal-ti IGI.DUḪ.A IGI
KK iii 1′ [IGI.D]UḪ.A [IGI]

40 NINDA nappalti ūmi u mūši ana 4 tanaššīma 2,40 nappalti tāmarti tammar
You multiply 40 NINDA, the interval-number for daytime and nighttime, by 4, and you find 2,40, the interval-number of the visibility.

<u>iii 16</u> DIŠ MUL$_5$.MUL$_5$ ŠIR^{meš}-šú SA$_5^{meš}$-ma KI.A SI.SÁ

D iii 16′ [DIŠ MU]L$_5$.MUL$_5$ ŠIR^{meš}-šú SA$_5^{meš}$-ma K[I.A SI.SÁ]
HH iii 16 DIŠ MUL$_5$.MUL$_5$ ŠIR^{meš}-šú SA$_5^{meš}$-ma KI.A SI.SÁ
OO 1′ [ ] SI.SÁ

šumma Zappu . . .-šu sāmūma ruṭibtu iššir
¶ If the . . .s of the Stars are red: the irrigated land will prosper.

<u>iii 17</u> DIŠ $^{mul}{}_5$Kár-šul ina ^{iti}ŠE uš-pa-lak-kam-ma BE ú-sa-naq-ma BE-nu

D iii 17′ [DIŠ ^{mu}]$^{l}{}_5$Kár-šul ina ^{iti}ŠE uš-pa-lak-kam-ma B[E]
HH iii 17 DIŠ $^{mul}{}_5$Kár-⸢šul⸣ ina ^{iti}ŠE uš-pa-la-ka-ma BE ú-sa-naq-ma BE-nu
KK iii 2′ [DIŠ $^{mul}{}_5$]Kár-šul ina ^{iti}ŠE uš-p[a-lak-kam-ma] 3′) BE-nu
OO 2′ [ ] BE ú-sa-naq-ma BE-nu

šumma Karšul ina Addari ušpalakkamma . . . usannaqma mūtānu
¶ If the constellation Karšul is opened wide in Month XII: . . ., deaths.

<u>iii 18</u> [DIŠ] ina lìb-bi $^{mul}{}_5$Kár-šul 1 MUL ma-gal KUR$_4$ ^{lú}KÚR

D iii 18′ [DIŠ ina lìb]-bi $^{mul}{}_5$Kár-šul 1 MUL ma-gal KUR$_4$ [ ]
HH iii 18 [DIŠ] ina ŠÀ $^{mul}{}_5$Kár-šú 1 ma-gal KUR$_4$-ma ^{lú}KÚR
OO 3′ [ ] ^{lú}KÚR

šumma ina libbi Karšul ištēn kakkabu magal baʾil nakru
¶ If one star inside of the constellation Karšul is very bright: the enemy.

<u>iii 19</u> DIŠ UD.DA 4 lu 2 GAL^{meš} SIG$_7^{meš}$ ma BE^{meš}

D iii 19′ [ ] ⸢x⸣ [l]u 2 GAL^{meš} SIG$_7$[^{meš} ma]
HH iii 19 DIŠ [UD.DA] 4 lu 2 GAL^{meš} SIG$_7^{me}$ ma BE^{meš}
KK iii 4′ [DIŠ U]D.DA [x l]u 2 GAL^{meš} SIG$_7^{meš}$ ma BE[^{meš}]
OO 4′ [ ]^{meš} ma BE^{meš}

šumma . . . 4 lu 2 rabûtu arqūma mūtānu
¶ If . . . 4 or 2 big ones are yellow: deaths.

<u>iii 20</u> DIŠ NIGIN ⸢x⸣ [x da]n-niš SA$_5^{meš}$-ma A.KAL u A.AN

HH iii 20 DIŠ NIGIN ⸢x⸣ [x da]n-niš SA$_5^{meš}$-ma A.KAL u PA.AN
KK iii 5′ [ ] u A.AN
OO 5′ [ ] ⸢u⸣ A.AN

šumma . . . danniš sāmūma mīlu u zunnu
¶ If . . . are very red: flood and rain.

iii 21 DIŠ $^{mul}{}_5$KU$_6$ ina ⌜x⌝ [x x] BE-ma SA$_5$ GAR u ba-il BE-ma un-nun u TUR BE-nu

HH iii 21 DIŠ $^{mul}{}_5$KU$_6$ ina ⌜x⌝ [x x] BE-ma SA$_5$ GAR u ba-il BE-ma un-nun u TUR BE-nu
KK iii 6′ [ ] ba-ìl BE-ma un-nun KAL BE-nu
OO 6′ [ ] u TUR BE-nu

šumma Nūnu ina . . . [. . .] šumma sūma šakin u baʾil šumma unnun u ṣeḫer mūtānu
¶ If the Fish in [. . .] either shows redness and is bright, or is . . . and small: deaths.

---

iii 22 DIŠ $^{mul}{}_5$U.RI.RI IGI.LÁ A.AN u A.KAL

E v 1′ [ ] ME
HH iii 22 DIŠ $^{mul}{}_5$U.RI.R[I IGI].LÁ A.AN u A.KAL
KK iii 7′ [DIŠ $^{mul}{}_5$U.RI.R]I ina ITI IGI A.A[N u A.KAL]
OO 7′ [A.K]AL

šumma . . . innamir zunnu u mīlu
¶ If the U.RI.RI-star becomes visible: rain and flood.

iii 23 DIŠ $^{mul}{}_5$U.RI.RI ana $^{mul}{}_5$ ^{giš}GIGIR KU.NU-ma ANŠE.PA+GÍN^{meš} BE^{meš}

E v 2′ [ ] ANŠE.PA+GÍN^{meš} GAM^{me}
HH iii 23 DIŠ $^{mul}{}_5$U.RI.R[I ana $^{mul}{}_5$ ^{giš}]GIGIR KU.NU-ma ANŠE.PA+GÍN^{meš} BE^{meš}
KK iii 8′ [DIŠ $^{mul}{}_5$U.RI].RI ana $^{mul}{}_5$ ^{giš}GIGIR KU.[NU-ma]

šumma . . . ana Narkabti iqribma sīsû imuttū
¶ If the U.RI.RI-star approaches the Chariot: horses will die.

iii 24 DIŠ $^{mul}{}_5$U.RI.RI ana $^{mul}{}_5$AB.SÍN KU.NU-ma ŠU.BI.AŠ.ÀM

E v 3′ [$^{mul}{}_5$AB.S]ÍN [K]U.NU-ma ŠU.BI.AŠ.ÀM
HH iii 24 DIŠ $^{mul}{}_5$U.RI.RI ana [$^{mul}{}_5$A]B.SÍN KU.NU-ma ŠU.BI.AŠ.ÀM
KK iii 9′ [DIŠ $^{mul}{}_5$U.RI].RI ana $^{mul}{}_5$AN ZI K[U.NU]-m[a]

šumma . . . ana Šerʾi iqribma ŠU.BI.AŠ.ÀM
¶ If the U.RI.RI-star approaches the Furrow: the same.

iii 25 DIŠ $^{mul}{}_5$U.RI.RI ana $^{mul}{}_5$ALLA KU.NU UR$_5$ MÁḪ GAM.ME

E v 4′ [ana] $^{mul}{}_5$ALLA KU.NU UR$_5$ [M]ÁḪ GAM.ME
HH iii 25 DIŠ $^{mul}{}_5$U.RI.RI ana $^{mul}{}_5$[AL]LA KU.NU UR$_5$ MÁḪ GAM.ME
KK iii 10′ [DIŠ $^{mul}{}_5$U.RI].RI ana $^{mul}{}_5$MUŠ KU.NU [ ]

šumma . . . ana Allutti iqrib tēret kabti imât
¶ If the U.RI.RI-star approaches the Crab: omen for an important person; he will die.

iii 26 DIŠ $^{mul}{}_5$U.RI.RI ana $^{mul}{}_5$ALLA 15 KU.NU UR$_5$ MÁḪ GAM.ME

E v 5′ [ ] ana $^{mul}{}_5$ALLA 15 KU.NU U[R$_5$ M]ÁḪ GAM.ME
HH iii 26 DIŠ $^{mul}{}_5$U.RI.RI ana $^{mul}{}_5$ALLA 15 KU.NU UR$_5$ MÁḪ GAM.ME
KK iii 11′ [DIŠ $^{mul}{}_5$U.RI].RI ana $^{mul}{}_5$MUŠ ZAG [KU.NU]

šumma . . . ana Allutti imitta iqrib: tēret kabti imât
¶ If the U.RI.RI-star approaches the Crab on the right: omen for an important person, he will die.

iii 27 DIŠ $^{mul}_{5}$U.RI.RI ana $^{mul}_{5}$ALLA 2,30 KU.NU IDIM GAM.ME

E v 6′ [DIŠ $^{mul}_{5}$U.RI.R]I ana $^{mul}_{5}$ALLA GÙB KU.NU [IDIM] GAM.ME
HH iii 27 DIŠ $^{mul}_{5}$U.RI.RI ana $^{mul}_{5}$ALLA 2,30 KU.NU IDIM GAM.ME
KK iii 12′ [DIŠ $^{mul}_{5}$U.RI].RI ana $^{mul}_{5}$MUŠ [ ]
TT r. 1′ [ ] ⸢NU$^{?}$⸣ [ ]

šumma . . . ana Allutti šumēla iqrib kabtu imât
¶ If the U.RI.RI-star approaches the Crab on the left: an important person will die.

---

iii 28 DIŠ $^{mul}_{5}$UG$_{5}$.GA ana id IM 1 KI.TA ina-pal ŠE.GIŠ.Ì SI.SÁ

E v 7′ [DIŠ $^{mul}_{5}$UG$_{5}$.G]A ana id IM 1 KI.TA ina-pal ŠE.GIŠ.Ì SI.SÁ
HH iii 28 DIŠ $^{mul}_{5}$UG$_{5}$.GA ana id IM 1 KI.TA ina-pal ŠE.GIŠ.Ì S[I.SÁ]
TT r. 2′ [IM] 1 KI ina-[pal] 3′) [ ] SI.SÁ

šumma Āribu ana id šūti šapliš innappal šamaššammu iššir
¶ If the Raven . . .s below to the direction of the South wind: sesame will prosper.

iii 29 DIŠ $^{mul}_{5}$UG$_{5}$.GA ana id IM 2 AN.TA ina-pal AB.SÍN ŠE NU SI.SÁ

E v 8′ [DIŠ ^{m}]$^{ul}_{5}$UG$_{5}$.GA ana id IM 2 AN.TA ina-pal AB.SÍN ŠE NU SI.SÁ
HH iii 29 DIŠ $^{mul}_{5}$UG$_{5}$.GA ana id IM 2 AN.[TA ina]-pal [AB.S]ÍN [ ]
TT r. 4′ [IM] 2 AN ina-pal 5′) [ ] ŠE NU SI.SÁ

šumma Āribu ana id iltāni elîš innappal šer'i še'i ul iššir
¶ If the Raven . . .s to the direction of the North wind: the barley crop will not prosper.

---

iii 30 DIŠ $^{mul}_{5}$UR.MAḪ MUL$_{5}^{meš}$-šú il-tap-pu-u 3,20 KI DU NÍG.È MUL$_{5}$ BI

E v 9′ DIŠ $^{mul}_{5}$UR.MAḪ MUL$_{5}^{meš}$-šú il-tap-pu-u 3,20 KI DU NÍG.È MUL$_{5}$ BI
HH iii 30 DIŠ ^{m}[$^{ul}_{5}$UR].MAḪ MUL$_{5}^{m}$[^{eš}-šú x x x] ⸢x⸣ ú 2,30 KI ⸢x⸣ NÍG.È M[UL$_{5}$ BI]
TT r. 6′ [ ]^{meš}-šú il-tap-pu-ú 7′) [ ] NÍG.È MUL$_{5}$ BI

šumma Nēšu kakkabūšu iltappû šarru ašar illaku lītu kakkabu šū
¶ If the stars of the Lion . . .: the king will be victorious wherever he goes. This star

iii 31 MUL$_{5}$ KASKAL

E v 9′ MUL$_{5}$ KASKAL
HH iii 31 MUL$_{5}$ KASKAL
TT r. 7′ MUL$_{5}$ KASKAL

kakkab ḫarrāni
is a campaign star.

iii 32 DIŠ $^{mul}_{5}$KAL.NE ÍB.TAG$_{4}$ RU ana 4 MUL$_{5}^{me}$ šá $^{mul}_{5}$AŠ.IKU TE UMUN URU GAM.ME

E v 10′ DIŠ $^{mul}_{5}$KAL.NE ÍB.TAG$_{4}$ RU ana 4 MUL$_{5}^{me}$ šá MUL$_{5}$.MUL$_{5}$ TE UMUN URU GAM

HH iii 32 DIŠ ^{mul_5}KAL.NE.N[E]$^?$ ⌜ÍB⌝.TAG$_4$ RU ana 4 MUL$_5^{me}$ šá MUL$_5$.MUL$_5$ TE UMUN URU GAM.ME
TT r. 8′ [ ] TAG$_4$ RU ana 4 MUL$_5^{meš}$ šá AŠ.IKU TE 9′) [ ] GAM.ME

šumma . . . ana 4 kakkabāni ša Ikî (var. Zappi) iṭḫi bēl āli imât
¶ If the KAL.NE-star . . .s and approaches the 4 stars of the Field (var. Stars): the lord of the city will die.

iii 33 DIŠ ^{mul_5} ^{d}EN.GIŠGAL.AN.NA KUR$_4$-ma A.AN u A.KAL ^{d}TIR.AN.NA UD ḪÉ.NUN MU.NE

E v 11′ DIŠ ^{d}EN.GIŠGAL.AN.NA KUR$_4$-ma A.AN u A.KAL 12) DIŠ ^{d}TIR.AN.NA UD ḪÉ.NUN MU.NE
HH iii 33 DIŠ ^{mul_5} ^{d}EN.URU.AN.NA KUR$_4$-ma A.KAL u A.AN : ^{d}TIR.AN.NA UD ḪÉ.NUN MU-šú
TT r. 10′ [A]N.NA KUR$_4$-ma A.AN u A. KAL

šumma EN.URU.AN.NA ba'ilma zunnu u mīlu : Manzât ūm$^?$ nuḫši šumša
¶ If Jupiter is bright: rain and flood. The name of the Rainbow is 'day$^?$ of abundance';

iii 34 DIŠ ina ^{im}U$_{18}$.LU A.AN ina ^{im}SI.SÁ A.KAL ina ^{im}KUR.RA A.AN ina ^{im}MAR GÌR.BAL

E v 13′ DIŠ ina ^{im}U$_{18}$ A.AN ina ^{im}SI.SÁ A.KAL ina ^{im}KUR A.AN ina ^{im}MAR GÌR.BAL
HH iii 34 ina ^{im}U$_{18}$.LU A.AN ina ^{im}SI.SÁ A.KAL ina ^{im}KUR.RA A.AN ina ^{im}MAR GÌR.BAL

ina šūti zunnu ina iltāni mīlu ina šadî zunnu ina amurri riḫṣu
¶ in the South, rain; in the North, flood; in the East, rain; in the West, devastation.

---

iii 35 DIŠ u$_4$-um ^{d}Li$_9$-si$_4$ IGI.LÁ 3 u$_4$-me mu-ši-ta LÚ NIGIN É-šú

E v 14′ DIŠ UD ^{d}Li$_9$-si$_4$ IGI.LÁ 3 u$_4$-mi mu-ši-ta LÚ NIGIN É-šú
HH iii 35 DIŠ u$_4$-um ^{d}Li$_9$-si$_4$ IGI.LÁ 3 u$_4$-me mu-ši-ta LÚ NIGIN É-šú

ūm Lisi innamru 3 ūmī mušīta amīlu siḫirti bītišu
¶ On the day the Lisi-star becomes visible, for 3 days a man should awaken at night all that is around his house,

iii 36 NAM.LÚ.U$_{18}$.LU GU$_4$ UDU.NÍTA ANŠE li-de-ek-ki

E v 15′ NAM.LÚ.U$_{18}$.LU GU$_4$ UDU.NÍTA ANŠE li-de-ek-ki
HH iii 36 NAM.LÚ.U$_{18}$.LU GU$_4$ UDU.NÍTA ANŠE li-de-ek-ki

amīlūta alpa immera imēra lidekki
people, cattle, sheep, donkeys,

iii 37 NU ina-al u ana ^{d}Li$_9$-si$_4$ lik-ru-ub KI NÍGIN É-šú uš-tak-lal

E v 15′ NU ina-al 16) u ana ^{d}Li$_9$-si$_4$ lik-ru-ub KI NÍGIN^{me} É-šú uš-tak-lal
HH iii 37 NU ina-al u ^{d}Li$_9$-⌜si$_4$⌝ lik-ru-ub DIB NÍGIN É-šú uš-tak-lal
KK iv 1′ [^{d}Li$_9$]-si$_4$ [ ]

lā inâl u ana Lisi likrub itti siḫirti bītišu uštaklal
and he must not sleep; he should pray to the Lisi-god, then he and all that is around his house will experience success.

---

iii 38 DIŠ ina ^{iti}GAN ina ^{iti}AB ina ^{iti}ZÍZ SI Sin 2,30 tar-ṣa-at-ma

E v 17′ DIŠ ina ^{iti}GAN ^{iti}AB ^{iti}ZÍZ SI Sin 2,30 tar-ṣa-at-ma
HH iii 38 DIŠ ina ^{iti}GAN [ina ^{iti}A]B ina ^{iti}ZÍZ SI Sin 2,30 tar-ṣa-at-ma
KK iv 2′ DIŠ ina [^{it}]^{i}GAN ^{iti}AB ^{iti}[ZÍZ]

šumma ina Kislīmi ina Ṭebēti ina Šabāṭi qaran Sin šumēla tarṣatma
¶ If in Month IX, in Month X, (or) in Month XI the left horn of the Moon is stretched out and

iii 39 KI ina-ṭal nu-uḫ-ḫu-ut ú-de-e

E v 18′ KI ina-ṭal nu-uḫ-ḫu-ut ú-de-e
HH iii 39 K[I] ina-[ṭal] nu-uḫ-ḫu-ut ú-de-e
KK iv 3′ K[I] ⸢x⸣ ḪU nu-uḫ-ḫu-[ut]

qaqqara inaṭṭal nuḫḫut udê
looks towards the earth: diminution? of trouble.

----

iii 40 DIŠ KUR ina ŠÀ ni-di KUR-ḫa 3,20 ŠÚR-ma ^{giš}TUKUL i-na-ši

HH iii 40 DIŠ KUR [ina Š]À? ŠUB KUR-ḫa 3,20 ŠÚR-ma ^{giš}TU[KUL] ⸢i-na⸣-ši
KK iv 4′ DIŠ ⸢x x⸣ ina ŠÀ ⸢ni-di⸣ KUR-ḫa ⸢x⸣ [ ]

šumma Šamaš ina libbi nīdi ippuḫa šarru izzizma kakka inašši
¶ If the Sun rises in a cumulus cloud: a king will become furious and raise weapons.

iii 41 DIŠ ^{d}UTU ina ŠÀ ni-di ŠÚ LUGAL BE

HH iii 41 DIŠ MIN ina MIN ŠÚ LUGAL BE
KK iv 5′ DIŠ ^{d}UTU ina ŠÀ [n]i-di ŠÚ [ ]

šumma Šamaš ina libbi nīdi irbi šarru imât
¶ If the Sun sets in a cumulus cloud: a king will die.

----

iii 42 DIŠ MUL TA ^{im}MAR SUR-ma ana ŠÀ ^{d}Li$_{9}$-si$_{4}$ KU$_{4}$ ḪI.GAR GÁL

HH iii 42 DIŠ MUL TA ^{im}MAR SUR-ma ana ŠÀ ^{d}Li$_{9}$-si$_{4}$ KU$_{4}$ ḪI.GAR GÁL
KK iv 6′ DIŠ MUL ⸢TA IM⸣.[4] SUR-ma ana ŠÀ [ ]

šumma kakkabu ištu amurri iṣrurma ana libbi Lisi īrub bārtu ibašši
¶ If a star flares up from the West and enters the Lisi-star: there will be revolution.

iii 43 DIŠ MUL TA ^{im}MAR SUR-ma ana ŠÀ ^{d}Ni-ri KU$_{4}$ ḪI.GAR GÁL

HH iii 43 DIŠ [MU]L TA ^{im}MAR SUR-ma ana ŠÀ ^{d}Ni-ri KU$_{4}$ ḪI.GAR GÁL
KK iv 7′ [DIŠ MU]L T[A] IM.4 SUR-ma ana ŠÀ [ ]

šumma kakkabu ištu amurri iṣrurma ana libbi Nīri īrub bārtu ibašši
¶ If a star flares up from the West and enters the Yoke: there will be revolution.

iii 44 DIŠ MUL TA ^{im}MAR SUR-ma ana ŠÀ ^{d}Sin KU$_{4}$ ḪI.GAR GÁL

HH iii 44 DIŠ MUL T[A ^{i}]^{m}MAR SUR-ma ana ŠÀ ^{d}Sin KU$_{4}$ ḪI.GAR GÁL
KK iv 8′ [DIŠ MUL] TA IM.4 SUR-ma ana ŠÀ [ ]

šumma kakkabu ištu amurri iṣrurma ana libbi Sin īrub bārtu ibašši
¶ If a star flares up from the West and enters the Moon: there will be revolution.

iii 45 DIŠ MUL [BI 3 šú]-nu È-ma ZI-bu NU kaš-du

HH iii 45 DIŠ ⸢MUL⸣ [BI 3 šú]-nu È-ma ZI-bu NU kaš-du
KK iv 9′ [ ]-nu È-ma Z[I-bu]

šumma kakkabu [šū 3-šu]nu ūṣima tību la kašdu
¶ If [this] star comes out (from the Moon) as three stars: unsuccessful attack.

---

iii 46 MUL [TA ^{i}]^{m}KUR ana ^{im}U$_{18}$.LU SUR-ma ^{mul}EN.TE.NA.BAR.ḪUM DIB-ma

U 1′ [KU]R ana ^{im}U$_{18}$.LU ⸢SUR⸣-[ma]
HH iii 46 MUL [TA ^{im}KUR] ana ^{im}U$_{18}$ SUR-ma ^{mul}EN.TE.NA.BAR.ḪUM DIB-ma
KK iv 10′ [MUL T]A ^{im}KUR ana ^{im}U$_{18}$ [SU]R-ma [ ]

<šumma> kakkabu [ištu] šadî ana šūti iṣrurma Ḫabaṣīrāna ītiqma
<If> a star flashes from the East towards the South, passes EN.TE.NA.BAR.ḪUM and

iii 47 ina ^{im}MAR ŠÚ 3 MU^{meš} KUR ḪÉ.NUN IGI

U 2′ [M]U^{meš} KUR nu-uḫ-šú [ ]
HH iii 47 ina [^{im}MAR ŠÚ 3] MU^{meš} KUR ḪÉ.NUN IGI
KK iv 11′ [ina] ^{i}[^{m}MA]R ŠÚ MU ⸢3⸣ KAM KUR [ ]

ina amurri irbi 3 šanāti mātu nuḫša immar
sets in the West: for three years the land will see abundance.

iii 48 [DIŠ MUL TA] ^{im}MAR ana ŠÀ ^{im}KUR DIB u$_{4}$-um 3 MU^{meš}

U 3′ [ ] ana ^{im}KUR.RA DIB-iq U[D]
HH iii 48 [DI]B u$_{4}$-um 3 MU^{meš}
KK iv 12′ [DIŠ MUL TA] ^{im}MAR ana ŠÀ ^{im}KUR DIB ⸢UD$^{?}$⸣ [ ]

[šumma kakkabu ištu] amurri ana libbi šadî ītiq ūm 3 šanāti
[¶ If a star] passes from the West to the middle of the East: (for) a period of three years

iii 49
HH iii 49 [KUR ḪUL] IGI.LÁ

[mātu lemutta] immar
[the land] will experience [evil.]

iii 50 [DIŠ MUL T]A MURUB$_{4}$ AN-e SUR-ma ina ^{d}UTU.ŠÚ.A ŠÚ-bi ZI.GA
U 4′ [S]UR-ma ina ^{d}UTU.ŠÚ.A ŠÚ-bi Z[I]
HH iii 50 [ina] ^{d}UTU.ŠÚ.A ŠÚ-bi ZI.GA
KK iv 13′ [DIŠ MUL T]A MURUB$_{4}$ AN-e SUR-ma ina ^{d}UTU.[ŠÚ].A ZI

[šumma kakkabu iš]tu qabal šamê iṣrurma ina ereb Šanši irbi ṣītu
[¶ If a star] flares up from the middle of the sky and sets in the West: a heavy loss

<u>iii 51</u> KALAG ina KUR È

U 4′ [ ]

HH iii 51 [KALAG ina KUR] È

KK iv 13′ KALAG ina KUR [È]

dannatu ina māti uṣṣi
will occur in the land.

<u>iii 52</u> [ ] ^{mul}GÍR.TAB IGI ^{im}U$_{18}$.LU GIN MU BI SIG$_5$

U 5′ [^{im}U$_{18}$.L]U GIN MU BI [ ]

HH iii 52 [^{i}]^{m}U$_{18}$ GIN MU B[I S]IG$_5$

KK iv 14′ [x] ⸢x x⸣ ^{mul}GÍR.TAB IGI ^{i}[^{m}]⸢U$_{18}$⸣ GIN MU BI SIG$_5$

[šumma] . . . Zuqāqīpi innamir šūtu illik šattu šī idammiq
[¶ If] . . . of the Scorpion becomes visible (and) the South wind blows: this year will be good.

<u>iii 53</u> ⸢DIŠ M⸣UL ⸢x x x x x x ṣir-ḫa NU TUK⸣ SIG$_5$

U 6′ [ ] ⸢x⸣ SIG$_5$$^{?}$ ṣir$^{?}$-ḫa NU T[UK]

HH iii 53 [ ] ⸢x⸣ [ ]

KK iv 15′ ⸢DIŠ M⸣UL ⸢x x x x x x ṣir-ḫa NU TUK⸣ SIG$_5$

šumma . . . ṣirḫa lā irašši idammiq
¶ If . . . does not have a flare: it will be good.

<u>Gap B 1</u> [DIŠ] MUL ^{d}AMAR.UTU ina SAG MU.AN.NA IGI MU BI AB.SÍN NÍG SI.SÁ

U 7′ [^{d}AMAR.U]TU ina SAG [M]U.AN.NA IGI.LÁ MU BI AB.S[ÍN]

KK iv 16′ [DIŠ] MUL ^{d}AMAR.UTU ⸢ina SAG⸣ MU.AN.NA I[GI] MU [B]I AB.SÍN NÍG SI.SÁ

[šumma] kakkab Marduk ina rēš šatti innamir ina šatti šâti šer'u iššir
[¶ If] the star of Marduk becomes visible at the beginning of the year: in this year the furrow will prosper

<u>Gap B 2</u> DIŠ MUL ^{d}AMAR.UTU MUL.MUL KUR-ud ina MU BI ^{d}IM RA

U 8′ ⸢DIŠ MUL⸣ ^{d}AMAR.UTU MUL.MUL KUR-ud MU BI ^{d}I[M]

KK iv 17′ DIŠ [MU]L ^{d}AMAR.UTU MUL.MUL KUR-ud ina MU BI ^{d}IM RA

[šumma] kakkab Marduk Zappa ikšud ina šatti šâti Adad iraḫḫiṣ
[¶ If] the star of Marduk reaches the Stars: in this year Adad will devastate.

<u>Gap B 3</u> DIŠ MUL ^{d}AMAR.UTU ^{mul}UGA KUR-ud ŠE.GIŠ.Ì NIM GIŠ

U 9′ DIŠ MUL ^{d}AMAR.UTU ^{mul}UGA^{mušen} KUR-ud ŠE.G[IŠ.Ì]

KK iv 18′ [DIŠ MU]L ^{d}AMAR.UTU ^{mul}UGA^{mušen} KUR-ud ŠE.GIŠ.Ì NIM GIŠ

šumma kakkab Marduk Āriba ikšud šamaššammu ḫarpu iššir
¶ If the star of Marduk reaches the Raven: early sesame will prosper.

Gap B 4 DIŠ MUL ^{d}AMAR.UTU pa-gar LÚ IGI be-en-nu DAB-su

U 10′ DIŠ MUL ^{d}AMAR.UTU pa-gar LÚ IGI be-en-n[i]
KK iv 19′ [DIŠ MUL] ^{d}AMAR.UTU pa-gar NA IGI be-en-nu DAB-su
PP 1′ [ ] pa-g[ar]

šumma kakkab Marduk pagar amīli īmur bennu iṣabbassu
¶ If the star of Marduk sees the body of a man: epilepsy$^{?}$ will seize him.

Gap B 5 DIŠ ina ma-ḫar MUL ^{d}AMAR.UTU LÚ A ir-muk NAM.TAG.GA GÁL-ši

U 11′ DIŠ ina ma-ḫar MUL ^{d}AMAR.UTU LÚ ⸢A^{meš}⸣ ir-muk [ ]
KK iv 20′ [DIŠ ina IGI] ^{d}AMAR.UTU NA A ir-⸢muk⸣ NAM.TAG.⸢GA⸣ GÁL-ši
PP 2′ [DIŠ ina I]GI ^{d}AMAR.[UTU L]Ú [ ]

šumma ina maḫar kakkab Marduk amīlu mê irmuk arnu ibašši
¶ If a man takes a bath in front of the star of Marduk: there will be guilt.

Gap B 6 DIŠ MUL ^{d}AMAR.UTU GI_{6}-ma IGI.LÁ MU BI A.SÌG GÁL-ši

U 12′ DIŠ MUL ^{d}AMAR.UTU GI_{6}-ma IGI.LÁ MU BI ⸢Á⸣.[SÌG]
FF vi 1′ [DIŠ MU]L ^{d}AMAR.UTU GI_{6}-ma IGI.LÁ ⸢MU⸣ B[I]
KK iv 21′ DIŠ MUL ^{d}AMAR.UTU GI_{6}-ma IGI.LÁ MU BI Á.[S]ÌG GÁL-ši
PP 3′ DIŠ MUL AMAR.UTU [ ]

šumma kakkab Marduk ṣalimma innamir šatta šâti asakku ibašši
¶ If the star of Marduk is dark when it becomes visible: in this year there will be *asakku*-disease.

Gap B 7 DIŠ ^{mul}ŠUDUN ina È-šú da-ʾi-im A.KAL up-pu-lu È

U 13′ DIŠ ^{mul}ŠUDUN ina È-šú da-ʾi-im A.KAL up-p[u-
FF vi 2′ [DIŠ] $^{mul}{}_{5}$ŠUDUN ina È-šú da-[ʾi-im] 3) A.KAL up-pu<-lu> È
KK iv 22′ DIŠ ^{m}[^{ul}ŠU]DUN ina È-šú da-ʾi-im A.KAL up-pu-⸢lu⸣ È
PP 4′ DIŠ ^{mul}ŠUDUN [ ]

šumma Nīru ina aṣîšu daʾim mīlu uppu<lu> uṣṣi
¶ If the Yoke is dim when it comes out: the late flood will come out.

Gap B 8 DIŠ ^{mul}ŠUDUN ina È-šú it-ta-na-an-paḫ A.KAL ḫar-pu

U 14′ DIŠ ^{mul}ŠUDUN ina È-[šú it-t]a-na-an-paḫ A.K[AL]
FF vi 4′ DIŠ $^{mul}{}_{5}$ŠUDUN ina È-šú it-ta-na-an-paḫ A.KAL ḫ[ar-pu]
KK iv 23′ DIŠ ^{mul}ŠUDUN ina È-šú it-ta-na-an-paḫ A.⸢KAL ḫar⸣-pu
PP 5′ DIŠ ^{mul}ŠUDUN [ ]

šumma Nīru ina aṣîšu ittananpaḫ mīlu ḫarpu
¶ If the Yoke keeps flaring up when it comes out: early flood.

iv 1 DIŠ ^{mul}ŠUDUN ina È-šú GIM IZI it-ta-na-an-paḫ $BURU_{14}$ SI.SÁ

U 15′ DIŠ ^{mul}ŠUDUN ina È-[šú GIM IZ]I it-ta-na-an-p[aḫ]
FF vi 5′ DIŠ $^{mul}{}_{5}$ŠUDUN ina È-šú GIM IZI MIN $BURU_{14}$ SI.SÁ

HH iv 1 [DIŠ ^{m}]^{ul}ŠUDUN ina È-šú GIM IZI it-ta-na-an-p[aḫ B]URU$_{14}$ SI.SÁ
KK iv 24′ DIŠ ^{mul}ŠU[DUN ina] È-šú [G]IM I[ZI] it-<ta>-na-an-paḫ B[URU$_{14}$]
PP 6′ DIŠ ^{mul}ŠUD[UN]

šumma Nīru ina aṣîšu kīma išāti ittananpaḫ ebūru iššir
¶ If the Yoke keeps flaring up like fire when it comes out: the harvest will prosper.

iv 2 DIŠ ^{mul}ŠUDUN ina È-šú šup-pul-ma da-ʾi-im A.KAL NU GÁL

U 16′ DIŠ ^{mul}ŠUDUN ina È-[šú šup-pul]-ma da-ʾa-am$^{?}$ ⌜x⌝ [ ]
FF vi 6′ DIŠ $^{mul}_{5}$ŠUDUN šup-pul-ma da-ʾi-im A.KAL NU GÁL
HH iv 2 [DIŠ ^{m}]^{ul}ŠUDUN ina È-šú šup-pul-ma DARA$_{4}$ A.KAL NU GÁL
KK iv 25′ DIŠ ⌜^{mul}⌝[ŠUDUN] ina È-šú šup-⌜pul⌝-ma da-ʾi-im A.KAL NU GÁL
PP 7′ DIŠ ^{mul}Š[UDUN]

šumma Nīru ina aṣîšu šuppulma daʾim mīlu ul ibašši
¶ If the yoke is very low and dim when it comes out: there will be no flood.

iv 3 DIŠ ^{mul}ŠUDUN ina È-šú ana ^{d}UTU.ŠÚ.A IGI-šú GAR-nu ^{im}MAR.TU ZI-ma

D iv 1′ [DIŠ ^{mu}]^{l}ŠUDUN ina [ ]
U 17′ [DIŠ ^{mul}]ŠUDUN ina⌜È⌝-[šú ana ^{d}UTU.ŠÚ].A IGI-šú šak-⌜nu⌝ [ ]
FF vi 7′ DIŠ $^{mul}_{5}$ŠUDUN ina È-šú ana ^{d}UTU.ŠÚ.A IGI-šú GAR-nu 8) ^{im}MAR.TU ZI-ma
HH iv 3 [DIŠ ^{m}]^{ul}ŠUDUN ina È-šú ana ^{d}UTU.ŠÚ.A IGI-šú GAR-nu ^{im}MAR.TU ZI-ma
KK iv 26′ DIŠ ^{mul}[ŠUDUN ^{d}U]TU.ŠÚ.A IGI-šú GAR-nu ^{im}[MAR.TU] ZI-ma

šumma Nīru ina aṣîšu ana ereb Šamši pānūšu šaknū amurru itbīma
¶ If the Yoke is turned towards sunset when it comes out, (if) the West wind rises and

iv 4 ana ^{im}U$_{18}$.LU is-ḫur ina ^{iti}KIN UD 10 KAM šal-pú-ti KUR GAR-an

D iv 2′ ana ^{im}U$_{18}$.LU is-[ḫur ina]
U 18′ [ana] ^{im}U$_{18}$.LU is-ḫur ina ^{iti}KIN ⌜UD 10 KAM⌝ [ ]
FF vi 8′ ana ^{im}U$_{18}$.LU is-ḫur 9) ina ^{iti}KIN UD 10 KAM šal-pú-ti KUR GAR-an
HH iv 4 ana ^{im}U$_{18}$ NIGIN ina ^{iti}KIN UD 10 KAM šal-pú-tì KUR GAR-an
KK iv 27′ ana ^{im}U$_{18}$ NIGIN ⌜ina ^{iti}KIN⌝ UD 10 KAM šal-pu-ti [KU]R GAR

ana šūti isḫur ina Ulūli UD 10 šalputti māti iššakkan
turns to South: on the 10th day of Month VI destruction of the land will be brought about.

iv 5 DIŠ ^{mul}ŠUDUN ina È-šú ana ^{d}UTU.TU.TU IGI-šú GAR-nu IGI AN-e IGI.BAR-ma

D iv 3′ [DIŠ ^{mu}]^{l}ŠUDUN ina È-šú [ ] IGI-šú GAR-nu [IGI AN-e] 4) IGI.BAR-ma
U 19′ [DIŠ ^{m}]^{ul}ŠUDUN ina È-šú ana ^{d}UTU.TU.[TU]
FF vi 10′ DIŠ $^{mul}_{5}$ŠUDUN ina È-šú ana ^{d}UTU.TU.TU IGI-šú GAR-nu 11) IGI AN-e IGI.BAR-ma
HH iv 5 [DIŠ ^{m}]^{ul}ŠUDUN ina È-šú ana ^{d}UTU.TU.TU IGI-šú GAR-nu IGI AN-e IGI.BAR-ma
KK iv 28′ DIŠ ^{mul}x ina È-[šú] ana ^{d}U[TU.T]U.TU IGI-šú GAR-nu IGI AN-[e IGI.BAR]-ma
RR 1′ [T]U IGI-šú GAR-nu [ ]

šumma Nīru ina aṣîšu ana ereb$^{?}$ Šamši pānūšu šaknū pān šamê ippalisma
¶ If the Yoke is turned towards Sunset$^{?}$ when it comes out and faces the front of the sky,

iv 6 IM mim-ma la i-zi-iq SU.KÚ GAR-an BAL NAM.GILIM.MA

D iv 4′ IM mim-ma la i-zi-qa SU.KÚ GAR-[an] 5) BAL NAM.GILIM.MA
U 20′ [I]M mim-ma la i-zi-qa [ ] 21) [BA]L ⸢NAM.GILIM⸣.MA
FF vi 11′ IM mim-ma la RI-qa 12) SU.KÚ GAR-an BAL NAM.GILIM.MA
HH iv 6 IM mim-ma la i-zi-iq SU.KÚ GAR BAL NAM.GILIM.MA
KK iv 28′ ⸢IM⸣ [mi]m-⸢ma la i⸣-z[i-i]q 29) SU.KÚ GAR-an 30) [B]AL NA[M.GIL]IM.MA
RR 2′ [ ] GAR BAL NAM.GILIM.[MA]

šāru mimma la izīq ḫušaḫḫu iššakkan palê šaḫluqti
and no wind blows: there will be famine; dynasty (ending in) catastrophe.

iv 7 šá I-bí-^{d}Sin LUGAL ŠEŠ.UNUG^{ki} šá ka-mu-us-su

D iv 5′ šá I-bí-^{d}Sin LUGAL ŠEŠ.UNUG^{ki} 6) šá ka-mu-us-su
U 21′ šá I-bí-[ ]
FF vi 13′ šá I-bí-^{d}Sin LUGAL ŠEŠ.UNUG^{ki} 14) ka-mu-us-su
HH iv 7 ŠÀ.BAD I-bí-^{d}Sin LUGAL ŠEŠ.UNUG^{ki} ka-mu-us-su
KK iv 30′ ŠÀ ⸢I-bi⸣-^{d}Sin ⸢LUGAL⸣ Š[EŠ.UNU]G^{ki} ka-mu-su
RR 3′ [š]á ka-mu-us-s[u]

ša (var. . . .) Ibbi-Sin šar Uri ša kamûssu
(omen) of Ibbi-Sin, king of Ur, who went in fetters

iv 8 a-na An-ša-an^{ki} DU-ku ERÍN-šú EGIR-šú i-bak-ku-ú KIMIN i-ma-aq-qu-tu

D iv 6′ a-na An-ša-an^{ki} DU-⸢ku⸣ 7) ERÍN-šú EGIR-šú i-bak-ku-ú KIMIN i-ma-aq-qu-tu
U 22′ [x x] ⸢x x x ŠU$^{?}$ ku$^{?}$ x⸣ [ ] 23) [x x x] ⸢x⸣ [x x] ⸢x x⸣ [ ]
FF vi 14′ ana An-ša$_{4}$-an^{ki} DU-ku 15) i-bak-ku-ú KIMIN i-ma-qu-tu
HH iv 8 [x] ⸢x ku$^{?}$⸣ UN^{meš} šá-an^{ki} DU i-ba-ak-ku-u KIMIN i-ma-qú-tu-ú
KK iv 30′ ⸢ana$^{?}$⸣ DU.DU 31) [x] DU i-[ba-a]k-ku-u u$^{?}$ [i-m]a-aq-qú-tu
RR 4′ [ ]-ku-u u i-mi-qu-[x x]

ana Anšan illiku ummānšu arkišu ibakkû KIMIN imaqqutū
to Anšan; after him his troops weep, variant: fall.

---

iv 9 DIŠ šum-ma LÚ ana NUN-ti GAR-ma ^{im}U$_{18}$.LU DU LÚ BI SIG$_{5}$

D iv 8′ DIŠ šum-ma LÚ ana NUN-ti GAR-ma ^{im}U$_{18}$.LU DU LÚ B[I] SIG$_{5}$
U 24′ [ ] ⸢x⸣ [ ]
FF vi 16′ [DIŠ šum-m]a LÚ ana NUN-ti GAR-ma ^{im}U$_{18}$.LU DU BAL SIG$_{5}$
HH iv 9 [DIŠ šum-m]a LÚ ana NUN-ti GAR-ma ^{im}U$_{18}$.LU DU LÚ BI SIG$_{5}$
KK iv 32′ DIŠ [B]E-ma LÚ [ana NUN-t]i GAR-ma IM-1 DU BAL SIG$_{5}$
QQ 1′ [L]Ú ana NUN-[ ]
RR 5′ [D]U NA BI SIG$_{5}$

šumma amīla ana rubûti iškunūma šūtu illik amīlu šū (variant: palû) idammiq
¶ If they make a man a ruler, and the South wind blows: this man (var.: the dynasty) will become good.

iv 10 DIŠ MIN-ma ^{im}SI.SÁ DU NINDA SIG KÚ

D iv 9′ DIŠ MIN-ma ^{im}SI.SÁ DU NINDA SIG [KÚ]
FF vi 17′ [DIŠ MIN-ma] ^{im}SI.SÁ DU NINDA SIG KÚ
HH iv 10 [ ] ^{im}SI.SÁ DU NINDA SIG KÚ

KK iv 33′ DIŠ IM-2 DU NINDA SIG [K]Ú?
QQ 2′ [BE]-ma LÚ ana NUN-ti [ ]
RR 6′ [D]U NINDA [ ]

šumma amīla ana rubûti iškunūma iltānu illik akala qatna ikkal
¶ If they make a man a ruler, and the North wind blows: he will eat thin? bread.

iv 11 DIŠ MIN-ma imKUR.RA DU UDme-šú LUGÚD.DAmeš

D iv 10′ DIŠ MIN-ma imKUR.RA DU UDme-šú LUGÚD.D[Ameš]
FF vi 18′ [DIŠ MIN-ma] imKUR.RA DU UDmeš-šú LUGÚD.DAmeš
HH iv 11 [ ] imKUR.RA DU UDme-šú LUGÚD.DAmeš
KK iv 33′ DIŠ IM-3 DU UDmeš-šú KU.D[A]
QQ 3′ BE-ma LÚ ana NUN-t[i]

šumma amīla ana rubûti iškunūma šadû illik ūmūšu ikarrû
¶ If they make a man a ruler, and the East wind blows: his days will be short.

iv 12 DIŠ MIN-ma imMAR.TU DU NU SI.SÁ

D iv 11′ DIŠ MIN-ma imMAR.TU DU NU SI.[SÁ]
FF vi 19′ [DIŠ MIN-ma imM]AR.TU DU NU SI.SÁ
HH iv 12 [ ] im[MA]R.TU DU NU SI.SÁ
KK iv 34′ [DIŠ] IM-4 DU NU S[I.SÁ]
QQ 4′ [BE-m]a LÚ ana NUN-t[i]

šumma amīla ana rubûti iškunūma amurru illik ul iššir
¶ If they make a man a ruler, and the West wind blows: he will not prosper.

Colophons

A

iv 40 [. . . D]U-ak DUB.1.KAM MUL.APIN
[. . . tra]vels. Tablet I of MUL.APIN

iv 41 [. . . kīma] SUMUN-šú ⸢SAR⸣-ma IGI
[. . . According] to its original written and checked.

D

iv 12 DIŠ mulSAG.ME.GAR dŠul-pa-è-[a?]
Jupiter (is) Šulpa'e.

iv 13 2 UŠ 41 ÀM MU.ŠID.BI DUB.2.KAM MUL.APIN NU AL.TIL gaba-ri Bár-sipak[i]
161 are its lines. Tablet II of MUL.APIN, not finished. Original from Borsippa.

iv 14 GIM SUMUN-šú SAR-ma IGI.TAB pa-liḫ dNa-bi-um ina sar-ti NU GIŠ-[šú?]
According to its original written and checked. He who reveres Nabû must not take it away fraudulently.

K

Upper edge 1 [. . . DUM]U ^{I}KI-^{d}ŠÚ-TIN A ^{I}Mu-še-zib
[. . . so]n of Itti-Marduk-balāṭu, descendant of Mušēzib.

2 [. . .] ^{d}Taš-me-tu$_{4}$ u ^{d}KI.ZA.ZA šá É-⌜zi$^{?}$⌝-[da$^{?}$]
[. . .] Tašmetu and . . . of Ezi[da$^{?}$]

3 [. . .] ^{I}Se-lu-ku LUGAL
[. . .] king Seleucus.

k

iv 1′ [. . .]^{meš}

AA

iv 1′ ⌜x⌝ [. . .]
. . . [. . .]

iv 2′ [AM]AR [. . .]
son of [. . .]

iv 3′ [AM]AR [. . .]
son of [. . .]

iv 4′ ⌜^{iti}⌝[. . .]
Month [. . .]

iv 5′ ⌜lim-mu ^{I}Man-nu⌝-[. . .]
Eponym Mannu-[kî-Adad$^{?}$ . . .]

DD

Rev. 8′ [GI]M SUMUN-šú SAR-ma bà-rì DU[B$^{?}$]
According to its original written and collated. Tab[let$^{?}$ . . .]

Rev. 9′ [^{lú}]ŠAMAN.LÁ TUR ša IR ^{d}UTU [ ]
small apprentice scribe. Whoever carries it away, may Šamaš [carry him away.]

Rev. 10′ [ša in]a dan-na-n[i] ⌜e⌝-kim-š[u]
[whoever] takes it away by force [. . .]

HH

iv 13 šà-ṭar ^{Id}PA-SAG-i-ši ^{lú}ŠAB.TUR daq-qu
Document of Nabû-rēšu-iši, small apprentice scribe,

iv 14 [mār ^{I}x x]-ri-bà ^{lú}A.BA BAL.TIL^{ki}-ú
[son of . . .]-rība, scribe from Assur,

iv 15 [DUM]U ^{I}x [x x]-šur ^{lú}A.BA-um-ma
son of . . . [. . .]-šur, also scribe,

iv 16 DUMU ^{I}Ḫa-ṭu-⸢x⸣ [x ^{lú}]A.BA-um-ma
son of Ḫaṭu[. . .], also scribe,

iv 17 [x x x x] ^{lú}A.BA-um-ma
[descendant of . . .,] also scribe.

iv 18 ^{iti}A-da-ri [U]D ⸢x⸣ KÁM
Month I, xth day,

iv 19 [lim]-mu ^{Id}Sin-PA[P]^{meš}-ri-bà LUGAL GAL [LUGAL d]an-nu
Eponymy of Sennacherib, the great king, the strong [king,]

iv 20 [LUG]AL KUR ^{d}[Aš]-šur
king of Assyria.

KK
iv 35 [DIŠ M]UL.APIN ZAG.T[IL].LA.BI.[ŠÈ]
MUL.APIN, to its end.

iv 36 [x] ^{Id}UTU-x-eri-ba ⸢x x⸣ Aš-šur$^{?}$ ⸢x⸣ [x x]
[Tablet$^{?}$ of] Šamaš-. . .-eriba, . . . of Assur, [. . .]

NN
rev. 10 [IM.GÍD].DA ^{Id}Na-bi-um-NUMUN-SUM.NA ^{lú}ŠAMAN.LÁ TUR
[Long] tablet of Nabû-zeru-iddin, young apprentice scribe.

Philological notes

Most of the text was well established at the time of the earlier edition in 1989. A few more manuscripts were found since; for Tablet I, they confirmed what was known. In Tablet II the gaps can now be bridged, although the damaged state of some passages still prevents complete understanding.

This commentary occasionally corrects the earlier edition or mentions additional material. The vertical wedge at the beginning of a line, transliterated DIŠ and represented in the translation by the sign ¶, was discussed in Watson and Horowitz (2011: 61f).

Tablet I

i 1ff.:
Many of the star names occur also in the 'Great Star List'; see Koch-Westenholz (1995: 187–205). Many god names can be found in the *Reallexikon der Assyriologie*. I only note additions that came to my attention.

i 3:
For the relation between the constellations ŠU.GI and En-me-šár-ra, see Schaumberger (1935: 327).

i 4:
DIŠ is restored at the beginning of this line because every constellation in this list is preceded by DIŠ. Sources BB and CC consistently omit DIŠ everywhere; in

AA and DD, the entry is given on the same line as the preceding entry, and DIŠ is normally omitted in those cases; the others are broken. For the writing of GÀM in manuscript BB, see Hätinen (forthcoming).

i 5:
The reading of the god name has been shown to be Lugalirra rather than Lugalgirra.

i 6:
The last sign in source AA may be MAḪ, as proposed by Weidner (1915: 142, n. 6), but is damaged on the tablet. For the god Alammuš, see Simons (2017). He is found together with Nin-gublaga also in Šurpu VIII 25; see Reiner (1958: 40).

i 11:
Eru has a date palm frond (*sissinnu*) in her right hand according to CAD s.v. sissinnu. CAD quotes LBAT No. 1510: 11; however, it is not at all clear that in this passage *sissinnu* has to do with Eru, mentioned in line 8′. The description of Eru in VAT 9428 r. 1–3 (Weidner 1927; Beaulieu et al. 2018) does not mention a *sissinnu.*

i 12:
ŠU.PA is frequently followed by Enlil, so ŠU.PA Enlil may mean 'ŠU.PA of Enlil'; reading and meaning are, however, still uncertain. A. L. Oppenheim in Pritchard (1969: 310, n. 8), proposed a derivation from Akk. šūpû 'shining forth', but one would expect an occasional variation in writing, such as šu-pu-ú or similar.

i 13:
For the different meanings of *sukkallu* see the CAD; we use 'minister' for convenience.

i 15:
Prayers to ^{mul}MAR.GÍD.DA are listed by Mayer (1976: 429f.).

i 21:
The star IBILA.É.MAḪ is the same as IBILA.AN.MAḪ; see Bezold et al. (1913: 43) and Gössmann (1950: No. 191). The latter occurs in the hemerologies 4R 32 i 48 and 4R 33* i 49. IBILA.AN.MAḪ fits better the Akkadian paraphrase māru reštû ša Anim here in MUL.APIN; IBILA.É.MAḪ is, however, the usual writing.

A prayer to IBILA.É.MAḪ occurs in Köcher (1980) No. 542 iii' 13ff. (I owe this reference to E. Reiner).

i 23:
DIŠ before the second constellation in this line is restored because F and probably DD have it. BB always omits it, and, in A and AA, both entries are in one line, in which cases DIŠ is omitted; see above to line i 4.

i 27:
For the reading of Nin-SAR as Nin-nisi(g) see Cavigneaux (1995: 65).

i 28:
^{mul}UD.KA.DUḪ.A probably has the Akkadian reading *nimru*. We retain the translation ‘Panther’ of the CAD for convenience; a literal translation is ‘Demon with the gaping mouth’. According to the *Reallexikon der Assyriologie und Vorderasiatischen Archäologie*, ’Leopard’ is more likely to be the correct identification.

i 29:
In Assyrian script, the signs ŠAḪ and ŠUL are different. Of the two Assyrian sources of this line, one has ŠAḪ, the other ŠUL. As ŠUL can be read šáḫ, the reading /šaḫ/ is preferred. The decision to read this star name as šaḫ is supported by a lexical compendium from Sippar (Fadhil and Hilgert 2007: 100), where the star names ^{mul}ŠAḪ = *šá-ḫu-u* and ^{mul}ANŠE.KUR.RA = *si-su-u* occur next to each other, as in MUL.APIN.

i 29f.:
Source BB has these two lines in inverse order, and spread over three lines.

i 36f.:
Unfortunately, no new evidence has come up to clarify this passage. My literal translation of *ugdammirūni* as ‘have been finished’ was chosen to fit the description of Jupiter’s visibility at sunrise, when all the stars have become invisible because of the light of the approaching sun; this explanation was given by Schaumberger (1935: 313). The word is translated by Horowitz (2014: 21) and by CAD s. v. nēberu mng. 3a as ‘have completed (their courses)’. I rather expect a preterite here (see von Soden 1995: § 172c) and therefore take the verb as Dt. The translation by Robson (2007), ‘have been assembled’, would refer to a different scenario when the stars of the path of Enlil are visible.

Horowitz (2014: 20–25) argues that Nēberu first was a name of Mercury, then, in the first millennium, mostly used for Jupiter. Furthermore, he understands the parallel passage in ‘Astrolabe B’ II rev. ii 13 as referring to the heliacal rising of Mercury at the New Year. This is a rare coincidence, and I do not see why Mercury would have been chosen when other planets can be seen at the New Year in their heliacal rising, equally rarely, but more easily visible than Mercury. But, even without the constraint of heliacal rising, Mercury’s visibility is less frequent than that of other planets.

Horowitz (2014: 22) takes BAR as a writing for *zâzu*, ‘to divide’. In CAD s. v. mašālu mng. 8, a reading *uštamšil* is proposed on the basis of parallels.

I cannot add to the collection of references given in the earlier edition, p. 126.

i 38:
The verb KÚR.KÚR-*ir* here and in the similar passages I ii 13ff. and II i 8 and 40 presents a reading problem. As the sentence contains both a subject (the planet) and an accusative object (*manzāssu*), the verb has to be transitive. Further, the intended form of *nakāru* should be present tense because it is in paratactic relation to *ibbir*, which certainly is present; we therefore expect *uttanakkar*. Unfortunately, the phonetic complement –*ir* after KÚR.KÚR does not agree with this, as it indicates either *ittanakkir* or *uttakkir*. Syllabically written parallels do in fact have *ut-ta-na-kar*, and our passage is therefore listed under *nukkuru* in CAD s. v. nakāru mng. 11g. Although there is no doubt about the meaning of these passages, the writing with –*ir* remains puzzling; it is assumed here that the Gtn-stem (*ittanakkir*) is meant, with a rare transitive usage, for which see CAD s. v. nakāru mng. 3a.

i 39:
A gate in the Aššur temple in the city of Assur was named after the 'Path of the Enlil stars'; see Frahm (1997: 165).

i 40:
In 'Astrolabe B' i 1 and 7, ^{mul}AŠ.IKU is the dwelling of Anu; see Horowitz (2014: 33).

i 44:
The translation of MUL.MUL as 'The Stars' takes the logogram literally. The Akkadian equivalent is *zappu*, 'bristle, mane'. The importance of this group of stars can be seen from the fact that they are used *pars pro toto* for the sign Taurus in later texts. Prayers addressed to them are listed in Mayer (1976: 431f).

ii 1:
The identification of *is lê* with *agê Anim* is also found in 'Astrolabe B' II obv. i 8 (see Horowitz 2014: 37, and CAD s. v. agû A mng. 1a – 2'b', where more references can be found).

ii 2:
On the name SIPA.ZI.AN.NA and its Akkadian equivalents, see Oelsner (2005: 120), with previous literature. Prayers to this constellation are listed in Mayer (1976: 431). In translating, we use the Sumerian logogram 'True Shepherd of Anu'.

ii 4:
For Lulal and Latarak, see Wiggermann (1992: 63f.).

ii 6:
KAK.SI.SÁ here is clearly an arrow; its identification with Sirius is certain from other sources. Less certain is which other stars belonged to this constellation; one

expects at least one more star to make a straight line, and Prokyon has been suggested already by Bezold et al. (1913: 49 and 59). In Pingree and Walker (1988: 315f.), KAK.SI.SÁ has a left foot and an elbow, suggesting a much larger image. Prayers addressing KAK.SI.SÁ are listed by Mayer (1976: 430f.).

ii 7:
In 'Astrolabe B' II obv. i 15 (Horowitz 2014: 37), the Elamite Ištar is called daughter of Anu.

ii 8:
For the snake god Niraḫ, see the *Reallexikon der Assyriologie und Vorderasiatischen Archäologie* s. v. In von Weiher (1988: No. 114A r. v 47), we find MUL.^{d}MUŠ = *ni-ra-ḫu* (Ḫḫ XXII), similarly in IM 132506 r. vi 11′, see Fadhil and Hilgert (2007: 100).

ii 9:
a-ri-bu is probably a gloss to ^{mul}UGA^{mušen}.

ii 10:
The reading *šer'u* is found in Ḫḫ XXII: ^{mul}AB.SÍN = *ši-ir-'u* (von Weiher 1988: No. 114A r. v 45), also in IM 132506 r. vi 7′; see Fadhil and Hilgert (2007: 100). A picture of Virgo with an ear of grain incised on a tablet can be found in Weidner (1967: pl. 10).

ii 12:
The logogram LÚ.BAD as a star name may have the reading *šalamtu*, as given in the star list in IM 132506 r. v 19′; see Fadhil and Hilgert (2007: 99).

ii 22:
The star name EN.TE.NA.BAR.ḪUM is to be read *ḫabaṣīrānu* according to the lexical list Ur$_5$-ra XXII; see von Weiher (1988: No. 114A r. iv 105). It seems to be related to *ḫabaṣīru* or *ḫumṣīru*, which is a kind of mouse. The logogram contains the word for 'cold' or 'winter', EN.TE.NA, but is otherwise unclear. As it is only used for the star name and not for the animal, its meaning may be different. We translate it by 'mouse', following Robson (2007).

ii 27:
The writing ŠÚ^{meš} of source A is probably an error.

^{mul}NU.MUŠ.DA has a reading *nammaššû*; see CAD s.v. nammaššû, and von Weiher (1988: No. 114A r. iv 127). The association with Adad is also attested in the lexical commentary ḪAR-gud B VI 48; see Reiner and Civil (1974: 41).

ii 34:
A syllabic writing of SUḪUR MÁŠ is attested once on a *kudurru* from Susa (see CAD s. v. *suḫurmašû*). The two signs may, however, have been read as two

words, as indicated by the writing SUḪUR *šá* MÁŠ in *Astronomical Diaries*; see Sachs and Hunger (1988: No. –567 rev. 10′).

ii 36f.:
These lines are quoted in a Neo-Assyrian letter, Parpola (1993: No. 62), which mentions a wooden writing board containing MUL.APIN.

ii 41ff.:
The beginnings of lines in this section on first visibilities are probably preserved on source EE col. ii. Unfortunately, little is legible. I assume that the third line from the end can be restored to DIŠ *ina* ^{iti}A[B . . .], which would correspond to iii 7 in the main text. The traces preceding it could also conform to the main text, but certainty cannot be achieved.

ii 42:
^{mul}UR.GU.LA is equated with *La-ta-rak* in the star list IM 132506 v 26′ (see Fadhil and Hilgert 2007: 99), and in parallel texts (see Oelsner 2003). Although these lists seem to consider Latarak as a reading of UR.GU.LA, the loanword *urgulû* is well attested.

ii 44a:
This line is present only in sources M and N, and possibly in Y (there would be enough space for it in the broken part of Y r. 7).

ii 46f.:
These two lines are excerpted on an exercise tablet; see Lambert (1960: pl. 73 VAT 8573 r. 10f; with variant IGI-*mar* for IGI).

iii 7:
SIM.MAḪ has the Akkadian reading *šinunūtu* 'swallow'; therefore, *šinunūtu* is most likely an explanatory gloss here, in spite of source V, which inserts *u* 'and' between the names. Of IM.ŠEŠ, not even the reading in this context is certain; see CAD s.v. marratu C; *marratu* is a word for 'rainbow'. We take it to be another gloss in view of the verb IGI.LÁ (singular) in sources A and H; admittedly, source E has a plural indicator (IGI.LÁ^{me}). So, there seems to have been some confusion about the identity of the three names in this line referring to only one constellation.

iv 2: KUR *u* ŠÚ could also be read *napāḫa u rabâ* here, but the same phrase occurs in iv 8, where clearly nouns are intended.

iv 8:
Source X has 'the chest of the observer of the sky' instead of 'your chest'.

iv 13:
kumāru is a word for 'border, edge'(?); *qumāru* is probably a part of the arm; see CAD s.vv. As UD.KA.DUḪ:A, whether it is an animal or of human shape, has

feet and knee, it is more likely that here too a body part is meant. In translating 'shoulder', we follow Parpola (1983: 93).

iv 31f.:
As there is no doubt that the Moon, a singular, is the subject of the second part of the relative clause, the writings DIB^{meš} and TAG^{meš} can only be explained as indicating iterative verbal forms, not plurals; this is appropriate as the passing of the Moon through the constellations is repeated regularly each month. *etēqu* is construed with the accusative, and so *ina* at the beginning of line 32 is probably a mistake; note that *ina* ought to be followed by a genitive, whereas *pi-rik-šu-nu* is better understood as accusative.

Tablet II

The gaps in this tablet could be partially filled from newly found manuscripts. It is now possible to provide an uninterrupted sequence of lines, even if some of them are completely destroyed. We nevertheless have not changed the line numbering of the earlier edition, except that Gap A is now longer than previously thought.

i 1–8: Readings given in Weidner (1923: 194) could only partially be verified by collation of source HH; see the copy in Hunger (1982: 128).

i 7f.:
The summary in line 7 adds the preceding planets and the Sun to make 6 gods, but one would have expected the Moon to be included as the seventh. In line 7, there does not seem to be enough space in the broken part of source HH to accommodate everything contained in D.

The reading *manzāzu* for NA was suggested in Sachs and Hunger (1988: 21) and has been confirmed several times since; see, for example, George (1992: 385).

In line 8 (and line i 40), one could read the verb KÚR.KÚR-*ru* as *uttanakkarū*, thereby avoiding the problem in reading Tablet I i 38 and ii 13–15 where the logogram is complemented by *-ir*.

i 11:
The head of the Lion can be identified with ε Leonis; it is among the 'Normal Stars' used for reference in the *Astronomical Diaries*; see Sachs and Hunger (1988: 18).

i 17:
The error of confusing UR.GU.LA and GU.LA is present in both the preserved sources (both Assyrian). Unfortunately, the Babylonian sources are broken here. UR.GU.LA instead of GU.LA also occurs twice in exemplars of the 'Astrolabe' tradition; see Horowitz (2014: 124).

i 20:
Source KK seems to have a writing error here.

i 21:
There is not enough space in the break in source HH to contain all that is in the duplicate KK; as *ina* is still visible just before the break, I expect IGI MUL.MUL to be broken away and EGIR ^{mul}ḪUN.GÁ left out.

i 26:
MÚ is here to be read *nipḫu*. Proof of this reading is the parallel passage in i 41 where KUR is written in place of MÚ; the only Akkadian reading common to both signs is *nipḫu*. *nipḫu* is the most frequent word for the 'rising' (lit., 'flaring up') of stars. Many omens derive predictions from the appearance of a celestial body at its *nipḫu* (see CAD s. v. nipḫu mng. 1).

i 27:
risnu, 'soaking', is taken to mean 'to pale, to expire' (said of a star or planet at heliacal rising when it disappears in the light of the rising sun) by Koch (1998: 112).

i 27–31:
The connection between horse, bitumen, and river water was explained by Freedman (2014) as follows: 'at low water and high temperature, . . . bitumen may cake horses' hooves and pollute watercourses. At high water and low temperature, the oil may be dilute and the bitumen solid to the touch'. The time of the year (Month VI, in line 25) is one of high temperature, and so the explanation given by Freedman fits. However, in lines 29–31, the injunction is reversed, and horses are allowed 'to touch bitumen and drink river water'. In the understanding of Freedman, a cooler time of year would be required to justify this change. This cooler season would have to be indicated by *ultatapûni*. This expression seems to mean that the stars mentioned are already well visible, as opposed to their first visibility in line 26. I do not see a change of season expressed by *ultatapûni*. It only takes a few days after first visibility to see stars well; so then, offerings could be made to them (line 30), and the horses need not be restrained any more.

In i 40–43, quite the same expressions are used in regard to the planets enumerated in i 38f., just before. Here, no indication of a time in the year is possible; therefore, the reason why horses may 'touch bitumen' is not obvious. Maybe it has to do with the offerings that are presented to the planets in the preceding line.

i 28:
The remnants of the verb in the beginning of this line could be combined into tunaṣṣar, reading *[tu-n]a-an-ṣar* in HH and *tu-na-a*[*ṣ-ṣar*] in JJ. Unfortunately, the D-stem of *naṣāru* is attested only in texts from outside Mesopotamia; see CAD s.v. naṣāru mng. 14.

i 29:
The reading and understanding of the verb in this line as third pers. plur. masc. perf. of *šūtapû* were suggested to me by W. von Soden.

i 32f.:
As in the preceding lines, the appearances of constellations in Months VIII and XII are mentioned in i 32f. and i 34–37. The wind blowing at this occasion is to be observed, but no mention of horses or any other action follows.

i 35f.:
These lines are largely parallel to i 26 and i 41, but still cannot be restored satisfactorily.

i 38:
Mercury frequently has the apposition *ša Ninurta šumšu*, 'whose name is Ninurta', also in astrological texts.

i 39:
The names 'The Scales' and 'Star of Šamaš' for Saturn are attested several times in cuneiform literature; see Parpola (1983: 342f.) and Brown (2000: 69f).

i 40:
For KÚR.KÚR-*ru*, see above to line i 8.

i 41f.:
The beginnings of these lines are restored from the similar passages i 7f. and i 27.

i 44:
Before *ereb Šamši*, *ina* has to be inserted to make the sentence conform to Akkadian syntax. *ina* is also missing before *ereb Šamši* in line 46; but there is no doubt that both instances are mistakes, as is shown by the parallel passages in the following paragraphs.

i 45:
The reading of KIMIN that introduces alternative words or sentences cannot be established in every case. It is sometimes to be read *šaniš*, sometimes *ašaršani*; other readings are possible too.

UD 15 KAM can be read *šapattu*, 'half a month'; in the similar passage i 55, the text writes 15 *ūmī* unambiguously.

i 49f.:
20 and 30 days as the normal duration of invisibility of Jupiter are quoted in a Neo-Assyrian letter; see Parpola (1993: No. 362) and Parpola (1983: 287, fn. 526).

i 53–59:
These lines have a parallel in Thureau-Dangin (1922: No. 16 rev. 36–42; *Enūma Anu Enlil* Tablet 56). There are only minor variants between the two texts: In i 55, the second KIMIN is shown to be an error for KI.3 by the parallel; on the other

hand, in this same line, ITU before 15 *ūmī* is erroneously omitted by the parallel. In i 58, Enūma Anu Enlil 56 writes É-MEŠ, 'summer', instead of BURU_{14}, 'harvest time'.

i 63:
From the parallel structure of red – bright, *unnun* – small, one would conclude that *unnun* is most likely a colour. The same expression occurs in iii 21.

I repeat the references to *unnun* in Enūma Anu Enlil provided by E. Reiner for the earlier edition:

K. 6021+8611 r. 5′: [. . .KI].GUB-*sà un-nun ú-tan-na-at-ma*

[If Venus . . .] her position is *unnun*, i.e. she becomes faint (see Reiner and Pingree 1998: 84)

K.229+7935:54: [. . . *un-nu-t*]*a*$^?$*-at* : *un-nu-na-at* TUR [. . .]

[If Venus . . . becomes] faint$^?$, i.e. she is *unnun* (and) small$^?$ [. . .] (see Reiner and Pingree 1998: 175)

K.11395:2′: BE-*ma* SA_5 GAR *u ba-il* BE-*ma un-nun u* SIG_7

Either it shows redness and is bright, or it is unnun and yellow (probably referring to Mercury).

i 64f.:
These lines are duplicated by Enūma Anu Enlil 56 r. 35f.; see above on i 53–59. Only the remark about the colour of Saturn is different: whereas it can be 'red' or 'white' according to MUL.APIN, it is said to 'show redness' in Enūma Anu Enlil 56 (SA_5 GAR, read *sūma šakin*).

i 68–71:
As stated in line 71, this section names the constellations by means of which one can establish the direction of a wind blowing at nighttime. In many omens, predictions vary according to the direction of the wind blowing at the moment of observation of some phenomenon. It was therefore necessary to have markers in the sky to identify the direction of a wind, even at night. The verb used for describing the position of the constellations mentioned, *parāku*, 'to lie across, to stretch', implies a certain imprecision. The passage cannot, therefore, be used to date the text, as was tried by Papke (1978: 42f).

ereqqu is fem., so GIL-át is correct, but *zuqāqīpu* is masc., so one expects just GIL. The end of the line is, however, damaged.

Gap A:
The length of gap A in manuscript HH can be estimated by comparing columns i and ii. In addition, it can be seen that the intercalation rules beginning in Gap A 8 go through the months of the year in sequence. The months can be restored reliably on the basis of the heliacal risings of the constellations, as given in Tablet I.

For Month IV in Gap A 12–15, to the appearance of Sirius an additional note is appended, similar to the one for Month X; only the last part of it is attested in UU. It is here provisionally restored in parallel to line ii 3, and to i 9–12. The length of Gap A was underestimated in the earlier edition.

Gap A 8f.:
This first intercalation rule ('Plejaden-Schaltregel') was discussed very early by Assyriologists; see Schaumberger (1935: 340–344). Other rules based on the date of conjunction of the Moon and Pleiades are found in Hunger and Reiner (1975).

Of the dates in these two lines, only day 3 is preserved in line 8. To find a meaningful intercalation rule, day 1 was always restored in line 7. However, other restorations are possible. In Virolleaud (1908–1911: 2nd Supp 19: 22; commentary *Sin ina tāmartišu* tablet IV), we read: [DIŠ *ina* ^{iti}B]ÁR UD 3 KAM MUL$_4$. MUL$_4$ *u sin ta-mur-šú-nu-ti-ma šit-qul-lu* MU BI *eš-ret*, 'if on the 3rd day of Month I you see the Pleiades and the Moon and they are in balance, this year is normal'. To agree with this, Gap A 7 would have to be restored with the date Month I day 3, and Gap A 8 with Month II day 3. This would be parallel to the intercalation rules following in MUL.APIN.

The practice of intercalation is discussed in letters to the Assyrian king: see Parpola (1993: Nos 42 and 253), with discussion in Parpola (1983: 45, 186, 285) and Hunger (1992: No. 98), discussed in Parpola (1983: 342).

Gap A 10ff.:
In the pairs of statements for normal and intercalary years, the first line is introduced by the marker DIŠ, the second by šumma, 'if'. Therefore (contrary to my earlier translation), the first lines contain statements of the 'normal' state of the calendar, and the second lines begin with 'If (however)', thus referring to the requirement of a correction of the calendar by intercalation. Whether this formulary was also used in the partly broken lines 8f. is uncertain.

Gap A 12:
To the appearance of Sirius, an additional note is appended, similar to the one for Month X in col. ii 3; only the last part of it is attested in source UU. It is here tentatively restored in parallel to line ii 3, and to i 9–12.

ii 1f.:
Only source UU preserves the names of Months VII and VIII in these lines. Thereby, Month VII is used twice, contrary to the overall layout of this section, which seems to have each month once. Under the assumption that each month occurs once, Months VIII and IX were restored in the earlier edition, but this is not necessary. The full moon near Pleiades in Month VII occurs in Tablet II i 14–16.

UU also seems to have mixed the rising of ŠU.PA and the conjunction of the full Moon with Pleiades in these lines, because LÁL ('is balanced') is preserved in UU 8′, where one expects IGI.LÁ ('become visible'). UU has a separation line after UU 9′ (= ii 1), which the other sources do not have.

A further problem is the gap between obverse and reverse of UU. According to Hätinen (forthcoming), there is a space of 1 or 2 broken lines both at the end of the obverse and at the beginning of the reverse. There is no text for such a gap available in the parallel source JJ, which continues with Month X. Therefore, it remains unclear what might have to be restored in this gap, and on which criteria a possible intercalation rule may have been based.

ii 5:
EE differs from the other manuscripts by adding the words *ina līlâti*, 'at night'; this would not fit the risings of the constellations Fish and Old Man, and so it is not certain which constellation should be restored in this partly broken source. As 'at night' does occur in the preceding line of the text, its repetition may just be a scribal error. The 15th day of Month XII is listed as the normal time for the heliacal rising of Fish and Old Man also in Tablet I iii 12.

It is not clear why source UU does not continue with this last intercalation rule but ends its excerpt with Month XI.

ii 7:
I do not know how this line is to be connected to the following line, whose beginning is unclear.

ii 8:
Readings are very uncertain. KK seems to have more text (at the beginning of the line) than the other manuscripts. The sense of 'you name this year' can only be guessed; a year could be 'named' either normal or intercalary. This is somehow arrived at from searching the risings of the fixed stars that are mentioned in line 7.

ii 9:
The computation mentioned here must lead to the decision of intercalating, as seen in line 10. Something like the 'excess days' may be meant.

ii 11:
As *šutākulu* is infinitive, I am inclined to read the DIŠ at the beginning of the line as *ana*; unfortunately, it is missing in HH. *šutākulu* means 'to multiply'; this does not make much sense here.

ii 14: *udazallû* is translated 'correction' because the real year is here assumed to differ by this amount from the schematic year of 360 days. See Sachs and Neugebauer (1956: 135, n. 4).

udazallû is rendered by Ossendrijver (2012: 599) as '*uddazallû*-coefficient', as most of the occurrences in procedure texts do not help in understanding the term. A constant 6,40 occurs as '*udazallû* of the day' in extispicy calculations, see Koch (2005: 457, r11′); its astronomical significance is unknown, if there is any.

ii 18–20:
Why these intercalary months are connected with certain reigns is unclear; all three do occur in documents from Old Babylonian times. In the first millennium, only Months XII and VI are attested as intercalary.

ii 19:
The reading of the intercalary month Addaru as *A. arkû* is frequently attested in Neo-Babylonian texts.

ii 22:
The expression x *ina ammati* for 'x cubits' is attested from the first half of the second millennium on, both in Assyria and Babylonia; see CAD A/2 s. v. ammatu A. Reports concerning the observation of the equinox are available in Hunger (1992: 140–142); see also Parpola (1983: 360).

ii 41:
The translation 'interval-number'" for *nappaltu* follows al-Rawi and George (1991–1992: 61f.).

iii 16ff.:
The section of omens that make up the rest of MUL.APIN from this point on is still unclear in many respects. Some of them are found in Enūma Anu Enlil; others appear so far only here. It is not apparent why these omens and no others were included in MUL.APIN.

I repeat the lines from Rm 308 + 79-7-8, 117+223 in the earlier edition, which are parallel to iii 16–19:
DIŠ MUL$_5$.MUL$_5$ ŠIR^{meš}-*šú* SI$_4$^{meš}-*ma* KI.A SI.SÁ
DIŠ MUL$_5$.KÁR.ŠUL *ina* ^{iti}ŠE *uš-pa-la-ka-ma* BE *ú-sa-naq-ma* BE-*nu*
DIŠ *ina* ŠÀ MUL$_5$.KÁR.ŠUL 1 MUL *ma-gal* KUR-*ma* ^{lú}KÚR
DIŠ ⸢UD$^?$.DA⸣ 4 *lu* 2 GAL^{me} SIG$_7$^{me}-*ma* [BE]^{meš}
[x] ⸢x⸣ NU u 3 SIG$_7$^{me}-*ma* [A.KAL] *u* A.AN

In this and the next section, the determinative for 'star' is written with the sign GÁN, which has a reading MUL$_5$. This is rare but nevertheless attested outside MUL.APIN as well (I changed the transliteration MUL$_4$ of the earlier edition to MUL$_5$, to conform to Borger (2003: 505)).

The constellation in iii 16 is therefore most likely to be read MUL$_5$.MUL$_5$, Pleiades. The following ŠIR is frequently a sign for *išku*, 'testicle'; this would imply that the constellation is a man or an animal. Pleiades, however, is the mane of the Bull, not the Bull itself. So either the constellation is not Pleiades, or ŠIR has a different meaning. Therefore I did not translate it.

iii 17:
The signs GÁN.ŠUL are attested in god lists, with the reading ^{d}Kár-šul, among names of the goddess Ištar (CT 25, 30 r. 16; CT 24, 41: 76; also Erimḫuš V 4, in Cavigneaux et al. 1985: 67). A personal name containing it occurs in a colophon in Hunger (1976: No. 39: 14′). Ištar can be represented by several stars, and especially by Venus, but Venus does not fit line iii 18, where Kár-šul has more than one star.

ušpalakkâmma (from *nepelkû*) means 'he/she/it opens' (transitive). No satisfactory sense can be found for this in the present context. The following words, BE *usannaqma*, are equally unclear. *usannaq* means 'he controls, checks'; the meaning 'to approach', frequent in celestial omens, is attested only for the G-stem of *sanāqu*.

The meaning of the apodoses here and in the following lines as referring to 'death' was found by George (1991: 303).

iii 19:
The reading UD.DA is uncertain also in the parallel Rm 308+, mentioned above. UD.DA usually is to be read *ṣētu*, 'light', but here one expects a constellation, although no determinative for 'star' is present.

iii 21:
unnun, as in i 63, is parallel to 'shows redness' and therefore seems to be a colour. In i 63 it occurs in a description of Mars. The Fish may be used for Mars according to Virolleaud (1908–1911: Supp. No. 49: 7f.), but the damage in the one preserved manuscript prevents a reading.

iii 22:
The U.RI.RI-star here and in the following lines is said to 'approach' other constellations and so it must be a planet (or some other moving celestial body). In Virolleaud (1908–1911: Ishtar 33: 8), it occurs (without star determinative) among omens derived from Mercury; so, it may be a name for this planet. In Virolleaud (1908–1911: Ishtar 29: 10), $^{mul}{}_{5}$U.RI.RI stands near to the shoulder of the Moon.

iii 23:
PA+GÍN was identified as a writing for ḪUR.SAG 'mountain' by Cavigneaux (1987). Confirmation can be found in George (1992: 314; in the temple name é.PA+GÍN.ti.la), and there are more references in Lambert (2007: 153), also for PA+GÍN as a writing for KUR, so that a translation 'horses' (elsewhere written ANŠE.KUR.RA) is completely justified.

iii 26f.:
According to these lines, the constellation ALLA had a right and a left part; or the text may just mean that U.RI.RI approaches ALLA from the right or from the left. The variant MUŠ in source KK may simply be due to a damaged original.

iii 28f.:

These lines also occur in Virolleaud (1908–1911: Ishtar 23: 5f. and 24: 6f.). There, the verb is written *in-na-pal*; the apodoses of the omens are partly different. No meaningful translation of the N-stem of *napālu* can be offered.

There seems to be no dividing line in HH after iii 29.

iii 30:

This line occurs also in Virolleaud (1908–1911: Supp. 2 No. 78 iv 4), and in Hunger (1992: No. 289: 3f., 54: 6f., 437: 3f). Reiner (2004: 6) suggests that *iltappû* 'refers to a great brightness', based on the explanation with Jupiter in Hunger (1992: No. 289: 3ff).

iii 32:

KAL.NE occurs in another omen in Virolleaud (1908–1911: Ištar 24: 9 and Supp. 2 No. 81: 3): DIŠ ^{mul}UG$_5$.GA *ana* ^{ul}KAL.NE *iṭḫi*, 'If the Raven approaches the KAL.NE star'.

ÍB.TAG$_4$ is a word for 'rest, remaining amount', in Akkadian *šapiltu* or *rēḫtu*. In astronomical context it occurs in Virolleaud (1908–1911: Sin 3: 84): DIŠ SIN *ina* ÍB.TAG$_4$ *innamir*, 'If the Moon appears in ÍB.TAG$_4$'. Here, ÍB.TAG$_4$ is something around the Moon, like a cloud or a halo. Under this assumption, one could take RU in the present line of MUL.APIN as ŠUB, logogram for *iddi* (from *nadû*), and translate 'if the KAL.NE-star produces an ÍB.TAG$_4$' (see CAD s.v. nadû mng. 3b).

MUL$_5$ and IKU are the same sign; in sources E and HH it is written twice, in source TT once. The two signs can therefore be understood as MUL$_5$.MUL$_5$, i.e. Pleiades; the single sign would be the Field. As the Field has 4 stars, and the Pleiades 7, I prefer the variant in TT, even if the two other manuscripts both have Pleiades. Of course, one can also assume that TT erroneously omitted one of the two signs.

iii 33:

My copy in Hunger (1982: 132) mistakenly omits the UD sign before ḪÉ.NUN.

The explanation UD *nu-uḫ-šú* MU.NE for TIR.AN.NA occurs also in CT 26 40 iv 6; see Weidner (1959–1960: 108) *ad* iii 29.

The variant EN.URU.AN.NA suggests a reading uru$_{17}$ for GIŠGAL here. EN.GIŠGAL.AN.NA is Jupiter; the omen is quoted, and EN.GIŠGAL.AN.NA is explained as SAG.ME.GAR, in the astrological report in Hunger (1992: No. 254: 7).

iii 34:

Here the appearance of a rainbow in each of the four wind directions is used as an omen.

iii 38f.:

These lines are also found in Pinches (1884: 46, No. 1: 54f.) and in Virolleaud (1908–1911: Sin 4: 23). *nuḫḫutu* means 'to trim, to clip'; the apodosis remains unclear, whether one translates *udû* as 'tools' or connects it with *uddû*, 'trouble, calamity', as is tentatively proposed in Caplice (1964: 63, n. 10). In the two texts quoted above, an ancient explanation is added (which unfortunately does not help us to understand the text): *šá* 3 ITI^{meš} *an-nu-ti* UD 14 KAM DINGIR KI DINGIR NU IGI : *šá* UD 30 KAM NU DIRI^{meš}, '(it means) that for these 3 months one god was not seen with the other on the 14th day (i.e. Sun and Moon were not opposite each other on the 14th day); (or,) that (the Moon) repeatedly did not complete the 30th day (i.e. the months were only 29 days long)'.

iii 40:
Source HH seems to have KUR (or another sign beginning like KUR) where one expects Šamaš from the parallels quoted in CAD s. v. nīdu B.

iii 42–45:
These lines have parallels in Virolleaud (1908–1911: Supp. 2, No. 63 iv 2–5). Line 45 can be restored from K 2292: 5, which is also parallel to this section.

iii 43:
A star/constellation *nīrum* is also attested in Mari and Tuttul, but it must be different from its Babylonian counterpart; see Marti (2002) and Reculeau (2002).

iii 46–51:
This section is parallel to Virolleaud (1908–1911: Supp. 2, No. 63: iv 6–9).

iii 53:
Cf. CT 40 40 r. 27, Virolleaud (1908–1911: Ishtar 5: 3): DIŠ ^{mul}*Dili-bat ṣir-ḫa* NU TUK SIG$_5$. Unfortunately, there are more traces than this in the line here.

Gap B 1:
The usual writing for *iššir* is SI.SÁ; NÍG SI.SÁ seems to be an error (only one source is preserved).

Gap B 2–5:
These omens also occur in K 6185+ (partly published in Virolleaud (1908–1911: Supp. 2 No. 69: 5–8) with slight variations.

Gap B 6:
This omen is quoted in the Neo-Assyrian letter in Parpola (1993: No. 67 r. 1–3).

Gap B 7 - iv 8:
These omens are also found in Enūma Anu Enlil Tablet 55 (as reconstructed by E. Reiner), but in different order: see Virolleaud (1908–1911: Ishtar 21: 1ff.); CT 51 144: 1ff.

Gap B 7:
Uppulu, 'late', is restored here because of the contrast to *ḫarpu*, 'early', in the following line. The last four signs of line 7 could be read *ár-bu-tú illak*(DU), but then *mīlu*(A.KAL) does not fit. A confusion may have arisen early in the manuscript tradition so that both preserved sources show *up-pu*. Instead of *mīlu uppu<lu> uṣṣi*, one could also amend the text to read *mīlu up-pu-lu*(text: UD) *illak*(DU).

Gap B 8:
Cf. Virolleaud (1908–1911: Ishtar 21: 5).

iv 1:
Cf. CT 51 144: 4.

iv 2:
Cf. Virolleaud (1908–1911: Ishtar 21: 4). This omen is quoted, but with a different apodosis, in the astrological report in Hunger (1992: No. 73: 1–3).

iv 3f.:
Cf. Virolleaud (1908–1911: Ishtar 21: 8f.) and CT 51 144: 7f. Quoted in Hunger (1992: No. 546, r. 4f.).

iv 5:
^{d}UTU.TU.TU may be a playful writing for *ereb šamši*, 'sunset', on the basis of TU (= KU$_4$) as logogram for *erēbu*; the parallel in Enūma Anu Enlil Tablet 55 (Virolleaud, 1908–1911: Ishtar 21: 12ff. and CT 51 144: 9) has ^{d}UTU.ŠÚ.A. The omen is quoted in Hunger (1992: No. 546, r. 6f.).

iv 7:
ŠÀ.BAD could stand for *amūtu*, 'omen', or another word of the same meaning; the parallel in Virolleaud (1908–1911: Ishtar 21: 13) has BÀ-*ut*.

iv 8:
The second part of the sentence may still be a dependent clause: '(and) after whom his troops weep . . . '.

I cannot read the remnants of signs in source U, despite the recent edition by Fincke (2017). In HH too, some mix-up seems to have occurred in the first part of the line: most of the signs are there, but their sequence is wrong.

In Virolleaud (1908–1911: Ishtar 21: 12f.), the apodosis is somewhat abbreviated to *ka-mu-us-su ana An-ša$_4$-an*^{ki} DU-*ku i-bak-ku-ú*, 'who went in fetters to Anšan, weeping'. In CT 51 144: 11, *kamūssu* (LAL-*su*) is preceded by what looks like É.⸢GAL⸣.

KIMIN may be an error for Ù; sources KK and RR have u. On the other hand, *imaqqutū* may be an old variant of *ibakkû* and therefore correctly marked by

KIMIN; the variant would have been faithfully copied until it became part of the established text and was then connected to the sentence by *ù* instead of the original KIMIN.

iv 9:
BAL in source KK is a mistake for NA BI. This mistake is also present in FF; it seems to have crept into the tradition early.

iv 9–12:
Paralleled by CT 40 39f., 52ff.; there, *iš-ku-nu* is written instead of GAR. Restoration of the beginnings of lines 10–12 in source HH is uncertain. To judge from line 12, where there is not enough space in the broken beginning for [DIŠ MIN-*ma*], the lines were probably just indented, and no repetition signs written.

Colophon of A:
At the end, the name of the scribe and possibly a date are broken.

Colophon of D:
iv 13:
The statement *ul qati* (NU AL.TIL) in colophons usually implies that another tablet of the same composition is to follow. Line iv 12 accordingly has to be considered a catch-line, with which the following tablet would begin. There are texts beginning with ^{mul}SAG.ME.GAR ^{d}Šul-pa-è, but they are not long enough to constitute a third tablet of MUL.APIN; they are also not called MUL.APIN (see Hunger and Pingree 1989: 8f.).

Colophon of K:
For the family of Mušezib, see Oelsner (2000: 810); he dates the scribe of K to the beginning of the second century BC.

Colophon of AA:
For a reading of AMAR as *māru*, see CAD s. v. *māru* lex. section; it does occur occasionally in colophons.
The name of the eponym is probably to be restored as Mannu-kî-Adad (who held the office in 683 BC), because the tablet comes from the same archive as source HH, which is dated to 687 BC.

Colophon of DD:
The last line's broken end will have contained a curse.

Composite text and translation

I i 1	DIŠ $^{mul\,giš}$APIN ^{d}En-líl a-lik pa-ni MUL^{meš} šu-ut ^{d}En-líl
I i 2	DIŠ ^{mul}UR.BAR.RA ^{giš}NÍNDA šá ^{mul}APIN
I i 3	DIŠ ^{mul}ŠU.GI ^{d}En-me-šár-ra
I i 4	[DIŠ] ^{mul}GÀM ^{d}Gam-lum
I i 5	DIŠ ^{mul}MAŠ.TAB.BA.GAL.GAL.LA ^{d}Lugal-ir$_{9}$-ra ù ^{d}Mes-lam-ta-è-a
I i 6	DIŠ ^{mul}MAŠ.TAB.BA.TUR.TUR ^{d}Alammuš ù ^{d}Nin-EZEN×GUD
I i 7	DIŠ ^{mul}AL.LUL šu-bat ^{d}A-nim
I i 8	DIŠ ^{mul}UR.GU.LA ^{d}La-ta-ra-ak
I i 9	DIŠ MUL šá ina GABA ^{mul}UR.GU.LA GUB-zu ^{mul}LUGAL
I i 10	DIŠ MUL^{meš} um-mu-lu-tu$_{4}$ šá ina KUN ^{mul}UR.GU.LA
I i 11	GUB-zu sis-sin-nu ^{d}E$_{4}$-ru$_{6}$ ^{d}Zar-pa-ni-tu$_{4}$
I i 12	DIŠ ^{mul}ŠU.PA ^{d}En-líl šá ši-mat KUR i-šim-mu
I i 13	DIŠ MUL šá ina IGI-šú GUB-zu ^{mul}Ḫé-gál-a-a-ú SUKAL ^{d}Nin-líl
I i 14	DIŠ MUL šá EGIR-šú GUB-zu MUL BAL.TÉŠ.A SUKAL ^{d}MÚŠ
I i 15	DIŠ ^{mul}MAR.GÍD.DA ^{d}Nin-líl
I i 16	DIŠ MUL šá KI za-ri-i šá ^{mul}MAR.GÍD.DA GUB-zu
I i 17	^{mul}KA$_{5}$.A ^{d}Èr-ra gaš-ri DINGIR^{meš}
I i 18	DIŠ MUL šá ina SAG.KI ^{mul}MAR.GÍD.DA GUB-zu ^{mul}U$_{8}$ ^{d}A-a
I i 19	DIŠ ^{mul}MU.BU.KÉŠ.DA ^{d}A-num GAL-ú šá AN-e
I i 20	DIŠ ^{mul}MAR.GÍD.DA.AN.NA ^{d}Dam-ki-an-na
I i 21	DIŠ MUL šá ina ṭur-ri-šú GUB-zu ^{mul}IBILA.É.MAḪ
I i 22	DUMU res-tu-ú šá ^{d}A-nu-um
I i 23	DIŠ ^{mul}DINGIR.GUB.BA^{meš} šu-ut É-kur <DIŠ> ^{mul}DINGIR.TUŠ.A^{meš} šu-ut É-kur
I i 24	DIŠ ^{mul}ÙZ ^{d}Gu-la
I i 25	DIŠ MUL šá ina IGI ^{mul}ÙZ GUB-zu ^{mul}UR.KU
I i 26	DIŠ MUL né-bu-ú šá ^{mul}ÙZ ^{d}LAMMA SUKAL ^{d}Ba-Ú
I i 27	DIŠ 2 MUL^{meš} šá EGIR-šú GUB^{meš}-zu ^{d}Nin-SAR u ^{d}Èr-ra-gal
I i 28	DIŠ ^{mul}UD.KA.DUḪ.A ^{d}U.GUR
I i 29	DIŠ MUL šá ina ZAG-šú GUB-zu ^{mul}ŠAḪ ^{d}Da-mu
I i 30	DIŠ MUL šá ina GÙB-šú GUB-zu ^{mul}ANŠE.KUR.RA
I i 31	DIŠ MUL šá EGIR-šú GUB-zu ^{mul}lu-lim SUKAL MUL.MUL
I i 32	DIŠ MUL^{meš} um-mu-lu-tu$_{4}$ šá ina GABA ^{mul}lu-lim
I i 33	GUB^{meš}-zu ^{d}Ḫar-ri-ru ^{d}TIR.AN.NA
I i 34	DIŠ MUL SA$_{5}$ né-bu-ú šá ina BIR ^{mul}lu-lim
I i 35	GUB-zu ^{mul}ZÚ.MUŠ.Ì.KÚ.E
I i 36	ki-ma MUL^{meš} šu-ut ^{d}En-líl ug-dam-mi-ru-ni
I i 37	1 MUL GAL UD.DA-su da-aʾ-mat AN-e BAR-ma GUB-zu MUL ^{d}AMAR.UD né-bi-ri
I i 38	DIŠ ^{mul}SAG.ME.GAR KI.GUB-su KÚR.KÚR-ir AN-e ib-bir
	--
I i 39	33 MUL^{meš} šu-ut ^{d}En-líl
	--

I i 1 ¶ The Plough, Enlil, who goes in front of the stars of Enlil.
I i 2 ¶ The Wolf, the seed-funnel of the Plough.
I i 3 ¶ The Old Man, Enmešarra.
I i 4 [¶] The Crook, Gamlu.
I i 5 ¶ The Great Twins, Lugalirra and Meslamtaea.

I i 6 ¶ The Small Twins, Alammuš and Nin-gublaga.
I i 7 ¶ The Crab, the seat of Anu.
I i 8 ¶ The Lion, Latarak.
I i 9 ¶ The star which stands in the chest of the Lion: the King.
I i 10 ¶ The scintillating stars which stand in the tail of the Lion:
I i 11 The Frond (of the date palm) of Eru, Zarpanitu.
I i 12 ¶ ŠU.PA, Enlil who decrees the fate of the land.
I i 13 ¶ The star which stands in front of it: the Abundant One, the minister of Ninlil.
I i 14 ¶ The star which stands behind it: the Star of Dignity, the minister of Tišpak.
I i 15 ¶ The Wagon, Ninlil.
I i 16 ¶ The star which stands in the shaft of the Wagon:
I i 17 the Fox, Erra, the strong one of the gods.
I i 18 ¶ The star which stands in the front part of the Wagon: the Ewe, Aja.
I i 19 ¶ The Hitched Yoke, great Anu of heaven.
I i 20 ¶ The Wagon of Heaven, Damkianna.
I i 21 ¶ The star which stands in its knot: the Heir of the Sublime Temple,
I i 22 the first-ranking son of Anu.
I i 23 ¶ The Standing Gods of Ekur. ¶ The Sitting Gods of Ekur.

I i 24 ¶ The Goat, Gula.
I i 25 ¶ The star which stands in front of the Goat: the Dog.
I i 26 ¶ The bright star of the Goat: Lamma, the minister of Baba.
I i 27 ¶ The two stars which stand behind it: Nin-nisig and Erragal.
I i 28 ¶ The Panther, Nergal.
I i 29 ¶ The star which stands on its right: the Pig, Damu.
I i 30 ¶ The star which stands on its left: the Horse.
I i 31 ¶ The star which stands behind it: the Stag, the minister of the Stars.
I i 32 ¶ The scintillating stars which stand in the chest of the Stag:
I i 33 The Vole, the Rainbow god.
I i 34 ¶ The bright red star which stands in the kidney of the Stag:
I i 35 The Deleter.
I i 36 When the stars of Enlil have been finished,
I i 37 one big star – (although) its light is dim – divides the sky in half and stands there: (that is) the star of Marduk, the Ford.
I i 38 ¶ Jupiter keeps changing its position and crosses the sky.

I i 39 33 stars of Enlil.

I i 40	DIŠ ^{mul}AŠ.IKU šu-bat ^{d}É-a a-lik IGI MUL^{meš} šu-ut ^{d}A-nim
I i 41	DIŠ MUL šá ina IGI-et ^{mul}AŠ.IKU GUB-zu ^{mul}Ši-nu-nu-tu$_{4}$
I i 42	DIŠ MUL šá EGIR ^{mul}AŠ.IKU GUB-zu ^{mul}A-nu-ni-tu$_{4}$
I i 43	DIŠ MUL šá EGIR-šú GUB-zu $^{mul\ lú}$ḪUN.GÁ ^{d}Dumu-zi
I i 44	DIŠ MUL.MUL ^{d}7.BI DINGIR^{meš} GAL^{meš}
I ii 1	DIŠ ^{mul}GU$_{4}$.AN.NA ^{d}is le-e AGA ^{d}A-nim
I ii 2	DIŠ ^{mul}SIPA.ZI.AN.NA ^{d}Pap-sukal SUKAL ^{d}A-nim u INNIN
I ii 3	DIŠ ^{mul}MAŠ.TAB.BA šá ina IGI-it ^{mul}SIPA.ZI.AN.NA
I ii 4	GUB^{meš}-zu ^{d}LÚ.LÀL u ^{d}La-ta-ra-ak
I ii 5	DIŠ MUL šá EGIR-šú GUB-zu ^{mul}DAR.LUGAL
I ii 6	DIŠ ^{mul}KAK.SI.SÁ šil-ta-ḫu UR.SAG GAL-ú ^{d}Nin-urta
I ii 7	DIŠ ^{mul}BAN ^{d}Iš-tar NIM.MA-tu$_{4}$ DUMU.SAL ^{d}En-líl
I ii 8	DIŠ $^{mul\ d}$MUŠ ^{d}Nin-giš-zi-da EN er-ṣe-tu$_{4}$
I ii 9	DIŠ ^{mul}UGA^{mušen} a-ri-bu MUL ^{d}IM
I ii 10	DIŠ ^{mul}AB.SÍN ^{d}Ša-la šu-bu-ul-tu$_{4}$
I ii 11	DIŠ ^{mul}ZI.BA.AN.NA SI ^{mul}GÍR.TAB
I ii 12	DIŠ MUL ^{d}Za-ba$_{4}$-ba$_{4}$ ^{mul}TI$_{8}$^{mušen} u ^{mul}AD$_{6}$
I ii 13	DIŠ ^{mul}Dili-bat KI.GUB-su KÚR.KÚR-ir-ma AN-e ib-bir
I ii 14	DIŠ ^{mul}Ṣal-bat-a-nu KI.GUB-su KÚR.KÚR-ir-ma AN-e ib-bir
I ii 15	DIŠ ^{mul}UDU.IDIM.SAG.UŠ KI.GUB-su KÚR.KÚR-ir-ma AN-e ib-bir
I ii 16	DIŠ ^{mul}UDU.IDIM.GU$_{4}$.UD šá ^{d}MAŠ MU.NI lu-ú ina ^{d}UTU.È.A
I ii 17	lu-ú ina ^{d}UTU.ŠÚ.A e-ma ITI IGI.LÁ-ma e-ma ITI TÙM

I ii 18	23 MUL^{meš} šu-ut ^{d}A-nim

I ii 19	DIŠ ^{mul}KU$_{6}$ ^{d}É-a a-lik IGI MUL^{meš} šu-ut ^{d}É-a
I ii 20	DIŠ ^{mul}GU.LA ^{d}É-a ^{mul}NUN^{ki} ^{d}É-a
I ii 21	DIŠ MUL šá ina 15-šú GUB-zu ^{mul}Nin-maḫ
I ii 22	DIŠ ^{mul}EN.TE.NA.BAR.ḪUM ^{d}Nin-gír-su
I ii 23	DIŠ MUL šá ina Á-šú GUB-zu $^{mul\ giš}$GÁN.ÙR ^{giš}TUKUL šá ^{d}A É
I ii 24	šá ina lìb-bi-šú ZU.AB i-bar-ru-ú
I ii 25	DIŠ 2 MUL^{meš} šá EGIR-šú GUB^{me}-zu ^{d}Šúllat u ^{d}Ḫániš ^{d}UTU u ^{d}IM
I ii 26	DIŠ MUL šá EGIR-šú-nu GUB-zu GIM ^{d}É-a KUR-ḫa
I ii 27	GIM ^{d}É-a ŠÚ-bi ^{mul}Nu-muš-da ^{d}IM
I ii 28	DIŠ MUL šá ina GÙB ^{mul}GÍR.TAB GUB-zu ^{mul}UR.IDIM ^{d}Kù-sù
I ii 29	DIŠ ^{mul}GÍR.TAB ^{d}Iš-ḫa-ra be-let da-ád-me
I ii 30	DIŠ ^{mul}GABA GÍR.TAB ^{d}Li$_{9}$-si$_{4}$ ^{d}AG
I ii 31	DIŠ 2 MUL^{meš} šá ina zi-qit ^{mul}GÍR.TAB GUB^{meš}-zu
I ii 32	^{d}Šár-ur$_{4}$ u ^{d}Šár-gaz
I ii 33	DIŠ MUL šá EGIR-šú-nu GUB-zu ^{mul}Pa-bil-sag
I ii 34	DIŠ ^{mul}MÁ.GUR$_{8}$ u ^{mul}SUḪUR.MÁŠ^{ku}$_{6}$

I ii 35	15 MUL^{meš} šu-ut ^{d}É-a

I i 40 ¶ The Field, the seat of Ea, who goes in front of the stars of Anu.
I i 41 ¶ The star which stands opposite the Field: the Swallow.
I i 42 ¶ The star which stands behind the Field: Anunitu.
I i 43 ¶ The star which stands behind it: the Hired Man, Dumuzi.
I i 44 ¶ The Stars, the Seven, the great gods.
I ii 1 ¶ The Bull of Heaven, the Jaw of the Bull, the crown of Anu.
I ii 2 ¶ The True Shepherd of Anu, Papsukal, the minister of Anu and Ištar.
I ii 3 ¶ The twin stars which stand opposite the True Shepherd of Anu:
I ii 4 Lulal and Latarak.
I ii 5 ¶ The star which stands behind it: the Rooster
I ii 6 ¶ The Arrow, the arrow of the great warrior Ninurta.
I ii 7 ¶ The Bow, the Elamite Ištar, the daughter of Enlil.
I ii 8 ¶ The Snake, Ningizzida, lord of the Netherworld.
I ii 9 ¶ The Raven, the star of Adad.
I ii 10 ¶ The Furrow, Šala, the ear of grain.
I ii 11 ¶ The Scales, the horn of the Scorpion.
I ii 12 ¶ The star of Zababa, the Eagle, and the Corpse.
I ii 13 ¶ Venus keeps changing its position and crosses the sky.
I ii 14 ¶ Mars keeps changing its position and crosses the sky.
I ii 15 ¶ Saturn keeps changing its position and crosses the sky

I ii 16 ¶ Mercury, whose name is Ninurta, rises or sets in the East
I ii 17 or in the West within a month.

I ii 18 23 stars of Anu.

I ii 19 ¶ The Fish, Ea, who goes in front of the stars of Ea.
I ii 20 ¶ The Great One, Ea; Eridu, Ea.
I ii 21 ¶ The star which stands at its right: Ninmaḫ.
I ii 22 ¶ The Mouse, Ningirsu.
I ii 23 ¶ The star which stands at its side: the Harrow, the weapon of Mār-bīti,
I ii 24 by means of which he sees the subterranean waters.
I ii 25 ¶ The two stars stand behind it: Šullat and Ḫaniš, Šamaš and Adad.
I ii 26 ¶ The star which stands behind them, rises like Ea
I ii 27 and sets like Ea: Numušda, Adad.
I ii 28 ¶ The star which stands at the left of the Scorpion: the Wild Dog, Kusu.
I ii 29 ¶ The Scorpion, Išḫara, lady of all inhabited regions.
I ii 30 ¶ The Chest of the Scorpion: Lisi, Nabû.
I ii 31 ¶ The two stars which stand in the sting of the Scorpion:
I ii 32 Šarur and Šargaz.
I ii 33 ¶ The star(s) which stand(s) behind them: Pabilsag,
I ii 34 ¶ the Barge, and the Goat-Fish.

I ii 35 15 stars of Ea.

I ii 36	DIŠ ina ^{iti}BÁR UD 1 KAM $^{mul\ lú}$ḪUN.GÁ IGI.LÁ
I ii 37	DIŠ ina ^{iti}BÁR UD 20 KAM ^{mul}GÀM IGI.LÁ
I ii 38	DIŠ ina ^{iti}GU$_4$ UD 1 KAM MUL.MUL IGI.LÁ
I ii 39	DIŠ ina ^{iti}GU$_4$ UD 20 KAM ^{mul}is le-e IGI.LÁ
I ii 40	DIŠ ina ^{iti}SIG$_4$ UD 10 KAM ^{mul}SIPA.ZI.AN.NA u ^{mul}MAŠ.TAB.BA.GAL.GAL IGI^{me}
I ii 41	DIŠ ina ^{iti}ŠU UD 5 KAM ^{mul}MAŠ.TAB.BA.TUR.TUR u ^{mul}AL.LUL IGI^{me}
I ii 42	DIŠ ina ^{iti}ŠU UD 15 KAM ^{mul}KAK.SI.SÁ ^{mul}MUŠ u ^{mul}UR.GU.LA
I ii 43	IGI^{me}-ma 4 MA.NA EN.NUN u$_4$-me 2 MA.NA EN.NUN GI$_6$
I ii 44	DIŠ ina ^{iti}IZI UD 5 KAM ^{mul}BAN u ^{mul}LUGAL IGI^{me}
I ii 44a	DIŠ ina ^{iti}KIN UD 1 KAM ^{mul}[ ]
I ii 45	DIŠ ina ^{iti}KIN UD 10 KAM ^{mul}NUN^{ki} u ^{mul}UGA^{mušen} IGI^{me}
I ii 46	DIŠ ina ^{iti}KIN UD 15 KAM ^{mul}ŠU.PA ^{d}En-líl IGI
I ii 47	DIŠ ina ^{iti}KIN UD 25 KAM ^{mul}AB.SÍN IGI
I iii 1	DIŠ ina ^{iti}DU$_6$ UD 15 KAM ^{mul}zi-ba-ni-tu$_4$ ^{mul}UR.IDIM ^{mul}EN.TE.NA.BAR.ḪUM
I iii 2	u ^{mul}UR.KU IGI^{me}-ma 3 MA.NA EN.NUN u$_4$-mi 3 MA.NA EN.NUN GI$_6$
I iii 3	DIŠ ina ^{iti}APIN UD 5 KAM ^{mul}GÍR.TAB IGI
I iii 4	DIŠ ina ^{iti}APIN UD 15 KAM ^{mul}ÙZ u ^{mul}GABA GÍR.TAB IGI^{me}
I iii 5	DIŠ ina ^{iti}GAN UD 15 KAM ^{mul}UD.KA.DUḪ.A ^{mul}TI$_8^{mušen}$
I iii 6	u ^{mul}Pa-bil-sag IGI^{meš}
I iii 7	DIŠ ina ^{iti}AB UD 15 KAM ^{mul}SIM.MAḪ ^{mul}ši-nu-nu-tu$_4$ ^{mul}IM.ŠEŠ
I iii 8	ina GIŠ.NIM IGI.LÁ u ^{mul}KAK.SI.SÁ ina li-la-a-ti
I iii 9	IGI.LÁ-ma 2 MA.NA EN.NUN u$_4$-me 4 MA.NA EN.NUN GI$_6$
I iii 10	DIŠ ina ^{iti}ZÍZ UD 5 KAM ^{mul}GU.LA ^{mul}AŠ.IKU u ^{mul}lu-lim IGI^{meš}
I iii 11	DIŠ ina ^{iti}ZÍZ UD 25 KAM ^{mul}A-nu-ni-tu$_4$ IGI.LÁ
I iii 12	DIŠ ina ^{iti}ŠE UD 15 KAM ^{mul}KU$_6$ u ^{mul}ŠU.GI IGI.LÁ^{me}

I iii 13	DIŠ MUL.MUL KUR-ma ^{mul}GÍR.TAB ŠÚ-bi
I iii 14	DIŠ ^{mul}GÍR.TAB KUR-ma MUL.MUL ŠÚ-bi
I iii 15	DIŠ ^{mul}GU$_4$.AN.NA KUR-ma ^{mul}ŠU.PA ŠÚ-bi
I iii 16	DIŠ ^{mul}SIPA.ZI.AN.NA KUR-ma ^{mul}Pa-bil-sag ŠÚ-bi
I iii 17	DIŠ ^{mul}KAK.SI.SÁ $^{mul\ d}$MUŠ u ^{mul}UR.GU.LA KUR^{me}-nim-ma
I iii 18	^{mul}GU.LA u ^{mul}TI$_8^{mušen}$ ŠÚ^{meš}
I iii 19	DIŠ ^{mul}BAN u ^{mul}LUGAL KUR^{me}-ma ^{mul}ÙZ ŠÚ-bi

I ii 36 ¶ On the 1st day of Month I, the Hired Man becomes visible.
I ii 37 ¶ On the 20th day of Month I, the Crook becomes visible.
I ii 38 ¶ On the 1st day of Month II, the Stars become visible.
I ii 39 ¶ On the 20th day of Month II, the Jaw of the Bull becomes visible.
I ii 40 ¶ On the 10th day of Month III, the True Shepherd of Anu and the Great Twins become visible.
I ii 41 ¶ On the 5th day of Month IV, the Small Twins and the Crab become visible.
I ii 42 ¶ On the 15th day of Month IV, the Arrow, the Snake, and the Lion
I ii 43 become visible; 4 minas is the watch of the day, 2 minas is the watch of the night.
I ii 44 ¶ On the 5th (var. 15th) of Month V, the Bow and the King become visible.
I ii 44a ¶ On the 1st day of Month VI, [ ]
I ii 45 ¶ On the 10th day of Month VI, Eridu and the Raven become visible.
I ii 46 ¶ On the 15th day of Month VI, ŠU.PA, Enlil, becomes visible.
I ii 47 ¶ On the 25th day of Month VI, the Furrow becomes visible.
I iii 1 ¶ On the 15th day of Month VII, the Scales, the Wild Dog, the Mouse,
I iii 2 and the Dog become visible; 3 minas is the watch of the day, 3 minas is the watch of the night.
I iii 3 ¶ On the 5th (var. 15th) day of Month VIII, the Scorpion becomes visible.
I iii 4 ¶ On the 15th (var. 25th) day of Month VIII, the Goat and the Chest of the Scorpion become visible.
I iii 5 ¶ On the 15th day of Month IX, the Panther, the Eagle
I iii 6 and Pabilsag become visible.
I iii 7 ¶ On the 15th day of Month X, SIM.MAḪ, (i. e.) the Swallow (or) IM.ŠEŠ,
I iii 8 becomes visible in the East, and the Arrow
I iii 9 becomes visible in the evening; 2 minas is the watch of the day, 4 minas is the watch of the night.
I iii 10 ¶ On the 5th (var. 15th) day of Month XI, the Great One, the Field, and the Stag become visible.
I iii 11 ¶ On the 25th day of Month XI, Anunitu becomes visible.
I iii 12 ¶ On the 15th day of Month XII, the Fish and the Old Man become visible.

I iii 13 ¶ The Stars rise, and the Scorpion sets.
I iii 14 ¶ The Scorpion rises, and the Stars set.
I iii 15 ¶ The Bull of Heaven rises, and ŠU.PA sets.
I iii 16 ¶ The True Shepherd of Anu rises, and Pabilsag sets.
I iii 17 ¶ The Arrow, the Snake, and the Lion rise, and
I iii 18 the Great One and the Eagle set.
I iii 19 ¶ The Bow and the King rise, and the Goat sets.

I iii 20	DIŠ ^{mul}NUN^{ki} u ^{mul}UGA^{mušen} KUR^{meš}-ma ^{mul}UD.KA.DUḪ.A ŠÚ-bi
I iii 21	DIŠ ^{mul}ŠU.PA ^{d}En-líl KUR-ma ^{mul}AŠ.IKU ŠÚ-bi
I iii 22	DIŠ ^{mul}Nin-maḫ KUR-ma ^{mul}A-nu-ni-tu$_{4}$ ŠÚ-bi
I iii 23	DIŠ ^{mul}zi-ba-ni-tu$_{4}$ ^{mul}UR.IDIM u ^{mul}EN.TE.NA.BAR.ḪUM
I iii 24	KUR^{me}-ma $^{\text{mul lú}}$ḪUN.GÁ ŠÚ-bi
I iii 25	DIŠ ^{mul}GÍR.TAB u ^{mul}UR.KU KUR^{me}-ma ^{mul}NUN^{ki} u MUL.MUL ŠÚ^{meš}
I iii 26	DIŠ ^{mul}GABA GÍR.TAB u ^{mul}ÙZ KUR^{meš}-ma ^{mul}ŠU.GI u ^{mul}SIPA.ZI.AN.NA ŠÚ^{meš}
I iii 27	DIŠ ^{mul}Pa-bil-sag ^{mul}Za-ba$_{4}$-ba$_{4}$ u DINGIR.GUB.BA^{meš} KUR^{meš}-ma
I iii 28	^{mul}KAK.SI.SÁ ^{mul}BAN u ^{mul}GÀM ŠÚ^{meš}
I iii 29	DIŠ ^{mul}UD.KA.DUḪ.A u ^{mul}TI$_{8}$^{mušen} KUR^{meš}-ma
I iii 30	^{mul}MAŠ.TAB.BA.GAL.GAL u ^{mul}MAŠ.TAB.BA.TUR.TUR ŠÚ^{meš}
I iii 31	DIŠ ^{mul}AŠ.IKU ^{mul}GU.LA u ^{mul}lu-lim KUR^{meš}-ma
I iii 32	^{mul}UR.GU.LA $^{\text{mul d}}$MUŠ u ^{mul}EN.TE.NA.BAR.ḪUM ŠÚ^{meš}
I iii 33	DIŠ ^{mul}KU$_{6}$ u ^{mul}ŠU.GI KUR^{meš}-ma ^{mul}AB.SÍN u ^{mul}UR.IDIM ŠÚ^{meš}

I iii 34	DIŠ TA KUR šá ^{mul}KAK.SI.SÁ 55 UD^{meš} ana KUR šá ^{mul}NUN^{ki}
I iii 35	DIŠ TA KUR šá ^{mul}KAK.SI.SÁ 1 ŠU UD^{meš} ana KUR šá ^{mul}ŠU.PA
I iii 36	DIŠ TA KUR šá ^{mul}ŠU.PA 10 UD^{meš} ana KUR šá ^{mul}AB.SÍN
I iii 37	DIŠ TA KUR šá ^{mul}AB.SÍN 20 UD^{meš} ana KUR šá ^{mul}zi-ba-ni-tu$_{4}$
I iii 38	DIŠ TA KUR šá ^{mul}zi-ba-ni-tu$_{4}$ 30 UD^{meš} ana KUR šá ^{mul}ÙZ
I iii 39	DIŠ TA KUR šá ^{mul}ÙZ 30 UD^{meš} ana KUR šá ^{mul}UD.KA.DUḪ.A
I iii 40	DIŠ TA KUR šá ^{mul}UD.KA.DUḪ.A 30 UD^{meš} ana KUR šá ^{mul}SIM.MAḪ
I iii 41	DIŠ TA KUR šá ^{mul}SIM.MAḪ 20 UD^{meš} ana KUR šá ^{mul}AŠ.IKU
I iii 42	DIŠ TA KUR šá ^{mul}AŠ.IKU 40 UD^{meš} ana KUR šá ^{mul}KU$_{6}$
I iii 43	DIŠ TA KUR šá ^{mul}KU$_{6}$ 35 UD^{meš} ana KUR šá ^{mul}GÀM
I iii 44	DIŠ TA KUR šá ^{mul}GÀM 10 UD^{meš} ana KUR šá MUL.MUL
I iii 45	DIŠ TA KUR šá MUL.MUL 20 UD^{meš} ana KUR šá ^{mul}GU$_{4}$.AN.NA
I iii 46	DIŠ TA KUR šá ^{mul}GU$_{4}$.AN.NA 20 UD^{meš} ana KUR šá ^{mul}SIPA.ZI.AN.NA
I iii 47	DIŠ TA KUR šá ^{mul}SIPA.ZI.AN.NA 35 UD^{meš} ana KUR šá ^{mul}KAK.SI.SÁ
I iii 48	DIŠ TA KUR šá ^{mul}KAK.SI.SÁ 20 UD^{meš} ana KUR šá ^{mul}BAN

I iii 49	u$_{4}$-mu 1 UŠ.TA.ÀM MUL^{meš} ina šèr-ti ana GI$_{6}$ KU$_{4}$^{meš}-ni
I iii 50	u$_{4}$-mu 1 UŠ.TA.ÀM MUL^{mes} ina li-la-a-ti ana u$_{4}$-me È^{meš}-ni

---

I iv 1	DIŠ MUL^{meš} šá ziq-pi šá ina KASKAL šu-ut ^{d}En-líl ina MURUB$_{4}$ AN-e
I iv 2	ina IGI-et GABA šá ŠEŠ AN-e GUB^{meš}-ma GI$_{6}$ KUR u ŠÚ-bi
I iv 3	šá MUL^{meš} ina lìb-bi-šú-nu im-ma-ru

I iii 20 ¶ Eridu and the Raven rise, and the Panther sets.
I iii 21 ¶ ŠU.PA, Enlil, rises, and the Field sets.
I iii 22 ¶ Ninmaḫ rises, and Anunitu sets.
I iii 23 ¶ The Scales, the Wild Dog, and the Mouse
I iii 24 rise, and the Hired Man sets.
I iii 25 ¶ The Scorpion and the Dog rise, and Eridu and the Stars set.

I iii 26 ¶ The Chest of the Scorpion and the Goat rise, and the Old Man and the True Shepherd of Anu set.
I iii 27 ¶ Pabilsag, Zababa, and the Standing Gods rise, and
I iii 28 the Arrow, the Bow, and the Crook set.
I iii 29 ¶ The Panther and the Eagle rise, and
I iii 30 the Great Twins and the Small Twins set.
I iii 31 ¶ The Field, the Great One, and the Stag rise, and
I iii 32 the Lion, the Snake, and the Mouse set.
I iii 33 ¶ The Fish and the Old Man rise, and the Furrow and the Wild Dog set.

I iii 34 ¶ From the rising of the Arrow 55 days to the rising of Eridu.
I iii 35 ¶ From the rising of the Arrow 60 days to the rising of ŠU.PA.
I iii 36 ¶ From the rising of ŠU.PA 10 days to the rising of the Furrow.
I iii 37 ¶ From the rising of the Furrow 20 days to the rising of the Scales.
I iii 38 ¶ From the rising of the Scales 30 days to the rising of the Goat.
I iii 39 ¶ From the rising of the Goat 30 days to the rising of the Panther.
I iii 40 ¶ From the rising of the Panther 30 days to the rising of the Swallow.
I iii 41 ¶ From the rising of the Swallow 20 (var. 10) days to the rising of the Field.
I iii 42 ¶ From the rising of the Field 40 days to the rising of the Fish.
I iii 43 ¶ From the rising of the Fish 35 days to the rising of the Crook.
I iii 44 ¶ From the rising of the Crook 10 days to the rising of the Stars.
I iii 45 ¶ From the rising of the Stars 20 days to the rising of the Bull of Heaven.
I iii 46 ¶ From the rising of the Bull of Heaven 20 days to the rising of the True Shepherd of Anu.
I iii 47 ¶ From the rising of the True Shepherd of Anu 35 days to the rising of the Arrow.
I iii 48 ¶ From the rising of the Arrow 20 days to the rising of the Bow.

I iii 49 The stars enter into the night in the morning 1 UŠ each day.
I iii 50 The stars come out into the day in the evening 1 UŠ each day.

I iv 1 ¶ The *ziqpu* stars that stand in the path of Enlil in the middle of the sky
I iv 2 opposite the chest of the observer of the sky, and
I iv 3 by means of which he observes the rising and setting of the stars at night:

I iv 4 DIŠ ^{mul}ŠU.PA MUL BAL.TÉŠ.A ^{mul}DINGIR.GUB.BA^{meš} ^{mul}UR.KU

I iv 5 ^{mul}ÙZ ^{mul}UD.KA.DUḪ.A ^{mul}lu-lim ^{mul}ŠU.GI ^{mul}GÀM

I iv 6 ^{mul}MAŠ.TAB.BA.GAL.GAL ^{mul}AL.LUL ^{mul}UR.GU.LA ^{mul}E$_4$-ru$_6$ u ^{mul}Ḫé-gál-la-a-a

---

I iv 7 PAP an-nu-tu MUL^{meš} šá ziq-pi šá KASKAL šu-ut ^{d}En-líl šá ina MURUB$_4$ AN-e

I iv 8 ina IGI-et GABA-ka GUB^{me}-zu-ma GI$_6$ SAR^{meš} u ŠÚ^{meš}

I iv 9 šá MUL^{meš} ina lìb-bi-šú-nu tam-ma-ru

I iv 10 BE-ma zi-iq-pa a-na a-ma-ri-ka ina ^{iti}BÁR UD 20 KAM

I iv 11 ina šèr-ti la-am ^{d}UTU KUR-ḫa GUB-ma ZAG-ka ^{im}MAR.TU

I iv 12 GÙB-ka ^{im}KUR.RA ni-iš IGI-ka ^{im}U$_{18}$.LU

I iv 13 qú-ma-ru šá ^{mul}UD.KA.DUḪ.A ina MURUB$_4$ AN-e

I iv 14 ina IGI-et GABA-ka GUB-ma ^{mul}GÀM KUR-ḫa

I iv 15 DIŠ ina ^{iti}GU$_4$ UD 1 KAM GABA šá ^{mul}UD.KA.DUḪ.A ina MURUB$_4$ AN-e

I iv 16 IGI-et GABA-ka GUB-ma MUL.MUL KUR-ḫa

I iv 17 DIŠ ina ^{iti}GU$_4$ UD 20 KAM ki-in-ṣu šá ^{mul}UD.KA.DUḪ.A

I iv 18 ina MURUB$_4$ AN-e IGI-et GABA-ka GUB-ma ^{mul}is le-e KUR-ḫa

---

I iv 19 DIŠ ina ^{iti}SIG$_4$ UD 10 KAM a-si-du šá ^{mul}UD.KA.DUḪ.A ina MURUB$_4$ AN-e

I iv 20 IGI-et GABA-ka GUB-ma ^{mul}SIPA.ZI.AN.NA KUR-ḫa

I iv 21 DIŠ ina ^{iti}ŠU UD 15 KAM MUL^{m}]^{eš} um-mu-lu-tú šá ^{mul}ŠU.GI ina MURUB$_4$ AN-e IGI-et GABA-ka GUB-ma ^{mul}KAK.SI.SÁ KUR-ḫa

---

I iv 22 DIŠ ina ^{iti}IZI UD 15 KAM MUL né-bu-ú šá ^{mul}ŠU.GI

I iv 23 ina MURUB$_4$ AN-e IGI-et GABA-ka GUB-ma ^{mul}BAN KUR-ḫa

---

I iv 24 DIŠ ina ^{iti}KIN UD 15 KAM ^{mul}MAŠ.TAB.BA.GAL.GAL ina MURUB$_4$ AN-e IGI-et GABA-ka GUB-ma ^{mul}ŠU.PA u ^{mul}NUN^{ki} KUR^{meš}-ni

---

I iv 25 DIŠ ina ^{iti}DU$_6$ UD 15 KAM ^{mul}UR.GU.LA ina MURUB$_4$ AN-e IGI-et GABA-ka GUB-ma ^{mul}zi-ba-ni-tu$_4$ KUR-ḫa

---

I iv 4 ¶ ŠU.PA, the Star of Dignity, the Standing Gods, the Dog,
I iv 5 the Goat, the Panther, the Stag, the Old Man, the Crook,
I iv 6 the Great Twins, the Crab, the Lion, Eru, and the Abundant One.

I iv 7 All these are the *ziqpu* stars of the path of the stars of Enlil that stand in the middle of the sky
I iv 8 opposite your chest, and by means of which you observe at night
I iv 9 the risings and settings of the stars.

I iv 10 If you are to observe the *ziqpu*, on the 20th of Month I, you stand
I iv 11 in the morning before sunrise, your right to the West,
I iv 12 your left to the East, your face directed towards the South;
I iv 13 the shoulder of the Panther stands in the middle of the sky
I iv 14 opposite your chest, and the Crook rises.

I iv 15 ¶ On the 1st day of Month II, the chest of the Panther stands in the middle of the sky
I iv 16 opposite your chest, and the Stars rise.

I iv 17 ¶ On the 20th day of Month II, the Knee of the Panther
I iv 18 stands in the middle of the sky opposite your chest, and the Jaw of the Bull rises.

I iv 19 ¶ On the 10th day of Month III, the Heel of the Panther stands in the middle of the sky
I iv 20 opposite your chest, and the True Shepherd of Anu rises.

I iv 21 ¶ On the 15th day of Month IV, the scintillating stars (var. bright star) of the Old Man stand in the middle of the sky opposite your chest, and the Arrow rises.

I iv 22 ¶ On the 15th (var. 5th) day of Month V, the bright star (var. scintillating stars) of the Old Man
I iv 23 stand in the middle of the sky opposite your chest, and the Bow rises.

I iv 24 ¶ On the 15th day of Month VI, the Great Twins stand in the middle of the sky opposite your chest, and ŠU.PA and Eridu rise.

I iv 25 ¶ On the 15th day of Month VII, the Lion stands in the middle of the sky opposite your chest, and the Scales rise.

I iv 26 DIŠ ina ^{iti}APIN UD 15 KAM ^{mul}E$_4$-ru$_6$ ina MURUB$_4$ AN-e IGI-et GABA-ka GUB-ma ^{mul}ÙZ KUR-ḫa

----

I iv 27 [DIŠ ina ^{iti}G]AN UD 15 KAM ^{mul}ŠU.PA MIN MIN ^{mul}UD.KA.DUḪ.A KUR-ḫa

----

I iv 28 DIŠ ina ^{iti}AB UD 15 KAM ^{mul}DINGIR.GUB.BA^{meš} MIN IGI-et GABA-ka GUB^{meš} ^{mul}SIM.MAḪ KUR-ḫa

----

I iv 29 DIŠ ina ^{iti}ZÍZ UD 15 KAM ^{mul}UR.KU MIN IGI-et GABA-ka GUB-ma ^{mul}AŠ.IKU KUR-ḫa

----

I iv 30 DIŠ ina ^{iti}ŠE UD 15 KAM ^{mul}ÙZ MIN IGI-et GABA-ka GUB-ma ^{mul}KU$_6$ KUR-ḫa

----

I iv 31 DINGIR^{meš} ša i-na KASKAL ^{d}Sin GUB^{meš}-ma ^{d}Sin e-ma ITI

I iv 32 {ina} pi-rik-šú-nu DIB^{meš}-ma TAG^{meš}-šú-nu-ti

I iv 33 MUL.MUL ^{mul}GU$_4$.AN.NA ^{mul}SIPA.ZI.AN.NA ^{mul}ŠU.GI

I iv 34 ^{mul}GÀM ^{mul}MAŠ.TAB.BA.GAL.GAL ^{mul}AL.LUL ^{mul}UR.GU.LA
I iv 35 ^{mul}AB.SÍN ^{mul}zi-ba-ni-tu$_4$ ^{mul}GÍR.TAB ^{mul}Pa-bil-sag
I iv 36 ^{mul}SUḪUR MÁŠ ^{mul}GU.LA KUN^{meš} ^{mul}SIM.MAḪ
I iv 37 ^{mul}A-nu-ni-tu$_4$ u $^{mul\ lú}$ḪUN.GÁ

I iv 38 PAP an-nu-tu$_4$ DINGIR^{meš} šá ina KASKAL ^{d}Sin GUB^{meš}-ma ^{d}Sin e-ma ITI
I iv 39 [pi-rik-šú-nu DIB]^{meš}-ma TAG^{meš}-šú-nu-ti

II i 1 DIŠ KASKAL ^{d}Sin DU-ku ^{d}UTU DU-ak
II i 2 DIŠ KASKAL ^{d}Sin DU-ku ^{d}Šul-pa-è-a DU-ak
II i 3 DIŠ KASKAL ^{d}Sin DU-ku ^{d}Dili-bat DU-ak
II i 4 DIŠ KASKAL ^{d}Sin DU-ku ^{d}Ṣal-bat-a-nu DU-ak
II i 5 DIŠ KASKAL ^{d}Sin DU-ku ^{mul}UDU.IDIM.GU$_4$.UD šá ^{d}Nin-urta MU-šú DU-ak
II i 6 DIŠ KASKAL ^{d}Sin DU-ku ^{mul}UDU.IDIM.SAG.UŠ DU-ak

II i 7 PAP 6 DINGIR^{meš} šá 1-en NA^{meš}-su-nu MUL^{me} AN-e

II i 8 TAG^{meš} NA^{meš}-su-nu KÚR.KÚR-ru

II i 9 DIŠ ina ^{iti}ŠU UD 15 KAM ^{mul}KAK.SI.SÁ IGI.LÁ-ma
II i 10 4 MA.NA EN.NUN u$_4$-mi 2 MA.NA EN.NUN GI$_6$
II i 11 ^{d}UTU šá ina id ^{im}SI.SÁ KI SAG.DU ^{mul}UR.GU.LA KUR-ḫa

I iv 26 ¶ On the 15th day of Month VIII, Eru stands in the middle of the sky opposite your chest, and the Goat rises.

* * *

I iv 27 ¶ On the 15th day of Month IX, ŠU.PA stands in the middle of the sky opposite your chest, and the Panther rises.

* * *

I iv 28 ¶ On the 15th day of Month X, the Standing Gods stand in the middle of the sky opposite your chest, and the Swallow rises.

* * *

I iv 29 ¶ On the 15th (error for 5th) day of Month XI, the Dog stands in the middle of the sky opposite your chest, and the Field rises.

* * *

I iv 30 ¶ On the 15th day of Month XII, the Goat stands in the middle of the sky opposite your chest, and the Fish rises.

* * *

I iv 31 The gods (var. stars) who stand in the path of the Moon, through whose region the Moon during a month
I iv 32 passes repeatedly and keeps touching them:

* * *

I iv 33 The Stars, the Bull of Heaven, the True Shepherd of Anu, the Old Man,
I iv 34 the Crook, the Great Twins, the Crab, the Lion,
I iv 35 the Furrow, the Scales, the Scorpion, Pabilsag
I iv 36 the Goat-Fish, the Great One, the Tails of the Swallow,
I iv 37 Anunitu, and the Hired Man.

* * *

I iv 38 All these are the gods who stand in the path of the Moon, through whose region the Moon during a month
I iv 39 [passes repeatedly] and keeps touching them.

* * *

II i 1 ¶ The Sun travels the (same) path the Moon travels.
II i 2 ¶ Jupiter travels the (same) path the Moon travels.
II i 3 ¶ Venus travels the (same) path the Moon travels.
II i 4 ¶ Mars travels the (same) path the Moon travels.
II i 5 ¶ Mercury whose name is Ninurta travels the (same) path the Moon travels.
II i 6 ¶ Saturn travels the (same) path the Moon travels.

* * *

II i 7 Together six gods whose places are one, (and) who touch the stars of the sky
II i 8 (and) keep changing their positions.

* * *

II i 9 ¶ On the 15th day of Month IV, the Arrow becomes visible, and
II i 10 4 minas is the watch of the day, 2 minas is the watch of the night.
II i 11 The Sun, which rises in the North with the head of the Lion,

II i 12	GUR-ma ana id ^{im}U$_{18}$.LU u$_{4}$-mu 40 NINDA.TA.ÀM ul-ta-nap-pal
II i 13	UD^{meš} LUGÚD.DA^{meš} GI$_{6}^{meš}$ GÍD.DA^{meš}
	--
II i 14	DIŠ ina ^{iti}DU$_{6}$ UD 15 KAM ^{d}UTU ina lìb-bi ^{mul}zi-ba-ni-tu$_{4}$ ina ^{d}UTU.È KUR-ḫa
II i 15	u ^{d}Sin ina IGI MUL.MUL EGIR $^{mul\ lú}$ḪUN.GÁ GUB-az-ma 3 MA.NA EN.NUN u$_{4}$-mi 3 MA.NA EN.NUN GI$_{6}$
	--
II i 16	DIŠ ina ^{iti}AB UD 15 KAM ^{mul}KAK.SI.SÁ ina li-la-a-ti IGI.LÁ-ma 2 MA.NA EN.NUN u$_{4}$-mi 4 MA.NA EN.NUN GI$_{6}$
II i 17	^{d}UTU šá ina id ^{im}U$_{18}$.LU KI SAG.DU ^{mul}UR.GU.LA KUR-ḫa GUR-ma ana id ^{im}SI.SÁ
II i 18	UD 40 NINDA.TA.ÀM un-da-na-ḫar UD^{meš} GÍD.DA^{meš} GI$_{6}^{meš}$ LUGÚD.DA^{meš}
	--
II i 19	DIŠ ina ^{iti}BÁR UD 15 KAM ^{d}Sin ina li-la-a-ti ina ŠÀ
II i 20	^{mul}zi-ba-ni-tú ina ^{d}UTU.È u ^{d}UTU ina ^{d}UTU.ŠÚ.A
II i 21	ina IGI MUL.MUL EGIR ^{mul}ḪUN.GÁ GUB-ma 3 MA.NA EN.NUN u$_{4}$-mi 3 MA.NA EN.NUN GI$_{6}$
	--
II i 22	DIŠ ina ^{iti}BÁR UD 15 KAM ina ^{iti}ŠU UD 15 KAM ina ^{iti}DU$_{6}$ UD 15 KAM ina ^{iti}AB UD 15 KAM
II i 23	KUR^{meš} šá ^{d}UTU NA^{meš} šá ^{d}Sin IGI.DUḪ.A^{meš} šá ^{mul}KAK.SI.SÁ
II i 24	ŠEŠ-ár UD^{meš} DIRI^{meš} IGI.LÁ
	--
II i 25	DIŠ ina ^{iti}KIN UD 10 KAM ^{mul}NUN^{ki} UD 15 KAM ^{mul}ŠU.PA IGI^{meš}
II i 26	MUL^{meš}-šú-nu ina u$_{4}$-mi IGI^{meš} MÚ^{meš}-šú-nu zi-me-šú-nu
II i 27	ri-is-ni-šú-nu ù IM šá DU-ku ŠEŠ ANŠE.KUR.RA^{meš}
II i 28	tu-na-an-ṣar-ma ina ÍD A^{meš} NU NAG^{meš}
II i 29	ki-i MUL^{meš}-šú-nu ul-ta-ta-pu-ni
II i 30	maḫ-ḫu-ri-šú-nu tu-maḫ-ḫar ANŠE.KUR.RA^{meš}
II i 31	ESIR TAG^{meš}-ma ina ÍD A^{meš} NAG^{meš}
	--
II i 32	DIŠ ina ^{iti}APIN UD 5 KAM ^{mul}GÍR.TAB UD 15 KAM ^{mul}GABA GÍR.TAB
II i 33	IGI^{meš} ina u$_{4}$-me IGI^{meš} IM šá [DU-ku ŠE]Š-ár
	--
II i 34	DIŠ ina ^{iti}ŠE UD 15 KAM ^{mul}KU$_{6}$ ina še-ri [IGI] ina li-la-a-ti ^{mul}NUN[^{ki} IGI]

II i 12 turns and keeps moving down towards the South 40 NINDA per day.
II i 13 The days become shorter, the nights become longer.

II i 14 ¶ On the 15th day of Month VII, the Sun rises within the Scales in the East,
II i 15 and the Moon stands in front of the Stars behind the Hired Man, 3 minas is the watch of the day, 3 minas is the watch of the night.

II i 16 ¶ On the 15th day of Month X, the Arrow becomes visible in the evening. 2 minas is the watch of the day, 4 minas is the watch of the night.
II i 17 The Sun, which rises in the South with the head of the Lion (error for: Great One?), turns and
II i 18 keeps coming up towards the North 40 NINDA per day. The days become longer, the nights become shorter.

II i 19 ¶ On the 15th day of Month I, the Moon stands in the evening within
II i 20 the Scales in the East, and the Sun in the West in front of the Stars behind
II i 21 the Hired Man. 3 minas is the watch of the day, 3 minas is the watch of the night.

II i 22 ¶ On the 15th day of Month I, on the 15th day of Month IV, on the 15th day of Month VII, on the 15th day of Month X,
II i 23 you observe the risings of the Sun, the positions of the Moon, the appearances of the Arrow,
II i 24 and you will find the days in excess.

II i 25 ¶ On the 10th day of Month VI, Eridu (and) on the 15th ŠU.PA become visible;
II i 26 on the day their stars become visible you observe their risings, their glow, and
II i 27 their 'soakings', and the wind that blows; you guard[?] the horses
II i 28 so that they do not drink water from the river.
II i 29 When their stars have been made visible,
II i 30 you present offerings to them; horses
II i 31 may touch bitumen and drink water from the river.

II i 32 ¶ On the 5th day of Month VIII, the Scorpion (and) on the 15th day the Chest of the Scorpion become visible;
II i 33 on the day they become visible you observe the wind that blows.

II i 34 ¶ On the 15th day of Month XII, the Fish [becomes visible] in the morning, in the evening Eridu [becomes visible;]

II i 35 MUL^{meš}-šú-nu MUL^{meš} ra ba [ ]
II i 36 ina u_4-me IGI^{meš} MÚ^{meš}-šú-nu zi-[ ]

II i 37 [r]i-is-ni-šú-nu IM š[á D]U-ku Š[EŠ-ár]

II i 38 ^{mul}Sag-me-gar ^{mul}Dili-bat ^{mul}[UDU.ID]IM.GU$_4$.UD šá ^{d}MAŠ MU-šú ^{mul}Ṣal-bat-a-nu ^{mul}UDU.IDIM.SAG.UŠ
II i 39 [KIMIN] ^{mul}zi-ba-ni-tu$_4$ MUL ^{d}UTU

II i 40 [N]A^{meš}-šú-nu u zi-me-šú-nu KÚR.KÚR-ru
II i 41 [MUL^{meš} AN]-e TAG^{meš} MUL^{meš}-šú-nu ina u_4-me IGI^{meš} KUR^{me}-šú-nu SUḪ^{meš}-šú-nu
II i 42 [ri-is-ni-šú-nu K]I IGI^{meš} IM šá DU-ku ŠEŠ-ár ina UD IGI^{meš} muḫ-ḫu-ri-šú-nu
II i 43 [tu-maḫ]-ḫa-ru ANŠE.KUR.RA^{meš} ESIR TAG^{meš}

II i 44 [DIŠ ^{mul}Di]li-bat <ina> ^{d}UTU.È TÙM-ma ITI ina AN-e uḫ-ḫa-ra

II i 45 [KIMIN] 1 ITI UD 15 KAM u_4-mi KIMIN 2 ITI uḫ-ḫa-ram-ma
II i 46 [ina] ^{d}UTU.ŠÚ.A IGI.LÁ

II i 47 DIŠ ^{mul}Dili-bat ina ^{d}UTU.ŠÚ.A TÙM-ma ina u_4-me TÙM ina ^{d}UTU.È KUR-ḫa KIMIN 3 u_4-mi
II i 48 KI.3 7 u_4-mi KI.4 14 u_4-mi uḫ-ḫa-ram.ma KUR-ḫa

II i 49 DIŠ ^{mul}Sag-me-gar ina ^{d}UTU.ŠÚ.A TÙM-ma 20 u_4-me ina AN-e uḫ-ḫa-ra
II i 50 KIMIN ITI uḫ-ḫa-ram-ma ina ^{d}UTU.È ina KASKAL ^{d}UTU MÚ-ḫa IGI.LÁ

II i 51 DIŠ ^{mul}Ṣal-bat-a-nu ina ^{d}UTU.ŠÚ.A TÙM-ma 2 ITI KIMIN 3 ITI 10 u_4-mi KIMIN 6 ITI
II i 52 20 u_4-mi ina AN-e uḫ-ḫa-ram-ma ina ^{d}UTU.È ina KASKAL ^{d}UTU MÚ-ḫa IGI.LÁ

II i 53 DIŠ ^{d}UDU.IDIM.SAG.UŠ ina ^{d}UTU.ŠÚ.A TÙM-ma 20 u_4-mi ina AN-e uḫ-ḫa-ram-ma

---

II i 54 DIŠ ^{mul}UDU.IDIM.GU$_4$.UD šá ^{d}MAŠ MU-šú lu ina ^{d}UTU.È lu ina ^{d}UTU.ŠÚ.A IGI.LÁ-ma
II i 55 7 u_4-mi KIMIN 14 u_4-mi KIMIN UD 21 KAM KI.4 ITI KI.5 ITI 15 u_4-mi ina AN-e GUB-ma

---

II i 35 their stars . . . [. . .];
II i 36 on the day they become visible you observe their risings, their glow,
II i 37 their 'soakings', (and) the wind that blows.

II i 38 Jupiter, Venus, Mercury, whose name is Ninurta, Mars, Saturn,

II i 39 [also called] 'the Scales' (or) 'Star of the Sun'.

II i 40 [ ] keep changing their positions and their glow, (and)
II i 41 touch [the stars of the sky]; on the day their stars become visible, you observe their risings, their glow,
II i 42 [their 'soakings',] where they become visible, (and) the wind that blows; on the day they become visible,
II i 43 you present offerings to them; horses may touch bitumen.

II i 44 ¶ Venus disappears in the East and remains (invisible) in the sky for a month,
II i 45 or for 1 month and 15 days, or it remains for 2 months, and
II i 46 becomes visible in the West.

II i 47 ¶ Venus disappears in the West and rises (again) in the East on the day it disappears; or, for 3 days,
II i 48 thirdly, for 7 days, fourthly, for 14 days, it remains (invisible) and then rises.

II i 49 ¶ Jupiter disappears in the West and remains (invisible) in the sky for 20 days,
II i 50 or remains for a month, and rises and becomes visible in the East in the path of the Sun.

II i 51 ¶ Mars disappears in the West and remains (invisible) in the sky for 2 months, or for 3 months and 10 days, or for 6 months
II i 52 and 20 days, and then rises and becomes visible in the East in the path of the Sun.

II i 53 ¶ Saturn disappears in the West, remains (invisible) in the sky for 20 days, and becomes visible in the path of the Sun.

II i 54 ¶ Mercury, whose name is Ninurta, becomes visible either in the East or in the West, and
II i 55 stands in the sky for 7 days, or for 14 days, or for 21 days, fourthly, for a month, fifthly, for a month and 15 days,

---

II i 56 ki-ma TÙM ma-la u$_{4}$-mi šá ina AN-e GUB-zu uḫ-ḫa-ram-ma lu ina ^{d}UTU.È

II i 57 lu ina ^{d}UTU.ŠÚ.A ina KASKAL ^{d}UTU MÚ-ḫa IGI.LÁ MUL BI ina EN.TE.NA IGI.LÁ-ma

II i 58 ina BURU$_{14}$ IGI.LÁ-ma zi-me-šú ri-is-ni-šú KI IGI.LÁ ù IM šá DU-ku ŠEŠ-ár

II i 59 MUL BI BE-ma SA$_{5}$ u ba-ìl BE-ma SIG$_{7}$ u GI$_{6}$

II i 60 [DIŠ] ^{mul}Sag-me-gar ina ^{d}UTU.È IGI-ma MU 1 KAM ina AN-e GUB-ma ina ^{d}UTU.ŠÚ.A TÙM

II i 61 DIŠ ^{mul}Dili-bat lu ina ^{d}UTU.È lu ina ^{d}UTU.ŠÚ.A IGI.LÁ-ma 9 ITI^{meš} ina AN-e GUB-ma i-tab-bal

----

II i 62 DIŠ ^{mul}Ṣal-bat-a-nu ina ^{d}UTU.È IGI.LÁ-ma MU 1 KAM 6 ITI KIMIN MU 1 KAM 10 ITI KIMIN 2 MU.AN.NA^{meš}

II i 63 ina AN-e GUB-ma ina ^{d}UTU.ŠÚ.A TÙM MUL BI BE-ma SA$_{5}$ GAR u ba-ìl BE-ma un-nu-un u TUR

II i 64 DIŠ ^{mul}UDU.IDIM.SAG.UŠ KIMIN ^{mul}zi-ba-ni-tu$_{4}$ MUL ^{d}UTU ina ^{d}UTU.È IGI.LÁ-ma

II i 65 MU 1 KAM ina AN-e GUB-ma ina ^{d}UTU.ŠÚ.A TÙM MUL BI BE-ma SA$_{5}$ BE-ma BABBAR

II i 66 DIŠ ^{mul}UDU.IDIM.GU$_{4}$.UD šá ^{d}Nin-urta MU-šú lu ina ^{d}UTU.È lu ina ^{d}UTU.ŠÚ.A

II i 67 e-ma ITI IGI.LÁ-ma e-ma ITI TÙM

II i 68 BE-ma mu-ṣe-e IM^{meš} ana IGI.LÁ-ka ^{mul}MAR.GÍD.DA ina ZI ^{im}SI.SÁ G[IL-á]t

II i 69 ^{mul}KU$_{6}$ ina ZI ^{im}U$_{18}$.LU GIL ^{mul}GÍR.TAB ina ZI ^{im}MAR.TU GIL-[á]t

II i 70 ^{mul}ŠU.GI u MUL.MUL ina ZI ^{im}KUR.RA GUB^{meš}-z[u]

II i 71 ina u$_{4}$-me EN.NUN-ka IM šá DU-ku MUL^{meš} ú-kal-la-mu-k[a]

II Gap A 1 [DIŠ] TA UD 1 KAM šá ^{iti}ŠE EN UD 30 KAM šá ^{iti}GU$_{4}$ ^{d}UTU ina KASKAL šu-ut ^{d}A-nim

II Gap A 2 GUB-ma zi-qu u UD.D[A]

II Gap A 3 [DIŠ] TA UD 1 KAM šá ^{iti}SIG$_{4}$ EN UD 30 KAM šá ^{iti}IZI ^{d}UTU

II Gap A 4 ina KASKAL šu-ut ^{d}En-líl GUB-ma BURU$_{14}$ u uš-šú

II i 56 and when it disappears it remains (invisible) for as many days as it stood in the sky,

II i 57 and rises and becomes visible either in the East or in the West in the path of the Sun. (If) this star becomes visible in winter, (there will be) rain and flood;

II i 58 (if) it becomes visible at harvest time, you observe its glow, its 'soakings', where it becomes visible, and the wind that blows.

II i 59 This star is either red and bright, or yellow and dark.

II i 60 ¶ Jupiter becomes visible in the East, stands in the sky for one year, and disappears in the West.

II i 61 ¶ Venus becomes visible either in the East or in the West, stands in the sky for 9 months, and disappears.

II i 62 ¶ Mars becomes visible in the East, stands in the sky for one year (and) 6 months, or for one year (and) 10 months, or for 2 years,

II i 63 and disappears in the West. This star shows either redness and is bright, or is . . . and small.

II i 64 ¶ Saturn, also (called) the Scales (or) star of the Sun, becomes visible in the East,

II i 65 stands in the sky for one year, and disappears in the West. This star is either red or white.

II i 66 ¶ Mercury, whose name is Ninurta, becomes visible within a month and disappears

II i 67 within a month, either in the East or in the West.

II i 68 If you are to see the direction of the winds: the Wagon lies across where the North wind rises,

II i 69 the Fish lies across where the South wind rises, the Scorpion lies across where the West wind rises,

II i 70 the Old Man and the Stars stand where the East wind rises.

II i 71 On the day of your watch the stars will show you which wind blows.

II Gap A 1 ¶ From the 1st day of Month XII until the 30th day of Month II, the Sun stands in the path of those of Anu:

II Gap A 2 wind and warm weather.

II Gap A 3 ¶ From the 1st day of Month III until the 30th day of Month V, the Sun

II Gap A 4 stands in the path of those of Enlil: harvest and heat.

II Gap A 5 [DIŠ T]A UD 1 KAM šá ^{iti}KIN EN UD 30 KAM šá ^{iti}APIN ^{d}UTU

II Gap A 6 ina KASKAL šu-ut ^{d}A-nim GUB-ma zi-qu u UD.DA

II Gap A 7 [DIŠ TA UD 1 K]AM šá ^{iti}GAN EN UD 30 KAM šá ^{iti}ZÍZ ^{d}UTU ina KASKAL šu-ut ^{d}É-a GUB-ma EN.TE.NA

II Gap A 8 [DIŠ ina ^{iti}BÁR$^{?}$ UD 1$^{?}$ K]AM MUL.MUL u ^{d}Sin šit-qu-lu MU BI GI.NA-ta

II Gap A 9 [BE-ma$^{?}$ ina ^{iti}BÁR$^{?}$ U]D 3 KAM MUL.MUL u ^{d}Sin LÁL MU BI DIRI-át

---

II Gap A 10 [DIŠ ina ^{iti}GU$_{4}$ UD 1 KAM] MUL.MUL IGI.LÁ MU BI GI.NA-ta

II Gap A 11 [BE-ma ina ^{iti}SIG$_{4}$ U]D 1 KAM MUL.MUL IGI.LÁ MU BI D[IRI-át]

II Gap A 12 [DIŠ ina ^{iti}ŠU UD 15 KAM ^{mul}KAK.SI.SÁ IGI.LÁ]

II Gap A 13 [^{d}UTU šá ina id ^{im}SI.SÁ KUR-ḫa]

II Gap A 14 [GUR-ma ana] ⌜id⌝ IM.⌜U$_{18}$⌝.L[U ultanappal$^{?}$]

II Gap A 15 [ ] ⌜x⌝ [ ] MU BI [GI.NA-át]

II Gap A 16 [B]E-ma ina ^{iti}IZI UD ⌜15⌝ KAM ^{mul}KAK.SI.SÁ IGI.LÁ MU BI DIRI-[át]

II Gap A 17 DIŠ ina ^{iti}KIN UD 15 KA[M] ^{mul}ŠU.PA IGI.LÁ MU BI [GI.NA-át]

II Gap A 18 [B]E-ma ina ^{iti}DU$_{6}$ UD 15 KAM ^{mul}ŠU.PA IGI.LÁ MU BI [DIRI-át]

II ii 1 [DIŠ ina $^{i]ti}$DU$_{6}$ UD 15 KAM MUL.MUL u ^{d}Sin LÁL MU BI [GI.N]A-át

---

II ii 2 [BE-m]a ina ^{iti}APIN UD 15 KAM MUL.MUL u ^{d}Sin LÁL MU BI DIRI-át

---

II ii 3 [DIŠ ina ^{iti}A]B UD 1[5 KA]M ^{mul}KAK.SI.SÁ ina li-la-a-ti ina ^{d}UTU.È [IGI.LÁ ^{d}UTU šá] ina id ^{im}U$_{18}$.LU KUR-ḫa GUR-ma ana id ^{im}SI.SÁ un-da-na-ḫar [MU B]I GI.NA-át

II ii 4 BE-ma ina ^{iti}ZÍZ UD 15 KAM ^{mul}KAK.SI.SÁ ina li-la-a-ti IGI MU BI DIRI-át

---

II ii 5 [DIŠ ina ^{iti}Š]E UD 15 KAM ^{mul}KU$_{6}$ ^{mul}ŠU.GI IGI.LÁ MU BI GI.NA-át

II Gap A 5 ¶ From the 1st day of Month VI until the 30th day of Month VIII, the Sun
II Gap A 6 stands in the path of those of Anu: wind and warm weather.

II Gap A 7 [¶ From the 1st day] of Month IX until the 30th day of Month XI, the Sun stands in the path of those of Ea: winter.

II Gap A 8 [¶ On the 1st$^{?}$ day of Month I$^{?}$] the Stars and the Moon are balanced; this year is normal.
II Gap A 9 [If] on the 3rd d[ay of Month I$^{?}$] the Stars and the Moon are balanced, this year is intercalary.

II Gap A 10 [¶ In Month II on the 1st day] the Stars become visible; this year is normal.
II Gap A 11 [If in Month III] on the 1st day the Stars become visible, this year is intercalary.
II Gap A 12 [¶ In Month IV on the 15th day the Arrow becomes visible;]
II Gap A 13 [the Sun, which rises in the North,]
II Gap A 14 [turns and keeps moving down towards] the South.
II Gap A 15 [ ] this year [is normal.]

II Gap A 16 If in Month V on the 15th day the Arrow becomes visible, this year is intercalary.

II Gap A 17 ¶ In Month VI on the 15th day ŠU.PA becomes visible; this year [is normal.]
II Gap A 18 If in Month VII on the 15th day ŠU.PA becomes visible, this year [is intercalary.]

II ii 1 [¶ In] Month VII on the 15th day the Stars and the Moon are balanced; this year is normal.

II ii 2 [If] in Month VIII on the 15th day the Stars and the Moon are balanced, this year is intercalary.

II ii 3 [¶ In Month X on the 15th] the Arrow [becomes visible] in the evening in the East; [the Sun, which] rises in the South, turns and keeps coming up towards the North: this [year] is normal.
II ii 4 If, in Month XI on the 15th day the Arrow becomes visible in the evening, this year is intercalary.

II ii 5 [¶ The Fish (and) the Old Man become visible (var.: at night) on the 15th day of Month XII; this year is normal.

II ii 6 [BE-ma] ina ^{iti}BÁR UD 15 KAM ^{mul}KU$_{6}$ ^{mul}ŠU.GI IGI^{meš} MU BI DIRI-át

---

II ii 7 MÚ^{meš} MUL^{meš} šá šu-ut ^{d}É-a šu-ut ^{d}A-nim šu-ut ^{d}En-líl
II ii 8 [. . . .] u MÚ^{meš}-šú-nu [K]IN.KI[N-m]a MU BI ta-nam-bi

---

II ii 9 ki-ma MUL^{meš} š[á . . . . IT]I u MU.AN.NA tuš-tab-bal-ma
II ii 10 ina 3 MU^{meš} ME-a GAR-ma MU [BI DI]RI.GA ME-bi

II ii 11 ana UD.NÁ.A 12 ITI^{meš} šu-ta-ku-lu ina 3 MU^{meš} ITI DIRI.GA ta-qab-bi

II ii 12 ina 12 ITI^{meš} 10 UD^{meš} DIRI^{meš} ŠID-at MU.AN.NA

II ii 13 šum-ma UD.DA.ZAL.LÁ-e u$_{4}$-mi ITI u MU.AN.NA ana IGI-ka
II ii 14 1,40 UD.DA.ZAL.LÁ-e u$_{4}$-me ana ITI ÍL-ma
II ii 15 50 UD.DA.ZAL.LÁ-e ITI IGI 50 UD.DA.ZAL.LÁ-e ITI

II ii 16 ana 12 ITI ÍL-ma 10 UD^{meš} DIRI^{meš} ŠID-at MU.AN.NA tam-mar

II ii 17 ina 3 MU^{meš} MU BI DIRI.GA ME-bi

II ii 18 DIŠ ^{iti}BÁR.ZAG.GAR 2 KAM-ma BAL-e ^{d}Šul-gi
II ii 19 DIŠ ^{iti}DIRI.ŠE.GUR$_{10}$.KU$_{5}$ BAL-e MAR.TU-i
II ii 20 DIŠ ^{iti}KIN.^{d}INNIN 2 KAM-ma BAL-e kaš-ši-i

II ii 21 DIŠ ina ^{iti}BÁR UD 15 KAM 3 MA.NA EN.NUN u$_{4}$-mi 3 MA.NA EN.NUN GI$_{6}$
II ii 22 1 ina 1 KÙŠ GIŠ.MI 2½ DANNA u$_{4}$-mu
II ii 23 2 ina 1 KÙŠ GIŠ.MI 1 DANNA 7 UŠ 30 NINDA u$_{4}$-mu
II ii 24 3 ina 1 KÙŠ GIŠ.MI ⅔ DANNA 5 UŠ u$_{4}$-mu

II ii 25 DIŠ ina ^{iti}ŠU UD 15 KAM 4 MA.NA EN.NUN u$_{4}$-mi 2 [MA.NA] EN.NUN GI$_{6}$
II ii 26 1 ina 1 KÙŠ GIŠ.MI 2 DANNA u$_{4}$-mu
2 ina 1 KÙŠ GI[Š.MI 1 DAN]NA u$_{4}$-mu
II ii 27 3 ina 1 KÙŠ GIŠ.MI ⅔ DANNA u$_{4}$-mu
4 ina 1 KÙŠ GIŠ.MI ½ DANNA u$_{4}$-mu
II ii 28 5 ina 1 KÙŠ GIŠ.MI 12 UŠ u$_{4}$-mu
6 ina 1 KÙŠ GIŠ.MI 10 UŠ u$_{4}$-mu
II ii 29 8 ina 1 KÙŠ GIŠ.MI 7 UŠ 30 NINDA u$_{4}$-mu
II ii 30 9 ina 1 KÙŠ GIŠ.MI 6 UŠ 40 NINDA u$_{4}$-mu
10 ina 1 KÙŠ GIŠ.MI 6 UŠ u$_{4}$-mu

II ii 6 [If] in Month I on the 15th day the Fish (and) the Old Man become visible, this year is intercalary.

II ii 7 The risings of the stars of Ea, Anu and Enlil.

II ii 8 You se[arch] for [. . .] and their risings, and you name this year.

II ii 9 When the stars . . ., you compute [. . . of] month$^{?}$ and year, and

II ii 10 in the third year (var. in three years) you make a pronouncement and pronounce this year as intercalary.

II ii 11 To . . . the day of disappearance of the Moon for 12 months, you pronounce an intercalary month in the third year (var. in three years);

II ii 12 10 days in excess in 12 months is the amount for one year.

II ii 13 If you are to see the correction for day, month, and year:

II ii 14 you multiply 1,40, the correction for a day, by a month, and

II ii 15 you find 50, the correction for a month; you multiply 50, the correction for a month,

II ii 16 by 12 months, and you find 10 days in excess, the amount for a year.

II ii 17 In the third year (var.: in three years) you pronounce this year as intercalary.

II ii 18 ¶ An intercalary Month I (belongs to) the reign of Šulgi;

II ii 19 ¶ an intercalary Month XII (belongs to) the Amorite reign;

II ii 20 ¶ an intercalary Month VI (belongs to) the Kassite reign.

II ii 21 ¶ On the 15th day of Month I, 3 minas is the watch of the day, 3 minas is the watch of the night.

II ii 22 1 cubit shadow 2½ bēru of daytime

II ii 23 2 cubits shadow 1 bēru 7 UŠ 30 NINDA daytime

II ii 24 3 cubits shadow ⅔ bēru 5 UŠ daytime

II ii 25 ¶ On the 15th day of Month IV, 4 minas is the watch of the day, 2 [minas] is the watch of the night.

II ii 26 1 cubit shadow 2 bēru daytime

2 cubits shadow [1] bēru daytime

II ii 27 3 cubits shadow ⅔ bēru daytime

4 cubits shadow ½ bēru daytime

II ii 28 5 cubits shadow 12 UŠ daytime

6 cubits shadow 10 UŠ daytime

II ii 29 8 cubits shadow 7 UŠ 30 NINDA daytime

II ii 30 9 cubits shadow 6 UŠ 40 NINDA daytime

10 cubits shadow 6 UŠ daytime

II ii 31 DIŠ ina ^{iti}DU$_6$ UD 15 KAM 3 MA.NA EN.NUN u$_4$-mi 3 MA.NA EN.NUN GI$_6$

II ii 32 1 ina 1 KÙŠ GIŠ.MI 2½ DANNA u$_4$-mu

II ii 33 2 ina 1 KÙŠ GIŠ.MI 1 DANNA 7 UŠ 30 NINDA u$_4$-mu

II ii 34 3 ina 1 KÙŠ GIŠ.MI ⅔ DANNA 5 UŠ u$_4$-mu

II ii 35 DIŠ ina ^{iti}AB UD 15 KAM 2 MA.NA EN.NUN u$_4$-mi 4 MA.NA EN.NUN GI$_6$

II ii 36 1 ina 1 KÙŠ GIŠ.MI 3 DANNA u$_4$-mu

2 ina 1 KÙŠ GIŠ.MI 1½ DANNA u$_4$-mu

II ii 37 3 ina 1 KÙŠ GIŠ.MI 1 DANNA u$_4$-mu

4 ina 1 KÙŠ GIŠ.MI ⅔ DANNA 2 UŠ 30 NINDA u$_4$-mu

II ii 38 5 ina 1 KÙŠ GIŠ.MI 18 UŠ u$_4$-mu

6 ina 1 KÙŠ GIŠ.MI ½ DANNA u$_4$-mu

II ii 39 8 ina 1 KÙŠ GIŠ.MI 11 UŠ 15 NINDA u$_4$-mu

9 ina 1 KÙŠ GIŠ.MI 10 UŠ u$_4$-mu

II ii 40 10 ina 1 KÙŠ GIŠ.MI 9 UŠ u$_4$-mu

II ii 41 BE-ma nap(!)-pal-ti 1 KÙŠ GIŠ.MI ana IGI-ka 40 nap-pal-ti u$_4$-m[i]

II ii 42 u GI$_6$ ana 7,30 ÍL-ma 5(!) nap-pal-ti GIŠ.MI 1 KÙŠ tam-[mar]

II ii 43 DIŠ ina ^{iti}BÁR UD 1 KAM 3 MA.NA 10 GÍN EN.NUN GI$_6$ 12 UŠ 40 NINDA ŠÚ šá Sin

II ii 44 DIŠ ina ^{iti}BÁR UD 15 KAM 3 MA.NA EN.NUN GI$_6$ 12 UŠ KUR šá Sin

---

II ii 45 DIŠ ina ^{iti}GU$_4$ UD 1 KAM 2 5/6 MA.NA EN.NUN GI$_6$ 11 UŠ 20 NINDA ŠÚ šá Sin

II ii 46 DIŠ ina ^{iti}GU$_4$ UD 15 KAM 2⅔ MA.NA EN.NUN GI$_6$ 10 UŠ 40 NINDA KUR šá Sin

---

II ii 47 DIŠ ina ^{iti}SIG$_4$ UD 1 KAM 2½ MA.NA EN.NUN GI$_6$ 10 UŠ ŠÚ šá Sin

II ii 48 DIŠ ina ^{iti}SIG$_4$ UD 15 KAM 2⅓ MA.NA EN.NUN GI$_6$ 9 UŠ 20 NINDA KUR šá Sin

---

II ii 49 DIŠ ina ^{iti}ŠU UD 1 KAM 2 MA.NA 10 GÍN EN.NUN GI$_6$ 8 UŠ 40 NINDA ŠÚ šá Sin

II ii 31 ¶ On the 15th day of Month VII, 3 minas is the watch of the day, 3 minas is the watch of the night.

II ii 32 1 cubit shadow 2½ bēru daytime

II ii 33 2 cubits shadow 1 bēru 7 UŠ 30 NINDA daytime

II ii 34 3 cubits shadow ⅔ bēru 5 UŠ daytime

II ii 35 ¶ On the 15th day of Month X, 2 minas is the watch of the day, 4 minas is the watch of the night.

II ii 36 1 cubit shadow 3 bēru daytime

2 cubits shadow 1½ bēru daytime

II ii 37 3 cubits shadow 1 bēru daytime

4 cubits shadow ⅔ bēru 2 UŠ 30 NINDA daytime

II ii 38 5 cubits shadow 18 UŠ daytime

6 cubits shadow ½ bēru daytime

II ii 39 8 cubits shadow 11 UŠ 15 NINDA daytime

9 cubits shadow 10 UŠ daytime

II ii 40 10 cubits shadow 9 UŠ daytime

II ii 41 If you are to see the interval-number for 1 cubit of shadow, you multiply 40, the interval-number for daytime

II ii 42 and night-time, by 7,30, and you see 5, the interval-number for a shadow of 1 cubit.

II ii 43 ¶ On the 1st day of Month I, 3 minas 10 shekels is the watch of the night; 12 UŠ 40 NINDA setting of the Moon.

II ii 44 ¶ On the 15th day of Month I, 3 minas is the watch of the night; 12 UŠ rising of the Moon.

II ii 45 ¶ On the 1st day of Month II, 2⅚ minas is the watch of the night; 11 UŠ 20 NINDA setting of the Moon.

II ii 46 ¶ On the 15th day of Month II, 2⅔ minas is the watch of the night; 10 UŠ 40 NINDA rising of the Moon.

II ii 47 ¶ On the 1st day of Month III, 2½ minas is the watch of the night; 10 UŠ setting of the Moon.

II ii 48 ¶ On the 15th day of Month III, 2⅓ minas is the watch of the night; 9 UŠ 20 NINDA rising of the Moon.

II ii 49 ¶ On the 1st day of Month IV, 2 minas 10 shekels is the watch of the night; 8 UŠ 40 NINDA setting of the Moon.

II ii 50 DIŠ ina ^{iti}ŠU UD 15 KAM 2 MA.NA EN.NUN GI$_6$ 8 UŠ [KUR šá Sin]

II ii 51 DIŠ ina ^{iti}IZI UD 1 KAM 2 MA.NA 10 GÍN EN.NUN GI$_6$ [8 UŠ 40 NINDA ŠÚ šá Sin]

II ii 52 DIŠ ina ^{iti}IZI UD 15 KAM 2⅓ MA.NA EN.NUN GI$_6$ 9 U[Š 20 NINDA KUR šá Sin]

II ii 53 DIŠ ina ^{iti}KIN UD 1 KAM 2½ MA.NA EN.NUN GI$_6$ 10 UŠ ŠÚ [šá Sin]

II ii 54 DIŠ ina ^{iti}KIN UD 15 KAM 2⅔ MA.NA EN.NUN GI$_6$ 10 UŠ 40 NINDA KUR [šá Sin]

II iii 1 DIŠ ina ^{iti}DU$_6$ UD 1 KAM 2 5/6 MA.NA EN.NUN GI$_6$ 11 UŠ 20 NINDA ŠÚ [šá Sin]

II iii 2 DIŠ ina ^{iti}DU$_6$ UD 15 KAM 3 MA.NA EN.NUN GI$_6$ 12 UŠ KUR [šá Sin]

II iii 3 DIŠ ina ^{iti}APIN UD 1 KAM 3 MA.NA 10 GÍN EN.NUN GI$_6$ 12 UŠ 40 NINDA ŠÚ šá Sin

II iii 4 DIŠ ina ^{iti}APIN UD 15 KAM 3⅓ MA.NA EN.NUN GI$_6$ 13 UŠ 20 NINDA KUR šá Sin

---

II iii 5 DIŠ ina ^{iti}GAN UD 1 KAM 3½ MA.NA EN.NUN GI$_6$ 14 UŠ ŠÚ šá Sin

II iii 6 DIŠ ina ^{iti}GAN UD 15 KAM 3⅔ MA.NA EN.NUN GI$_6$ 14 UŠ 40 NINDA KUR šá Sin

---

II iii 7 DIŠ ina ^{iti}AB UD 1 KAM 3 5/6 MA.NA EN.NUN GI$_6$ 15 UŠ 20 NINDA ŠÚ šá Sin

II iii 8 DIŠ ina ^{iti}AB UD 15 KAM 4 MA.NA EN.NUN GI$_6$ 16 UŠ KUR šá Sin

---

II iii 9 DIŠ ina ^{iti}ZÍZ UD 1 KAM 3 5/6 MA.NA EN.NUN GI$_6$ 15 UŠ 20 NINDA ŠÚ šá Sin

II iii 10 DIŠ ina ^{iti}ZÍZ UD 15 KAM 3⅔ MA.NA EN.NUN GI$_6$ 14 UŠ 40 NINDA KUR šá Sin

---

II iii 11 DIŠ ina ^{iti}ŠE UD 1 KAM 3½ MA.NA EN.NUN GI$_6$ 14 UŠ ŠÚ šá Sin

II iii 12 DIŠ ina ^{iti}ŠE UD 15 KAM 3⅓ MA.NA EN.NUN GI$_6$ 13 UŠ 20 NINDA KUR šá Sin

---

II ii 50 ¶ On the 15th day of Month IV, 2 minas is the watch of the night; 8 UŠ [rising of the Moon.]

II ii 51 ¶ On the 1st day of Month V, 2 minas 10 shekels is the watch of the night; 8 UŠ 40 NINDA setting of the Moon.

II ii 52 ¶ On the 15th day of Month V, 2⅓ minas is the watch of the night; 9 U[Š 20 NINDA rising of the Moon.]

II ii 53 ¶ On the 1st day of Month VI, 2½ minas is the watch of the night; 10 UŠ setting of the Moon.

II ii 54 ¶ On the 15th day of Month VI, 2⅔ minas is the watch of the night; 10 UŠ 40 NINDA rising [of the Moon.]

II iii 1 ¶ On the 1st day of Month VII, 2⅚ minas is the watch of the night; 11 UŠ 20 NINDA setting [of the Moon.]

II iii 2 ¶ On the 15th day of Month VII, 3 minas is the watch of the night; 12 UŠ rising of the Moon.

II iii 3 ¶ On the 1st day of Month VIII, 3 minas 10 shekels is the watch of the night; 12 UŠ 40 NINDA setting of the Moon.

II iii 4 ¶ On the 15th day of Month VIII, 3⅓ minas is the watch of the night; 13 UŠ 20 NINDA rising of the Moon.

II iii 5 ¶ On the 1st day of Month IX, 3½ minas is the watch of the night; 14 UŠ setting of the Moon.

II iii 6 ¶ On the 15th day of Month IX, 3⅔ minas is the watch of the night; 14 UŠ 40 NINDA rising of the Moon.

II iii 7 ¶ On the 1st day of Month X, 3⅚ minas is the watch of the night; 15 UŠ (var.: half a bēru) 20 NINDA setting of the Moon.

II iii 8 ¶ On the 15th day of Month X, 4 minas is the watch of the night; 16 UŠ rising of the Moon.

II iii 9 ¶ On the 1st day of Month XI, 3⅚ minas is the watch of the night; 15 UŠ (var.: half a bēru) 20 NINDA setting of the Moon.

II iii 10 ¶ On the 15th day of Month XI, 3⅔ minas is the watch of the night; 14 UŠ 40 NINDA rising of the Moon.

II iii 11 ¶ On the 1st day of Month XII, 3½ minas is the watch of the night; 14 UŠ setting of the Moon.

II iii 12 ¶ On the 15th day of Month XII, 3⅓ minas is the watch of the night; 13 UŠ 20 NINDA rising of the Moon.

II iii 13 4 igi-gub-bé-e IGI.DUḪ.A šá ^{d}Sin 3 MA.NA EN.NUN GI$_{6}$

II iii 14 ana 4 ÍL-ma 12 IGI.DUḪ.A šá ^{d}Sin IGI

II iii 15 40 NINDA nap-pal-ti u$_{4}$-mi u GI$_{6}$ ana 4 ÍL-ma 2,40 nap-pal-ti IGI.DUḪ.A IGI

II iii 16 DIŠ MUL$_{5}$.MUL$_{5}$ ŠIR^{meš}-šú SA$_{5}^{meš}$-ma KI.A SI.SÁ

II iii 17 DIŠ $^{mul_{5}}$Kár-šul ina ^{iti}ŠE uš-pa-lak-kam-ma BE ú-sa-naq-ma BE-nu

II iii 18 [DIŠ] ina lìb-bi $^{mul_{5}}$Kár-šul 1 MUL ma-gal KUR$_{4}$ ^{lú}KÚR

II iii 19 DIŠ UD.DA 4 lu 2 GAL^{meš} SIG$_{7}^{meš}$ ma BE^{meš}

II iii 20 DIŠ NIGIN ⸢x⸣ [x da]n-niš SA$_{5}^{meš}$-ma A.KAL u A.AN

II iii 21 DIŠ $^{mul_{5}}$KU$_{6}$ ina ⸢x⸣ [x x] BE-ma SA$_{5}$ GAR u ba-ìl BE-ma un-nun u TUR BE-nu

-----

II iii 22 DIŠ $^{mul_{5}}$U.RI.RI IGI.LÁ A.AN u A.KAL

II iii 23 DIŠ $^{mul_{5}}$U.RI.RI ana $^{mul_{5}\,giš}$GIGIR KU.NU-ma ANŠE.PA+GÍN^{meš} ÚŠ^{meš}

II iii 24 DIŠ $^{mul_{5}}$U.RI.RI ana $^{mul_{5}}$AB.SÍN KU.NU-ma ŠU.BI.AŠ.ÀM

II iii 25 DIŠ $^{mul_{5}}$U.RI.RI ana $^{mul_{5}}$ALLA KU.NU UR$_{5}$ MÁḪ GAM.ME

II iii 26 DIŠ $^{mul_{5}}$U.RI.RI ana $^{mul_{5}}$ALLA 15 KU.NU UR$_{5}$ MÁḪ GAM.ME

II iii 27 DIŠ $^{mul_{5}}$U.RI.RI ana $^{mul_{5}}$ALLA 2,30 KU.NU IDIM GAM.ME

II iii 28 DIŠ $^{mul_{5}}$UG$_{5}$.GA ana id IM 1 KI.TA ina-pal ŠE.GIŠ.Ì SI.SÁ

II iii 29 DIŠ $^{mul_{5}}$UG$_{5}$.GA ana id IM 2 AN.TA ina-pal AB.SÍN ŠE NU SI.SÁ

II iii 30 DIŠ $^{mul_{5}}$UR.MAḪ MUL$_{5}^{meš}$-šú il-tap-pu-u 3,20 KI DU NÍG.È MUL$_{5}$ BI

II iii 31 MUL$_{5}$ KASKAL

II iii 32 DIŠ $^{mul_{5}}$KAL.NE ÍB.TAG$_{4}$ RU ana 4 MUL$_{5}^{me}$ šá $^{mul_{5}}$AŠ.IKU TE U URU GAM.ME

II iii 33 DIŠ $^{mul_{5}}$ ^{d}EN.GIŠGAL.AN.NA KUR$_{4}$-ma A.AN u A.KAL ^{d}TIR.AN.NA UD ḪÉ.NUN MU.NE

II iii 34 DIŠ ina ^{im}U$_{18}$.LU A.AN ina ^{im}SI.SÁ A.KAL ina ^{im}KUR.RA A.AN ina ^{im}MAR GÌR.BAL

II iii 35 DIŠ u$_{4}$-um ^{d}Li$_{9}$-si$_{4}$ IGI.LÁ 3 u$_{4}$-me mu-ši-ta LÚ NIGIN É-šú

II iii 13 4 is the coefficient for the visibility of the Moon; you multiply 3 minas, the nighttime watch,

II iii 14 by 4, and you find 12, the visibility of the Moon.

II iii 15 You multiply 40 NINDA, the interval-number for daytime and nighttime, by 4, and you find 2,40, the interval-number of the visibility.

II iii 16 ¶ If the . . .s of the Stars are red: the irrigated land will prosper.

II iii 17 ¶ If the constellation Karšul is opened wide in Month XII: . . ., deaths.

II iii 18 ¶ If one star inside the constellation Karšul is very bright: the enemy.

II iii 19 ¶ If . . . 4 or 2 big ones are yellow: deaths.

II iii 20 ¶ If . . . are very red: flood and rain.

II iii 21 ¶ If the Fish in [. . .] either shows redness and is bright, or is . . . and small: deaths.

II iii 22 ¶ If the U.RI.RI-star becomes visible: rain and flood.

II iii 23 ¶ If the U.RI.RI-star approaches the Chariot: horses will die.

II iii 24 ¶ If the U.RI.RI-star approaches the Furrow: the same.

II iii 25 ¶ If the U.RI.RI-star approaches the Crab: omen for an important person; he will die.

II iii 26 ¶ If the U.RI.RI-star approaches the Crab on the right: omen for an important person; he will die.

II iii 27 ¶ If the U.RI.RI-star approaches the Crab on the left: an important person will die.

II iii 28 ¶ If the Raven . . .s below to the direction of the South wind: sesame will prosper.

II iii 29 ¶ If the Raven . . .s to the direction of the North wind: the barley crop will not prosper.

II iii 30 ¶ If the stars of the Lion . . .: the king will be victorious wherever he goes. This star

II iii 31 is a campaign star.

II iii 32 ¶ If the KAL.NE-star . . .s and approaches the 4 stars of the Field (var. Stars): the lord of the city will die.

II iii 33 ¶ If Jupiter is bright: rain and flood. The name of the Rainbow is ‘day$^{?}$ of abundance’;

II iii 34 ¶ in the South, rain; in the North, flood; in the East, rain; in the West, devastation.

II iii 35 ¶ On the day the Lisi-star becomes visible, for 3 days a man should awaken at night all that is around his house,

II iii 36	NAM.LÚ.U_{18}.LU GU_{4} UDU.NÍTA ANŠE li-de-ek-ki
II iii 37	NU ina-al u ana $^{d}Li_{9}$-si_{4} lik-ru-ub KI NÍGIN É-šú uš-tak-lal
	---
II iii 38	DIŠ ina ^{iti}GAN ina ^{iti}AB ina ^{iti}ZÍZ SI Sin 2,30 tar-ṣa-at-ma
II iii 39	KI ina-ṭal nu-uḫ-ḫu-ut ú-de-e

II iii 40	DIŠ KUR ina ŠÀ ni-di KUR-ḫa 3,20 ŠÚR-ma ^{giš}TUKUL i-na-ši
II iii 41	DIŠ ^{d}UTU ina ŠÀ ni-di ŠÚ LUGAL ÚŠ

II iii 42	DIŠ MUL TA ^{im}MAR SUR-ma ana ŠÀ $^{d}Li_{9}$-si_{4} KU_{4} ḪI.GAR GÁL
II iii 43	DIŠ MUL TA ^{im}MAR SUR-ma ana ŠÀ ^{d}Ni-ri KU_{4} ḪI.GAR GÁL
II iii 44	DIŠ MUL TA ^{im}MAR SUR-ma ana ŠÀ ^{d}Sin KU_{4} ḪI.GAR GÁL
II iii 45	DIŠ MUL [BI 3 šú]-nu È-ma ZI-bu NU kaš-du

II iii 46	MUL [TA ^{i}]^{m}KUR ana $^{im}U_{18}$.LU SUR-ma ^{mul}EN.TE.NA.BAR.ḪUM DIB-ma
II iii 47	ina ^{im}MAR ŠÚ 3 $MU^{meš}$ KUR ḪÉ.NUN IGI
II iii 48	[DIŠ MUL TA] ^{im}MAR ana ŠÀ ^{im}KUR DIB u_{4}-um 3 $MU^{meš}$
II iii 49	[KUR ḪUL] IGI.LÁ
II iii 50	[DIŠ MUL T]A $MURUB_{4}$ AN-e SUR-ma ina ^{d}UTU.ŠÚ.A ŠÚ-bi ZI.GA
II iii 51	KALAG ina KUR È
II iii 52	[ ] ^{mul}GÍR.TAB IGI $^{im}U_{18}$.LU GIN MU BI SIG_{5}

II iii 53	⸢DIŠ M⸣UL ⸢x x x x x x ṣir-ḫa NU TUK⸣ SIG_{5}

II Gap B 1	[DIŠ] MUL ^{d}AMAR.UTU ina SAG MU.AN.NA IGI MU BI AB.SÍN NÍG SI.SÁ
II Gap B 2	DIŠ MUL ^{d}AMAR.UTU MUL.MUL KUR-ud ina MU BI ^{d}IM RA
II Gap B 3	DIŠ MUL ^{d}AMAR.UTU ^{mul}UGA KUR-ud ŠE.GIŠ.Ì NIM GIŠ
II Gap B 4	DIŠ MUL ^{d}AMAR.UTU pa-gar LÚ IGI be-en-nu DAB-su
II Gap B 5	DIŠ ina ma-ḫar MUL ^{d}AMAR.UTU LÚ A ir-muk NAM.TAG.GA GÁL-ši

II iii 36 people, cattle, sheep, donkeys,
II iii 37 and he must not sleep; he should pray to the Lisi-god, then he and all that is around his house will experience success.

II iii 38 ¶ If in Month IX, in Month X, (or) in Month XI the left horn of the Moon is stretched out and
II iii 39 looks towards the Earth: diminution[?] of trouble.

II iii 40 ¶ If the Sun rises in a cumulus cloud: a king will become furious and raise weapons.
II iii 41 ¶ If the Sun sets in a cumulus cloud: a king will die.

II iii 42 ¶ If a star flares up from the West and enters the Lisi-star: there will be revolution.
II iii 43 ¶ If a star flares up from the West and enters the Yoke: there will be revolution.
II iii 44 ¶ If a star flares up from the West and enters the Moon: there will be revolution.
II iii 45 ¶ If [this] star comes out (from the Moon) as three stars: unsuccessful attack.

II iii 46 <If> a star flashes from the East towards the South, passes EN.TE.NA.BAR.ḪUM and
II iii 47 sets in the West: for three years the land will see abundance.
II iii 48 [¶ If a star] passes from the West to the middle of the East: (for) a period of three years
II iii 49 [the land] will experience [evil.]
II iii 50 [¶ If a star] flares up from the middle of the sky and sets in the West: a heavy loss
II iii 51 will occur in the land.
II iii 52 [If] . . . of the Scorpion becomes visible (and) the South wind blows: this year will be good.

II iii 53 ¶ If . . . does not have a flare: it will be good.

II Gap B 1 [¶ If] the star of Marduk becomes visible at the beginning of the year: in this year the furrow will prosper.
II Gap B 2 [¶ If] the star of Marduk reaches the Stars: in this year Adad will devastate.
II Gap B 3 ¶ If the star of Marduk reaches the Raven: early sesame will prosper.
II Gap B 4 ¶ If the star of Marduk sees the body of a man: epilepsy[?] will seize him.
II Gap B 5 ¶ If a man takes a bath in front of the star of Marduk: there will be guilt.

II Gap B 6	DIŠ MUL ^{d}AMAR.UTU GI$_{6}$-ma IGI.LÁ MU BI A.SÌG GÁL-ši

----

II Gap B 7	DIŠ ^{mul}ŠUDUN ina È-šú da-ʾi-im A.KAL up-pu-lu È
II Gap B 8	DIŠ ^{mul}ŠUDUN ina È-šú it-ta-na-an-paḫ A.KAL ḫar-pu
II iv 1	DIŠ ^{mul}ŠUDUN ina È-šú GIM IZI it-ta-na-an-paḫ BURU$_{14}$ SI.SÁ
II iv 2	DIŠ ^{mul}ŠUDUN ina È-šú šup-pul-ma da-ʾi-im A.KAL NU GÁL
II iv 3	DIŠ ^{mul}ŠUDUN ina È-šú ana ^{d}UTU.ŠÚ.A IGI-šú GAR-nu ^{im}MAR.TU ZI-ma
II iv 4	ana ^{im}U$_{18}$.LU is-ḫur ina ^{iti}KIN UD 10 KAM šal-pú-ti KUR GAR-an
II iv 5	DIŠ ^{mul}ŠUDUN ina È-šú ana ^{d}UTU.TU.TU IGI-šú GAR-nu IGI AN-e IGI.BAR-ma
II iv 6	IM mim-ma la i-zi-iq SU.KÚ GAR-an BAL NAM.GILIM.MA
II iv 7	šá I-bí-^{d}Sin LUGAL ŠEŠ.UNUG^{ki} šá ka-mu-us-su
II iv 8	a-na An-ša-an^{ki} DU-ku ERÍN-šú EGIR-šú i-bak-ku-ú KIMIN i-ma-aq-qu-tu

----

II iv 9	DIŠ šum-ma LÚ ana NUN-ti GAR-ma ^{im}U$_{18}$.LU DU LÚ BI SIG$_{5}$
II iv 10	DIŠ MIN-ma ^{im}SI.SÁ DU NINDA SIG KÚ
II iv 11	DIŠ MIN-ma ^{im}KUR.RA DU UD^{me}-šú LUGÚD.DA^{meš}
II iv 12	DIŠ MIN-ma ^{im}MAR.TU DU NU SI.SÁ

==

II Gap B 6 ¶ If the star of Marduk is dark when it becomes visible: in this year there will be *asakku*-disease.

II Gap B 7 ¶ If the Yoke is dim when it comes out: the late flood will come out.

II Gap B 8 ¶ If the Yoke keeps flaring up when it comes out: early flood.

II iv 1 ¶ If the Yoke keeps flaring up like fire when it comes out: the harvest will prosper.

II iv 2 ¶ If the yoke is very low and dim when it comes out: there will be no flood.

II iv 3 ¶ If the Yoke is turned towards sunset when it comes out, (if) the West wind rises and

II iv 4 turns to South: on the 10th day of Month VI, destruction of the land will be brought about.

II iv 5 ¶ If the Yoke is turned towards Sunset$^{?}$ when it comes out and faces the front of the sky,

II iv 6 and no wind blows: there will be famine; dynasty (ending in) catastrophe.

II iv 7 (omen) of Ibbi-Sin, king of Ur, who went in fetters

II iv 8 to Anšan; after him his troops weep (var.: fall).

II iv 9 ¶ If they make a man a ruler, and the South wind blows: this man (var.: the dynasty) will become good.

II iv 10 ¶ If they make a man a ruler, and the North wind blows: he will eat thin$^{?}$ bread.

II iv 11 ¶ If they make a man a ruler, and the East wind blows: his days will be short.

II iv 12 ¶ If they make a man a ruler, and the West wind blows: he will not prosper.

===

Commentary

I i 1 – I ii 35

MUL.APIN begins with three lists of stars of Enlil, Anu, and Ea. The Akkadian term *kakkabu*, translated here as 'star', refers to a broader group of celestial objects than the English word 'star'. For example, single stars, small groups of stars, constellations, and even non-stellar objects such as comets and, on occasions, planets may be designated as 'stars'. Most of the stars given in these lists are in fact constellations (e.g. the Crab, the Lion, and the Wagon) or star groups (e.g. the two stars which stand in the sting of the Scorpion, called Šarur and Šargaz).[1] The five planets visible to the naked eye (Mercury, Venus, Mars, Jupiter, and Saturn) are also included.

Each of the three lists of stars is followed by a summary statement giving the number of stars which appear in that list. Entries within the lists themselves give the name of the star, often accompanied by the name of a god with whom the star is associated. For some stars, additional short comments are provided, usually referring to the position of the star relative to an earlier star in the list. In some of these cases, both the constellation and individual parts of that constellation are mentioned as separate stars. For example, the Goat and the Bright Star of the Goat are listed as two separate Enlil stars, the Scorpion and the Chest of the Scorpion are given as separate Ea stars, with a further part of the Scorpion, the Horn of the Scorpion, listed among the Anu stars, and the Lion is followed in the list of Enlil stars by the King, which is explained to be the star in the Lion's chest.

On most of the manuscripts, the entries for each star are written on a separate line and preceded by a DIŠ sign acting as an item marker (note that sources BB and CC always omit the DIŠ sign). Occasionally, however, two stars are given on the same line. In such cases, the DIŠ sign is only given at the beginning of the line; the second star does not have an item marker. As a consequence, the number of item markers in the lists does not tally with the number of stars given in the summary

1 For attempts to identify the stars and constellations referred to in MUL.APIN and other cuneiform texts with various degrees of success, see Kugler (1913), van der Waerden (1949), and Reiner and Pingree (1981). We refrain from attempting to make identifications and instead simply refer to the stars by their ancient name.

statements: in our composite edition, which follows the structure of source A, for example, where the summary states that there are 33 Enlil stars, we count only 31 item markers, for the 23 Anu stars there are only 20 item markers, and for the 15 Ea stars there are only 13 item markers. The lack of explicit item markers can occasionally cause ambiguities within the text, where it is not clear whether the text refers to two entries or whether what appears to be a second star name is a gloss to the first star. As a result, reconstructions of the lists of 33 Enlil, 23 Anu, and 15 Ea stars by previous scholars have not all agreed with one another. Most of these problems can be resolved using evidence from other parts of MUL.APIN and from other texts.

Table 1 details the Enlil, Anu, and Ea stars as we reconstruct the three lists. In addition to the star names, we include in this table any gods associated with the stars and any additional information (usually relative positions between stars) given in the text. We briefly explain below the reconstruction of each of the three lists.

According to the summary statement, there should be 33 Enlil stars. In our reconstructed text, 31 of these stars are indicated by DIŠ markers. Thus, there must be two additional stars not marked by DIŠ signs, because they are written on the same line. One of these cases is clearly at line I i 23. This line refers to two stars, the Standing Gods of Ekur and the Sitting Gods of Ekur. Although they are placed together in source A, which we follow for the structure of our edition, and in sources Z and AA, sources F, BB, and GG separate them on to two lines. Furthermore, the Standing Gods appear without the Sitting Gods in the list of *ziqpu* stars at lines I iv 4 – I iv 6. The other case is less straightforward. Kugler and Pingree took lines I i 10 – I i 11 to refer to two stars: the Scintillating Stars which stand in the Tail of the Lion and the Frond of Eru.[2] This explanation is attractive in that several Neo-Assyrian and *ziqpu* star lists mention two neighbouring stars: the Single Star from his (the Lion's) tail and Eru. However, the phrasing of the entry at I i 10 – I i 11 does not seem to support this interpretation. The entry is written exactly like the previous entry, which refers to the star the King. Furthermore, in source AA, the line break occurs between the end of 'the scintillating stars which stand in the tail of the Lion' and 'the Frond (of the date palm) of Eru, Zarpanitu'. Source AA regularly uses the DIŠ sign as an item marker at the beginning of lines, and so we would expect a DIŠ sign at the beginning of both lines. No DIŠ sign is given before the Frond of Eru, however. Thus, it seems certain that the phrase 'the scintillating stars which stand in the tail of the Lion' is to be understood as a description of the star the Frond, not as a separate star. We propose instead to take the Ford in line I i 37 as a separate star in order to reach the total of 33 Enlil stars. The entry for the Ford is unusual in that it is given a longer description than most stars, because of its role (for example, in the Three Stars Each tradition) in dividing the sky in half. Because the Ford is said to be the star of Marduk, and because Jupiter is associated with Marduk, Pingree took them both to be part of

2 Kugler (1913: 54) and Hunger and Pingree (1989: 137).

Table 1 The primary catalogue of Enlil, Anu, and Ea stars.

Position in list	*Star name*	*Associated gods*	*Additional information*
Enlil			
Enlil 1	The Plough	Enlil	Who goes in front of the stars of Enlil
Enlil 2	The Wolf		The seed-funnel of the Plough
Enlil 3	The Old Man	Enmešarra	
Enlil 4	The Crook	Gamlu	
Enlil 5	The Great Twins	Lugalirra and Meslamtaea	
Enlil 6	The Small Twins	Alammuš and Nin-gublaga	
Enlil 7	The Crab		The seat of Anu
Enlil 8	The Lion	Latarak	
Enlil 9	The King		The star which stands in the chest of the Lion
Enlil 10	The Frond of Eru	Zarpanitu	The scintillating stars which stand in the tail of the Lion
Enlil 11	ŠU.PA	Enlil who decrees the fate of the land	
Enlil 12	The Abundant One	The minister of Ninlil	The star which stands in front of it (SU.PA)
Enlil 13	The Star of Dignity	The minister of Tišpak	The star which stands behind it (SU.PA)
Enlil 14	The Wagon	Ninlil	
Enlil 15	The Fox	Erra, the strong one of the gods	The star which stands in the shaft of the Wagon
Enlil 16	The Ewe	Aja	The star which stands in the front part of the Wagon
Enlil 17	The Hitched Yoke	Great Anu of Heaven	
Enlil 18	The Wagon of Heaven	Damkianna	
Enlil 19	The Heir of the Sublime Temple	The first-ranking son of Anu	The star which stands in its (the Wagon of Heaven's) knot
Enlil 20	The Standing Gods of Ekur		
Enlil 21	The Sitting Gods of Ekur		
Enlil 22	The Goat	Gula	
Enlil 23	The Dog		The star which stands in front of the Goat
Enlil 24	The Bright Star of the Goat	Lamma, the minister of Baba	
Enlil 25	Nin-nisig and Erragal		The two stars which stand behind it (the Goat)
Enlil 26	The Panther	Nergal	

Enlil 27	The Pig	Damu	The star which stands on its (the Panther's) right
Enlil 28	The Horse		The star which stands on its (the Panther's) left
Enlil 29	The Stag	The minister of the Stars	The star which stands behind it (the Panther)
Enlil 30	The Vole	The Rainbow god	The scintillating stars which stand in the chest of the Stag
Enlil 31	The Deleter		The bright red star which stands in the kidney of the Stag
Enlil 32	The Ford	The star of Marduk	When the stars of Enlil have been finished, one big star – (although) its light is dim – divided the sky in half and stands there
Enlil 33	Jupiter	Marduk, the Ford	Keeps changing its position and crosses the sky
Anu			
Anu 1	The Field	The seat of Ea	Who goes in front of the stars of Anu
Anu 2	The Swallow		The star which stands opposite the Field
Anu 3	Anunitu		The star which stands behind the Field
Anu 4	The Hired Man	Dumuzi	The star which stands behind it
Anu 5	The Stars	The Seven, the great gods	
Anu 6	The Bull of Heaven, the Jaw of the Bull	The crown of Anu	
Anu 7	The True Shepherd of Anu	Papsukal, the minister of Anu and Ištar	
Anu 8	Lulal and Latarak		The twin stars which stand opposite the True Shepherd of Anu
Anu 9	The Rooster		The star which stands behind it (the True Shepherd of Anu)
Anu 10	The Arrow	The arrow of the great warrior Ninurta	
Anu 11	The Bow	The Elamite Ištar, the daughter of Enlil	
Anu 12	The Snake	Ningizzida, lord of the Netherworld	
Anu 13	The Raven	The star of Adad	
Anu 14	The Furrow	Šala, the ear of grain	
Anu 15	The Scales		
Anu 16	The Horn of the Scorpion		

(continued)

Table 1 (continued)

Position in list	*Star name*	*Associated gods*	*Additional information*
Anu 17	The star of Zababa		
Anu 18	The Eagle		
Anu 19	The Corpse		
Anu 20	Venus		Keeps changing its position and crosses the sky
Anu 21	Mars		Keeps changing its position and crosses the sky
Anu 22	Saturn		Keeps changing its position and crosses the sky
Anu 23	Mercury	Ninurta	Keeps changing its position and crosses the sky
Ea			
Ea 1	The Fish	Ea	Who goes in front of the stars of Ea
Ea 2	The Great One	Ea	
Ea 3	Eridu	Ea	
Ea 4	Ninmaḫ		The star which stands at its (Eridu's) right
Ea 5	The Mouse	Ningirsu	
Ea 6	The Harrow	The Weapon of Mār-bīti, by means of which he sees the subterranean waters	The star which stands at its (the Mouse's) side
Ea 7	Šullat and Ḫaniš	Šamaš and Adad	The two stars which stand behind it (the Mouse)
Ea 8	Numušda	Adad	The star which stands behind them (Šullat and Ḫaniš), rises like Ea, and sets like Ea
Ea 9	The Wild Dog	Kusu	The star which stands at the left of the Scorpion
Ea 10	The Scorpion	Išḫara, lade of all inhabited regions	
Ea 11	The Chest of the Scorpion	Lisi, Nabû	
Ea 12	Šarur and Šargaz		The two stars which stand in the sting of the Scorpion
Ea 13	Pabilsag		The stars which stand behind them (Šarur and Šargaz)
Ea 14	The Barge		
Ea 15	The Goat-fish		

the same entry. However, the entry for Jupiter is preceded by a DIŠ marker, which would be unusual if it is continuing an entry from a previous line.[3] Furthermore, in the Three Stars Each tradition, the Ford and Jupiter are clearly separate stars (in Astrolabe B, the Ford is among the stars of Anu, whereas Jupiter is listed with the stars of Enlil). Thus, we take the Ford and Jupiter as separate entries in the list.

There are 20 DIŠ markers in the list of Anu stars in our reconstructed text, leaving three additional stars which must be accounted for. Two are straightforward: line I ii 12 clearly refers to three stars: the star of Zababa, the Eagle, and the Corpse. These stars are the last in the list before the planets, and the presence of more than one star is highlighted by the use of 'and' (*u*) before the third star on this line. There are two possibilities for the other star. Pingree assumed that line I ii 1, which reads '¶ The Bull of Heaven, the Jaw of the Bull, the crown of Anu', refers to two stars: the Bull of Heaven and a second star, which forms part of the same constellation, called the Jaw of the Bull, which is associated with the crown of Anu.[4] In support of this conclusion, it can be remarked that other constellations in MUL.APIN appear both as generic constellations and as stars which constitute their parts, as explained above. Furthermore, a star named the Jaw of the Bull is often used as a Normal Star in Late Babylonian observational texts. Against this conclusion, however, is the fact that the Bull of Heaven and the Jaw of the Bull seem to be used interchangeably in other sections of MUL.APIN. For example, the list of the dates of first appearances of stars in I ii 36 – I iii 12 includes an entry for the Jaw of the Bull, with a first visibility date of the 20th of Month II, but does not mention the Bull of Heaven. This same date for the first visibility of the Jaw of the Bull appears in the list of simultaneous culminations and risings at first visibility in I iv 10 – I iv 30. However, in the list of intervals between first visibilities of stars in I iii 34 – I iii 48, the Jaw of the Bull is not included, but the Bull of Heaven is named, with the same implied date of first visibility. We find the same switching between the Bull of Heaven and the Jaw of the Bull in other early astronomical texts. For example, in the list of Ea stars in Astrolabe B, the Jaw of the Bull, again identified with the crown of Anu, and said to be 'the star which stands after the Stars', is given, but, in the clearly related star catalogue HS 1897, the Jaw of the Bull is replaced by the Bull of Heaven, accompanied by exactly the same remarks about its identification with the crown of Anu and its place after the Stars. A later duplicate to HS 1897, BM 55502, switches back to the Jaw of the Bull.[5] Furthermore, the lexical text URA = *hubullu* Tablet 22 line 273 equates the Bull of Heaven (^{mul}GU$_4$.AN.NA) with the Jaw of the Bull (is le-e). Finally, the uranology text MLC 1884 Rev. 15' seems to take the Jaw of the Bull as an alternative name for the Bull of Heaven: '[The Bull of Heav]en, the Jaw of the Bull, a bull', mirroring the previous line, which reads '[The Stars,] the seven gods, the great gods'.[6] The uranology texts draw heavily on MUL.APIN for their repertoire of

3 Noted already by Horowitz (2014: 25).

4 Hunger and Pingree (1989: 138).

5 Horowitz (2014: 103).

6 Beaulieu, Frahm, Horowitz, and Steele (2018).

stars, and so it seems that the author of this uranology text understood MUL.APIN to state that the Jaw of the Bull was an alternative name for the Bull of Heaven. An alternative suggestion is to understand line I ii 11, which reads '¶ The Scales, the horn of the Scorpion', as two stars.[7] The Scorpion constellation appears as a star in the list of Ea stars, accompanied by a second star, the Chest of the Scorpion. The Scorpion faces the Scales, and, in some Greek traditions, the Scales (Libra) were known as the 'Claws of the Scorpion'. It is possible that MUL.APIN refers to such an equivalent Babylonian tradition, where the Scales (a weighing balance) were seen as the claws ('horns') of the Scorpion.[8] However, it is more likely that the Horn of the Scorpion was a separate star, located near to the Scales. In support of this possibility, we note that the Horn of the Scorpion seems to appear as a separate star in the so-called 'GU text' (BM 78161),[9] and the Horn of the Scorpion is mentioned in various omen texts as a distinct part of the Scorpion (some omen texts refer to the left and right horns of the Scorpion as separate stars).[10] We therefore consider it likely that the Horn of the Scorpion is a separate star to the Scales and list it, rather than the Jaw of the Bull, as an Anu Star.

There are 13 DIŠ markers for 15 Ea stars. Fortunately, in this case, it is easy to identify the lines which contain more than one star. Line I ii 20 reads, '¶ The Great One, Ea; Eridu, Ea', and clearly refers to two stars, the Great One and Eridu. The Great One and Eridu appear separately and with very different dates in the list of dates of first visibilities. In addition, source X separates these entries over two lines, both beginning with a DIŠ sign. Furthermore, if Eridu was a gloss on the name of the Great One, then we would not expect the god Ea's name to be repeated. Line I ii 34 names two stars, the Barge and the Goat-fish, separated by the word 'and' (*u*), implying that they are different stars. In addition, source d separates these two stars over two lines.

Many of the associations between stars and gods in the lists of Enlil, Anu, and Ea stars are found in other texts, such as Section 2 of the so-called 'Astrolabe B' Three Stars Each text and the Great Star list, and therefore seem to be part of a long-standing, widespread tradition.[11] In later parts of MUL.APIN (and elsewhere), for a few stars the god's name is sometimes used in place of the star name. For example, the Frond of Eru (*sissinnu* ^{d}*Eru*) is often written using the name Eru with the star determinative (^{mul}*Eru*).

The grouping of stars into three categories, those of Enlil, Anu, and Ea, follows a tradition that can be traced back to at least the middle of the second millennium. A Middle Babylonian prayer to the gods of the night from Boghazkoi (the ancient Hittite capital Hattuša) contains a list of stars in order of their first appearances,

7 This suggestion has already been made by Koch (1989: 114–115).

8 Kugler (1913: 63).

9 BM 78161 21–22 (Pingree and Walker 1988).

10 See, for example, 91-5-9, 164 10' (Reiner and Pingree 2005: 88–89) and K 2568+ Obv. Ii 8'–9' (Reiner and Pingree 2005: 92–93).

11 Hunger and Pingree (1999: 59–61) provide a full comparison of the associations found in MUL. APIN with those in Astrolabe B.

followed by a reference to the stars of Ea, Anu, and Enlil.[12] A roughly contemporary star list, probably from Nippur, contains three lists of stars of Ea, Anu, and Enlil. Each list is followed by a summary statement noting that there are ten stars in each list, using exactly the same terminology as in MUL.APIN.[13] The Three Stars Each texts list three stars, one from each of those of Ea, Anu, and Enlil, for each month of the year. Note that these earlier sources give the three lists in the order Ea, Anu, and Enlil, whereas MUL.APIN reverses that order to Enlil, Anu, and Ea.

The three groups of stars, those of Enlil, Anu, and Ea, can be associated with the three 'paths' (*ḫarrānu*) of Enlil, Anu, and Ea mentioned elsewhere in MUL.APIN (II Gap A 1 – II Gap A 7, which describes the Sun's motion among the three paths over the course of the year, and I iv 1 and I iv 7, which both describe the *ziqpu* stars standing in the path of Enlil). The three paths also appear in celestial omens and occasionally in accounts of observations. The stars in the three paths fall roughly into three regions of declination: the Enlil stars to the north of about +17° declination, the Anu stars to between about +17° and –17° declination, and the Ea stars to the south of about –17° declination.[14] Most scholars have interpreted the three paths as bands of declination stretching across the sky from the eastern to the western horizon.[15] Pingree, however, has argued for a stricter interpretation of the paths as segments of the eastern horizon through which stars rise.[16] Several objections can be raised against Pingree's interpretation.[17] First, the list of Enlil stars in MUL.APIN contains a group of circumpolar stars, including the Wagon, which is said explicitly elsewhere to be visible all year and to circle around the sky.[18] By definition, circumpolar stars cannot rise across the eastern horizon.[19] Second, some reports of observations of comets found in the *Astronomical Diaries* refer to the comet as being within one of the three paths. In some cases, on the night that the comet was observed, it was already close to setting at the western horizon when it first became visible shortly after sunset and, therefore, could not have been observed to rise across a segment of the eastern horizon. It seems more likely, therefore, that the three paths correspond to rough bands across the sky stretching from the eastern to the western horizon: the middle band, Anu, corresponds roughly to about ±17° of declination; Enlil, to everywhere to the north of this (including the circumpolar regions); and Ea, everywhere to the south of it.

12 KUB 4 47 rev. 47–48; see Weidner (1915: 60–62) and Horowitz (1998: 158).

13 HS 1897; see Oelsner and Horowitz (1997–1998).

14 This was first recognized by Bezold, Kopff, and Boll (1913: 8), and the declination boundaries were refined by Schaumberger (1935: 321–322).

15 In addition to Bezold, Kopff, and Boll (1913: 8) and Schaumberger (1935: 321–322), see, for example, Weidner (1915: 46–49) and van der Waerden (1949).

16 Reiner and Pingree (1981: 17–18), Hunger and Pingree (1989: 137), Hunger and Pingree (1999: 61).

17 See Lambert (1987), Steele (2007: 299), and Horowitz (2014: 11–15).

18 K 4292 28c: [mul]MAR.GÍD.DA kal MU DU-az ma-a i-lam-ma-a, 'The Wagon stands all year, namely, it circles around' (Reiner and Pingree 1981: Text III).

19 Pingree argues that the circumpolar stars are interpolations into the list.

Almost all of the stars referred to in other parts of MUL.APIN are taken from the three lists of Enlil, Anu, and Ea stars. Thus, these three lists can be understood as the primary star catalogue within MUL.APIN, presenting the full repertoire of stars from which the other lists draw. In Table 2, we give the dates of the first appearances of stars found in I ii 36 – I iii 12, whether the star is included in the list of rising and setting stars (I iii 13 – I iii 33), whether the star is included in the list of intervals between the first appearances of stars (I iii 34 – I iii 48), whether the star appears in the list of *ziqpu* stars (I iv 1 – I iv), whether the star appears as a rising star in the list of simultaneously rising and culminating stars (I iv 15 – I iv 30), and whether the star appears in the list of stars in the path of the Moon (I iv 33 – I iv 37). It is noticeable that most of these subsequent lists use a very similar sub-repertoire of stars drawn from the longer primary list.

With a small number of exceptions, the three lists of Enlil, Anu, and Ea stars are arranged in order of the successive first appearances of the stars within that path. These exceptions fall into three groups: First are stars whose position is recorded with reference to another star. In these cases, the reference star appears first in the list, with the stars that refer to it following. In such cases, stars that are 'in front of' (meaning further to the east and so rise before) the reference star are given before stars that are 'behind' (meaning further to the west and so rise after) the reference star. Second, circumpolar stars are inserted in the list of Enlil stars after the star Dignity, probably because the Wagon, which is the most frequently mentioned circumpolar star in cuneiform texts, is near the star Dignity. Third, the planets, whose position changes relative to the fixed stars, are placed at the ends of the Enlil and Anu lists.

As already noted, the notion of assigning stars to the three paths can be traced back at least to the Middle Babylonian period. The Three Stars Each tradition gives one star from each path for each month of the year, making a total of 12 stars for each path and 36 stars overall. The repertoire of stars in MUL.APIN is therefore considerably greater than found in the Three Stars Each tradition. More importantly, however, those stars that appear in both sources are frequently not assigned to the same path. For example, comparing the stars that appear in Section 3 of the so-called Astrolabe B (Table 3), we see that 13 stars listed as being in the path of Enlil in MUL.APIN are included in Astrolabe B, but 5 of them are there said to be in the path of Anu, and, of the 12 Anu stars from MUL.APIN that are given in Astrolabe B, only 4 are said to be in this path, with 5 assigned to the path of Ea and 3 assigned to the path of Enlil. Although slightly different Three Stars Each lists are known, none of these texts demonstrates a close agreement with the MUL.APIN lists.[20] Thus, the Three Stars Each star lists and the MUL.APIN star lists seem to form separate traditions. Much closer agreement in the paths assigned to stars is found between MUL.APIN and the star list CT 33 9. This partially preserved list gives twelve stars for each of the three paths. All four of the surviving Enlil stars are placed in the same path in MUL.APIN; 11 out of 12 Anu stars are in the same path, and 9 out of 12 Ea stars (two stars listed in this path in

20 See Hunger and Pingree (1999: 58–63) and Horowitz (2014).

Table 2 The appearance of stars from the primary lists of Enlil, Anu, and Ea stars in other star lists in MUL.APIN.

Position in list	*Star name*	*Date of first visibility*	*List of rising/ setting stars*	*List of intervals between first visibility*	*List of ziqpu stars*	*List of rising stars with culmination of a ziqpu star*	*List of stars in the path of the Moon*
Enlil							
Enlil 1	The Plough						
Enlil 2	The Wolf						
Enlil 3	The Old Man	XII 15	r & s		y		y
Enlil 4	The Crook	I 20	s	y	y	y	y
Enlil 5	The Great Twins	III 10	s		y		y
Enlil 6	The Small Twins	IV 5	s				
Enlil 7	The Crab	IV 5			y		y
Enlil 8	The Lion	IV 15	r & s		y		y
Enlil 9	The King	V 5 (var. 15)	r				
Enlil 10	The Frond of Eru				y		
Enlil 11	ŠU.PA	VI 15	r & s	y	y	y	
Enlil 12	The Abundant One				y		
Enlil 13	The Star of Dignity				y		
Enlil 14	The Wagon						
Enlil 15	The Fox						
Enlil 16	The Ewe						
Enlil 17	The Hitched Yoke						
Enlil 18	The Wagon of Heaven						
Enlil 19	The Heir of the Sublime Temple						
Enlil 20	The Standing Gods of Ekur		r		y		
Enlil 21	The Sitting Gods of Ekur						
Enlil 22	The Goat		r & s	y	y	y	
Enlil 23	The Dog	VII 15	r		y		

(continued)

Table 2 (continued)

Position in list	*Star name*	*Date of first visibility*	*List of rising/ setting stars*	*List of intervals between first visibility*	*List of ziqpu stars*	*List of rising stars with culmination of a ziqpu star*	*List of stars in the path of the Moon*
Enlil 24	The Bright Star of the Goat						
Enlil 25	Nin-nisig and Erragal						
Enlil 26	The Panther	IX 15	r & s	y	y	y	
Enlil 27	The Pig						
Enlil 28	The Horse						
Enlil 29	The Stag	XI 5 (var. 15)	r		y		
Enlil 30	The Vole						
Enlil 31	The Deleter						
Enlil 32	The Ford						
Enlil 33	Jupiter						
Anu							
Anu 1	The Field	XI 5 (var. 15)	r & s	y		y	
Anu 2	The Swallow	X 15		y		y	y
Anu 3	Anunitu	XI 25	s				y
Anu 4	The Hired Man	I 1	s				y
Anu 5	The Stars	II 1	r & s	y		y	y
Anu 6	The Bull of Heaven, the Jaw of the Bull	II 20	r	y		y	y
Anu 7	The True Shepherd of Anu	III 10	r & s	y		y	y
Anu 8	Lulal and Latarak						
Anu 9	The Rooster						
Anu 10	The Arrow	IV 15	r & s	y		y	
Anu 11	The Bow	V 5 (var. 15)	r & s	y		y	
Anu 12	The Snake	IV 15	r & s				
Anu 13	The Raven	VI 10	r				
Anu 14	The Furrow	VI 25	s	y			y
Anu 15	The Scales	VII 15	r	y		y	y

Anu 16	The Horn of the Scorpion					
Anu 17	The star of Zababa		r			
Anu 18	The Eagle	IX 15	r & s			
Anu 19	The Corpse					
Anu 20	Venus					
Anu 21	Mars					
Anu 22	Saturn					
Anu 23	Mercury					
Ea						
Ea 1	The Fish	XII 15	r	y	y	
Ea 2	The Great One	XI 5 (var. 15)	r & s			y
Ea 3	Eridu	VI 10	r & s	y	y	
Ea 4	Ninmaḫ		r			
Ea 5	The Mouse	VII 15	r & s			
Ea 6	The Harrow					
Ea 7	Šullat and Ḫaniš					
Ea 8	Numušda					
Ea 9	The Wild Dog	VII 15	r & s			
Ea 10	The Scorpion	VIII 5 (var. 15)	r & s			y
Ea 11	The Chest of the Scorpion	VIII 5 (var. 15)	r			
Ea 12	Šarur and Šargaz					
Ea 13	Pabilsag	IX 15	r & s			y
Ea 14	The Barge					
Ea 15	The Goat-fish					y

Table 3 A comparison of the paths of stars mentioned in both MUL.APIN and Astrolabe B Section 3.

Star	*Path in MUL.APIN*	*Path in Astrolabe B Section 3*
The Plow	Enlil	Enlil
The Old Man	Enlil	Anu
The Great Twins	Enlil	Anu
The Little Twins	Enlil	Anu
The Crab	Enlil	Anu
The Lion	Enlil	Anu
The King	Enlil	Enlil
ŠU.PA	Enlil	Enlil
The Wagon	Enlil	Enlil
The Fox	Enlil	Enlil
The Goat	Enlil	Enlil
The Panther	Enlil	Enlil
Jupiter	Enlil	Enlil
The Field	Anu	Ea
The Swallow	Anu	Anu
Anunitu	Anu	Enlil
The Stars	Anu	Ea
The Arrow	Anu	Ea
The Bow	Anu	Ea
The Snake	Anu	Enlil
The Raven	Anu	Anu
The Scales	Anu	Anu
The Eagle	Anu	Enlil
Venus	Anu	Anu
Mars	Anu	Ea
The Fish	Ea	Ea
The Great One	Ea	Ea
Ninmah	Ea	Ea
EN.TE.NA.BAR.HUM	Ea	Enlil
Numušda	Ea	Ea
The Mad Dog	Ea	Ea
The Scorpion	Ea	Anu

CT 33 9 are not given in MUL.APIN).[21] It is tempting to assume, as many previous authors have done, that the MUL.APIN lists represent a later attempt to revise assignments of the stars to the paths in the Three Stars Each texts, to make them fit astronomical reality better. In this model, CT 33 9 would represent an intermediate stage in this process. However, although MUL.APIN is almost certainly a later text than the Three Stars Each tradition, the continued use of the Three Stars List assignments well into the late first millennium BC – for example, in the

21 Horowitz (2014: 209–214).

microzodiac rising time scheme texts[22] – makes it problematical to assume such a linear progress in astronomical knowledge. Instead, it may be that the assignment of the stars to the three paths in the Three Stars Each tradition was not intended to be astronomically accurate, but was instead based upon a range of mythological and other reasons.

The entry for the Ford (Nēberu), the 32nd Enlil star, differs in style from all other entries in these lists. Instead of a DIŠ sign, the entry begins with the phrase, 'When the stars of Enlil have finished', and the star is not only named but described and given a role: 'one big star – (although) its light is dim – divides the sky in half and stands there: (that is) the star of Marduk, the Ford'. A similar description of this star is found in the list of 12 Anu stars in Astrolabe B:

> DIŠ MUL SA$_5$ šá ina ZI ^{im}U$_{18}$.LU EGIR DINGIR^{meš} GI$_6$-ti ug-da-mi-ru-nim-ma AN-e BAR-ma GUB-ma MUL BI ^{d}né-bi-ru ^{d}AMAR.UD
>
> ¶ The red star which stands in the south, after the gods of the night have finished, divides the sky in half and stands there: that star is the Ford, Marduk.

The Ford is also mentioned in *Enūma Eliš* V 6, where it is said to have been placed by Marduk in its heavenly stand (*manzāzu*) in order to fix the intervals of the stars and keep them moving in order.[23] It also appears in Neo-Assyrian astrological reports and in omen texts and commentaries.[24] The role of the Ford and its identification have been investigated by many previous scholars, without a consensus having been reached.[25] Sometimes, the name was used to refer to planets: in the Neo-Assyrian period, Jupiter could be named the Ford, and, in earlier times, there is evidence that Mercury (and possibly Venus) could be called by this name.[26] The fact that one or more planets could be called the Ford, however, does not require that the Ford could not also refer to a constellation. Planets were often called by the name of stars or constellations (for example, later in MUL.APIN, Saturn is said to also be called the Scales).[27]

The inclusion of the planets among the stars in the three paths has also puzzled scholars. Unlike the fixed stars, the planets move between the three paths over the course of their motion through the zodiac and up and down in celestial latitude. This characteristic of the planets is noted explicitly for Jupiter, Venus, Mars, and Saturn, whose names are followed by the phrase 'keeps changing its position and crosses the sky'. Mercury receives a slightly different gloss: 'Mercury, whose name is Ninurta, rises or sets in the east or in the west within a month'. This phrase is almost exactly repeated in II i 66–67, a section of the text presenting the intervals of visibility and invisibility for the planets. Planets also appear in the Three Stars Each texts. For example, in Section 3 of Astrolabe B, Mars is placed in the

22 Steele (2017).
23 Lambert (2013: 98–99).
24 For a summary of references to the Ford, see Hunger and Pingree (1989: 126).
25 See, for example, Schaumberger (1935: 313–314), Schott (1936), Koch (1991), Horowitz (2014: 20–25).
26 Brown (2000: 58).
27 Brown (2000: 53–81), Reiner (2004).

path of Ea, Venus in the path of Anu, and Jupiter in the path of Enlil. In MUL. APIN, Jupiter is placed at the end of the list of Enlil stars, and the other four planets are placed at the end of the list of Anu stars. Pingree suggests that the planets were initially placed in the path of Anu because this path lies roughly in the middle of the extreme northern and southern rising points of the ecliptic on the horizon. Jupiter was then moved to the path of Enlil because, in *Enūma Eliš*, the god Marduk established Nēberu (the Ford) as the gatekeeper.[28] This legend is alluded to in I i 37. Pingree's argument is possible, but does not account for the appearance of the planets in different paths in the Three Stars Each texts. A speculative, alternative interpretation would be to see the names of the planets as referring to the position of the planet at its *bīt niṣirti*. The *bīt niṣirti* of the planets, which roughly correspond to the Greek astrological concept of planetary exaltations, are already referred to in *Enūma Anu Enlil* and in a royal inscription of Esarhaddon.[29] Three of the planets are given in the position of their *bīt niṣirti* in the preserved part of the so-called GU text (BM 78161), which lists stars in 'strings' stretching out from a *ziqpu* star (or a distance behind a *ziqpu* star): Jupiter, 'which stands behind the Crab in front of the Lion', Mercury, 'which stands with the Furrow in front of the Raven', and Saturn, 'which stands in front of the Scales'.[30] The uranology texts that describe constellations also include the positions of the planets in their *bīt niṣirti*.[31] The preserved entries refer to Jupiter placed between the Crab and the Lion, and Venus in the area of the Swallow and Anunitu. Drawings of the planets in the position of their *bīt niṣirti* appear on two microzodiac tablets from Late Babylonian Uruk.[32] A variety of Late Babylonian astrological texts also refer to the *bīt niṣirti*. These texts confirm the positions of Mercury, Venus, Jupiter, and Saturn's *bīt niṣirti*s and show that Mars's *bīt niṣirti* is in the zodiacal sign of Capricorn, corresponding to the constellation the Goat-fish. The positions of the constellations containing these *bīt niṣirti* in MUL.APIN would place Jupiter's *bīt niṣirti* in the path of Enlil, Mercury, Venus, and Saturn's *bīt niṣirti*s in the path of Anu, and Mars's *bīt niṣirti* in the path of Ea. Only Mars's *bīt niṣirti* is in a different path to that given for the planet in the star lists. Given the appearance of planets in their *bīt niṣirti* in other star lists, we suggest that the planets are included in the lists of stars in the three paths by reference to their *bīt niṣirti*.[33]

28 Hunger and Pingree (1989: 139).

29 See Rochberg-Halton (1988a: 53–57) and Hunger and Pingree (1999: 28–29) for a summary of the evidence.

30 Pingree and Walker (1988). See also Hunger and Pingree (1999: 90–100) and Steele (2017: 95–96). On the appearance of the *bīt niṣirti* in this text, see Koch (1999).

31 Beaulieu, Frahm, Horowitz, and Steele (2018).

32 Weidner (1967).

33 It is worth noting that, in Astrolabe B, Mars is assigned to the path of Ea, which is the path in which (according to MUL.APIN) we would expect the Goat-fish to be placed. If the *bīt niṣirti*s are the reason for including the planets in the Three Stars Each texts, this would imply that the concept of the *bīt niṣirti* can be traced back to at least the Middle Babylonian period.

I ii 36 – I iii 12

This section contains a list of the dates of the first visibility (heliacal rising) of at least 35 stars drawn from the lists of stars in the three paths in I i 1 – I ii 35. Each entry begins with the DIŠ sign acting as an item marker. As the Sun moves along the ecliptic, there will be a critical date when it is sufficiently far away from a star that the star will be visible for the first time shortly before sunrise. On this date, known as heliacal rising, the star will rise over the horizon and be visible in the sky for a short period of time before disappearing in the light of dawn. Many of the stars given in this list are actually constellations. Not all of the stars that constitute a constellation will have their first visibility on the same date. It is therefore unclear exactly what the first visibility of a constellation refers to: the first visibility of one star that is part of the constellation, the first visibility of enough stars to make the constellation clearly recognizable, or the first visibility of all of the stars that make up the constellation?

Table 4 summarizes the dates of first visibilities of the stars given in the list. Three entries contain additional remarks about the length of day and night: Month IV Day 15, Month VII Day 15, and Month X Day 15, corresponding to the dates of the summer solstice, the autumnal equinox, and the winter solstice in the schematic 360-day calendar. The lengths of day and night are specified in terms of weights using the unit mina: at the summer solstice, day is given as 4 minas and night as 2 minas; at the autumnal equinox, both day and night are given as 3 minas; and, at the winter solstice, day is given as 2 minas and night as 4 minas. Identical statements about the length of day and night at the solstices and equinoxes appear in II i 9 – II i 21 and II ii 21–40, and a scheme for the variation in the length of night over the course of the schematic year is presented in II ii 43 – II iii 12. See the commentary to II i 9 – II i 21 for a detailed discussion of these statements.

The placement of the solstices and equinoxes on the 15th day of Months IV, VII, and X (and by implication also Month I) shows that the dates given in this section are in the schematic 360-day calendar. The dates of the first visibilities are clearly schematic as well: all of the day numbers are a multiple of 5, with the exception of three instances of Day 1. These three cases have clearly been adjusted from Day 30 of the previous month. Section I iii 34 – I iii 48 contains statements of the number of days between the first visibilities of selected stars from the present list. These statements only agree with the present list if the Day 1 entries are moved to Day 30 of the previous month.

The known manuscripts for this part of MUL.APIN attest to four variants. In line I ii 44, the Bow and the King are said to have their first visibility on the 5th of Month V in sources A and H, and on the 15th of Month V in sources M and N. Line I iii 48 states that the rising of the Bow takes place 20 days after the rising of the Arrow (the number is preserved in sources A and FF), which would be the 5th of Month V. Line I iv 22 states that the Bright Star of the Old Man culminates as the Bow rises. Here again, we find two variants for the date of this event. Sources

Table 4 Dates of the first visibility of stars given in I ii 36 – I iii 12. For reference, the positions of the mentioned stars in the three lists of the stars in the paths of Enlil, Anu, and Ea are included.

Date	*Star*	*Position in primary star list*
I 1	The Hired Man	Anu 4
I 20	The Crook	Enlil 4
II 1	The Stars	Anu 5
II 20	The Jaw of the Bull	Anu 6
III 10	The True Shepherd of Anu	Anu 7
	The Great Twins	Enlil 5
IV 5	The Small Twins	Enlil 6
	The Crab	Enlil 7
IV 15	The Arrow	Anu 10
	The Snake	Anu 12
	The Lion	Enlil 8
V 5 (var. 15)	The Bow	Anu 11
	The King	Enlil 9
VI 1	[. . .]	[. . .]
VI 10	Eridu	Ea 3
	The Raven	Anu 13
VI 15	ŠU.PA	Enlil 11
VI 25	The Furrow	Anu 14
VII 15	The Scales	Anu 15
	The Wild Dog	Ea 9
	The Mouse	Ea 5
	The Dog	Enlil 23
VIII 5 (var. 15)	The Scorpion	Ea 10
VIII 15 (var. 25)	The Goat	Enlil 22
	The Chest of the Scorpion	Ea 11
IX 15	The Panther	Enlil 26
	The Eagle	Anu 18
	Pabilsag	Ea 13
X 15	The Swallow	Anu 2
	Arrow (acronychal rising)	Anu 10
XI 5 (var. 15)	The Great One	Ea 2
	The Field	Anu 1
	The Stag	Enlil 29
XI 25	Anunitu	Anu 3
XII 15	The Fish	Ea 1
	The Old Man	Enlil 3

A and O give the date as the 15th of Month V, whereas source AA gives it as the 5th of Month V. It is particularly troubling that source A gives both dates in different parts of the text. A Late Babylonian text that clearly draws on MUL.APIN,

BM 37175, gives the date as Month V Day 15,[34] whereas another Late Babylonian text gives the date of the first visibility of the Bow as the 5th of Month V.[35] We consider the 5th of Month V to be the more likely date.

Line I iii 3 presents two variants for the date of the first visibility of the Scorpion. Sources E, H, and GG give the date as the 5th of Month VIII, whereas sources M and N give it as the 15th of Month VIII. Source M gives the same date for the next entry in the list, the Goat and the Chest of the Scorpion, suggesting that the date in line I iii 3 in this source is simply a scribal error. Line II i 32 gives the date of the first visibility of the Scorpion as the 5th of Month VIII (preserved in sources HH and JJ). Thus, it seems likely that M and N have scribal errors here, and the correct date is the 5th of Month VIII.

Line I iii 4 presents two variants for the date of the first visibility of the Goat and the Chest of the Scorpion. Sources A, E, H, M, and GG give the date as the 15th of Month VIII, whereas source L gives it as the 25th of Month VIII. Line II i 32 gives the date of the first visibility of the Chest of the Scorpion as the 15th of Month VIII (preserved in sources HH and JJ). Thus, it seems likely that L is in error here, and the correct date is the 15th of Month VIII.

Line I iii 10 presents two variants for the date of the first visibility of the Great One, the Field, and the Stag. Sources A, E, H, O, GG, and SS give the date as the 5th of Month XI, whereas source M gives the date as the 15th of Month XI. Lines I iii 41 and I iii 42 state that there are 20 days between the rising of the Swallow and the rising of the Field, and 40 days between the rising of the Field and the rising of the Fish. These intervals imply that the first visibility of the Field is on the 5th of Month XI. However, I iv 29 states that the Dog culminates while the Field rises on the 15th of Month XI (preserved only on source A). Given the known problems with the entries in the section concerning the simultaneous culminations and risings of stars in source A (see the commentary to I iv 10 – I iv 30), it is likely that the correct date is the 5th.

The Arrow receives special attention in this list. In later texts, the Arrow is clearly used as a name for the star Sirius, and it seems likely that in MUL.APIN it referred either to Sirius alone or to a group of stars that included Sirius. The Arrow's first visibility is placed on the 15th of Month IV, the date of the summer solstice. In reality, in Babylon, Sirius's first visibility takes place approximately three weeks after the summer solstice. A Late Babylonian scheme for the dates of the phenomena of Sirius, attested in use during the last three centuries BC, sets the first visibility of the star 21 days (more accurately, 21 *tithi*s or 30ths of a synodic month) after the solstice.[36] Uniquely among the stars given in this list, the date of the acronychal rising of Sirius is presented, in addition to the date of its first visibility. The date given for this event is the 15th of Month X, which is the date of the winter solstice, exactly 6 months or 180 days later in the schematic calendar.

34 BM 37175 Obv. 9'. On this text, see, provisionally, Steele (in press a).

35 BM 77054 Obv. 10'–12' (George 1991). On this text, see further the commentary to I iv 10 – I iv 30 below.

36 Sachs (1952). A variant scheme known from a tablet from Uruk, SpTU V 269, gives the interval as 20 days; see Steele (in press b) and Hunger and Pingree (1999: 152).

In the Late Babylonian schemes, the interval between Sirius's first visibility and its acronychal rising is 170 *tithi*s. Clearly, the author of MUL.APIN made a deliberate decision to align these two phenomena of Sirius with the two solstices.

This section was copied on to an excerpt tablet, our source M, a Late Babylonian tablet from Nippur, along with a very badly preserved, unidentified text on the other side of this tablet. It is also quoted on the unpublished fragment BM 37630.[37]

I iii 13 – I iii 33

This section contains a list of simultaneously rising and setting stars. As usual, each entry in the list is preceded by a DIŠ sign used as an item marker. Table 5 summarizes this list. The list is arranged according to the order in which the rising stars cross the horizon, with the exception of the second entry, which reverses the pairing of the first entry concerning the Stars and the Scorpion rising and setting. For reference, in Table 5, we also include the date given in I ii 36 – I iii 12 for the first visibility of the star.

The meanings of 'rises' (KUR) and 'sets' (ŠÚ) in this section are ambiguous. The term 'rises' is used in Sections I iii 34 – I iii 48 and I iv 10 – I iv 30 to refer to the first visibility of a star, as can be seen by comparing the data in those sections with the dates of first visibility given in I ii 36 – I iii 12, which use the less ambiguous phrase 'becomes visible' (IGI.LÁ). Thus, in the present section, 'rises' could also be interpreted as referring to the first visibility of the star and 'sets' to its last visibility. This interpretation was assumed in the notes to the first publication of one source for this part of MUL.APIN by King in 1912.[38] However, 'rising' and 'setting' could also be used in the more basic sense of simply referring to the stars' crossing the horizon at the same moment on any given night when they are visible. Kugler makes the case that it is in this looser sense that we should understand this section.[39] In support of Kugler's conclusion, it can be pointed out that, in a few cases, where several stars are said to rise together, these groups of stars are not always identical with the groups of stars that have the same date for their first visibility in I ii 36 – I iii 12.[40] For example, according to lines I iii 1 – I iii 3, the Scales, the Wild Dog, the Mouse, and the Dog have their first visibility on the 15th of Month VII, whereas the Scorpion's first visibility is on the 5th of Month VIII. However, according to lines I iii 23 – I iii 24, the Scales, the Wild Dog, and the Mouse rise together, and the Scorpion and the Dog rise together. If rising referred to the first visibility (i.e. heliacal rising), then the Dog should be listed with the first group of stars rather than with the Scorpion. This discrepancy can be explained, however, if we assume that the text is simply referring to the simultaneous rising of stars on any night of the year when they are visible. Because the first visibility of a star depends upon its magnitude and its

37 The first four lines of this tablet preserve the ends of MUL.APIN I iii 9 – I iii 12. Following a horizontal ruling, the tablet continues with a text we are not able to identify or understand, but is clearly not MUL.APIN. We thank Jeanette Fincke for identifying and bringing this tablet to our attention.

38 King (1912: 5).

39 Kugler (1913: 22). Reiner and Pingree (1981: 6) agree with Kugler's interpretation.

40 See also Hunger and Pingree (1999: 67).

Table 5 Rising and setting stars in I iii 13 – I iii 33. For reference the positions of the mentioned stars in the three lists of the stars in the paths of Enlil, Anu, and Ea are included.

Rising stars			*Setting stars*	
Star name	*Position in primary star list*	*Date of first visibility in I ii 36 – I iii 12*	*Star name*	*Position in primary star list*
The Stars	Anu 5	II 1	The Scorpion	Ea 10
The Scorpion	Ea 10	VIII 5 (var. 15)	The Stars	Anu 5
The Bull of Heaven	Anu 6	–	ŠU.PA	Enlil 11
The True Shepherd of Anu	Anu	III 10	Pabilsag	Ea 13
The Arrow The Snake The Lion	Anu 10 Anu 12 Enlil 8	IV 15 IV 15 IV 15	The Great One The Eagle	Ea 2 Anu 18
The Bow The King	Anu 11 Enlil 9	V 5 (var. 15) V 5 (var. 15)	The Goat	Enlil 22
Eridu The Raven	Ea 3 Anu 13	VI 10 VI 10	The Panther	Enlil 26
ŠU.PA	Enlil 11	VI 15	The Field	Anu 1
Ninmaḫ	Ea 4	–	Anunitu	Anu 3
The Scales The Wild Dog The Mouse	Anu 15 Ea 9 Ea 5	VII 15 VII 15 VII 15	The Hired Man	Anu 4
The Scorpion The Dog	Ea 10 Enlil 23	VIII 5 VII 15	Eridu The Stars	Ea 3 Anu 5
The Chest of the Scorpion The Goat	Ea 10 Enlil 22	VIII 15 (var. 25) VIII 15 (var. 25)	The Old Man The True Shepherd of Anu	Enlil 3 Anu 7
Pabilsag Zababa The Standing Gods	Ea 13 Anu 17 Enlil 20	IX 15 – –	The Arrow The Bow The Crook	Anu 10 Anu 11 Enlil 4
The Panther The Eagle	Enlil 26 Anu 18	IX 15 IX 15	The Great Twins The Small Twins	Enlil 5 Enlil 6
The Field The Great One The Stag	Anu 1 Ea 2 Enlil 29	XI 5 (var. 15) XI 5 (var. 15) XI 5 (var. 15)	The Lion The Snake The Mouse	Enlil 8 Anu 12 Ea 5
The Fish The Old Man	Ea 1 Enlil 3	XII 15 XII 15	The Furrow The Wild Dog	Anu 14 Ea 9

relative position in right ascension and declination with respect to the Sun, stars that cross the horizon together may not be seen for this first time together (put simply, some stars will need to be higher in the sky at sunrise in order to be seen than other stars). Furthermore, because many of the 'stars' are actually constellations, the first star of the constellation that rises above the horizon is not necessarily the first star that can be seen to rise heliacally. The way that the stars are grouped in this section, therefore, demonstrates that the list has not simply been constructed from the list of dates of first visibilities in the previous section.

A list of simultaneously rising and setting stars is also found in the so-called Astrolabe B Three Stars Each text. In that text, and in later texts related to it, the rising and setting stars mirror one another. In other words, if star A rises as star B sets, then star B rises and star A sets. Astronomically, this relationship only holds if the stars are situated on the celestial equator or have equal but opposite declinations. Most of the star pairings given in Astrolabe B do not fulfil this criterion, and so the list must be seen as purely schematic. However, in the list of simultaneously rising and setting stars in MUL.APIN, it is only occasionally that we find mirrored entries. In most cases, if star A rises as star B sets, when star B appears in the list as a rising star, it is paired with a different star, C, which sets. As a result, about one-third of the rising stars do not appear as setting stars, and about a quarter of setting stars do not appear as rising stars.

The lack of precise agreement between the groupings of stars in this section and in the list of dates of first visibilities of stars in the previous section, coupled with the inclusion of stars here that do not appear in that list and the fact that the list of rising and setting stars follows astronomical reality in not simply assuming that pairs of stars that rise and set simultaneously also set and rise simultaneously, indicates that the present section was not derived from the list of heliacally rising stars in Section I ii 36 – I iii 12 but was probably instead based upon accumulated observational experience.

I iii 34 – I iii 48

This section lists intervals in days between the 'rising' (KUR) of two stars (see Table 6). Each entry in the list is given on a separate line, which begins with a DIŠ sign as an item marker. With two exceptions, the intervals correspond to the number of days between the dates of the first visibilities of the same stars given in Section I ii 36 – I iii 12, assuming that we work with the schematic 360-day calendar. The two exceptions both concern the Stars, which is the only star in this list whose first visibility occurs on Day 1 of a month, rather than a day that is a multiple of 5. It seems certain that, in this case, the date of the first visibility of the Stars has been adjusted or rounded from the 1st of Month II to the 30th of Month I, in order to ensure that all of the intervals in days in the list are a multiple of 5.

The list begins and ends with the Arrow. Most of the list progresses through a straightforward cycle of stars, with the second star in one line being the first star in the next line. The beginning and the end of the list break with this pattern, however. The first two and the final entries all begin with the Arrow: 55 days from the Arrow to Eridu, 60 days from the Arrow to ŠU.PA, and 20 days from the Arrow to the Bow, rather than 20 days from the Arrow to the Bow, 25 days from the Bow

Table 6 Intervals between the first visibilities of stars given in I iii 34 – I iii 48. For reference, the positions of the mentioned stars in the three lists of the stars in the paths of Enlil, Anu, and Ea and the dates of first visibility of the stars from I ii 36 – I iii 12 are included.

Interval in days	*Star from*			*Star to*		
	Star name	*Position in primary star list*	*Date of first visibility in I ii 36 – I iii 12*	*Star name*	*Position in primary star list*	*Date of first visibility in I ii 36 – I iii 12*
55	The Arrow	Anu 10	IV 15	Eridu	Ea 3	VI 10
60	The Arrow	Anu 10	IV 15	ŠU.PA	Enlil 11	VI 15
10	ŠU.PA	Enlil 11	VI 15	The Furrow	Anu 14	VI 25
20	The Furrow	Anu 14	VI 25	The Scales	Anu 15	VII 15
30	The Scales	Anu 15	VII 15	The Goat	Enlil 22	VIII 15 (var. 25)
30	The Goat	Enlil 22	VIII 15 (var. 25)	The Panther	Enlil 26	IX 15
30	The Panther	Enlil 26	IX 15	The Swallow	Anu 2	X 15
20 (var. 10)	The Swallow	Anu 2	X 15	The Field	Anu 1	XI 5 (var. 15)
40	The Field	Anu 1	XI 5 (var. 15)	The Fish	Ea 1	XII 15
35	The Fish	Ea 1	XII 15	The Crook	Enlil 4	I 20
10	The Crook	Enlil 4	I 20	The Stars	Anu 5	II 1
20	The Stars	Anu 5	II 1	The Bull of Heaven	Anu 6	(II 20)
20	The Bull of Heaven	Anu 6	(II 20)	The True Shepherd of Anu	Anu 7	III 10
35	The True Shepherd of Anu	Anu 7	III 10	The Arrow	Anu 8	IV 15
20	The Arrow	Anu 10	IV 15	The Bow	Anu 9	V 5 (var. 15)

to Eridu, and 5 days from Eridu to ŠU.PA, which is what we might have expected. Nevertheless, the total number of days going around the circuit, from the Arrow to the Arrow again, is 360 days, as it should be in the schematic calendar. As discussed in the commentary to Section I ii 36 – I iii 12, the Arrow's first visibility is placed on the date of the summer solstice in the schematic calendar. This almost certainly explains why the list begins with the Arrow, rather than with the Hired Man, as in Section I ii 36 – I iii 12. The summer solstice, rather than the beginning of the year, was often taken as the beginning point of numerical schemes in other texts of schematic astronomy.[41]

Although the present section is clearly based upon the list of the dates of first visibilities given in Section I ii 36 – I iii 12, not all of the stars in that latter list appear in the present section. In particular, where two or more stars are listed as having their first visibility on the same day in Section I ii 36 – I iii 12, only one of those stars (usually the first in the list) is named in the present list. Furthermore, there are no entries in the present list corresponding to four dates in Section I ii 36 – I iii 12: Month I Day 1 (first visibility of the Hired Man), Month IV Day 5 (the Small Twins and the Crab), Month VI Day 1 (unknown star), and Month VIII Day 5 (var. 15; the Scorpion). We do not know why these dates were not considered in this section.

I iii 49 – I iii 50

This short section contains two complementary statements concerning the motion of the celestial sphere. The section breaks with the pattern of the preceding sections, which contained lists with each entry of the list (at least if it appears on a new line) beginning with the DIŠ sign used as an item marker. Instead, the present section contains statements about the behaviour of stars generally. These statements are not preceded by the DIŠ sign, which, as noted already by Watson and Horowitz,[42] suggests that the author of MUL.APIN considered these statements to be of a different kind to those found in the preceding sections: a difference between statements of what we might call data and rules or descriptions of general behaviour.

The two statements refer to the fact that the stars that are visible at night gradually change over the course of the year. A complete cycle of the sky takes one full year. Thus, on average, working with the schematic calendar of 360 days, 1/360 of the sky will be visible one day but not the next, and 1/360 of the sky that is not visible one day will be visible the next day; 1/360 corresponds to 1 UŠ of distance, where there are 360 UŠ in a circle.

These two statements are the only place within MUL.APIN where the unit UŠ appears as a measure of celestial distance. However, in other texts, the distance in front of or behind a *ziqpu* star is usually recorded with the unit UŠ or its subunit

41 See, for example, the date-based rising time schemes on BM 34639, BM 38704, and A 3414+ discussed by Steele (2017) and the shadow-length schemes on BM 45721 discussed by Steele (2013).

42 Watson and Horowitz (2011: 75).

NINDA (60 NINDA = 1 UŠ). In modern terms, distances in front of or behind *ziqpu* stars correspond to differences in right ascension. It seems very likely that the reason why this section appears here in MUL.APIN is to introduce the *ziqpu* stars. These stars are the subject of the next section. Furthermore, these two lines from MUL.APIN are quoted in the Late Babylonian text BM 38369+38694, immediately after a list of the distances between *ziqpu* stars.[43]

I iv 1 – I iv 9

This section comprises three subsections: an introductory statement (I iv 1 – I iv 3), a list of 14 stars (I iv 4 – I iv 6), and a concluding statement (I iv 7 – I iv 9) that almost duplicates the introductory statement. The section introduces the so-called *ziqpu* stars. The word *ziqpu* means the apex or highest point. Later astronomical texts refer to the moment when a star 'goes to its *ziqpu*-point' (*ana ziqpi* DU), in other words the culmination of a star when it reaches its highest point in the sky. For most stars, the culmination corresponds to the passage of the star across the north–south meridian. Circumpolar stars will cross the meridian twice: once at culmination and once when reaching their lowest point. The *ziqpu* stars are therefore a group of stars that culminate at known intervals.

The first subsection (I iv 1 – I iv 3) introduces the stars as a group. The stars are named the '*ziqpu* stars' after their particular role. In the Late Babylonian period, the group of stars used as reference points in stating the position of the Moon or a planet were similarly named as a group according to their use within astronomy: 'counting stars' (MUL ŠID.MEŠ = *kakkabū minâti*).[44] After naming the stars, the text very succinctly describes their location, observation, and function. The stars are located 'in the path of Enlil in the middle of the sky opposite the chest of the observer of the sky'. As discussed in the commentary to lines I i 1 – I ii 35, the stars in the path of Enlil are the northern stars with declinations greater than about +17°. The phrase 'in the middle of the sky' has been interpreted by many authors to imply that the stars culminate at the zenith, that is, directly overhead.[45] However, to then also be 'opposite the chest of the observer of the sky' would require that the observer was lying on their back on the ground. This contradicts the instructions in the next section of MUL.APIN, where the observer is told to stand with 'your right to the West, your left to the East, your face directed towards the South'. It seems more likely, therefore, that 'middle of sky' refers not to the zenith but instead to the north–south meridian, which splits the sky into two halves. In support of this conclusion, it can be noted that some of the *ziqpu* stars that can be securely identified do not culminate at the zenith but instead

43 BM 38369+38694 ii 25–28 (Horowitz 1994).

44 On the Normal Stars, see, for example, Sachs and Hunger (1988: 17–19), Jones (2004), Roughton, Steele and Walker (2004), and Steele (2007). Modern scholarship refers to these stars as Normal Stars, following the German term *Normalstern* introduced by Epping (1889) before the ancient name was known.

45 Hunger and Pingree (1989: 141).

lower, towards the south. Finally, it is stated that the *ziqpu* stars are observed in order to determine the 'rising and setting' of the stars at night. This passage is quoted almost verbatim in AO 6478 (Thureau-Dangin 1922: No. 21), Obv. 2–4, before a list of the distances between *ziqpu* stars. It is interesting that no reference is made here to the use of *ziqpu* stars in marking the time of an event. From the Neo-Assyrian period onward, *ziqpu* stars were sometimes used to mark the moment when an event took place (or should take place). *Ziqpu* star timings are most commonly attested in astronomical texts – for example, in records of lunar eclipses – but they are also known from non-astronomical contexts, including a letter referring to a storm that took place during the night, and ritual texts.[46]

The second subsection (I iv 4 – I iv 6) contains a list of 14 stars taken from the list of Enlil stars in I i 1 – I ii 35 (see Table 7). The stars are listed in the order in which they rise and cross the meridian. The list begins with ŠU.PA and goes through a full circuit to the Abundant One.[47] The list simply gives the names of the *ziqpu* stars, without any indication of their distribution around this circuit. The complete circuit itself is implied in I iii 49 – I iii 50 to be 360 UŠ or 12 *bēru*. This value for the length of the circuit is stated explicitly in a Neo-Assyrian tablet from Sultanepe, STT 340, which contains a blessing that includes the statement:

> 12 DANNA MUL^{meš} [z]iq-pi šá KASKAL šu-ut ^{d}En-líl
>
> 12 *bēru* are the *ziqpu* stars of the path of Enlil.[48]

A Neo- or Late Babylonian tablet, BM 38369+38694, also refers to the 12 *bēru* circuit of the *ziqpu* stars:

> [PA]P$^{?}$ 12 DANNA kip-pat zi-[iq-pi] bi-rit MUL^{meš} šá KASKAL šu-ut ^{d}[En-líl]
>
> [Tot]al$^{?}$: 12 *bēru* is the circle of the *zi*[*qpu*] amidst the stars of the path of Enlil.[49]

The word 'circle' (*kippatu*) should probably not be interpreted literally to imply that the *ziqpu* stars lie upon a great circle.[50] The stars do not all have the same declination, and so do not follow exactly the same path through the sky. Instead, they are spread in a band centred on a circle of declination that represents their mean distribution. A circle cannot be drawn directly through all of the *ziqpu* stars. Thus, the 'circle' referred to here is actually a circuit.[51]

46 Steele (2014).
47 The Abundant One is placed after ŠU.PA in the list in I i 1 – I ii 35, but is said there to stand in front of ŠU.PA.
48 STT 340 12. See also Horowitz (1994: 97).
49 BM 38369+38694 II 20–21 (Horowitz 1994).
50 Contra Horowitz (1994: 96–97).
51 An analogy may be drawn here to the zodiacal band through which the Moon, Sun, and planets move. Only the centre of that band, the ecliptic, is a circle.

Table 7 The 14 *ziqpu* stars listed in I iv 4 – I iv 6.

Star	*Position in primary star list*
ŠU.PA	Enlil 11
The Star of Dignity	Enlil 13
The Standing Gods	Enlil 21
The Dog	Enlil 23
The Goat	Enlil 22
The Panther	Enlil 26
The Stag	Enlil 29
The Old Man	Enlil 3
The Crook	Enlil 4
The Great Twins	Enlil 5
The Crab	Enlil 7
The Lion	Enlil 8
Eru	Enlil 10
The Abundant One	Enlil 12

Many of the stars given in the MUL.APIN list of *ziqpu* stars are actually large constellations. Some of these constellations are divided into individual *ziqpu* stars in Section I iv 10 – I iv 30 below: the Panther is split into the Shoulder of the Panther, the Chest of the Panther, the Knee of the Panther, and the Heel of the Panther, and the Old Man is split into the Scintillating Stars of the Old Man and the Bright Star of the Old Man.

More extensive lists of *ziqpu* stars are found outside MUL.APIN on tablets dating from the Neo-Assyrian to the Seleucid period.[52] These lists often include statements of the distance between successive *ziqpu* stars. The commonest form of *ziqpu* star list contains 25 stars. Part of this list, from the Panther to Eru, is based upon the *ziqpu* stars in MUL.APIN, although again the large constellations are divided into their constituent parts: the Panther is again split into its Shoulder, the Bright Star of its Chest, its Knee, and its Heel; the Old Man is split into the Scintillating Stars, the Bright Star of the Old Man, and Naṣrapu; the Crook is split into the Crook and the Handle of the Crook; and the Lion is split into the Two Stars of its Head, the Four Stars of its Chest, the Two Stars of its Thigh, and the Single Star of its Tail. However, most of the stars in the other part of the list do not follow the MUL.APIN list: the Abundant One, the Star of Dignity, the Standing Gods, and the Dog are replaced by the Harness, the Rear Harness, the Circle, the Star from the Doublets, the Star from the Triplets, and the Single Star; the Goat is usually renamed the Lady of Light; and ŠU.PA is usually renamed the Yoke.

Following the list of *ziqpu* stars, Subsection I iv 7 – I iv 9 repeats the summary of the *ziqpu* stars and their use from I iv 1 – I iv 3, but with one small but important

52 For a detailed discussion of these texts and references to their publication, see Steele (2014).

difference. Whereas lines I iv 1 – I iv 3 are written as a third-person description with an anonymous 'observer of the sky', I iv 7 – I iv 9 switches to the second person, turning the description into an instruction ('you observe'), and the DIŠ marker at the beginning of the passage is replaced by the words 'all these' (PAP an-nu-tu). All previous sections of the text have been purely descriptive. From here onwards, however, second-person instructions appear intermittently in the text.[53]

I iv 10 – I iv 30

This section contains statements of simultaneously culminating and rising stars on days in the schematic 360-day calendar. The dates chosen are taken from the list of first appearances of stars in I ii 36 – I iii 12, indicating that 'rising' is here to be understood as heliacal rising or first visibility. The section is divided into subsections for each entry. The first subsection begins with a short procedure written in the second person, explaining how to observe the culmination of the *ziqpu* stars. The procedure begins with the remark 'if you are to observe', a familiar phrase for the start of procedures (see II i 68 and II ii 13 for other examples of its use in MUL.APIN). We are then told to stand in the morning before sunrise, with west to our right, east to our left and our face towards the south. The reference to observing in the morning before sunrise confirms that the reason that the *ziqpu* stars are being observed in this section is because they culminate as another star rises heliacally. Following this preamble, we are told that a *ziqpu* star 'stands in the middle of the sky opposite your chest' as another star rises. These remarks on the relative positions of the observer and the culminating star confirm that culmination refers to the star crossing the meridian rather than directly overhead.

Subsequent sections omit the procedure and instead begin with a DIŠ sign used as an item marker. Each entry provides three pieces of information: a date in the schematic 360-day calendar, a star that has its first visibility or heliacal rising on that day, and a star that culminates at the moment when the star becomes visible. The entries in this section are summarized in Table 8. The rising stars are a subset of those given in I ii 36 – I iii 12. This subset is almost the same as the one found in the list of the number of days between first visibilities in I iii 34 – I iii 48. As in that list, where multiple stars are said to have their first visibility on a single date in the list of first appearances in I ii 36 – I iii 12, only one star, usually the first in the group, is given here. There are three differences between the list of rising stars in the current section and those in I iii 34 – I iii 48. First, the Furrow, which has its first visibility on the 25th of Month VI, is omitted here but included in I iii 34 – I iii 48. Second, the Bull is referred to as the Jaw of the Bull (like in I ii 36 – I iii 12), rather than the Bull of Heaven (as in I iii 34 – I iii 48). And third, ŠU.PA and Eridu are given together as having their first visibility on the 15th of Month VI, whereas, in I ii 36 – I iii 12 and by implication in I iii 34 – I iii 48, Eridu has its first visibility on the 10th of Month VI, 5 days before that of ŠU.PA. The dates of

53 On the possible significance of this transition, see Watson and Horowitz (2011: 78 and 127–128).

two of the entries in this list are problematical. In line I iv 22, source A gives the 15th of Month V for the date of the first visibility of the Bow, whereas source AA gives the 5th of Month V. As discussed above in the commentary to I ii 36 – I iii 12, both the 5th and the 15th are attested there too. Second, in line I iv 29, source A gives the 15th of Month XI for the first visibility of the Field. None of the other sources preserves the day number, but all but one of the sources for I iii 10 give the date as the 5th of Month XI, with only source, M, giving the 15th. As we will see, source A contains other errors in this section, and so we consider it the least trustworthy evidence for this part of the text.

The repertoire of *ziqpu* stars used in this section is based upon the list in the previous section, but, as noted in the commentary to that section, some of the stars that are in fact large constellations are divided into individual stars or small star groups to allow a more precise indication of the position to be given. In particular, the Panther is divided into its Shoulder, Chest, Knee, and Heel, and the Old Man is divided into the Scintillating Stars and its Bright Star. Without this splitting up of large constellations into smaller parts, the same *ziqpu* star would culminate at the first appearance of several different stars. The preserved sources offer variant *ziqpu* stars for two of the entries in the list. At I iv 21, sources A and, possibly, AA give the *ziqpu* star as the Bright Star of the Old Man, whereas sources T and R give the star as the Scintillating Stars of the Old Man. In the following line, I iv 22, sources A and, probably, O and AA give the *ziqpu* star as the Scintillating Stars of the Old Man, whereas source T names it the Bright Star of the Old Man. From the later *ziqpu* star lists, it is clear that the Scintillating Stars

Table 8 Simultaneous culminations and heliacal risings (first visibilities) of stars from I iv 10 – I iv 30.

Date	*Rising star*	Ziqpu *star*
I 20	Crook	The Shoulder of the Panther
II 1	The Stars	The Chest of the Panther
II 20	The Jaw of the Bull	The Knee of the Panther
III 10	The True Shepherd of Anu	The Heel of the Panther
IV 15	The Arrow	The Scintillating Stars of the Old Man (var. The Bright Star of the Old Man)
V 15 (var. 5)	The Bow	The Bright Star of the Old Man (var. The Scintillating Stars of the Old Man)
VI 15	ŠU.PA and Eridu	The Great Twins
VII 15	The Scales	The Lion
VIII 15	The Goat	Eru
IX 15	The Panther	ŠU.PA
X 15	The Swallow	The Standing Gods
XI 15 (error for 5?)	The Field	The Dog
XII 15	The Fish	The Goat

are in front of the Bright Star of the Old Man and, therefore, should culminate with the earlier heliacal rising date. Thus, sources T and R probably preserve the correct text, whereas sources A and, probably, O and AA mistakenly reverse the order of the stars.

A close parallel to I iv 10 – I iv 30 is preserved on the Late Babylonian tablet BM 77054. This tablet was identified and first published by George (1991), who considered it a late copy of a possible forerunner to MUL.APIN. It has been re-edited and studied by Steele (forthcoming a). The text more or less follows the pattern of MUL.APIN I iv 10 – I iv 30. Its contents are summarized and compared with MUL.APIN in Table 9. BM 77054 contains at least two additional entries to the scheme in MUL.APIN. The first of these entries concerns the 1st of Month IV and does not correspond to anything in MUL.APIN. However, the 10th of Month VI, the date of the second of these entries, is the date when Eridu and the Raven have their first visibilities, according to the list of first visibilities in MUL.APIN I ii 36 – I iii 12. In the MUL.APIN scheme, Eridu has been moved to the 15th of Month VI to be paired with ŠU.PA. A puzzling feature of BM 77054 is the inclusion of the statement that, '4 minas is the watch of the [day]', immediately after the entry for the culmination of the Heel of the Panther with the first appearance of the True Shepherd of Anu on the 10th of Month III. Statements of the length of day and night at the solstices and equinoxes are included in the list of dates of first visibilities in MUL.APIN I ii 36 – I iii 12, but do not appear in the present section. As noted by George, the placement of the summer solstice on the 15th of Month III is characteristic of what are often assumed to be earlier texts than MUL.APIN (see the commentaries to I ii 36 – I iii 12, II i 9 – II i 21, and II ii 43 – II iii 12). He therefore suggested that BM 77054 contains a copy of an early work that predated MUL.APIN. Two objections to this conclusion can be put forward. First, it does not appear that BM 77054 explicitly places the summer solstice on the 15th of Month III; rather, it appears to be associated with the entry for the 10th of Month III. Second, and more significant, if the summer solstice was placed on the 15th of Month III, rather than on the 15th of Month IV, as in MUL.APIN, then the dates of the first visibilities of the stars should also be one month earlier than their dates in MUL.APIN, but this is not the case.

The scheme presented in this section of MUL.APIN is related to Late Babylonian so-called 'rising time' schemes that connect the culmination of *ziqpu* stars (or points behind them) to the rising and setting of the Sun.[54] Two types of Late Babylonian rising time scheme are known. In one, the culminating point is given for the moment of sunrise and sunset on dates in the schematic 360-day calendar. In the other, the culminating point is given for positions in the zodiac. These two types are both based upon the same basic scheme, because, in schematic astronomy, where the Sun moves through the zodiac at 1 UŠ per day, the date in the schematic calendar will equal the sun's position in the zodiac at sunrise. These schemes seem to be derived from the assumption of a 2:1 ratio for the length of

54 A detailed discussion of the rising time schemes may be found in Steele (2017).

Table 9 A comparison of MUL.APIN I iv 10 – I iv 30 and BM 77054.

MUL.APIN			*BM 77054*		
Date	*Rising star*	Ziqpu *star*	*Date*	*Rising star*	Ziqpu *star*
I 20	Crook	The Shoulder of the Panther	[. . .]	[. . .]	[. . .]
II 1	The Stars	The Chest of the Panther	[. . .]	[. . .]	[. . .]
II 20	The Jaw of the Bull	The Knee of the Panther	[. . .]	[. . .]	[. . .]
III 10	The True Shepherd of Anu	The Heel of the Panther	III 10	The True Shepherd of Anu	The Heel of the Panther
–	–	–	IV 1	[. . .]	TIR.AN.NA
IV 15	The Arrow	The Scintillating Stars of the Old Man	IV 16	The Arrow	The Three Stars of the Old [Man?]
V 15 (var. 5)	The Bow	The Bright Star of the Old Man	V 5	The Bow and [. . .]	The Four Stars [of the Old Man?]
–	–	–	VI 10	[. . .]	The [Great?] Tw[ins]
VI 15	ŠU.PA and Eridu	The Great Twins	VI [15]	ŠU.PA and [. . .]	[The Great Twins?]
VII 15	The Scales	The Lion	VII 15	The Scales	The Head [of the Lion]
VIII 15	The Goat	Eru	VIII 15	The Goat	The Fro[nd]
IX 15	The Panther	ŠU.PA	IX 15	The Panther	ŠU.PA
X 15	The Swallow	The Standing Gods	X 15	The Swallow	The Standing Gods
XI 15 (error for 5?)	The Field	The Dog	XI 5	The Field	The Dog
XII 15	The Fish	The Goat	XII 15	The Fish	[The Goat]

the longest to the shortest night and follow MUL.APIN in placing the equinoxes and solstices on the 15th day of Months I, IV, VII, and X. The date-based version of the rising time scheme is summarized in Table 10. The scheme assumes that the culminating point at sunrise changes by 20 UŠ per month between the winter solstice and the summer solstice and by 40 UŠ per month between the summer solstice and the winter solstice.

Comparing the Late Babylonian rising time scheme with the present section of MUL.APIN, we find broad agreement in most of the entries. For example, the MUL.APIN scheme refers to the culmination of the Shoulder of the Panther on the 20th of Month I with the heliacal rising of the Crook. In the Late Babylonian rising time scheme, the Shoulder of the Panther culminates at sunrise on the 15th of Month I, and the point 3;20 UŠ behind the Shoulder of the Panther culminates at sunrise on the 20th. Similarly, in the MUL.APIN scheme, the Chest of the Panther culminates with the heliacal rising of the Stars on the 1st of Month II. In the Late Babylonian rising time scheme, the point 0;40 UŠ behind the Bright Stars of its (i.e. the Panther's) Chest culminates at sunrise on the date. Not all of the entries agree so well, however. In particular, in Months VII, VIII, and IX, the Late Babylonian scheme gives positions that are roughly one constellation in front of those given in MUL.APIN. It should be remembered, however, that the Late Babylonian scheme refers to the moment of sunrise, whereas MUL.APIN presents information for the moment of the heliacal rising of a star, which will be somewhat before sunrise. Furthermore, the author of MUL.APIN is working with a shorter, and somewhat different, list of *ziqpu* stars, and neither his list nor the entries in this section give distances between the stars or positions in front of or behind the stars. Whereas the Late Babylonian rising time scheme is a mathematically derived and mathematically precise scheme, this section of MUL.APIN instead provides only a qualitative description of the phenomenon.

Table 10 The Late Babylonian rising time scheme.

Date	*Culminating point at sunrise*	*Difference from the culminating point in the next month*
I 15	The Shoulder of the Panther	20 UŠ
II 15	10 UŠ behind the Bright Star of its (the Panther's) Chest	20 UŠ
III 15	10 UŠ behind the Knee of the Panther	20 UŠ
IV 15	The Four (Stars) of the Horn of the Stag	40 UŠ
V 15	*Naṣrapu*	40 UŠ
VI 15	½ *bēru* behind the Handle of the Crook	40 UŠ
VII 15	5 UŠ behind the Crab	40 UŠ
VIII 15	½ *bēru* behind the Four Stars of his (the Lion's) Chest	40 UŠ
IX 15	½ *bēru* behind Eru	40 UŠ
X 15	The Circle	20 UŠ
XI 15	The Star of the Triplets	20 UŠ
XII 15	The Lade of Life	20 UŠ

I iv 31 – I iv 39

This section contains a list of the zodiacal constellations that stand in the path of the Moon. The section is divided into three subsections: an introduction explaining the property of the following list of stars, namely that the Moon passes through them every month (I iv 31 – I iv 32); a list of 17 stars (I iv 33 – I iv 37); and a closing summary statement that repeats the introductory statement, with the addition of the words 'all these are' at the beginning (I iv 38 – I iv 39). This division of the section into three subsections (introduction, list, summary) mirrors that of the list of *ziqpu* stars in I iv 1 – I iv 9.

The introductory statement classifies the following group of stars by their function as defining regions through which the Moon moves and that it touches every month. Source E refers to these constellations as 'gods' (DINGIR^{meš}), whereas source F refers to them as 'stars' (MUL^{meš}).

The constellations listed in the second subsection are summarized in Table 11. The list begins with the Stars and is ordered in increasing celestial longitude, following the path of the Moon in its monthly cycle. The list begins with the Stars because the Moon is assumed to be within that constellation at the beginning of the year (see the commentary to II Gap A 8 – II ii 6). There has been considerable uncertainty in previous scholarship whether there are 17 or 18 stars in the list. This uncertainty is caused by the mention of the 'Tails': are these a separate star, or are they part of the star referred to as the Swallow? Unfortunately, the question cannot be resolved on philological grounds: because the words 'Tails' and 'Swallow' are written using only logograms, we could read this as either 'the

Table 11 Stars in the path of the Moon listed in I iv 33 – I iv 37.

Star	*Position in primary star list*
The Stars	Anu 5
The Bull of Heaven	Anu 6
The True Shepherd of Anu	Anu 7
The Old Man	Enlil 3
The Crook	Enlil 4
The Great Twins	Enlil 5
The Crab	Enlil 7
The Lion	Enlil 8
The Furrow	Anu 14
The Scales	Anu 15
The Scorpion	Ea 10
Pabilsag	Ea 13
The Goat-Fish	Ea 15
The Great One	Ea 2
The Tails of the Swallow	Anu 2
Anunitu	Anu 3
The Hired Man	Anu 4

Tails of the Swallow' or 'The Tails, the Swallow'.[55] The Tails appear in many Late Babylonian texts as the name of a constellation and the zodiacal sign Pisces. However, a strong case can be made that here the Tails are to be interpreted as part of the name of the Swallow. Unlike every other entry in this list, the Tails do not appear as a star in the primary star list in I i 1 – I ii 35. Furthermore, it is clear from evidence outside MUL.APIN that both the Swallow and Anunitu have tails that cross one another. For example, the uranology text MLC 1866 i 4–7 describes the tails as follows:

> [MUL šá ina] miḫ-rat ^{mul}IKU GUB-⸢zu⸣ ^{mul}Sí-⸢nu⸣-nu-tú ⸢MUŠEN⸣ MUL KAP.ḪI.A mut-tap-ri-iš šá kap-pi ⸢ra⸣-šu-ú MUL šá EGIR^{meš} ^{mul}IKU GUB-zu ^{mul}A-nun-ni-tu$_4$ na-a-ru ⸢^{mul}⸣Sí-nu-nu-tú ù ^{mul}A-nun-ni-tu$_4$ ina KUN⸢^{meš}-šú⸣-nu it-gu-ru-ú-ma
>
> [The star which] stands opposite the Field (is) the Swallow. (It is) a bird, a star with wings, flying, that is it has wings. The star which stands after the Field is Anunitu, a river. [Th]e Swallow and Anunitu at their tails cross one another.[56]

This passage demonstrates that the Swallow is in front of and facing away from Anunitu, such that their tails are together. Thus, if the Tails were a separate constellation to the Swallow, we would expect that the order of entries in the list would be the Swallow, the Tails, Anunitu. This is not what we find in the list, however, suggesting that the Tails must here be interpreted as part of the name of the Swallow.

The list of constellations in the path of the Moon formed the basis for two systems of tracking the motion of heavenly bodies during the Late Babylonian period: the Normal Stars and the zodiac. The Normal Stars are a group of stars distributed fairly unevenly in a band around the zodiac.[57] The majority of the Normal Stars were named as parts of constellations. Of the 17 zodiacal constellations listed in MUL.APIN, only the Old Man, the Crook, and Anunitu do not appear in the names of Normal Stars, and only one constellation, the Chariot, not in this list was used to name Normal Stars. The zodiac is an abstract division of the zodiacal band into twelve equal parts, with each part named after a zodiacal constellation contained within it. Although there is considerable variation in the names given to the signs of the zodiac, particularly before the early third century BC, with the single and rare exception of naming Pisces the 'Field', all of the attested names are drawn from the constellations listed in the present section of MUL.APIN.[58]

55 See Kugler (1913: 70) and Hoffmann (2017: 323). Kugler (1913: 70) and Hunger and Pingree (1989) assume that the text refers to one star, whereas van der Waerden (1952–1953: 219) assumes that the Tails and the Swallow are two stars.

56 Beaulieu, Frahm, Horowitz, and Steele (2018).

57 Twenty-eight Normal Stars were used, regularly supplemented by another dozen or so that were used occasionally. See Jones (2004) and Roughton, Steele, and Walker (2004).

58 Steele (forthcoming b).

II i 1 – II i 8

This section contains statements asserting that the Sun and the five planets travel the same path as the Moon. The section is divided into two subsections: the first containing a series of six statements, one for the Sun and one for each planet, each introduced by a DIŠ sign (II i 1 – II i 6), and the second a summary statement without an initial DIŠ sign. The summary statement groups the Sun and the five planets together as 'gods' who share the property of being in the same places, touching the same stars, and who keep changing their positions. The phrase 'keep changing their positions' was also used in I i 38 and I ii 13 – I ii 17 to distinguish the planets from the fixed stars whose position remains constant, and appears again in II i 40 to refer to the five planets.

The series of statements that the Sun and the five planets travel the same path as the Moon imply that the Sun and the planets move through the same 17 zodiacal constellations as listed in I iv 33 – I iv 37. However, these statements mark a shift in the way that MUL.APIN presents information.[59] Up to this point in the text, the primary topic of interest is the stars, which are grouped in various ways because of their own behaviours, their relationship to other stars, or because the Moon interacts with them. Here, however, it is the behaviour of the Sun and the planets (that they move along a path) that is the subject of the discussion. Furthermore, this behaviour is not itself explained in detail, but rather through an analogy with the motion of the Moon. We are not told that the Sun and the planets move through the stars in the path of the Moon, nor are these stars listed. Instead, the text compares the motion of the Sun and the planets to that of the Moon. The Moon is, in effect, the model for the Sun and the planets, a form of reasoning that we find quite often in other areas of Babylonian astronomy.

The Sun and the planets are given in the following order: Sun, Jupiter, Venus, Mars, Mercury, and Saturn. A standard order for the planets emerged in the Late Babylonian period: Jupiter, Venus, Mercury, Saturn, and Mars. The Late Babylonian order is based upon the benefic and malefic characteristics of the planets in astrology.[60] In earlier texts, however, there is no clear evidence of a fixed order, except that Jupiter usually comes first, often followed by Venus.[61] Different sections of MUL.APIN attest to different orders. The five planets are listed in the order Jupiter, Venus, Mercury, Mars, and Saturn at II i 38–39. In the primary lists of Enlil, Anu, and Ea stars in I i 1 – I ii 35, Jupiter appears by itself at the end of the Enlil stars, and Venus, Mars, Saturn, and Mercury appear in that order at the end of the Anu stars.

The names of the Sun, Moon, and the five planets in this section are written with the divine determinative, rather than the star determinative. In addition, Jupiter is written ^{d}Šul-pa-è-a rather than SAG.ME.GAR, which is used everywhere else in MUL.APIN. It is unclear whether there is any significance to this.

59 See Watson and Horowitz (2011: 87).

60 Rochberg-Halton (1988b).

61 Jones and Steele (2011).

II i 9 – II i 21

This section concerns the length of daylight and the motion of the Sun at the solstices and equinoxes. It is divided into four subsections, each of which contains the date of the solstice or equinox in the schematic 360-day calendar, a statement of the length of day and night, the position of the Sun, and a statement of a stellar phenomenon. Table 12 summarizes the statements given in each subsection. Note that, neither here, nor elsewhere, is any term for solstice and equinox used. In later astronomical texts, these phenomena are referred to by the phrases 'the Sun stands' (šamaš GUB) and '(day and night are) balanced' (LÁL-tim, Akk. *šitqultu*). This terminology suggests that the solstices and equinoxes were understood both in terms of the variation in the rising point of the Sun and the variation in the length of daylight. The same understanding is apparent in this section of MUL.APIN, which defines the four solstices and equinoxes in terms of both the length of day and night and the rising point of the Sun.

The first subsection (I i 9 – I i 13) concerns the summer solstice, which is placed on the 15th of Month IV in the schematic calendar. The text begins by stating that, on that day, the Arrow has its first visibility, and that the length of day is equal to 4 minas and night to 2 minas. This statement parallels the entry at I ii 42 – I ii 43 in the list of first visibilities of stars, except that, there, two other stars, the Snake and the Lion, are listed with the Arrow as having their first visibility on that day. The text continues with the statement that the Sun rises in the north with the head of the Lion, turns and keeps moving to the south by 40 NINDA per day. As already noted, according to I ii 42 – I ii 43, the Lion has its first visibility on this date.[62] Finally, the subsection concludes with the statement that the days become shorter and the nights become longer.

The subsection concerning the winter solstice (I i 16 – I i 18) is almost a mirror image of the summer solstice section. Instead of the first visibility of the Arrow, the winter solstice is said to coincide with its first evening visibility (acronychal rising), and day is equal to 2 minas and night to 4 minas. Both statements parallel I iii 7 – I iii 9, although again that entry includes additional information, namely that the Swallow has its first visibility on that date. The Sun is now said to rise in the south and to turn and move to the north at the same rate of 40 NINDA per day. Only two of the known sources for this section preserve the name of the star with which the Sun rises (sources HH and KK). Both sources give the star as the Head of the Lion, exactly paralleling the situation at the summer solstice. The Sun cannot rise with the same star at both summer and winter solstices, however.[63] In all

62 The Head of the Lion is not otherwise known from MUL.APIN, and it is not clear whether it is here used to indicate a particular star within the Lion or to mean the beginning of the Lion constellation. In the Late Babylonian period, the Head of the Lion is one of the Normal Stars and can be confidently identified as ε Leonis. This star had a declination of about +32½° in 700 BC. The Sun's declination at summer solstice is about +23½°, and so this star would rise considerably further north than the Sun. This fact may point to a looser interpretation of the meaning of the term Head here.

63 The Sun's declination at winter solstice is about –23½° compared with +23½° at summer solstice, but the declination of a star does not change over the course of the year. Furthermore, after six months, the Sun and a constellation will be on roughly opposite horizons at sunrise.

Table 12 Length of day and night, stellar phenomena, and the position of the Sun at the solstices and equinoxes according to II i 9 – II i 21.

Date	*Day length*	*Night length*	*Stellar phenomenon*	*Position of the Sun*
IV 15 (Summer solstice)	4 minas	2 minas	First visibility of the Arrow	Rising in the north with the Head of the Lion
VII 15 (Autumnal equinox)	3 minas	3 minas	Moon stands in front of the Stars behind the Hired Man	Rising within the Scales
X 15 (Winter solstice)	2 minas	4 minas	Acronychal rising of the Arrow	Rising in the south with the Head of the Lion (error for: Great One)
I 15 (Spring equinox)	3 minas	3 minas	Moon stands within the Scales	In the west in front of the Stars behind the Hired Man

likelihood, therefore, the Head of the Lion is a mistake. An obvious alternative is to assume an error for the Head of the Great One, because the writing of the Lion (^{mul}UR.GU.LA) is very similar to that of the Great One (^{mul}GU.LA; see further the discussion in the philological notes). However, according to I iii 10, the Great One's first visibility is on the 5th (var. 15th) of Month XI. Thus, it should not be visible at the winter solstice. We would expect the Swallow, which has its first appearance on the date of the solstice, to be given instead. It is possible, therefore, that the error in mentioning the Head of the Lion is best explained by the similarity of this subsection to the subsection for the summer solstice. The subsection ends with a statement that the days become longer and the nights become shorter.

The entries for the equinoxes differ slightly in style from those for the solstices. Instead of referring to the date of the heliacal or acronychal rising of a star, these sections mention the position of the Moon relative to one or more stars. The subsection for the autumnal equinox (II i 14–15) states that the Sun rises within the Scales in the east, and the Moon stands in front of the Stars and behind the Hired Man, and that, on that date, both day and night are 3 minas in length. In I iii 1–2, this same date is given for the first appearance of the Scales (and the Wild Dog, the Mouse, and the Dog), and there is an identical statement about the length of day and night. Thus, following the logic of MUL.APIN, the Sun should rise within the Scales as stated on this date. The date of the equinox is set as the 15th of Month VII. The 15th is the assumed date of full Moon in the schematic calendar, and so on this date the Moon should be opposite the Sun. Furthermore, assuming simple mean motion of the Sun and Moon, working within the schematic calendar, the position of the Moon on the 15th of Month VII should be the position of the Sun on the 15th of Month I. This is indeed what we find in the subsection for the vernal equinox (II i 19 – II i 21), which simply mirrors the entry for the autumnal equinox: on the 15th of Month I, the Moon is said to stand behind the

Scales in the east, and the Sun stands in front of the Stars and behind the Hired Man in the west.

The statements giving the length of day and night are repeated in Sections I ii 36 – I iii 12 (summer solstice, autumnal equinox, and winter solstice only) and II ii 21–40 (all four solstices and equinoxes). The length of day and night, called the 'watch of the day/night' (EN.NUN u_4-mi/GI_6), is presented with the weight unit mina. Neugebauer (1947: 40), followed by Hunger and Pingree (1989: 153), assumed that the phrase 'watch of the day/night' referred to each of the three watches into which day/night could be divided, and therefore that these time intervals referred to one-third of the length of day or night. However, as already suggested by Weidner and convincingly demonstrated by al-Rawi and George (1991–1992: 60), Neugebauer was in error here, and the phrase refers to the length of the complete day or night. Two pieces of evidence lead to this conclusion. First, in Table B of *Enūma Anu Enlil* 14, the duration of visibility of the Moon on the 15th day (full Moon) of an equinoctial month is given as 3 minas. This table assumes that the Moon is visible all night on the day of full Moon. Thus, the length of the night is also 3 minas on the 15th of an equinoctial month. Table C of *Enūma Anu Enlil* 14 gives this same value of 3 minas, which it calls the 'watch of the night'. Thus, the 'watch of the night' refers to the whole of the night. Second, a commentary text to *Enūma Anu Enlil* 20 (K 3145) contains the statement that, '3 minas is the watch of the night of Month I, 1 mina for each of the three watches' (3 ma-na EN.NUN GI_6 šá ^{iti}BÁR 1 ma-na-a-a a-na 3 EN.NUN SUM$^!$-in).[64] As the same value, 3 minas for the watch of the night in Month I, is given here in MUL.APIN, it can be assumed that here too the phrases 'watch of the night' and, by analogy, 'watch of the day' refer to the whole of the night and day.

The weights given for the length of day and night almost certainly correspond to the weight of water in a water clock.[65] Late Babylonian water clocks were very likely outflow clocks, where the water dripped out of a large vessel kept with a constant head of water.[66] In such devices, time is directly proportional to the volume (or equivalently weight) of water that is collected. Although we should not assume that a vessel of exactly this kind was what the author of MUL.APIN had in mind, it seems certain nevertheless that here, too, weight and time are assumed to be proportional.[67]

64 For this text, see Rochberg-Halton (1988c: 226); for the correct interpretation of this passage, see al-Rawi and George (1991–1992: 60 fn. 24).

65 Kugler (1913: 95).

66 Brown, Fermor, and Walker (1999–2000), Fermor and Steele (2000).

67 Neugebauer's (1947) attempt to explain the inaccuracy of the ratio for the length of longest to shortest night by means of an outflowing water clock, where weight of water and time are not directly proportional, can be rejected on multiple grounds, including a detailed consideration of the physics of outflow water clocks, experiments with reconstructed water clocks, and, more crucially, direct textual evidence. See Friberg, Hunger, and al-Rawi (1990: 497), Gehlken (1991), Høyrup (1998–1999), Brown, Fermor, and Walker (1999–2000), and Fermor and Steele (2000).

The length of daylight is given as 4 minas at the summer solstice, 3 minas at the equinoxes, and 2 minas at the winter solstice. The lengths of night are the mirror of the length of day: 2 minas at summer solstice, 3 minas at the equinox, and 4 minas at the winter solstice. Thus, the length of a complete day plus night is equal to 6 minas. The ratio between the length of the longest to the shortest day (or equivalently night) is 4 minas to 2 minas, or 2:1, which, as has long been known, is a great exaggeration for anywhere within Mesopotamia. The values for the length of night given for the solstices and equinoxes agree with those found in II ii 43 – II iii 12, which give the length of night for the 1st and 15th days of every month. The values for the length of night in this later section follow a linear zig-zag function, with extremes of 4 minas and 2 minas (see further the commentary to II ii 43 – II iii 12).

The 2:1 ratio for the longest to shortest night is found in many other texts, both earlier and later than MUL.APIN.[68] The earliest known example is the Old Babylonian tablet BM 17175+17284.[69] This tablet is divided into four sections. Each section begins with the date of a solstice and equinox and a statement of the length of day and night. These lengths are given as numbers without units. The text continues by stating how much the lengths of day and night change by the time of the next solstice and equinox. The solstices and equinoxes are placed one month earlier in the schematic calendar than in MUL.APIN. A fuller scheme, giving values for each of the twelve months of the schematic calendar is found in some of the Three Stars Each texts. Like the scheme on BM 17175+17284, the Three Stars Each texts present the length of daylight as sexagesimal numbers without units and place the solstices and equinoxes one month earlier than in MUL.APIN. A full scheme for the length of day and night every 15 days is found in the so-called Table C of *Enūma Anu Enlil* 14.[70] This last text gives the length of daylight using the units mina and shekel (60 shekels = 1 mina), but again places the solstices and equinoxes one month earlier than in MUL.APIN.

The subsections for the two solstices (I i 9 – I i 13 and I i 16 – I i 18) add the remark that the Sun 'keeps moving down/coming up towards the south/north 40 NINDA per day'. These passages are a little ambiguous in that they combine the change in the rising point of the Sun with a daily change given in the units NINDA. However, a good argument can be made that the 40 NINDA per day refers to the change in the length of day, not the change in the rising position of the Sun. Between the summer solstice and the winter solstice, the length of daylight changes between 4 minas and 2 minas. Thus, over 180 days, the length of daylight changes by 2 minas. The total length of day plus night is 6 minas, which must equal 12 *bēru* or 360 UŠ. Two minas therefore equal 4 *bēru* or 120 UŠ. Dividing 120 UŠ by 180 days yields a change in the length of daylight of 0;40 UŠ or 40 NINDA per day.

68 For an overview of these texts and selected translations, see Hunger (1999).

69 Hunger and Pingree (1989: 163–164). See also Hunger (1999).

70 Al-Rawi and George (1991–1992).

Finally, these two sections end with the phrase 'the days become shorter/longer, the nights become longer/shorter'. These phrases are also found in Table C of *Enūma Anu Enlil* 14.

II i 22 – II i 24

This short section instructs the reader to observe the risings of the Sun, the positions of the Moon, and the appearances of the Arrow on the dates of the solstices and equinoxes in order to find the 'days in excess'. What is to be observed here is taken from what was described in the previous section: the position of the Sun along the horizon and with certain stars at its rising, the heliacal and acronychal rising of the Arrow, and the position of the Moon with respect to the Stars and the Hired Man or the Scales. By observing the dates of these phenomena, we will find the 'days in excess'.

The phrase we translate as 'position of the Moon' (NA^{meš} šá ^{d}Sin) requires some explanation. In Late Babylonian observational and related texts, NA can be used for the duration of the visibility of the Moon on the 1st day of the month and the time between sunrise and moonset on the day on which the Moon set for the first time after sunrise in the middle of the month. It would be possible, therefore, to translate NA^{meš} šá ^{d}Sin as 'visibility times of the Moon', as it was indeed translated in Hunger and Pingree (1989: 78). However, this use of NA to mean visibility time is only attested in Late Babylonian texts. In lines II ii 43 – II iii 12, these intervals are referred to by the terms ŠÚ šá Sin, 'setting of the Moon', and KUR šá Sin, 'rising of the Moon'. The same intervals are designated IGI.DU$_8$.A šá ^{d}Sin, 'visibility of the Moon', and KUR šá ^{d}Sin, 'rising of the Moon', in Table D of *Enūma Anu Enlil* 14. The possibility of translating NA as 'position', however, is assured by phrases that refer to the motion of the planets in lines II i 8 and II i 40.[71] Given these points, and that the preceding section includes a statement referring to the position of the Moon relative to particular stars and does not mention visibility times, it seems certain that the text refers to the Moon's position here.

The term 'days in excess' (UD^{meš} DIRI^{meš}) appears also in lines II ii 12 and II ii 16. Those lines contain calculations of the nominal number of extra days in a year that would result from intercalating every three years. It is likely, therefore, that here too 'days in excess' refers to the discrepancy between the year and the solar year. Determination of these 'days in excess' may have had one or more of at least three purposes. First, comparing the schematic dates with observed dates could allow the maximum discrepancy between the schematic calendar and the civil calendar to be determined. Second, this same type of comparison could form the basis of an intercalation rule: if the observed 'days in excess' are greater than some predetermined limit, then it is necessary to intercalate. And third, as suggested by Brack-Bernsen (2005), the 'days in excess' could be used to correct

71 NA^{meš} appears in the same place in these phrases as KI.GUB in the parallel phrases in I i 38 and I ii 13 – I ii 15.

calculations made using the schematic calendar to make them applicable to the civil calendar.[72]

II i 25 – II i 37

This section marks a significant shift in topic from the preceding section. It is divided into three subsections, each of which begins with the date(s) of the first visibility of two stars. These dates are taken from the list in I ii 36 – I iii 12. The first subsection (II i 25 – II i 31) gives the dates of the first appearance of Eridu on the 10th of Month VI and of ŠU.PA on the 15th of the same month; the second subsection (II i 32 – II i 33) refers to the first visibility of the Scorpion on the 5th of Month VIII and the Chest of the Scorpion on the 15th of the same month; and the third subsection (II i 34 – 37) refers to the first visibility of the Fish on the 15th of Month XII and the evening visibility (acronychal rising) of Eridu on the same evening. We do not know why these dates and stars were chosen. Pingree notes that these months were next to the months of the equinoxes,[73] but we do not know why this should be significant, or why no entry from Month II is given if this was the reason behind this section. Whereas Eridu, ŠU.PA, and the Fish appear in all of the star lists in MUL.APIN that draw on the list of dates of first visibilities, the Scorpion and the Chest of the Scorpion do not (see Table 2 above).

Following the dates of the first visibilities, the reader is told to make certain observations. The first subsection gives the longest account. We are told that, on the day when the stars become visible (the phrase 'their stars' is presumably a reference to the fact that the 'stars' Eridu and ŠU.PA are constellations), we should observe their risings (*nipḫu*), glow (*zīmu*), and soakings (*risnu*). On the day of the first visibility of a star, the star rises above the eastern horizon shortly before dawn. Shortly afterwards, the light of dawn will fill the sky, and the star will be lost to the Sun's glow. The three terms 'rising', 'glow', and 'soaking' almost certainly refer to the rising of the star, its appearance as it stands above the horizon, and its disappearance as it is 'soaked' in the light of dawn as it sweeps in.[74] In addition, we are told to observe which wind blows (i.e. the wind direction). The reason for making these observations may well be connected to celestial divination and ritual practice. The rising and appearance of stars and other celestial bodies and the direction of the wind appear frequently in the protases of celestial omens. The following text seems to support a ritual context for the observations: First, we are told to prevent horses from drinking water until after the stars have

72 Brack-Bernsen goes further in noting that the solstices and equinoxes do not generally fall on the dates of full moon, as implied in the preceding section, and so calculations made using the schematic calendar would need to be corrected, not only against the solar year, but also against the lunar month. She provides a method by which this might have been achieved. Although we consider this interpretation possible, we note that understanding NA[meš] to refer to the Moon's position, not its visibility time, which seems to us to be certain, removes a piece of circumstantial evidence in support of her interpretation.

73 Hunger and Pingree (1989: 152).

74 Koch (1998: 112 fn. 10). Steele independently came to the same interpretation, adding support to Koch's conclusion.

appeared. Once this has happened, we are told to present offerings to the stars,[75] after which the horses may touch bitumen and drink water.[76] The second and third subsections present shortened versions of this material. The second subsection only refers to the observation of the wind direction. The third subsection tells us to observe the risings, glow, soakings, and wind direction, but does not include the reference to the ritual. A more or less identical passage appears in the introduction to the section on planetary visibilities and invisibilities at lines II i 41 – II i 43.

The reference to the acronychal rising of Eridu on the 15th day of Month XII in the third subsection is the only place in MUL.APIN that refers to the acronychal rising of this star. Indeed, the only other star whose acronychal rising is mentioned in MUL.APIN is the Arrow. Eridu's acronychal rising is assumed to take place six months and five days after its first appearance.

II i 38 – II i 67

The topic of the text switches again here to discuss the duration of the phases of visibility and invisibility of the planets. The section begins with a short subsection listing the five planets. The planets are listed in the order Jupiter, Venus, Mercury, Mars, and Saturn. The names of the planets are written with the star determinative (^{mul}), as was the case in the primary lists of Enlil, Anu, and Ea stars, rather than the divine determinative (^{d}), which was used in II i 1 – II i 6. Additional names are given for two of the planets. Mercury is given the additional name Ninurta (as it was in lines I ii 12 and II i 5); this additional name is also given in the following subsections dealing with this planet (II i 54 – II i 55 and II i 66 – II i 67). Saturn is given the additional names 'the Scales' and the 'Star of the Sun'. Both of these associations are traditional and are used often in commentaries on celestial omens and in the Neo-Assyrian astrological reports.[77] Saturn is given these additional names also in the subsection II i 64 – II i 65, but strangely not in the subsection II i 53.

75 For other references to the presentation of offerings to stars, along with prayers and other activities associated with gods, see Reiner (1995: 15–24).

76 Freedman (2014) notes that, in the early autumn (corresponding to Month VI), the level of water discharged by the Tigris and Euphrates basins into the alluvial plain is low, and the temperature in Iraq is sufficiently high that bitumen 'may be oily and sticky with a consistency similar to molasses', and consequently 'may cake horses' hooves and pollute watercourses'. He therefore proposes to understand this passage as an instruction not to let horses drink the polluted water or go near to bitumen at this time, but only later in the year when the water level is high and the temperature lower. Although this is an attractive hypothesis, and ancient knowledge of the changing nature of bitumen throughout the year can probably be assumed and so may well lie behind the concern with water and bitumen expressed here, the text is explicit that the horses may touch bitumen on the days mentioned in Month VI once the offerings to the stars have been made. Thus, we seem to have here a reference to a ritual rather than a practical instruction. Furthermore, the same reference to bitumen is made in II i 43 in the context of observations of the planets. The first visibilities of the planets can take place at any time of year and so are not correlated with the annual cycle of hardening and softening of bitumen.

77 Brown (2000: 68–70), Reiner (2004), van der Sluijs and James (2013). The Babylonian tradition of naming Saturn 'the Sun' persisted and was known to the Greek author Diodorus, who refers to it in his *Bibliotheca Historica* 2.30 (see Jones and Steele 2018).

Following this first introductory subsection is a second introductory subsection (II i 40 – II i 43). This second introduction begins by noting that the planets change their positions and their appearance. The phrase 'keep(s) changing their/its position' is also used to distinguish the planets from fixed stars in the primary list of Enlil, Anu, and Ea stars (Jupiter in line I i 38 and Venus, Mars, and Saturn in lines I ii 13 – I ii 15; Mercury is instead given the alternative distinguishing feature that it rises and sets within a month in both the east and the west in line I ii 16–17) and in the summary following the list of the Sun and the planets that travel in the path of the Moon (II i 8). The second introduction continues by stating that, on the day that they become visible, the reader should observe their risings, glow, soakings, where they become visible, and the wind direction. This passage is an almost exact duplicate of the instructions in II i 25 – II i 31. The risings, glow, and soakings must here too refer to the rising of the planet across the horizon before dawn, its appearance as it stands above the horizon, and its disappearance as the sky fills with the glow from the Sun, although this only makes sense for the outer planets and for the eastern (morning) visibility of the inner planets, which suggests that the passage is based directly upon the case of stellar first visibilities presented in II i 25 – II i 31. The text continues by stating that, when the planets become visible, you should present offerings to them, and then horses may touch bitumen, a statement that has again clearly been copied from the previous section. Indeed, further evidence that this passage is based directly upon the earlier section is in the reference to 'their stars' (MUL^{meš}-šú-nu). 'Their stars' makes sense when discussing a constellation, but the possessive plural form is not appropriate when referring to a planet. The passage does add one remark to the passage in the earlier section: in addition to the risings, glow, and soakings, the reader is told to observe the position of the planet. The position of a star, either relative to other stars or along the horizon, does not change, and so there is no purpose to observing it. However, planets do move, both relative to stars and in the position of their rising point, and so observing the position makes sense here.[78]

The following 12 subsections present values for the duration of visibility and invisibility of the planets. These data in these subsections are summarized in Table 13. The subsections are arranged first to give the periods of invisibility and then the periods of visibility. Venus has two periods of invisibility, which are given in two separate subsections: from last visibility in the east to first visibility in the west, and from last visibility in the west to first visibility in the east. Venus also has two periods of visibility, one in the east and one in the west, but the text combines them in one subsection, saying that the periods of visibility are the same in the east and west. Mercury also has two periods of invisibility and visibility. In both cases, the duration of invisibility or visibility is said to be the same whether in the east or west. Mercury's period of invisibility is said to be the same as its period of visibility.

78 Many celestial omens refer to the position of the rising point of a planet. See Reiner and Pingree (1998: 18–19).

Table 13 Duration of visibility and invisibility of the planets given in II i 44 – II i 67.

Lines	*Planet*	*Phase*	*Duration*	*Additional information*
II i 44 – II i 46	Venus	Invisibility (east)	1 month 1 month 15 days 2 months	
II i 47 – II i 48	Venus	Invisibility (west)	same day 3 days 7 days 14 days	
II i 49 – II i 50	Jupiter	Invisibility	20 days 1 month	
II i 51 – II i 52	Mars	Invisibility	2 months 3 months 10 days 6 months 20 days	
II i 53	Saturn	Invisibility	20 days	
II i 54 – II i 55	Mercury	Visibility (east or west)	7 days 14 days 21 days 1 month 1 month 15 days	
II i 56 – II i 59	Mercury	Invisibility (east or west)	'As many days as it stood in the sky'	Observation instructions. Red and bright or yellow and dark
II i 60	Jupiter	Visibility	1 year	
II i 61	Venus	Visibility (east or west)	9 months	
II i 62 – II i 63	Mars	Visibility	1 year 6 months 1 year 10 months 2 years	Redness and is bright or is . . . and is small
II i 64 – II i 65	Saturn	Visibility	1 year	Red or white
II i 66 – II i 67	Mercury	Invisibility and visibility (east or west)	Within 1 month	

The subsections for Saturn and Mercury are duplicated on AO 6450 (Thureau-Dangin 1922: No. 16) Rev. 35–42, with only very minor discrepancies (see the philological notes). According to its colophon, this tablet contains (a copy of?) a commentary to *Enūma Anu Enlil* 56 written in Uruk in the Seleucid period.[79] The ordering of the material is slightly different to that found in MUL.APIN. On AO 6450, Saturn's visibility period (corresponding to MUL.APIN II i 64 – II i 65) is given first, followed directly by its invisibility period (corresponding to MUL.APIN II i 53), separated from the visibility material by a two-wedge 'colon' sign (Rev. 35–37). In MUL.APIN, these two subsections are separated by material concerning the other planets. The Mercury material on AO 6450 (Rev. 38–43) corresponds to the two MUL.APIN subsections II i 54 – II i 55 and II i 56 – II i 59, followed by about a line and a half of further material not found in MUL.APIN. The two Mercury subsections from MUL.APIN are presented as a single section, with no break between them. The final Mercury subsection in MUL.APIN (II i 66 – II i 67) is not duplicated on AO 6450.

The durations of visibility and invisibility of the planets given in this section are clearly traditional and not intended to provide precise astronomical information.[80] As already noted, the Mercury and Saturn material is directly paralleled in the commentary to *Enūma Anu Enlil* 56, which may indicate that this material was part of *Enūma Anu Enlil* 56, a text composed either earlier than, or contemporary with, MUL.APIN. The nine-month period of visibility of Venus is also attested in a Neo-Assyrian omen text that may or may not be part of *Enūma Anu Enlil*.[81] A letter sent by the scholar Mar-Issar of Babylon to the Neo-Assyrian king refers to Jupiter's period of invisibility as being between 20 and 30 days,[82] the two lengths for this period given in MUL.APIN. It is also evident from the durations of visibility and invisibility themselves that they are not meant to be astronomically precise. It is striking, for example, that the first three visibility periods for Mercury are 7 days, 14 days, and 21 days, all multiples of 7, and that the final invisibility period for Mars, 6 months 20 days, is double the second period, 3 months 10 days. Furthermore, there is no astronomical reason why several discrete periods are given: the actual period can be any number of days between a minimum and a maximum.

Three of the subsections contain statements about the colour and brightness of the planet. Mercury is said to be either red and bright or yellow and dark (II i 56 – II i 59), Mars is said to be either red and bright or 'unnun' (a colour that we are

79 For an edition of this tablet, see Largement (1957).

80 See Brown (2000: 118). See also Swerdlow (1998: 24–26), who compares the periods of visibility and invisibility and the total synodic periods implied in MUL.APIN with modern computation. As Swerdlow notes, although the periods agree to some extent with modern computation, they are sufficiently inaccurate that they would be rejected if compared with observations made over one or two decades.

81 K 2346+3904+8725 Obv. 22 (Reiner and Pingree 1998: 224).

82 K 1551 (Parpola 1993: no. 362).

unable to identify) and small (II i 62 – II i 63), and Saturn is said to be either red or white (II i 64 – II i 65). The colour and the brightness of a planet (and of other astronomical bodies) are often mentioned in the protases of celestial omens, but we cannot identify a clear, single tradition of colours for the planets, nor a reason why these colours were chosen.

The subsection on Mercury's invisibility (II i 56 – II i 59) states that the planet is invisible for as many days as it is visible. It then contains an omen stating that, if Mercury becomes visible in winter, there will be rain and flood, followed by the instruction to the reader that, if it becomes visible at harvest time, you observe its glow, its soaking, where it becomes visible, and the wind direction, you present offerings, and then horses may touch bitumen. This passage echoes the statement in II i 40 – II i 43.

II i 68 – II i 71

This short section contains a procedure instructing the reader how to determine the direction of the winds. The wind direction is important in its own right because of its role in celestial divination, and, as discussed above, the wind direction is one of the things we are told to observe along with the rising, glow, and soaking of a star or planet at its first visibility. But the cardinal directions were also named for the winds. Thus, in Section II i 9 – II i 21, the rising point of the Sun (towards the north, east, etc) is written using the names of the winds, and, therefore, the procedure outlined in this section probably refers both to determining the wind direction and to determining the cardinal points.

As discussed by Neugebauer and Weidner (1931–1932: 271) and Horowitz (1998: 195–200), wind directions, at least when used to refer to winds themselves, seem to relate to 90° ranges in azimuth roughly centred on the cardinal directions. Thus, the east wind refers to the range from north-east to south-east.

The directions indicated by the stars are listed in Table 14. The stars are meant to be rough indicators of direction, nothing more, as is clear from the phrase 'lies across' indicating the star's position.[83] The Wagon is a circumpolar star and so is

Table 14 Stars and wind directions.

Wind	*Star*
North	The Wagon
South	The Fish
West	The Scorpion
East	The Old Man and the Stars

83 Contra the interpretations proposed by Papke (1978) and Koch (1995–1996).

an obvious candidate to indicate north. The Scorpion sets somewhat to the south of west, and the Stars rise somewhat to the north of east. No star can rise directly to the south, but the Fish is a southern star. The exact meaning of 'lies across' and 'stands' in these statements therefore cannot be determined.

Pingree notes that similar ideas to those presented in this section are found in Vedic material.[84]

II Gap A 1 – II Gap A 7

This section outlines the motion of the Sun through the three paths of Enlil, Anu, and Ea over the course of the schematic year. The section is divided into four subsections, each of which covers a three-month period centred on one of the solstices or equinoxes. In addition, a brief statement is given about the prevailing weather conditions in each quarter of the year. Table 15 summarizes the content of this section.

II Gap A 8 – II ii 6

This section contains a series of criteria for determining whether or not it is necessary to intercalate. It is divided into seven subsections, each of which contains a pair of statements.[85] The first statement, which is preceded by a DIŠ sign used as an item marker, gives the date of a phenomenon, followed by the remark that this is a normal year. The second statement, preceded this time not by DIŠ but by the word *šumma*, 'if' (written BE-ma), contains an alternative date for the same phenomenon, with the remark that, in this case, the year is intercalary. Thus, we have a set of rules stating that, if the phenomenon is observed on the first date, the year is normal, but, if it is not observed until the second date, then it is necessary to intercalate.

The phenomena that appear in this section can be divided into two groups: the first visibility or acronychal rising of a star and the 'balancing' of the Moon and

Table 15 The Sun's motion through the paths of Enlil, Anu, and Ea over the course of the year and associated weather.

Date range	*Midpoint*	*Path*	*Weather*
XII 1 to II 30	I 15 (vernal equinox)	Anu	Wind and warm weather
III 1 to V 30	IV 15 (summer solstice)	Enlil	Harvest and heat
VI 1 to VIII 30	VII 15 (autumnal equinox)	Anu	Wind and warm weather
IX 1 to XI 30	X 15 (winter solstice)	Ea	Winter

84 Hunger and Pingree (1989: 152).

85 Note, however, that the preserved sources are not consistent in their use of horizontal rulings to indicate the boundaries between subsections and occasionally even have rulings between two statements that are part of the same subsection.

the Stars (Pleiades). So far as they are preserved, the first visibility and acronychal rising dates agree with those given in the list in Section I ii 36 – I iii 12. The intercalation criterion is simple in these cases. If the phenomenon occurs on the date given in Section I ii 36 – I iii 12, then the year is normal, but, if it does not occur until one month later, then it is necessary to intercalate. The former date – that is, the date in a normal year – can be understood as the earliest date on which the phenomenon occurs; if it occurs anytime between this date and the date one month later, then the year is normal, and only if it is more than one month later than the first date – that is, after the second date – should the year become intercalary.

Lines II Gap A 12 – II Gap A 15 and II ii 3, which concern the first appearance and acronychal rising of the Arrow on the 15th of Months IV and X (i.e. the dates of the summer and winter solstices), quote the statements about the rising point of the Sun in lines II i 10 – II i 13 and II i 16 – II i 18.

The two subsections concerning the balancing of the Moon and the Stars present greater difficulties in their interpretation. These subsections have been investigated by several scholars, most notably Schaumberger, who named the first of these subsections the 'Pleiaden-Schaltregel'.[86] There are two problems with understanding this material. First, what is the meaning of 'balanced'? This term is written using the logogram LÁL for the Akkadian word *šitqulū*, which has the general sense of being equally balanced (e.g. in weight). In other astronomical contexts, LÁL is used in two ways: (1) to refer to the circumstance of the Sun and the Moon being 'balanced' on opposite horizons at sunrise or sunset; and (2) as a supplemental remark added to statements of the measurement of the distance between two celestial bodies, either 'in front of' or 'behind' (roughly equivalent to differences in celestial longitude) or 'above' or 'below' (roughly equivalent to differences in celestial latitude). LÁL only appears on occasions when only one of these measurements is given, and in most cases it seems to be used when the two objects were at the same latitude or longitude (but note that there are many measurements of this kind where LÁL is not used, suggesting that it is a redundant statement that is usually omitted). Thus, it seems most likely that, in MUL. APIN, 'balanced' means that the Moon and the Stars were at the same celestial longitude, that is, when they were in conjunction.[87]

The greater difficulty, however, is with the dates given in the scheme. Although the entry in lines II ii 1 – II ii 2 is now fully preserved (contrary to in the earlier edition, where the restored dates can now be seen to be in error), little remains of the dates in the first rule at II Gap A 8 – II Gap A 9 in the known sources. The rule in II ii 1 – II ii 2 states that the year is normal if the Moon and the Stars are

86 Schaumberger (1935: 340–344). This and related schemes have recently been re-examined by Ratzon (2016). Unfortunately, Ratzon's arguments are undermined by the new reading of lines II ii 1 – II ii 2, which shows that the dates for the occurrence of the Moon in conjunction with the Pleiades are the 15th of Months VII and VIII, not Months VIII and IX.

87 Koch's (1997) proposal to understand LÁL in observation statements as an indication of their precision (or lack thereof) and in MUL.APIN to refer to the Moon and the Pleiades having the same duration of visibility before they set is not, in our opinion, plausible.

balanced on the 15th of Month VII, and intercalary if they are balanced on the 15th of Month VIII. The criterion here, then, is similar to the other rules in this section, namely a one-month difference in when the phenomenon occurs.

The rule at II Gap A 8 – II Gap A 9 can be restored in several different ways. No part of the date of the first statement for the normal year is preserved, and only the day number 3 is preserved of the second statement for the intercalary year. Previous scholarship has unanimously assumed that the date of conjunction of the Moon and the Stars in a normal year is the 1st of Month I, and the date for an intercalary year is the 3rd of Month I. This interpretation can be traced back to the first publication of a summary of a then recently discovered tablet (our source GG) containing this rule, by George Smith in 1875. Smith gave a translation of these lines with the day numbers given as the 1st of Month I and the 3rd of Month I, noting that his translation includes 'some slight restorations, which are easily supplied by the regular character of the text', but without noting where he made these restorations.[88] He also gave a short astronomical interpretation of the passage. The first copy of the text was published by Weidner (1913) and shows the tablet as it is today, with the first dates of the conjunction of the Moon and the Stars in a normal year lost and only the day number for the case of an intercalary year preserved. It is unknown, therefore, whether Smith restored the dates when he translated the text in 1875 or whether the part of the tablet containing those dates was lost to damage between 1875 and 1913. The former option seems the most likely explanation. Smith's restored dates have been followed by all scholars up to the present day.

The traditional interpretation of this passage finds some support by comparing the rule in II Gap A 8 – II Gap A 9 with that in II ii 1 – II ii 2. In the second rule, the year is normal if the Moon and the Stars are in conjunction on the 15th of Month VII, and intercalary if they are in conjunction on the 15th of Month VIII. On the 15th of Month VII, which is the date of the autumnal equinox in the schematic calendar, the Moon will be directly opposite the Sun. Thus, working within the framework of the schematic calendar and assuming mean motion for the Sun and Moon, the Moon will be at the position of the Sun on the 15th of Month I. Thus, the Stars must be located at the same position as the Sun on the 15th of Month I in that year. On the 1st of Month I, the Sun will therefore be located 14 UŠ in longitude in front of the Stars. The Moon, however, will be 12 UŠ in front of the Sun at sunset on the 1st day of the month, and so will be 2 UŠ in front of the Stars. This is fairly close to being in conjunction with the Stars. By contrast, on the 3rd day, the Moon will have moved by 26 UŠ and thus be well beyond the Stars. Similarly, in the intercalary year, if the Moon is in conjunction with the Stars on the 15th of Month VIII, this implies that the Sun will be in conjunction with the Stars on the 15th of Month II, 30 UŠ in front of the Stars on the 15th of Month I, and 44 UŠ in front of the Stars on the 1st of Month I. The Moon will be 12 UŠ behind the Sun on day 1 of Month I, and so 32 UŠ in front of the Stars. On

88 Smith (1875: 401–402).

day 2, the Moon will have moved 13 UŠ and so will be 19 UŠ in front of the Stars, and, on day 3, it will have moved another 13 UŠ and so will be 6 UŠ in front of the Stars. The following night, it would be beyond the Stars. Thus, the two rules in II Gap A 8 – II Gap A 9 and II ii 1 – II ii 2 are more or less compatible.[89]

Alternative possibilities should not be ruled out, however. For example, it would be possible to restore the dates of the conjunction of the Moon and the Stars as the 3rd of Month I for a normal year and the 3rd of Month II for an intercalary year. This restoration has the advantage that the criterion would then be the same in the other rules in this section, namely a 1-month difference between the date of the phenomenon in a normal year and the date in one in which it is necessary to intercalate. As we will see, the possibility finds some support in other texts.

Methods for determining whether or not to intercalate are contained in several other texts that date from the Neo-Assyrian period, if not earlier. The so-called Babylonian Diviner's Manual refers to the dates of the first visibilities of stars and the balancing of the Moon with the Stars in the context of intercalation.[90] Although this text does not provide specific criteria for determining intercalation, it clearly refers to rules of the kind found in this section of MUL.APIN.

Specific criteria are found in two other texts, however. The fourth tablet, *Šumma Sîn ina Tāmartišu*, a commentary series to *Enūma Anu Enlil*, contains the following passage:

> [DIŠ MUL$_4$].⸢MUL$_4$ pa-ni⸣-ma Sin ⸢ar-ki MU⸣ BI eš-⸢ret⸣ : DIŠ MUL$_4$.MUL$_4$ ar-ki-ma Sin pa-ni MU BI TAG$_4$-et
>
> [DIŠ ina ^{iti}B]ÁR UD 3 ⸢KAM MUL$_4$⸣.MUL$_4$ u ⸢sin ta-mur-šú⸣-nu-ti-ma šit-qul-lu MU BI eš-ret [ip]-pal-si-ḫu TAG$_4$-et
>
> [¶ If] the Stars (go) in front and the Moon behind, this year is normal. If the Stars (go) behind and the Moon in front, this year is intercalary.
>
> [¶] If on the 3rd day of Month I you see the Stars and the Moon and they are in balance, this year is normal. If they are apart, this year is intercalary.[91]

The first rule implies that, if the Moon is at a lower celestial longitude than the Stars, the year is normal, but, if it is at a higher longitude, the year is intercalary. No date on which this criterion is to be tested is given. The second rule states that, if the Moon and the Stars are in balance on the 3rd of Month I, the year is normal, but, if they are not yet in balance, then the year is intercalary. In order for this

89 It should be noted that there is no evidence from MUL.APIN itself of this type of argument, or for assuming a mean motion of the Moon of 13 UŠ per day (or even of celestial longitudes), although this value and the type of argument do appear in Late Babylonian texts that draw on MUL.APIN.

90 Oppenheim (1974). For a detailed study of this passage, see Williams (2002).

91 K 3123 (= ACh 2nd Supp. 19) Rev. 21–22. For a full edition of this work and a discussion of this passage, see Wainer (forthcoming).

rule to be in agreement with the rule in MUL.APIN, we would have to restore the dates in the MUL.APIN rule as the 3rd of Month I for a normal year and the 3rd of Month II for an intercalary year. This restoration could still fit with the rule in lines II ii 1 – II ii 2 where we saw that, in an intercalary year determined by the conjunction of the Moon with the Stars on the 15th of Month VIII, the Moon would still be slightly short of the Stars on the 3rd of Month I.

Yet another rule is known from a text preserved in three Neo-Assyrian copies.[92] This text gives criteria for intercalation based upon the date on which the Moon and the Stars are in conjunction on different months of the year. The basic rule is that, if the conjunction occurs on day (27 – 2n) of month n, the the year is normal, but, if not, then the year is intercalary. According to this rule, therefore, the Moon and the Stars are in conjunction on the 25th of Month I in a normal year. Clearly, this scheme is at odds with both the MUL.APIN and the *Šumma Sîn ina Tāmartišu* rules and requires that the beginning of the year be one month earlier than in the *Šumma Sîn ina Tāmartišu* scheme. This shift could be explained by the difference between the placement of the solstices and equinoxes in earlier texts and in MUL.APIN.

It remains an open question, therefore, how the first intercalation rule given in this section should be restored. In the absence of convincing evidence either way, we have retained the traditional interpretation of the Pleiaden-Schaltregel following Schaumberger in our edition and translation, but this restoration must be regarded as hypothetical.

Finally, it is worth noting that the Pleiaden-Schaltregel, however it is interpreted, was probably not intended to be a more accurate rule than the other rules in this section.[93]

We have no evidence that any of the intercalation criteria given in this section were applied in practice. Until the introduction of a fixed intercalation pattern based on the 19-year cycle around the early fifth century BC, intercalation was determined by the king on a variety of grounds, including the advice of his scholars. A possible reference to intercalation on the basis of the first visibilities of stars occurring one month too late is found in a report sent by the Neo-Assyrian scholar Balasi to the king (K 760 = Hunger 1992: No. 98), which states, 'Let them intercalate a month: all the stars of the sky have fallen behind'.[94] It is worth noting that this section was copied on to an excerpt tablet (our source UU) from Assur, which perhaps points to its utility to scholars.

II ii 7 – II ii 8

This short section complements the preceding section by explaining that intercalation ('naming the year') can be determined by observing the risings of the stars.

92 The text is edited and discussed by Hunger and Reiner (1975).

93 As already argued by Brown (2000: 118–119) and Ratzon (2016: 148).

94 Hunger (1992: no. 98)

II ii 9 – II ii 17

This section, which is divided into three subsections, continues with the theme of intercalation. Rather than provide a method for determining intercalation, however, this section presents the mathematical consequences of intercalation.

The first subsection (II ii 9 – II ii 10), the beginning of which is very badly preserved, refers to the computation of something to do with the stars, the months, and the year, with the result that an intercalation is to be performed every three years. This fact forms the basis of the calculations in the following two sections.

The second subsection (II ii 11 – II ii 12) begins with a reference to the day of disappearance of the Moon, but we are not sure what is done with or to this day. The text then reiterates that intercalation takes place every three years and then gives a value of 10 'days in excess' for 12 months, which is the amount for one year. The 'days in excess' appeared already in line II i 24, which gave a procedure for determining its value by observing the risings of the Sun, the position of the Moon, and the first visibility and acronychal rising of the Arrow.

The value 10 days for the 'days in excess' is derived in the third subsection (II ii 13 – II ii 17). This short procedure, written as normal in the second person, instructs the reader to obtain the 'correction' (UD.DA.ZAL.LÁ-e) for the day, month, and year. The procedure starts with the correction for a day given without justification as 0;1,40. We then multiply 0;1,40 by one month of 30 days to obtain 0;50, which is called the 'correction for one month'. Finally, we multiply 0;50 by 12 months to find 10 days, which are the 'days in excess' for one year. The subsection concludes by repeating the statement that intercalation occurs every three years. The procedure as given has clearly been computed backwards from this final statement. The intercalary month of 30 days that is added every three years is divided by three to give 10 days in each year that contribute to that intercalary month. Thus, 10 days is then divided by 12 months to give 0;50 days per month, and then by 30 days to give 0;1,40 days per day, which is the extra amount each day that accumulated to make up the full intercalary month in three years.

A Late Babylonian text that is based upon MUL.APIN gives a slightly fuller version of this procedure:

> 1,40 UD.DA.ZAL.LÁ UD 1,40 [ana 30 UD^{meš} ÍL-ma 50 50 ana] 12 ITI^{meš} ÍL-ma 10 UD^{meš} DI[RI 10 UD^{meš} ana] 3 MU$^{⌜\text{meš}⌝}$ ÍL-ma 30 UD^{meš} ⌜x⌝ [. . .] [x$^{?}$] ⌜x⌝ BI ITI ta-de-ri-ma IT[I . . .]
>
> 1,40 is the correction for a day. [You multiply] 1,40 [by 30 days and you find 50.] You multiply [50] by 12 months and you find 10 days in ex[cess]. You multiply [10 days] by 3 years and you find 30 days [. . .] . . . month you intercalate and mo[nth . . .].[95]

95 BM 37175 Rev. I 6′–9′ (Steele in press a).

The procedure runs more or less parallel to the procedure in MUL.APIN, except that it takes the final step in deriving 30 (i.e. one month) as the amount of days in excess after three years.

The figures 1,40 for the correction for a day, 50 for the correction for a month, and 10 for the correction for the year are also given in the second part of the composition i.NAM.giš.ḫur.an.ki.a. The relevant passage reads:

> 1,40 UD.DA.ZAL-e u_4-mu [50 UD.DA.ZAL]-e ITI 10 UD.DA.ZAL.LÁ-e MU.AN.NA
>
> 1,40 is the correction for a day. [50 is the correction]n for a month. 10 is the correction for a year.[96]

Although the mathematics contained in this section of MUL.APIN have long been understood, differing interpretations of the section as a whole and its relation to the intercalation criteria set out in II Gap A 8 – II ii 6 have been proposed. Britton, for example, claims that the purpose of the criteria in the earlier section is to provide a method for improving on the basic rule of intercalating every three years.[97] Brown, however, has argued that the earlier criteria are simply an embodiment of the three-year rule.[98] We agree with Brown on this point. The meaning of the 10 'days in excess' has also been debated. Horowitz (1998) and Britton (2007: 119), for example, assume that the 10 days are to be added to the lunar year (which they take to be equal to 354 days by multiplying 29.5 days by 12), thus producing a solar year of 364 days. Koch (1996) and Brown (2000: 119–120), however, argue that the year in MUL.APIN is always the schematic 360-day year, and so, as Brown puts it, the 'ideal intercalated year' is 370 days. In our opinion, these claims miss the point of this section. What MUL.APIN is doing here, as elsewhere, is aiming to provide a unified description of astronomical phenomena using the schematic calendar as its base. The 10 days in excess, the once every three years intercalation rule, and the intercalation criteria based upon one-month discrepancies in the date of the first visibility of stars are all clearly based upon the 360-day calendar, but describe an astronomical phenomenon that only makes sense in a true luni-solar calendar. Thus, the intercalation rules and the 10-day excess in the length of the year as found in MUL.APIN are schematic interpretations of astronomical reality that merge the 360-day schematic calendar and the true luni-solar calendar in order to produce the scheme.

This section is quoted in the Late Babylonian tablet BM 36766.[99] Unfortunately, this tablet is fragmentary, and the remainder of its contents is not understood.

96 K 2164+2195+3510 Obv. 26–27; edited by Livingstone (1986: 24), but mistranslated and incorrectly understood by him.

97 Britton (2007: 120).

98 Brown (2000: 118–119).

99 See provisionally Steele (in press a).

Table 16 Intercalation criteria in II Gap A 8 – II ii 6.

Lines	*Phenomenon*	*Date in normal year*	*Date in intercalary year*
II Gap A 8 – II Gap A 9	The Stars and the Moon are balanced	[I$^?$ 1$^?$]	[I$^?$] 3
II Gap A 10 – II Gap A 11	First visibility of the Stars	[II 1]	[III] 1
II Gap A 12 – II Gap A 16	First visibility of the Arrow	[IV 15]	V 15
II Gap A 17 – II Gap A 18	First visibility of ŠU.PA	VI 15	VII 15
II ii 1 – II ii 2	The Stars and the Moon are balanced	VII 15	VIII 15
II ii 3 – II ii 4	Acronychal rising of the Arrow	[X 15]	XI 15
II ii 5 – II ii 6	First visibility of the Fish and the Old Man	XII 15	I 15

II ii 18 – II ii 20

MUL.APIN's discussion of intercalation finishes with this short passage, which associates intercalary months with the reign of periods in earlier Mesopotamian history. The section gives three possible months that may be intercalary, Month I, Month XII, and Month VI, and associates them with the reigns of Šulgi, the reign of the Amorites, and the reign of the Kassites. During the first millennium BC, only Months VI and XII were used as intercalary months, although Month I is known to have been used in the Old Babylonian period (early second millennium BC). The month names used in this section are longer versions than are used elsewhere in the text.

II ii 21 – II ii 42

This section presents a mathematical scheme relating the length of shadow cast by a vertical gnomon and the time after sunrise (or, equivalently, before sunset) for different months of the year.[100] The section is divided into five subsections. Four subsections contain data for the 15th of Months I, IV, VII, and X (i.e. the days of the equinoxes and solstices). The final subsection contains a summary procedure.

The four subsections each begin with a DIŠ sign acting as an item marker, followed by the date of the equinox or solstice and a statement of the length of day and night in minas. These statements are identical to statements found in Sections I ii 36 – I iii 12 (summer solstice, autumnal equinox, and winter solstice only) and

100 For a detailed study of this and other Babylonian shadow-length schemes, see Steele (2013).

II i 9 – II i 21 (all four equinoxes and solstices). Following this statement of the date, the subsections then list the time at which the shadow is a given number of cubits in length. The entries in the list are not preceded by the DIŠ sign, indicating that the list as a whole is to be considered an item. The list is arranged from shortest to longest shadow length. For the two equinoxes, the entries are for 1, 2, and 3 cubits of shadow. For the solstices, the entries are for 1, 2, 3, 4, 5, 6, 8, 9, and 10 cubits (the reason why 7 cubits is omitted will be explained below). The whole scheme is summarized in Table 17.

As recognized already by van der Waerden and Neugebauer, the scheme is based upon the simple mathematical relation that the length of the shadow multiplied by the time after sunrise is equal to a constant whose value depends upon the month.[101] For the equinoxes (the 15th of Months I and VII), this constant is equal to 75 UŠ per cubit; for the summer solstice (the 15th of Month IV), it is equal to 60 UŠ per cubit; and, for the winter solstice (the 15th of Month X), it is equal to 90 UŠ per cubit.[102] Surprisingly, this basic rule works quite well for the latitude of Babylon.[103] It also explains why no value for the time at which the shadow reaches 7 cubits is given in the scheme: the result of dividing 60, 75, or 90 by 7 is a non-terminating sexagesimal fraction that cannot be represented by whole numbers or simple fractions of bēru, UŠ, and NINDA. One further consequence of this mathematical rule should be mentioned: according to the scheme, the shadow is 1 cubit in length 3 bēru after sunrise on the winter solstice. However, at the winter solstice, it is stated that daylight is equal to 2 minas, which corresponds to 2,0 UŠ = 4 bēru. Thus, noon takes place 2 bēru after sunrise. Three bēru after sunrise is in the middle of the afternoon, and so the shadow is already getting longer again. In fact, at the winter solstice, the shadow length can never be as short as 1 cubit: according to the scheme, the noon shadow will be 1½ cubits in length. This point emphasizes the mathematical rather than observational basis of the scheme.

The concluding subsection contains a short procedure that expands the scheme just presented to allow it to be applied to the other months of the year.[104] The procedure instructs the reader how to find the 'interval-number' for 1 cubit of shadow, which refers to the amount by which the time corresponding to 1 cubit of shadow changes by each step of a function, in this case its monthly change. The procedure starts with the number 40, which is called the 'interval-number for daytime and nighttime'. This number corresponds to the daily change in the length of daylight, which is equal to 40 NINDA or 0;40 UŠ, was given already in Section

101 van der Waerden (1951), Neugebauer (1975: 544–545).

102 Neugebauer (1975: 545), followed by Pingree in Hunger and Pingree (1989: 153), noted that the ratio between the constants 60 and 90 for the two solstices is equal to 3:2, which he incorrectly believed was the ratio between the longest and shortest day found in MUL.APIN. The ratio between the longest and shortest night used throughout MUL.APIN is, however, 2:1. For a detailed explanation of the problems with Neugebauer's interpretation, see Steele (2013: 11).

103 Steele (2013: 9–10).

104 This procedure was first correctly explained by Friberg, Hunger and al-Rawi (1990: 498–499).

Table 17 The shadow-length scheme in II ii 21 – II ii 42.

Shadow length	*Time after sunrise*			
	I 15 (vernal equinox)	IV 15 (summer solstice)	VII 15 (autumnal equinox)	X 15 (winter solstice)
1 cubit	2½ bēru (= 75 UŠ)	2 bēru (= 60 UŠ)	2½ bēru (= 75 UŠ)	3 bēru (= 90 UŠ)
2 cubit	1 bēru 7 UŠ 30 NINDA (= 37;30 UŠ)	1 bēru (= 30 UŠ)	1 bēru 7 UŠ 30 NINDA (= 37;30 UŠ)	1½ bēru (= 45 UŠ)
3 cubit	⅔ bēru 5 UŠ (= 25 UŠ)	⅔ bēru (= 20 UŠ)	⅔ bēru 5 UŠ (= 25 UŠ)	1 bēru (= 30 UŠ)
4 cubits		½ bēru (= 15 UŠ)		⅔ bēru 2 UŠ 30 NINDA (= 22;30 UŠ)
5 cubits		12 UŠ		18 UŠ
6 cubits		10 UŠ		½ bēru (= 15 UŠ)
8 cubits		7 UŠ 30 NINDA (= 7;30 UŠ)		11 UŠ 15 NINDA (= 11;15 UŠ)
9 cubits		6 UŠ 40 NINDA (= 6;40 UŠ)		10 UŠ
10 cubits		6 UŠ		9 UŠ

II i 9 – II i 21 and is also found in a coefficient list.[105] It is then multiplied by 7,30 to give the result 5, which is stated to be the desired interval number. Thus, the procedure relates the change in the length of daylight to the change in time at which the shadow reaches 1 cubit in length.

As this final subsection makes clear, the shadow-length scheme can be extrapolated to each month of the year (see Table 18). The time after sunrise at which the shadow reaches a given number of cubits in length varies according to a linear zigzag function.

The mathematical scheme relating the length of shadow to the time after sunrise found in MUL.APIN underlies several later texts concerning shadow lengths.[106] For example, the Late Babylonian tablet BM 29371 contains a scheme for the length of shadow cast by a gnomon at 1⅔ bēru after sunrise, at intervals of five days through the schematic 360-day year. The shadow lengths agree exactly with those that can be extrapolated from the MUL.APIN scheme by following the rule in the final subsection.

II ii 43 – II iii 15

This section presents a mathematical scheme for the variation in the length of night and the 'rising' and 'setting' of the Moon over the course of the schematic 360-day year. The section is divided into 13 subsections. The first twelve subsections contain two statements each: the length of night and the rising of the Moon on the 1st day of a month, and the length of night and the setting of the Moon on the 15th day of a month. The final subsection is a short procedure connecting the variability in the length of night to the variability in the rising/setting of the Moon.

Table 19 summarizes the data given in this section. The length of night is given using the weight units mina and shekel, and, as discussed in the commentary to II i 9 – II i 21, these weights refer to the weight of water as measured by a water clock and are in direct proportion to the passage of time, such that 1 mina corresponds to 60 UŠ (= 2 bēru). The entries for the length of night follow a linear zigzag function with maximum 4 minas, minimum 2 minas, a difference per line of ⅙ mina (= 10 shekels), and a period of 1 schematic year. One caveat must be raised, however. Strictly speaking, the entries given for the length of night on the 1st of a month should be for the 30th of the previous month. The date has been changed to the 1st because the first visibility of the Moon takes place on the 1st not the 30th of a month.

The second part of each entry gives a time in UŠ for either the 'setting' (on the 1st of the month) or the 'rising' (on the 15th of the month) of the Moon. These time intervals are equal to 1/15 of the length of night on the same day. The 'setting' of the Moon is the time between the first appearance of the new Moon crescent after sunset and the setting of the Moon. Although it is not explicitly

105 CBS 10996 iii 14'; see Robson (1999: 129).

106 See Steele (2013) for a detailed examination of these schemes and their relation to MUL.APIN.

Table 18 Extrapolation of the shadow-length scheme to all months of the year. The time intervals are given in UŠ.

Shadow length	*Time after sunrise*											
	Month I	*Month II*	*Month III*	*Month IV*	*Month V*	*Month VI*	*Month VII*	*Month VIII*	*Month IX*	*Month X*	*Month XI*	*Month XII*
1 cubit	1,15	1,10	1,5	1,0	1,5	1,10	1,15	1,20	1,25	1,30	1,25	1,20
2 cubits	37;30	35	32.30	30	32.30	35	37;30	40	42;30	45	42;30	40
3 cubits	25	23;20	21;40	20	21;40	23;20	25	26;40	28;20	30	28;20	26;40
4 cubits	18;45	17;30	16;15	15	16;15	17;30	18;45	20	21;15	22;30	21;15	20
5 cubits	15	14	13	12	13	14	15	16	17	18	17	16
6 cubits	12;30	11;40	10;50	10	10;50	11;40	12;30	13;20	14;10	15	14;10	13;20
8 cubits	9;22,30	8;45	8;7,30	7;30	8;7,30	8;45	9;22,30	10	10;37,30	11;15	10;37,30	10
9 cubits	8;20	7;46,40	7;13,20	6;40	7;13,20	7;46,40	8;20	8;53,20	9;26,40	10	9;26,40	8;53,20
10 cubits	7;30	7	6;30	6	6;30	7	7;30	8	8;30	9	8;30	8

Table 19 The length of daylight and the rising and setting of the Moon.

Date	*Length of night*	*Rising/setting of the Moon*
I 1	3 minas 10 shekels	12 UŠ 40 NINDA
I 15	3 minas	12 UŠ
II 1	2⅚ minas	11 UŠ 20 NINDA
II 15	2⅔ minas	10 UŠ 40 NINDA
III 1	2½ minas	10 UŠ
III 15	2⅓ minas	9 UŠ 20 NINDA
IV 1	2 minas 10 shekels	8 UŠ 40 NINDA
IV 15	2 minas	8 UŠ
V 1	2 minas 10 shekels	8 UŠ 40 NINDA
V 15	2⅓ minas	9 UŠ 20 NINDA
VI 1	2½ minas	10 UŠ
VI 15	2⅔ minas	10 UŠ 40 NINDA
VII 1	2⅚ minas	11 UŠ 20 NINDA
VII 15	3 minas	12 UŠ
VIII 1	3 minas 10 shekels	12 UŠ 40 NINDA
VIII 15	3⅓ minas	13 UŠ 20 NINDA
IX 1	3½ minas	14 UŠ
IX 15	3⅔ minas	14 UŠ 40 NINDA
X 1	3⅚ minas	15 UŠ 20 NINDA
X 15	4 minas	16 UŠ
XI 1	3⅚ minas	15 UŠ 20 NINDA
XI 15	3⅔ minas	14 UŠ 40 NINDA
XII 1	3½ minas	14 UŠ
XII 15	3⅓ minas	13 UŠ 20 NINDA

noted in MUL.APIN, this interval is also the daily change in the duration of visibility of the Moon until it reaches full Moon. On the night of the full Moon, the Moon is assumed to be visible all night long, rising at sunset and setting at sunrise. The following night, the Moon rises a certain amount of time after sunset. The next night, it rises the same interval later again, until, on the 30th, the Moon is assumed not to be visible at all, rising at sunrise with the Sun and setting at sunset with the Sun. This nightly change in the time at which the Moon rises after sunset in the second half of the month is what is termed the 'rising' of the Moon in this section. Both the rising and the setting of the Moon given in this text can, therefore, be interpreted as the daily retardation of moonrise and moonset throughout the month.[107]

Almost identical schemes for both the length of night and the daily retardation of the Moon are found in Tablet 14 of *Enūma Anu Enlil*, Tables C and D.[108] The

107 For the term 'daily retardation', see van der Waerden (1951: 20–21).

108 Al-Rawi and George (1991–1992).

only difference is that the schemes in *Enūma Anu Enlil* place the solstices and equinoxes 1 month earlier than in MUL.APIN, as already noted, and that Table C of *Enūma Anu Enlil* Tablet 14 gives the day numbers of the entries as the 15th and the 30th, as they should be, rather than the 1st and the 15th as in MUL.APIN. Another version of the scheme is found in the second part of the composition i.NAM.giš.ḫur.an.ki.a,[109] which contains a section that almost mirrors the present section of MUL.APIN. In i.NAM.giš.ḫur.an.ki.a, both the length of night and the setting/rising of the Moon are given as sexagesimal numbers without units. In addition, the setting/rising of the Moon is explicitly computed by multiplying the length of night by 4. Multiplying by 4 is the same as dividing by 15 when working in a floating-point sexagesimal place value system.

Following the presentation of the scheme, the final subsection contains two short procedures relating to it. Both procedures are presented in the same subsection, without any textual mark such as a DIŠ sign to indicate that one procedure has ended and the other has begun. Unlike the other procedures in MUL.APIN, these procedures do not begin with a statement of what is to be found. Instead, the text jumps straight into the calculations. The first procedure begins with the number 4, which is called the 'coefficient for the visibility of the Moon' (igi-gub-bé-e IGI.DUḪ.A šá ^{d}Sin). We are then told to multiply 3 minas, which is the length of the night, by this coefficient and we arrive at 12, which is the visibility (i.e. the daily retardation) of the Moon. This calculation involves a metrological shift between minas and UŠ, which is hidden within the coefficient. Exactly the same procedure is performed in a commentary to *Enūma Anu Enlil* 14.[110] The calculation uses as an example the case of an equinoctial month when the length of night is equal to 3 minas. The result, 12 (UŠ) for the visibility of the Moon – that is, for its rising and setting – is found in the coefficient list CBS 10996 III 10–11, immediately before the coefficient 40 for the daily change in the length of day and night.[111]

The second procedure performs the same multiplication by 4 to find the daily change (called the 'interval-number') of the duration of visibility of the Moon from the daily change in the length of night. This procedure, therefore, at least in principle, allows the daily retardation of the Moon to be calculated precisely for any night, rather than taking the mid-month value to apply to the whole month, as in Tables A and B of *Enūma Anu Enlil* Tablet 14. In doing so, this section demonstrates that the author of MUL.APIN sought to produce a completely self-consistent scheme of astronomical phenomena, eschewing some of the simplifications found in other, probably earlier, works.

This section was copied on to an excerpt tablet (our source NN) at Assur.

109 For an edition of this text, see Livingstone (1986), and, for a correct understanding of this part of the text, see Al-Rawi and George (1991–1992: 62).

110 On this commentary, see most recently Ossendrijver (2014) and Wainer and Steele (forthcoming).

111 See the commentary to the final subsection of II ii 21 – II ii 42 above.

II iii 12 – II iv 12

The final part of MUL.APIN contains a collection of celestial omens. It is divided into 13 subsections. As is frequently the case in omens texts, the entries within a subsection share a common theme. Roughly one-third of the subsections are known from other omen texts, including tablets that are believed to be part of *Enūma Anu Enlil* (for details of the parallels, see the philological notes). Given the large number of unpublished tablets containing omens, it is quite possible that more parallels will be found in the future.

The omens chosen for inclusion are mostly related to stars, which is appropriate given the prominence of stars within MUL.APIN as a whole. With the exception of references to the U.RI.RI-star and the KAL.NE-star, which may be coded references to planets as these stars can approach other stars, all but one of the stars mentioned in the omens are found in the primary star lists in I i 1 – I ii 35. The only star not found in this list is the Chariot, mentioned in line II iii 23, a constellation in Taurus that becomes important in Late Babylonian observational astronomy.

In addition to the stellar omens, there are omens for Jupiter (but none of the other planets), the horns of the Moon, the rising of the Sun in a cloud, and winds. No omens referring to other astronomical phenomena that make up a large part of the omen tradition, such as eclipses and the many other aspects of the appearance of the Sun and Moon, are included. This again points to the fact that the omens have been selected to complement the material in the rest of MUL.APIN.

Lines II iii 35 – II iii 37 contain what appears to be a description of ritual rather than an omen. The ritual shares some similarities with the ritual mentioned in II i 25 – II i 31, in particular its concern with animals and in praying to a god/star. Whereas the ritual in II i 25 – II i 31 is written in the second person as a set of instructions, here the ritual is written in the third person.

It is worth noting that, in the first part of the collection of omens (II iii 16 – II iii 34), MUL_5 is used rather than MUL to write the word 'star'. In the later half of the collection (II iii 42 – II iv 12), MUL is used in most sources, including in HH, which straddles the two parts and uses MUL_5 in the earlier part. This might be evidence that the earlier omens were taken from a different source to the later omens, but it is also possible that the author of MUL.APIN intended to convey some meaning that is not clear to us by using the two signs in different parts of the text.

Plates

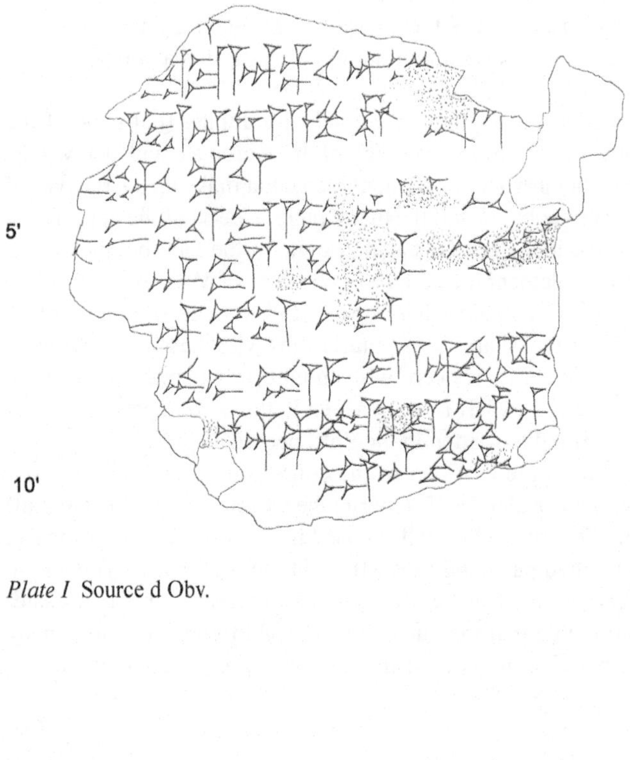

Plate I Source d Obv.

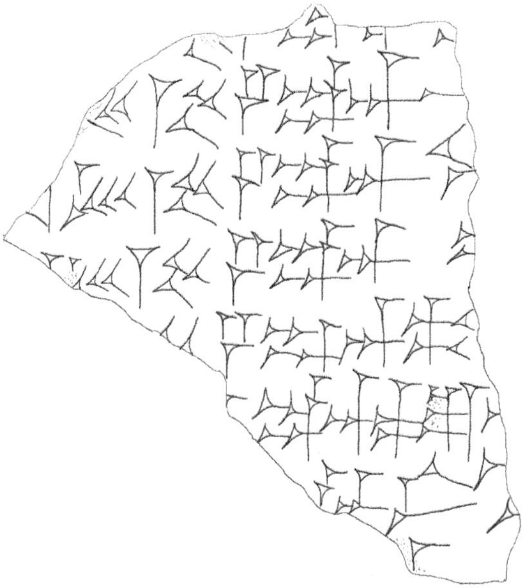

5'

Plate II Source d Rev.

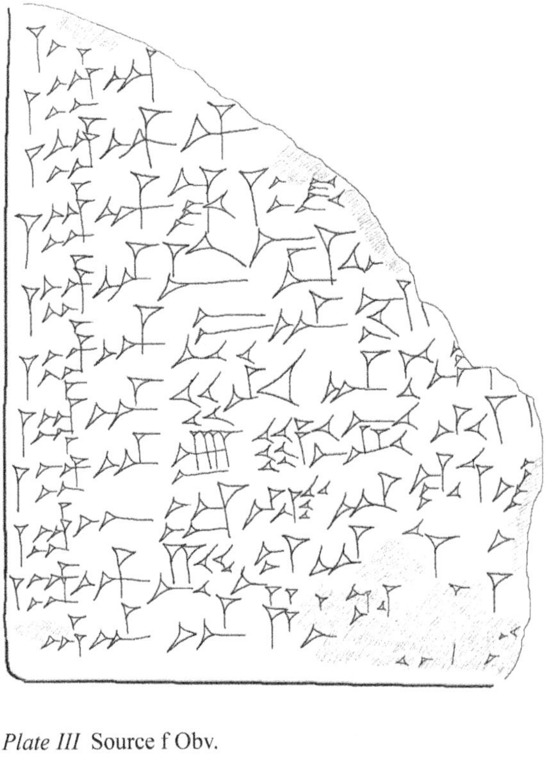

5'

10'

Plate III Source f Obv.

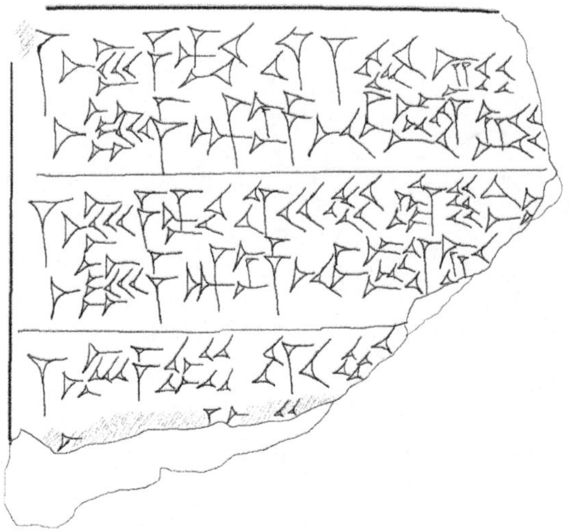

Plate IV Source f Rev.

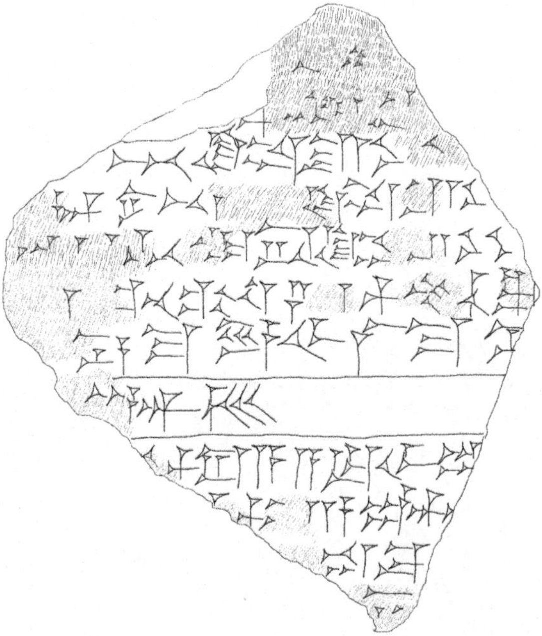

Plate V Source g Obv.

5'

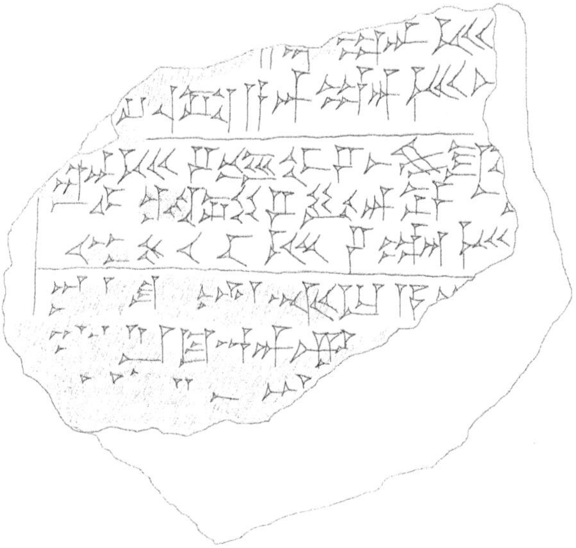

Plate VI Source g Rev.

i ii

5 5

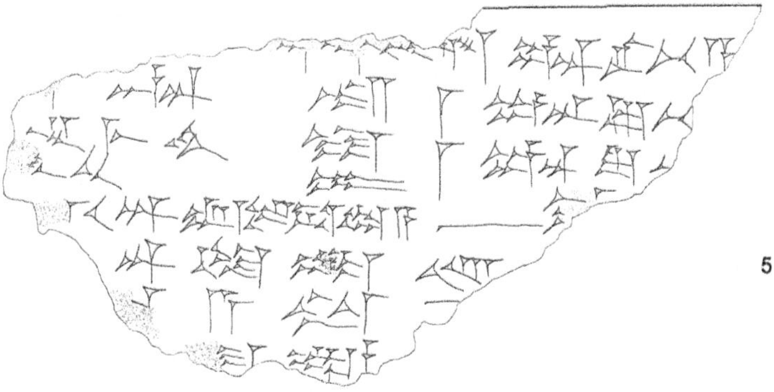

Plate VII Source k Obv.

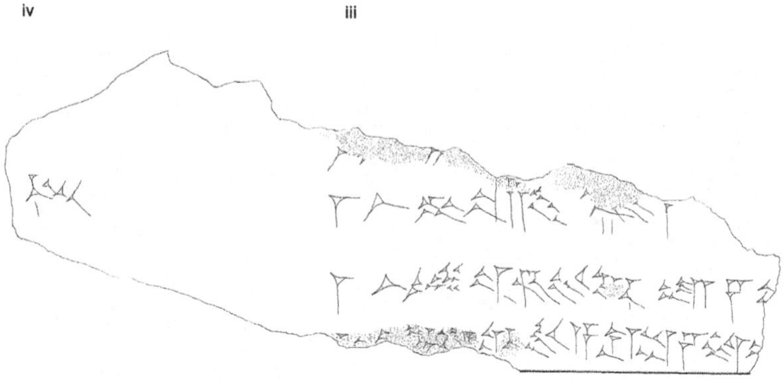

Plate VIII Source k Rev.

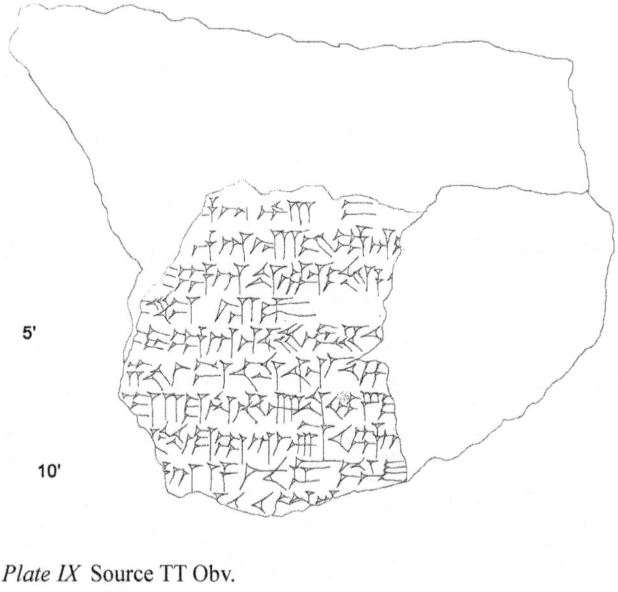

Plate IX Source TT Obv.

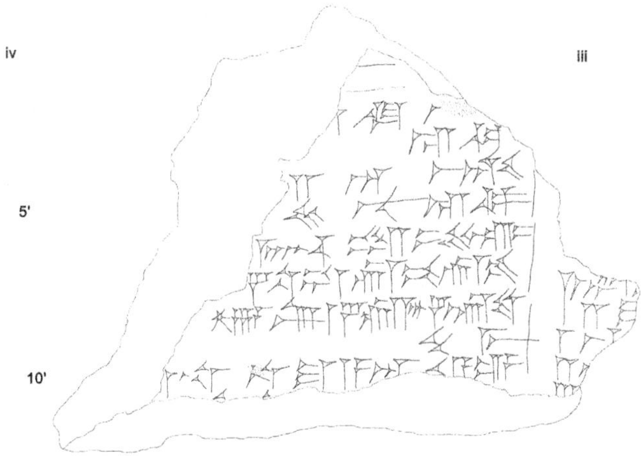

Plate X Source TT Rev.

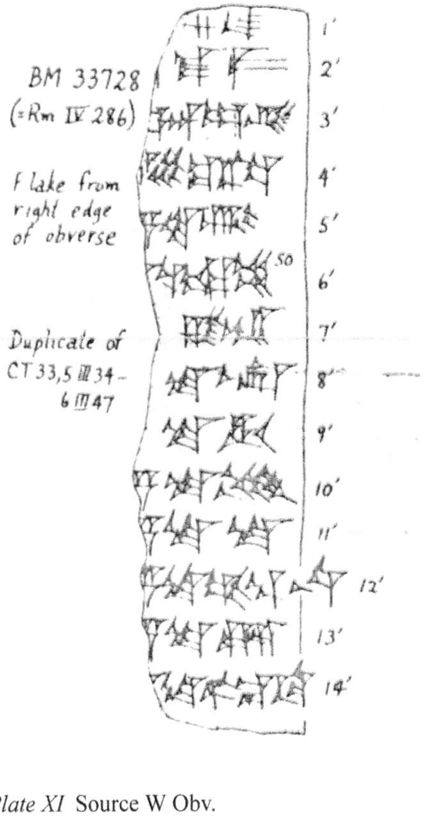

Plate XI Source W Obv.

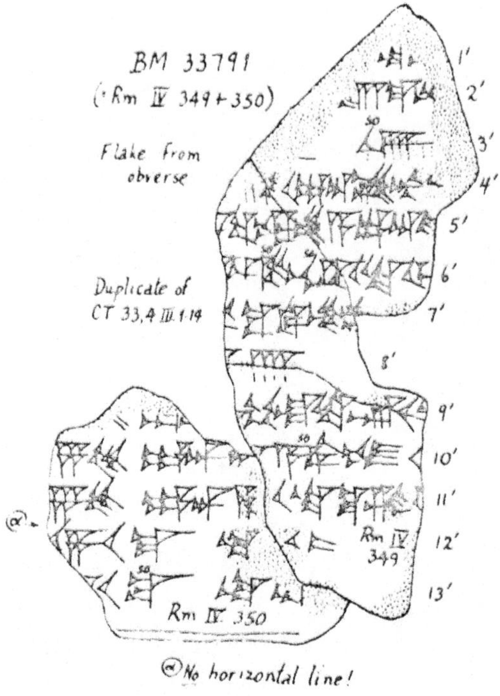

Plate XII Source V Obv.

Bibliography

Al-Rawi, F., and George, A., 1991–1992, 'Enūma Anu Enlil 14 and Other Early Astronomical Tables', *Archiv für Orientforschung* 38–39, 52–73.

Beaulieu, P.-A., Frahm, E., Horowitz, W., and Steele, J. M., 2018, *The Cuneiform Uranology Texts: Drawing the Constellations* (Philadelphia: American Philosophical Society).

Bezold, C., Kopff, A., and Boll, F., 1913, *Zenit- und Äquatorialgestirne am babylonischen Fixsternhimmel* (Heidelberg: Carl Winters Universitätsbuchhandlung).

Black, J. A., and Wiseman, D. J., 1996, *Literary Texts from the Temple of Nabû* (London: British School of Archaeology in Iraq).

Bloch, Y., 2012, 'Middle Assyrian Lunar Calendar and Chronology', in J. Ben-Dov, W. Horowitz, and J. M. Steele (eds), *Living the Lunar Calendar* (Oxford: Oxbow Books), 19–62.

Borger, R., 2003, *Mesopotamisches Zeichenlexikon* (Münster: Ugarit-Verlag).

Brack-Bernsen, L., 2005, 'The "Days in Excess" from MUL.APIN: On the "First Intercalation" and "Water Clock" schemes from MUL.APIN', *Centaurus* 47, 1–29.

Brack-Bernsen, L., 2007, 'The 360-Day Year in Mesopotamia', in J. M. Steele (ed.), *Calendars and Years: Astronomy and Time in the Ancient Near East* (Oxford: Oxbow Books), 83–100.

Brack-Bernsen, L., and Hunger, H., 2002, 'TU 11: A Collection of Rules for the Prediction of Lunar Phases and of Month Lengths', *SCIAMVS* 3, 3–90.

Britton, J. P. 2007, 'Calendars, Intercalations and Year-Lengths in Mesopotamian Astronomy', in J. M. Steele (ed.), *Calendars and Years: Astronomy and Time in the Ancient Near East* (Oxford: Oxbow Books), 115–132.

Brown, D., 2000, *Mesopotamian Planetary Astronomy-Astrology* (Groningen: Styx).

Brown, D., Fermor, J., and Walker, C., 1999–2000, 'The Water Clock in Mesopotamia', *Archiv für Orientforschung* 47, 130–148.

Caplice, R., 1964, 'Akkadian UD(D)Û', in R. D. Biggs and J. A. Brinkman (eds), *Studies Presented to A. Leo Oppenheim* (Chicago: Oriental Institute), 62–66.

Cavigneaux, A., 1987, 'PA.DÙN = hursag et le dieu Amurru', *Nouvelles assyriologiques brèves et utilitaires*, 26.

Cavigneaux, A., 1995, 'MAŠ-HUL-DÚB-BA', in U. Finkbeiner, R. Dittmann, and H. Hauptmann (eds), *Beiträge zur Kulturgeschichte Vorderasiens. Festschrift für Rainer Michael Boehmer* (Mainz: Philipp von Zabern), 53–69.

Cavigneaux, A., Güterbock, H. G., and Roth, M. T., 1985, *MSL XVII. The Series Erim-ḫuš = anantu and An-ta-gál = šaqû* (Rome: Pontificium Institutum Biblicum).

Epping, J., 1889, *Astronomisches aus Babylon* (Freiburg im Breisgau: Herder'sche Verlagshandlung).
Fadhil, A., and Hilgert, M., 2007, 'Zur Identifikation des lexikalischen Kompendiums 2R 50+', *Revue d'Assyriologie* 101, 95–105.
Falkenstein, A., 1931, *Literarische Keilschrifttexte aus Uruk* (Berlin: Staatliche Museen).
Fermor, J., and Steele, J. M., 2000, 'The Design of Babylonian Waterclocks: Astronomical and Experimental Evidence', *Centaurus* 42, 210–222.
Fincke, J. C., 2001, 'Der Assur-Katalog der Serie *enūma anu Enlil* (EAE)', *Orientalia* 70, 19–39.
Fincke, J. C., 2014, 'Another Fragment of MUL.APIN from Babylonia (BM 43871)', *Nouvelles assyriologiques brèves et utilitaires* 84.
Fincke, J. C., 2017, 'Additional MUL.APIN Fragments in the British Museum', *Journal of Cuneiform Studies* 69, 247–260.
Frahm, E., 1997, *Einleitung in die Sanherib-Inschriften*, Archiv für Orientforschung Beiheft 26 (Vienna: Institut für Orientalistik).
Freedman, I., 2014, 'On Horses and Bitumen in ^{mul}APIN', *Nouvelles assyriologiques brèves et utilitaires* 53–54.
Friberg, J., Hunger, H., and al-Rawi, F., 1990, 'Seeds and Reeds', *Baghdader Mitteilungen* 21, 483–557.
Gehlken, E., 1991, 'Der längste Tag in Babylon (MUL.APIN und die Wasseruhr)', *Nouvelles assyriologiques brèves et utilitaires*, 65–66.
Gehlken, E., 1996, *Uruk, Spätbabylonische Wirtschaftstexte aus dem Eanna-Archiv, Teil II* (Mainz: Philipp von Zabern).
Geller, M., 1990, 'Astronomy and Authorship', *Bulletin of the School of Oriental & African Studies* 53, 209–213.
George, A. R., 1991, 'Review of Hunger and Pingree, *MUL.APIN: An Astronomical Compendium in Cuneiform*', *Zeitschrift für Assyriologie* 81, 301–306.
George, A. R., 1992, *Babylonian Topographical Texts* (Louvain: Peeters).
Gössmann, F., 1950, *Planetarium Babylonicum oder die sumerisch-akkadischen Stern-Namen* (Rome: Pontificio Istituto Biblico).
Gurney, O. R., 1989, *Literary and Miscellaneous Texts in the Ashmolean Museum*. OECT XI (Oxford: Clarendon Press).
Gurney, O. R., and Hulin, P., 1963, *The Sultantepe Tablets II* (London: British Institute of Archaeology at Ankara).
Hätinen, A., forthcoming, 'Fragmente des Kompendiums MUL.APIN und ein astrologisch-astronomischer Kommentar aus Assur'.
Hobson, R., 2012, *Transforming Literature into Scripture at Nineveh and Qumran* (Sheffield: Equinox).
Hoffmann, S. M., 2017, *Hipparchs Himmelsglobus: Ein Bindeglied in der babylonisch-griechischen Astrometrie?* (Wiesbaden: Springer Spektrum).
Høyrup, J., 1998–1999, 'A Note on Water-Clocks and on the Authority of Texts', *Archiv für Orientforschung* 44–45, 192–194.
Horowitz, W., 1989–1990, 'Two Mul-Apin Fragments', *Archiv für Orientforschung* 36–37, 116–117.
Horowitz, W., 1994, 'Two New Ziqpu-Star Texts and Stellar Circles', *Journal of Cuneiform Studies* 46, 89–98.
Horowitz, W., 1998, *Mesopotamian Cosmic Geography* (Winona Lake: Eisenbrauns).
Horowitz, W., 2014, *The Three Stars Each: The Astrolabes and Related Texts*, Archiv für Orientforschung Beiheft 33 (Horn: Berger & Söhne).
Hunger, H., 1976, *Spätbabylonische Texte aus Uruk I* (Berlin: Gebr. Mann).

Hunger, H., 1982, 'Zwei Tafeln des astronomischen Textes MUL.APIN im Vorderasiatischen Museum zu Berlin', *Forschungen und Berichte* 22, 127–135.

Hunger, H., 1992, *Astrological Reports to Assyrian Kings*, State Archives of Assyria 8 (Helsinki: Helsinki University Press).

Hunger, H., 1999, 'Babylonische Quellen für die Länge von Tag und Nacht', *Res Orientales* 12, 129–136.

Hunger, H., and Pingree, D., 1989, *MUL.APIN: An Astronomical Compendium in Cuneiform*, Archiv für Orientforschung Beiheft 24 (Horn: Berger & Söhne).

Hunger, H., and Pingree, D., 1999, *Astral Sciences in Mesopotamia* (Leiden: Brill).

Hunger, H., and Reiner, E., 1975, 'A Scheme for Intercalary Months from Babylonia', *Wiener Zeitschrift für die Kunde des Morgenlandes* 67, 21–28.

Jeffers, J., 2017, 'The Nonintercalated Lunar Calendar of the Middle Assyrian Period', *Journal of Cuneiform Studies* 69, 151–191.

Jones, A., 2004, 'A Study of Babylonian Observations of Planets near Normal Stars', *Archive for History of Exact Sciences* 58, 475–536.

Jones, A., and Steele, J. M., 2011, 'A New Discovery of a Component of Greek Astrology in Babylonian Tablets: The "Terms"', *ISAW Papers* 1.

Jones, A., and Steele, J. M., 2018, 'Diodorus on the Chaldeans', in C. J. Crisostomo, E. A. Escobar, T. Tanaka, and N. Veldhuis (eds), *The Scaffolding of Our Thoughts: Essays on Assyriology and the History of Science in Honor of Francesca Rochberg* (Leiden: Brill), 334–353.

de Jong, T., 2007, 'Astronomical Dating of the Rising Star List in MUL.APIN', *Wiener Zeitschrift für die Kunde des Morgenlandes* 97, 107–202.

King, L. W., 1912, *Cuneiform Texts from Babylonian Tables, &c., in the British Museum. Part XXXIII* (London: The British Museum).

Koch, J., 1989, *Neue Untersuchungen zur Topographie des babylonischen Fixsternhimmels* (Wiesbaden: Harrassowitz).

Koch, J., 1991, 'Der Mardukstern Nēberu', *Die Welt des Orients* 22, 48–72.

Koch, J., 1995–1996, 'MUL.APIN II i 68–71', *Archiv für Orientforschung* 42–43, 155–162.

Koch, J., 1996, 'AO 6478, MUL.APIN und das 364 Tage-Jahr', *Nouvelles assyriologiques brèves et utilitaires* 111, 97–99.

Koch, J., 1997, 'Zur Bedeutung von LÁL in den "Astronomical Diaries" und in der Plejaden-Schaltregel', *Journal of Cuneiform Studies* 49, 83–101.

Koch, J., 1998, 'Zur Bedeutung von ina UGU ṭur-ri . . . in zwei Astronomical Diaries', *Die Welt des Orients* 29, 109–123.

Koch, J., 1999, 'Die Planeten-Hypsomata in einem babylonischen Sternenkatalog', *Journal of Near Eastern Studies* 58, 19–31.

Koch, U., 2005, *Secrets of Extispicy* (Münster: Ugarit-Verlag).

Koch-Westenholz, U., 1995, *Mesopotamian Astrology* (Copenhagen: Museum Tusculanum Press).

Köcher, F., 1980, *Die babylonisch-assyrische Medizin in Texten und Untersuchungen*, Band VI, Keilschrifttexte aus Ninive 2 (Berlin: Walter de Gruyter).

Kugler, F. X., 1907, *Sternkunde und Sterndienst in Babel. I* (Münster: Aschendorffsche Verlagsbuchhandlung).

Kugler, F. X., 1913, *Sternkunde und Sterndienst in Babel. Ergänzungen zum I. und II. Buch* (Münster: Aschendorffsche Verlagsbuchhandlung).

Kurtik, G. E., 2007, *The Star Heaven of Ancient Mesopotamia: The Sumero-Akkadian Names of Constellations and Other Heavenly Bodies* (St Petersburg: ALETHEIA). [In Russian]

Lambert, W. G., 1960, *Babylonian Wisdom Literature* (Oxford: Clarendon Press).

Lambert, W. G., 1987, 'Babylonian Astrological Omens and Their Stars', *Journal of the American Oriental Society* 107, 93–96.

Lambert, W. G., 2007, *Babylonian Oracle Questions* (Winona Lake: Eisenbrauns).

Lambert, W. G., 2013, *Babylonian Creation Myths* (Winona Lake: Eisenbrauns).

Largement, R., 1957, 'Contribution à l'Etude des Astres errants dans l'Astrologie chaldéenne (1)', *Zeitschrift für Assyriologie* 52, 235–264.

Livingstone, A., 1986, *Mystical and Mythological Explanatory Works of Assyrian and Babylonian Scholars* (Oxford: Oxford University Press).

Mayer, W. R., 1976, *Untersuchungen zur Formensprache der babylonischen 'Gebetsbeschwörungen'*. Studia Pohl series maior 5 (Rome: Pontificio Istituto Biblico).

Marti, L., 2002, 'Les étoiles de Tuttul', *Nouvelles assyriologiques brèves et utilitaires*, 61–62.

Neugebauer, O., 1947, 'Studies in Ancient Astronomy. VIII. The Waterclock in Babylonian Astronomy', *Isis* 37, 37–43.

Neugebauer, O., 1975, *A History of Ancient Mathematical Astronomy* (Berlin: Springer).

Neugebauer, P. V., and Weidner, E. F., 1931–1932, 'Die Himmelsrichtungen bei den Babyloniern', *Archiv für Orientforschung* 7, 269–271.

Oelsner, J., 1986, *Materialien zur babylonischen Gesellschaft und Kultur in hellenistischer Zeit* (Budapest: Eötvös University).

Oelsner, J., 2000, 'Von Iqīšâ und einigen anderen spätgeborenen Babyloniern', in S. Graziani (ed.), *Studi sul Vicino Oriente antico dedicati alla memoria di Luigi Cagni* (Naples: Istituto Universitario Orientale), 797–814.

Oelsner, J., 2003, 'BM 54609 Rs. 1-9', *Nouvelles assyriologiques brèves et utilitaires*, 82.

Oelsner, J., 2005, 'Der "Hilprecht-Text"', *Archiv für Orientforschung* 51, 108–124.

Oelsner, J., and Horowitz, W., 1997–1998, 'The 30-Star-Catalogue HS 1897 and the Late Parallel BM 55502', *Archiv für Orientforschung* 44–45, 176–185.

Oppenheim, A. L., 1974, 'A Babylonian Diviner's Manual', *Journal of Near Eastern Studies* 33, 197–220.

Ossendrijver, M., 2012, 'A New Join between Fragments of MUL.APIN from Uruk', *Nouvelles assyriologiques brèves et utilitaires*, 100.

Ossendrijver, M., 2014, 'Some New Results on a Commentary to *Enūma Anu Enlil* Tablet 14,' *Nouvelles Assyriologiques Brèves et Utilitaires*, 158–161.

Papke, W., 1978, *Die Keilschriftserie MUL.APIN: Dokument Wissenschaftlicher Astronomie im 3. Jahrtausend*, PhD dissertation, Universität Tübingen.

Parpola, S., 1983, *Letters from Assyrian Scholars to the Kings Esarhaddon and Assurbanipal*, Part II (Kevelaer: Butzon & Bercker, and Neukirchen-Vluyn: Neukirchener Verlag).

Parpola, S., 1993, *Letters from Assyrian and Babylonian Scholars*, State Archives of Assyria 10 (Helsinki: Helsinki University Press).

Pedersén, O., 1995, *Archives and Libraries in the Ancient Near East 1500–300 B.C.* (Bethesda: CDL Press).

Pinches, Th. G., 1884, *The Cuneiform Inscriptions of Western Asia, Vol. V* (London)

Pingree, D., and Walker, C., 1988, 'A Babylonian Star-Catalogue: BM 78161', in E. Leichty et al. (eds), *A Scientific Humanist: Studies in Memory of Abraham Sachs* (Philadelphia: University Museum), 313–322.

Pritchard, J. B., 1969, *Ancient Near Eastern Texts Relating to the Old Testament* (Princeton: Princeton University Press).

Ratzon, E., 2016, 'Early Mesopotamian Intercalation Schemes and the Sidereal Month', *Mediterranean Archaeology & Archaeometry* 16, 143–151.

Reculeau, H., 2002, 'Données nouvelles sur l'astronomie amorrite', *Nouvelles assyriologiques brèves et utilitaires*, 62–63.

Reiner, E., 1958, *Šurpu, A Collection of Sumerian and Akkadian Incantations* (Graz: Ernst Weidner).

Reiner, E., 1995, *Astral Magic in Babylonia*, Transactions of the American Philosophical Society 85/4 (Philadelphia: American Philosophical Society).

Reiner, E., 1998, 'Celestial Omen Tablets in the British Museum', in S. M. Maul (ed.), *Festschrift für Rykle Borger zu seinem 65. Geburtstag am 24. Mai 1994* (Groningen: Styx), 215–302.

Reiner, E., 2004, 'Constellation into Planet', in C. Burnett, J. P. Hogendijk, K. Plofker, and M. Yano (eds), *Studies in the History of the Exact Sciences in Honour of David Pingree* (Leiden: Brill), 3–15.

Reiner, E., and Civil, M., 1974, *MSL XI. The Series ḪAR-ra = ḫubullu. Tablets XX – XXIV* (Rome: Pontificium Institutum Biblicum).

Reiner, E., and Pingree, D., 1981, *Babylonian Planetary Omens. Part II: Enūma Anu Enlil Tablets 50–51* (Malibu: Undena).

Reiner, E., and Pingree, D., 1998, *Babylonian Planetary Omens. Part III* (Groningen: Styx).

Reiner, E., and Pingree, D., 2005, *Babylonian Planetary Omens. Part IV* (Leiden: Brill).

Robson, E., 1999, *Mesopotamian Mathematics, 2100–1600 BC: Technical Constants in Bureaucracy and Education* (Oxford: Clarendon Press).

Robson, E., 2007, Transliteration and translation of Mul-Apin 1 (http://oracc.museum.upenn.edu/cams/gkab/Q002715/html) and 2 (http://oracc.museum.upenn.edu/cams/gkab/Q002716/html), accessed August 2017.

Rochberg-Halton, F., 1988a, 'Elements of the Babylonian Contribution to Hellenistic Astrology', *Journal of the American Oriental Society* 108, 51–62.

Rochberg-Halton, F., 1988b, 'Benefic and Malefic Planets in Babylonian Astrology', in E. Leichty (ed.), *A Scientific Humanist: Studies in Memory of Abraham Sachs* (Philadelphia: University Museum), 323–328.

Rochberg-Halton, F. 1988c, *Aspects of Babylonian Celestial Divination: The Lunar Eclipse Tablets of Enūma Anu Enlil*, Archiv für Orientforsching Beiheft 22 (Horn: Berger & Söhne).

Roughton, N. A., Steele, J. M., and Walker, C. B. F., 2004, 'A Late Babylonian Normal and *Ziqpu* Star Text', *Archive for History of Exact Sciences* 58, 537–572.

Sachs, A., 1952, 'Sirius Dates in Babylonian Astronomical Texts of the Seleucid Period', *Journal of Cuneiform Studies* 6, 105–114.

Sachs, A., and Hunger, H., 1988, *Astronomical Diaries and Related Texts from Babylonia. Volume I: Diaries from 652 B.C. to 262 B.C.* (Vienna: Österreichische Akademie der Wissenschaften).

Sachs, A., and Neugebauer, O., 1956, 'A Procedure Text Concerning Solar and Lunar Motion: B.M. 36712', *Journal of Cuneiform Studies* 10, 131–136.

Schaumberger, J., 1935, *Sternkunde und Sterndienst in Babel. 3. Ergänzungsheft zum ersten und zweiten Buch* (Münster in Westfalen: Aschendorffsche Verlagsbuchhandlung).

Schott, A., 1936, 'Marduk und sein Stern', *Zeitschrift für Assyriologie* 43, 124–145.

Simons, F., 2017, 'Alammuš Redux', *Nouvelles assyriologiques brèves et utilitaires*, 8–13.

Smith, G., 1875, *Assyrian Discoveries: An Account of Explorations and Discoveries on the Site of Nineveh, During 1873 and 1874* (New York: Scribner, Armstrong & Co.).

Steele, J. M., 2007, 'Celestial Measurement in Babylonian Astronomy', *Annals of Science* 64, 293–325.

Steele, J. M., 2013, 'Shadow-Length Schemes in Babylonian Astronomy', *SCIAMVS* 14, 3–39.

Steele, J. M., 2014, 'Late Babylonian *Ziqpu*-star Lists: Written or Remembered Traditions of Knowledge', in D. Bawanypeck and A. Imhausen (eds), *Traditions of Written Knowledge in Ancient Egypt and Mesopotamia* (Münster: Ugarit-Verlag), 123–151.

Steele, J. M., 2017, *Rising Time Schemes in Babylonian Astronomy* (Dordrecht: Springer).

Steele, J. M., in press a, 'The Continued Relevance of MUL.APIN in Late Babylonian Astronomy', in M. Ossendrijver (ed.), *Scholars, Priests and Temples: Babylonian and Egyptian Science in Context* (Berlin: TOPOI).

Steele, J. M., in press b, 'Astronomical Activity in the "House of the *āšipus*" in Uruk', in C. Proust and J. M. Steele (eds), *Scholars and Scholarship in Late Babylonian Uruk*, in press

Steele, J. M., forthcoming a, 'Comments on BM 77054'.

Steele, J. M., forthcoming b, 'The Development of the Babylonian Zodiac: Some Preliminary Observations'.

Swerdlow, N. M., 1998, *The Babylonian Theory of the Planets* (Princeton: Princeton University Press).

Thureau-Dangin, F., 1922, *Tablettes d'Uruk à l'usage des prêtres du Temple d'Anu au temps des Séleucides* (Paris: Paul Geuthner).

van der Sluijs, M. A., and James, P., 2013, 'Saturn as the "Sun of Night" in Ancient Near Eastern Texts', *Aula Orientalis* 31, 279–321.

van der Waerden, B. L., 1949, 'Babylonian Astronomy. II. The Thirty-Six Stars', *Journal of Near Eastern Studies* 8, 6–26.

van der Waerden, B. L., 1951, 'Babylonian Astronomy. III. The Earliest Astronomical Computations', *Journal of Near Eastern Studies* 10, 20–34.

van der Waerden, B. L., 1952–1953, 'History of the Zodiac', *Archiv für Orientforschung* 16, 216–230.

van der Waerden, B. L., 1968, *Die Anfänge der Astronomie* (Basel and Stuttgart: Birkhäuser).

Virolleaud, Ch., 1908–1911, *L'Astrologie chaldéenne* (Paris: Geuthner).

von Soden, W., 1995, *Grundriss der akkadischen Grammatik* (Rome: Pontificio Istituto Biblico).

von Weiher, E., 1988, *Spätbabylonische Texte aus Uruk*, Teil III (Berlin: Gebr. Mann).

Wainer, Z., forthcoming, *The Series 'If the Moon at Its Appearance' and Mesopotamian Scholarship of the First Millennium BCE* (Leiden: Brill).

Wainer, Z., and Steele, J. M., forthcoming, 'Celestial-Divinatory Commentaries within the Mesopotamian Received Tradition', in K. Chemla, L. Daston, M. Geller, and G. Most (eds), *Commentaries in the Mathematical Sciences.*

Watson, R., and Horowitz, W., 2011, *Writing Science Before the Greeks: A Naturalistic Analysis of the Babylonian Astronomical Treatise MUL.APIN* (Leiden: Brill).

Weidner, E. F., 1913, 'Die Entdeckung der Präzession, Eine Geistestat babylonischer Astronomen', *Babyloniaca* 7, 1–19.

Weidner, E. F., 1915, *Handbuch der babylonischen Astronomie. Erster Band* (Leipzig: J. C. Hinrichs'sche Buchhandlung),

Weidner, E. F., 1923, 'Ein babylonisches Kompendium der Himmelskunde', *The American Journal of Semitic Languages & Literatures* 40, 186–208.

Weidner, E. F., 1927, 'Eine Beschreibung des Sternenhimmels aus Assur', *Archiv für Orientforschung* 4: 73–85.

Weidner, E. F., 1939, 'Neue Bruchstücke des Berichtes über Sargons achten Feldzug', *Archiv für Orientforschung* 12, 144–148, Pl. XII.
Weidner, E. F., 1959–1960, 'Ein astrologischer Sammeltext aus der Sargonidenzeit', *Archiv für Orientforschung* 19, 105–113.
Weidner, E. F., 1967, *Gestirn-Darstellungen auf babylonischen Tontafeln* (Graz: Hermann Böhlaus Nachf.).
Wiggermann, F. A. M., 1992, *Mesopotamian Protective Spirits* (Groningen: Styx).
Williams, C., 2002, 'Signs from the Sky, Signs from the Earth: The Diviner's Manuel Revisited', in J. M. Steele and A. Imhausen (eds), *Under One Sky: Astronomy and Mathematics in the Ancient Near East* (Münster: Ugarit-Verlag), 473–485.

Index of words and names

Note: StN = Star name. Keywords are written as in CAD.

abālu: tuš-tab/ta-bal II ii 9.
Absinnu s. šer'u
AD$_6$ s. Pagru
Adad: ^{d}IM I ii 9.25.27. II B 2.
Agru: $^{mul\ lú}$ḪUN.GÁ I i 43.ii 36.iii 24.iv 37. II i 15.21.
agû: AGA ^{d}Anim I ii 1.
aḫāru: D ina šamê uḫ-ḫa-ra II i 44.49; uḫ-ḫa-ram-ma II i 45.48.50.52.53.56.
Aja: ^{d}A-a I i 18.
akalu: NINDA qatna ikkal II iv 10.
akālu: šu-ta-ku-lu II ii 11; akala qatna KÚ II iv 10.
alāku: a-lik pāni I i 1.40. ii 19; ḫarrān Sin DU-ku StN DU-ak II i 1–6; šāru ša DU-ku II i 27.33.37.42.58.71; IM . . . DU II iv 9–12; ša . . . ana Anšan DU-ku II iv 8.
Alammuš: ^{d}LÀL (var. MUŠ.LÀL) I i 6.
ALLA s. Alluttu
AL.LUL s. Alluttu
Alluttu: ^{mul}AL.LUL I i 7.ii 41.iv 6.34; $^{mul}{}_{5}$ALLA II iii 25–27.
alpu: GU$_4$ II iii 36.
Alû: ^{mul}GU$_4$.AN.NA I ii 1.iii 15.45f.iv 33.
ālu: bēl URU II iii 32.
amāru: IGI.LÁ, IGI I ii 17.36–41.43–47.iii 2–4.6.8–12. II i 9.16.24f.33.36.46.50. 52–54.57f.60–62.64.67. A 10f.14f. ii 4–6.iii 22.35.47.49.52. B 4.6; ana IGI. LÁ-ka II i 68; ana IGI-ka II ii 13.41; ziqpa ana a-ma-ri-ka I iv 10; ša . . . nipḫa u rība . . . im-ma-ru I iv 3; tam-ma-ru I iv 9; tam-mar/IGI II ii 15f.42.iii 14f.
amīlu: pagar LÚ/NA II B 4; LÚ/NA mê irmuk II B 5; LÚ ana rubûti iškunū II iv 9–12; LÚ BI II iv 9.
amīlūtu: NAM.LÚ.U$_{18}$.LU II iii 36.
ammatu: x ina 1 KÙŠ II ii 22–40.42.
Amurrû: MAR.TU-i II ii 19.
Angubbû s. Dingirgubbû
Anšan: An-ša/ša$_4$-an^{ki} II iv 8.
ANŠE.KUR.RA s. Sīsû
ANŠE.PA+GÍN s. sīsû
Antušû s. Dingirtušû
Anu: I i 7.19.22.40.ii 1f. II A 1.6.ii 7.
Anunītu: ^{mul}A-nu-ni-tu$_4$ I i 42.iii 11.22.iv 37.
^{giš}APIN s. Epinnu
apsû: ša ina libbišu ZU.AB ibarrû I ii 24.
apû: Š kî kakkabūšunu ul-ta-ta-pu-ni II i 29.
arāku: mūšâtu GÍD.DA^{meš} II i 13; ūmū GÍD.DA^{meš} II i 18.
arāqu: SIG$_7$ II i 59; SIG$_7$^{meš} II iii 19.
arḫu: ēma ITI I iv 31.38. II i 67; ITI II i 50f.55.61f.ii 13–16; ITI^{meš} II i 61.ii 11f.
Āribu: ^{mul}UGA^{mušen} a-ri-bu I ii 9; s. I ii 45.iii 20. II B 3; $^{mul}{}_{5}$UG$_5$.GA II iii 28f.
arki: EGIR-šú I i 14.27.31.43.ii 5.25; EGIR-šú-nu I ii 26.33; EGIR StN I i 42. II i 15.21; EGIR-šú ibakkû II iv 8.
arnu: NAM.TAG.GA ibašši II B 5.
asakku: Á.SÌG ibašši II B 6.
asīdu: a-si-du ša Nimri I iv 19.
aṣû: ana ūmi È^{meš}-ni I iii 50; StN ina È-šú II B 7f.iv 1–3.5; kakkabu . . . È II iii 45; ṣītu . . . È II iii 51; mīlu . . . È II B 7.
AŠ.IKU s. Ikû
atāru: DIRI-át II A 9.11.16.ii 2.4.6.
atru: ūmī DIRI^{meš} II i 24.ii 12.16; arḫa DIRI.GA II ii 11; šatta . . . DIRI.GA II ii 10.17.

ba'ālu: ba-ìl II i 59.63.iii 21; KUR$_4$ II iii 18.33.
Baba: ^{d}Ba-Ú I i 26.

Subject index

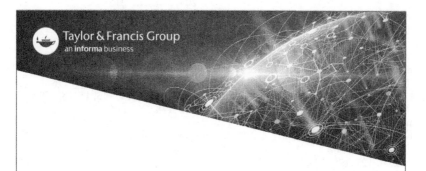